History of the War in Afghanistan Vol. I

Kaye, John William, Sir

Copyright © BiblioLife, LLC

This historical reproduction is part of a unique project that provides opportunities for readers, educators and researchers by bringing hard-to-find original publications back into print at reasonable prices. Because this and other works are culturally important, we have made them available as part of our commitment to protecting, preserving and promoting the world's literature. These books are in the "public domain" and were digitized and made available in cooperation with libraries, archives, and open source initiatives around the world dedicated to this important mission.

We believe that when we undertake the difficult task of re-creating these works as attractive, readable and affordable books, we further the goal of sharing these works with a global audience, and preserving a vanishing wealth of human knowledge.

Many historical books were originally published in small fonts, which can make them very difficult to read. Accordingly, in order to improve the reading experience of these books, we have created "enlarged print" versions of our books. Because of font size variation in the original books, some of these may not technically qualify as "large print" books, as that term is generally defined; however, we believe these versions provide an overall improved reading experience for many.

HISTORY

OF

THE WAR IN AFGHANISTAN.

By JOHN WILLIAM KAYE, F.R.S.

THIRD EDITION.

IN THREE VOLUMES.

VOL. I.

LONDON:
WM. H. ALLEN & CO., 13, WATERLOO PLACE,
Publishers to the India Office.
1874.

Dedication.

IF PUBLIC CLAIMS ALONE WERE TO BE REGARDED, I KNOW NOT TO WHOM I COULD MORE FITLY INSCRIBE THESE VOLUMES, THAN TO THE OFFICERS OF A REGIMENT, ON THE ROLLS OF WHICH ARE THE NAMES OF POLLOCK, MACGREGOR, TODD, SHAKESPEAR, LAWRENCE, ABBOTT, ANDERSON, AND OTHERS, DISTINGUISHED IN THE ANNALS OF THE AFGHAN WAR; BUT IT IS IN GRATEFUL RECOLLECTION OF SOME OF THE HAPPIEST YEARS OF MY LIFE THAT I DEDICATE THESE VOLUMES TO THE

OFFICERS OF THE BENGAL ARTILLERY.

BLETCHINGLEY,
Oct. 30, 1851.

ADVERTISEMENT TO THIRD EDITION.

THE present Edition of the "History of the War in Afghanistan" is a reproduction of the three-volumed Edition of 1857, which was thoroughly revised, and much improved by the kindly aid of many of the chief actors in the scenes described. I do not think that I can make it any better.

Only one alleged error has been brought to my notice since the last Edition was published. It is stated, in Chapter IV., page 55, that "Mr. Harford Jones, a civil servant of the Company, who was made a Baronet for the occasion, was deputed to Teheran to negotiate with the Ministers of the Shah." This was first published in 1851. After a lapse of twenty-three years, I have recently been informed by the son of Sir Harford Jones, that his father was not made a Baronet in consideration of prospective but of past services. It is certain that Mr. Harford Jones rendered good service to the East India Company, but it is equally certain that His Majesty's Government were not very prodigal in their grants of honours to the Company's servants. The Baronetcy was created in 1807, when the Persian Mission was under consideration; but I must admit that there is a difference between coincidences and consequences—and, therefore, as I cannot establish the fact stated, I am willing to withdraw the assertion of it, whatever may be my own convictions.

J. W. K.

Rose-Hill,
March 1874.

PREFACE TO SECOND EDITION.

THE present Edition of the History of the War in Afghanistan has been thoroughly revised; and several alterations have been made, which I hope may be fairly regarded also as emendations. Some of the notes have been abridged; and others, when the importance of their subject-matter seemed to warrant it, have been incorporated with the text. I have freely and gratefully availed myself of such information and such suggestions as have been furnished to me by others since the first appearance of the Work, whilst my own more recent historical and biographical researches have enabled me to illustrate more fully in some places my original conceptions, and in others to modify or to correct them.

The material corrections, however, are not numerous. As almost every statement in the book was based upon copious documentary evidence, I have now, as regards my historical facts, very little to withdraw or to amend.

I think I may, without unreasonable self-congratulation, assert that few works of contemporary history containing so large a body of facts have been so little questioned and controverted. The numerous communications, which I have received alike from friends and strangers, have contained little but confirmatory or illustrative matter; and, if they have cast any doubt upon the statements in the Work, it has been mainly on those advanced by the actors in the events described, and which therefore have appeared only in a dramatic sense in these pages. When, however, an opportunity has been afforded me of placing before the reader any new facts, or counter-statements, which may possibly cause him to modify his previous opinions, I have always turned them to account. As I have no other object than that of declaring the truth, I cannot but rejoice in every added means of contributing to its completeness.

In this present Edition, the History of the War in Afghanistan is divided into three Volumes. This is a change in the outer form of the Work, which may appear to be scarcely worthy of notice; but I believe it to be an improvement, and a suggestive one. I doubt whether there is a series of events in all history, which falls more naturally into three distinct groupes, giving the epic completeness of a beginning. a middle, and an end to the entire Work. It is true that some very generous and good-natured people have given me credit for the unity of design and of construction apparent in this; but in truth all the parts of the Work fell so naturally into their proper places, that there was little left for art to accomplish; and I am conscious that I owe to the nature of my subject the largest part of the praise which has been so encouragingly bestowed on myself.

I should have nothing more to say in this place, if I did not desire to express my gratitude to the friends who have taken an interest in this new edition of my History, and have aided me with verbal corrections of my text, or suggestions of greater moment. I might not please them by any more special recognition of their kindness; but there is one whom such praise and gratitude as mine can no longer reach, and whom I may therefore name without offence. Among others who were at the trouble to re-peruse this book, for the purpose of aiding its revision for the present edition, the appearance of which has been retarded by accidental circumstances, was the late Sir Robert Harry Inglis. I believe that this, which he assured me was a labour of love, was the last literary task which he ever set himself. His final list of *corrigenda* was sent to me, indeed, only a few days before the occurrence of that event which, although there be good and wise and genial men still among us, has left a gap in society, which cannot easily be filled by one so good, so wise, and so genial. Of all the privileges of literature, the greatest, perhaps, is that it makes for its followers kind and indulgent friends, who sometimes transfer to the writer the interest awakened by his book. I owe to this Work some cherished friendships; but none more cherished than that which has now become both a pleasing and a painful reminiscence.

LONDON,
January, 1857.

PREFACE TO THE ORIGINAL EDITION.

CIRCUMSTANCES having placed at my disposal a number of very interesting and important letters and papers, illustrative of the History of the War in Afghanistan, I undertook to write this Work. There was nothing that peculiarly qualified me for the task, beyond the fact that I enjoyed the confidence of some of the chief actors in the events to be narrated, or—for death had been busy among those actors—their surviving relatives and friends. I had been in India, it is true, during the entire period of the War; but I never took even the humblest part in its stirring scenes, or visited the country in which they were enacted.

It was not, therefore, until I considered that no more competent person might be disposed to undertake the Work; that the materials placed in my hands might not in the same number and variety be placed in the hands of any other writer; and that those best qualified by a full knowledge of the subject to write the History of the War, were restrained by the obligations of official position from that fulness of revelation and freedom of discussion, which a work of this kind demands—that entered upon the perilous undertaking. The necessities of the subject have rendered the task peculiarly painful, and, but for the encouragement I have received in the progress of its execution, alike from strangers and from friends who have freely placed new materials in my hands, and expressed a lively interest in my labours, I might have shrunk from its completion. I now lay before the public the result of much anxious thought and laborious investigation, confident that, although the Work might have been done more ably, it could not have been performed more conscientiously, by another.

I have been walking, as it were, with a torch in my hand over a floor strewn thickly with gunpowder. There is the chance of an explosion at every step. I have been treading all along on dangerous ground. But if I cannot confidently state that I have asserted nothing which I cannot prove, I can declare my belief that, except upon what I had a right to consider as good and sufficient authority, I have advanced absolutely nothing. It will be seen how careful I have been to quote my authorities. Indeed, I have an uneasy misgiving in my mind that I have overburdened my Work with quotations from the letters and documents in my possession. But this has been done with design and deliberation. It was not sufficient to refer to these letters and documents, for they were singly accessible only to a few, and collectively, perhaps, to no one but myself. They have, therefore, been left to speak for themselves. What the Work has lost by this mode of treatment in compactness and continuity, it has gained in trustworthiness and authenticity. If the narrative be less animated, the history is more genuine. I have had to deal with unpublished materials, and to treat of very strange events; and I have not thought it sufficient to fuse these materials into my text, and to leave the reader to fix or not to fix his faith upon the unsupported assertions of an unknown writer.*

I would make another observation regarding the execution of this Work. The more notorious events of the War, which stand fully revealed in military despatches and published blue-books, have not been elaborated with the care, and expanded into the amplitude, which their importance may seem to demand. These Volumes may be thought, perhaps, rather deficient in respect of military details. Compelled to condense somewhere, I have purposely abstained from enlarging upon those events, which have already found fitting chroniclers. The military memoir-writers, each one on his own limited field, have arrayed before us all the strategical operations of the Campaign from the assemblage of Fane's army in 1838, to the return of Pollock's at the close of 1842; but the political history of the War

---

* In most cases I have had the original letters and documents in my possession—in the rest, authenticated copies. The translations are official translations, verified, in some of the most important instances, as in the treaties in Book V., by one of the most accomplished Persian scholars in the kingdom.

has never been written. For information on many points of military interest, not sufficiently dwelt upon in these volumes, I would therefore refer the reader to the works of Havelock, Hough, Barr, Eyre, Stacy, Neill, and other soldierly writers. The progress of events in Upper Sindh after the capture of Khelat, I have not attempted to narrate. The military operations in that part of the country have found an intelligent annalist in Dr. Buist.

I need only now, after gratefully acknowledging my obligations to all who have aided me with original papers, or with information otherwise conveyed (and I have largely taxed the patience of many during the progress of this work), offer one more word of apology. I know that my scholarly Oriental friends will revolt against my spelling of Oriental names. I have only to bow beneath their correcting hand, and fling myself upon their mercy. I have written all the names in the old and vulgar manner, most familiar to the English eye, and, in pronunciation, to the English ear; and I believe that the majority of readers will thank me for the barbarism.

BLETCHINGLEY,
October, 1851.

CONTENTS.

BOOK I.—INTRODUCTION.

[1800—1837]

CHAPTER I.

[1800—1801.]

PAGE

Shah Zemaun and the Douranee Empire—Threatened Afghan Invasion—Malcolm's First Mission to Persia—Country and People of Afghanistan—Fall of Zemaun Shah 1

CHAPTER II.

[1801—1808.]

The Early Days of Soojah-ool-Moolk—Disastrous Commencement of his Career—Defeat of Shah Mahmoud—Reign of Shah Soojah—The Insurrection of Prince Kaysur—Tidings of the British Mission 25

CHAPTER III.

[1801—1808.]

France and Russia in the East—Death of Hadjee Khalil Khan—The Mission of Condolence—Aga Nebee Khan—Extension of Russian Dominion in the East—French Diplomacy in Persia—The pacification of Tilsit—Decline of French influence in Teheran 36

CHAPTER IV.

[1808—1809.]

The Second Mission to Persia—Malcolm's Visit to Bushire—Failure of the Embassy—His Return to Calcutta—Mission of Sir Harford Jones—His Progress and Success . . . 55

CHAPTER V.

[1808—1809.]

The Missions to Lahore and Caubul—The Aggressions of Runjeet Singh—Mr. Metcalfe at Umritsur—Treaty of 1809—Mr. Elphinstone's Mission—Arrival at Peshawur—Reception by Shah Soojah—Withdrawal of the Mission—Negotiations with the Ameers of Sindh 77

CHAPTER VI.

[1809—1816.]

The Mid-Career of Shah Soojah—His Wanderings and Misfortunes—Captivity in Cashmere—Imprisonment at Lahore—Robbery of the Koh-i-noor—Reception of the Shah by the Rajah of Kistawar—His Escape to the British Territories . . . 97

CHAPTER VII.

[1816—1837.]

Dost Mahomed and the Barukzyes—Early days of Dost Mahomed—The fall of Futteh Khan—Defeat of Shah Mahmoud—Supremacy of the Barukzyes—Position of the Empire—Dost Mahomed at Caubul—Expedition of Shah Soojah—His Defeat—Capture of Peshawur by the Sikhs 107

CHAPTER VIII.

[1810—1837.]

Later Events in Persia—The Treaty of Goolistan—Arrival of Sir Gore Ouseley—Mr. Morier and Mr. Ellis—The Definitive Treaty—The War of 1826-27—The Treaty of Toorkomanchai—Death of Futteh Ali Shah—Accession of Mahomed Shah—His Projects of Ambition—The Expedition against Herat . 139

BOOK II.

[1835—1838.]

CHAPTER I.

[1835—1837.]

The Commercial Mission to Caubul—Arrival of Lord Auckland—His Character—Alexander Burnes—His Travels in Central Asia—Deputation to the Court of Dost Mahomed—Reception by the Ameer—Negotiations at Caubul—Failure of the Mission 166

CHAPTER II.

[1837—1839.]

The Siege of Herat—Shah Kamran and Yar Mahomed—Return of the Shah—Eldred Pottinger—Preparations for the Defence—Advance of the Persian Army—Progress of the Siege—Negotiations for Peace—Failure of the Attack—The Siege raised . 211

CHAPTER III.

[1837—1838.]

Policy of the British-Indian Government—Our Defensive Operations—Excitement in British India—Proposed Alliance with Dost Mahomed—Failure of Burnes's Mission considered—The claims of the Suddozye Princes—The Tripartite Treaty—Invasion of Afghanistan determined—Policy of the Movement 300

CHAPTER IV.

[July—October: 1838.]

The Simlah Manifesto—The Simlah Council—Influence of Messrs. Colvin and Torrens—Views of Captains Burnes and Wade—Opinions of Sir Henry Fane—The Army of the Indus—The Governor-General's Manifesto—Its Policy considered . 350

BOOK III.

[1838—1839.]

CHAPTER I.

The Army of the Indus—Gathering at Ferozepore—Resignation of Sir Henry Fane—Route of the Army—Passage through Bahwulpore—The Ameers of Sindh—The Hyderabad Question—Passage of the Bolan Pass—Arrival at Candahar. . 388

CHAPTER II.

[April—August: 1839.]

Arrival at Candahar—The Shah's Entry into the City—His Installation—Nature of his Reception—Behaviour of the Douranees—The English at Candahar—Mission to Herat—Difficulties of our Position—Advance to Ghuznee . . 437

CHAPTER III.

[June—August: 1839.]

The Disunion of the Barukzyes—Prospects of Dost Mahomed—Keane's Advance to Ghuznee—Massacre of the Prisoners—Fall of Ghuznee—Flight of Dost Mahomed—Hadjee Khan, Khaukur—Escape of Dost Mahomed—Restoration of Shah Soojah—Success of the Campaign 454

APPENDIX 481

THE WAR IN AFGHANISTAN.

BOOK I.—INTRODUCTION.

[1800—1837]

CHAPTER I.

[1800—1801.]

Shah Zemaun and the Douranee Empire—Threatened Afghan Invasion—Malcolm's First Mission to Persia—Country and People of Afghanistan—Fall of Zemaun Shah.

AT the dawn of the present century, Zemaun Shah reigned over the Dourance Empire. The son of Timour Shah, and the grandson of the illustrious Ahmed Shah, he had sought, on the death of his father, the dangerous privilege of ruling a divided and tumultuous people. Attaining by intrigue and violence what did not rightfully descend to him by inheritance, he soon began to turn his thoughts towards foreign conquest, and to meditate the invasion of Hindostan. His talents were not equal to his ambition, and his success fell far short of the magnitude of his designs There was too little security at home to ensure for him prosperity abroad. And so it happened, that he was continually marching an army upon the frontier, eager to extend the Douranee Empire to the banks of the Ganges; and continually retracing his steps in alarm, lest his own sovereignty should be wrested from him in his absence. For many years Zemaun Shah's descent upon Hindostan kept the British Indian Empire in a chronic state of unrest. But he never advanced further than Lahore, and then was compelled precipitately to retire. Starvation threatened his troops; a brotherly usurper his throne; and he hastened back lest he should find Prince Mahmoud reigning at Caubul in his stead.

This was in 1797,[*] when Sir John Shore was Governor-General of India. We smile now at the alarm that was created along the whole line of country from the Attock to the Hooghly, by the rumoured approach of this formidable invader. But half a century ago, the English in India knew little of the resources of the Douranee Empire, of the national characteristics of the people, of the continually unsettled state of their political relations, or of the incompetency of the monarch himself to conduct any great enterprise. Distance and ignorance magnified the danger: but the apprehensions, which were then entertained, were not wholly groundless apprehensions. All the enemies of the British Empire in India had turned their eyes with malicious expectancy upon Caubul. Out of the rocky defiles of that romantic country were to stream the deliverers of Islam from the yoke of the usurping Franks. The blood of the Mahomedan princes of India was at fever heat. From northern Oude and from southern Mysore had gone forth invitations to the Afghan monarch. With large promises of aid, in money and in men, Vizier Ali and Tippoo Sultan had encouraged

[*] And again in the cold weather of 1798-99 he advanced as far as Lahore, but was recalled by the invasion of Khorassan by the Persian troops. Lord Wellesley had by this time succeeded to the government of India. The danger was then considered sufficiently cogent to call for an augmentation of the native army.

him to move down upon Hindostan at the head of an army of true believers. Others, with whom he could claim no community of creed, extended to him the hand of fellowship. The Rajah of Jyneghur offered him a lakh of rupees a day as soon as the grand army should enter his district.* We, who in these times trustingly contemplate the settled tranquillity of the north-western provinces of India, and remember Zemaun Shah only as the old blind pensioner of Loodhianah, can hardly estimate aright the real importance of the threatened movement, or appreciate the apprehensions which were felt by two governors-general of such different personal characters as Sir John Shore and Lord Wellesley.†

The new century had scarcely dawned upon the English in India, when the perils which seemed to threaten them from beyond the Indus began to assume a more complicated and perplexing character. The ambition of a semi-barbarous monarch and the inflammatory zeal of hordes of Mussulman fanatics, were sources of danger, which, however alarming, were at least plain and intelligible. But when it was suspected that there was intrigue of a more remote and insidious character to be combated—

* I find this fact, which however is to be referred rather to dread of the Mahrattas than to hatred of the British, stated, among other answers to queries put in 1800-1 by Captain Malcolm to Mahomed Sadik.—*MS.*

† Of the two, perhaps, Lord Wellesley regarded the movements of the Douranee monarch with the livelier concern. Sir John Shore wrote : "Report speaks of an invasion of Hindostan by Zemaun Shah, and with respect to his intention is entitled to credit. . . . The execution of his intentions will be hazardous unless he can obtain the co-operation of the Sikhs and hostages for the continuance of it ; and I have great doubt as to his success." Lord Wellesley, two or three years later, spoke of the threatened invasion "creating the liveliest sensation throughout India ;" and added, "Every Mahomedan, even in the remotest region of the Deccan, waited with anxious expectation for the advance of the champion of Islam."

when intelligence, only too credible, of the active efforts of French diplomacy in Persia, reached the Calcutta Council-Chamber, and it was believed that the emissaries of Napoleon were endeavouring to cement alliances hostile to Great Britain in every quarter of the Eastern world, the position of affairs in Central Asia was regarded with increased anxiety, and their management demanded greater wisdom and address. It was now no longer a question of mere military defence against the inroads of a single invader. The repeated failures of Zemaun Shah had, in some degree, mitigated the alarm with which his movements were dimly traced in Hindostan. The Douranee monarch had lost something of his importance as an independent enemy; but as the willing agent of a hostile confederacy, he appeared a more formidable opponent, and might have become a more successful one. An offensive alliance between France, Persia, and Caubul, might have rendered the dangers, which once only seemed to threaten us from the north-west, at once real and imminent. To secure the friendship of Persia, therefore, was the great aim of the British Government. It was obvious that, whilst threatened with invasion from the west, Zemaun Shah could never conduct to a successful issue an expedition against Hindostan; and that so long as Persia remained true to Great Britain, there was nothing to be apprehended from French intrigue in the countries of Central Asia. It was determined, therefore, to despatch a mission to the Court of the Persian Shah, and Captain John Malcolm was selected to conduct it.

The choice could not have fallen on a fitter agent. In the fullest vigour of life, a young man, but not a young soldier—for, born in that year of heroes which witnessed the nativity of Wellington, of Napoleon, and of Mehemet Ali, he had entered the service of the Company at the early age of thirteen—Captain Malcolm brought to the difficult and responsible duties entrusted to him, extraordinary energy of mind and activity of body—talents of the most available and useful character—some experience of native courts and acquaintance with the Oriental languages. He had been successively military secretary to the commander-in-chief of Madras, town-major of Fort St. George, assistant to the Resident at Hyderabad, and commandant of the infantry of the Nizam's contingent. When that army took the field in Mysore, and shared in the operations against Tippoo Sultan, Captain Malcolm accompanied it in the capacity of political agent, which was virtually the chief command of the force; and, after the reduction of Seringapatam and the death of Tippoo, was associated with General Wellesley, Colonel Close, and Captain Munro,* in the commission that was then appointed for the settlement of the Mysore country.

This was in 1799. In that same year he was selected by Lord Wellesley to fill the post of envoy to the Court of Persia. With such address had he acquitted himself in all his antecedent appointments; so great had been the knowledge of native character, the diplomatic tact, and the sound understanding he had evinced in all his negotiations, that at an age when the greater number of his contemporaries were in the discharge of no higher duties than those entailed by the command of a company of sepoys, Captain Malcolm was on his way to the presence of the great defender of Islamism, charged with one of the most important missions that has ever been despatched by the British-Indian Government to the Court of a native potentate.

The mission, says Captain Malcom, was "completely successful"—a declaration repeated more emphatically by

* Men who lived to occupy a space in history, as the Duke of Wellington, Sir Barry Close, and Sir Thomas Munro. Malcolm was Secretary to the Commission, and Munro his assistant.

Lord Wellesley.* But time and circumstance did more for us than diplomacy. It was the ostensible object of the mission to instigate the Shah of Persia to move an army upon Herat, and so to withdraw Shah Zemaun from his threatened invasion of Hindostan. But the move, which was to do so much for our security in India, had been made before the British ambassador appeared at the Persian Court; and the work, which was thus commenced by Futteh Ali, was completed by Prince Mahmoud.† "You may rest assured," wrote Captain Malcolm, from Ispahan, in October, 1800, "that Zemaun Shah can do nothing in India before the setting in of the rains of 1801. He has not time, even if he had the power for such an

* "Captain Malcolm," he wrote to the Secret Committee, "returned from his embassy in the month of May, after having completely succeeded in accomplishing every object of his mission, and in establishing a connection with the government of the Persian Empire, which promises to the interests of the British nation in India political and commercial advantages of the most important description."—[*MS. Records.*]

† A writer in the *Calcutta Review*, who betrays an acquaintance with his subject such as could only have been acquired in the countries of which he writes, or by the examination of an immense mass of contemporary records, justly observes: "That the storm was dissipated in the manner suggested by Lord Wellesley was creditable to his lordship's foresight, but was entirely independent of his measures. The second expedition of Futteh Ali Khan into Khorassan in 1800, which drew Shah Zemaun from Candahar to Herat, took place almost simultaneously with Captain Malcolm's journey from the south of Persia to the capital. His majesty received the British mission at Subzewar; and the subsequent proceedings of Shah Mahmood, which led, in the sequel, to his dethronement, so far from originating in British instigation or in Persian support, were in reality indebted for their success to their entire independence of all foreign aid. As the minion of Persia, Shah Mahmood could never have prevailed against his elder brother. As the popular Douranee champion he was irresistible."—[*Calcutta Review*, vol. xii.] Malcolm was at Shiraz in June, 1800, when he received intelligence of the Shah's successes in Khorassan.

attempt; and by the blessing of God he will for some years to come be too much engaged in this quarter to think of any other."* But some years to come of empire he was not destined to see. Even as Malcolm wrote, the days of his sovereignty were numbered, and the bugbear of Afghan invasion was passing into tradition.

The envoy was empowered either to offer a subsidy of from three to four lakhs of rupees for a term of three years, or by a liberal distribution of presents to the king and his principal ministers, to bribe them into acquiescence. Malcolm chose the latter course. He threw about his largesses with an unstinting hand, and everything went smoothly with him. The farther he advanced into the interior, the greater was the attention shown to the Mission, for the greater was the renown of the liberality of the Christian *Elchee*. Every difficulty melted away beneath the magic touch of British gold.† There had been at the outset some trifling disputes about formalities—about titles and designations—but these were soon cleared away; and the serious business of the Mission proceeded in the midst of feasts and formalities to a satisfactory completion. A commercial and a political treaty were negotiated at Teheran by Malcolm and Hadjee Ibrahim; and the Shah stamped their validity by prefixing to each a firman, or mandate, under the royal seal,

---

* *MS. Correspondence of Sir John Malcolm.*

† Before Malcolm left Shiraz he began to have some misgivings on the score of his lavish expenditure. "I trust I will not disappoint your hopes," he writes from that place, under date July 26, 1800, "but the expense I have incurred is heavy, and it is on that score alone I am alarmed. Not that it is one farthing more than I have to the best of my judgment thought necessary to answer, or rather further, the ends of my mission, and to support the dignity of the British Government; but people sometimes differ in their opinions on such points. However, ' All's well that ends well.' "—[*MS. Correspondence of Sir John Malcolm.*]

calling upon all the officers of the state to perform its prescribed conditions. Of all the terms proposed by the English envoy, but one was demurred to by the Persian Court. "And that even," writing some years afterwards, he said, "was not rejected."* This proposal related to the occupation by the English of the islands of Kishm, Angani, and Khargh (or Kharrack),† in the Persian Gulf, on the expediency of which, though much and ably controverted by others, Malcolm never ceased to expatiate so long as he had a hand in the game of Persian diplomacy.

This provision, which was to have been contained in the commercial treaty, was said to contemplate only commercial objects; but, there was to be a permission to fortify; and commerce, with an occasional permission of this kind, had made India a British dependency, and the Persians were not unreasonably jealous, therefore, of a commencement which might have had a similar end.

In February, 1801, Captain Malcolm reported that he had accomplished the object of his mission, and brought his labours to a close. "Whether with credit or not," he added in a private letter, "it is the province of my superiors to judge. I can only say, in self-defence, that I have done as much as I was able; and no man can do more. I am far from admiring my own work, or considering it (as termed in one of the preambles) *a beautiful image in the mirror of perpetuity*. It is, on the contrary, I know, a very incorrect performance; and I can hope it to meet with a favourable consideration only on the grounds of the difficulties I had to encounter in a

* *Brigadier-General Malcolm to Lord Minto*, October, 1810.
† Kishm is a large island, and Angani a small one at the entrance of the Persian Gulf. They properly belonged to the Arabs. Kharrack is at the further end of the Gulf, nearly opposite Bushire.

first negotiation with a government not two stages removed from a state of barbarism."*

The political treaty, indeed, called for apology; but not on the grounds indicated in this deprecatory letter. It stipulated that if ever again the Douranee monarch should be induced to attempt the invasion of Hindostan, the King of Persia should be bound to lay waste, with a great army, the country of the Afghans; and conclude no peace with its ruler that was not accompanied with a solemn engagement to abstain from all aggressions upon the English. But it was remarkable chiefly for the bitterness with which it proscribed the French. "Should an army of the French nation," it stated, "actuated by design and deceit, attempt to settle, with a view of establishing themselves on any of the islands or shores of Persia, a conjoint force shall be appointed by the two high contracting parties to act in co-operation, and to destroy and put an end to the foundation of their treason." The firman prefixed to this treaty contained a passage addressed to the rulers and officers of the ports, sea-coasts, and islands of Fars and Koorgistan, saying, "Should ever any persons of the French nation attempt to pass your boundaries, or desire to establish themselves either on the shores or frontiers of the kingdom of Persia,

---

* *MS. Correspondence.*—In another letter Malcolm says: "Had I to do with men of sense and moderation I should not fear, but I have to deal with a race that are possessed of neither." The necessity of adopting in all his negotiations the most flowery language, somewhat puzzled him at first; but in time he fell into the right vein of discourse. On one occasion, wishing to demonstrate the advantages of simplicity of style, he produced a copy of an Indian treaty, when the Meerza, after reading two articles of it, declared that he would "give in his resignation to his sovereign rather than that such a document should be copied into the records of the office over which he presided."

you are at full liberty to disgrace and slay them."* These proceedings have been severely censured by French writers, and even English politicians have declared them to be "an eternal disgrace to our Indian diplomacy." But those were days when, even in India, men's minds were unhinged and unsettled, and their ideas of right and wrong confounded by the monstrosities of the French revolution. It would be unjust to view these measures with the eyes of to-day, or to forget the desperate evils to which these desperate remedies were applied. It was conceived that there was a great and pressing danger, and Captain Malcolm was sent to combat it. But the treaty was never formally ratified; and the Persian Court practically ignored its obligations as soon as it was no longer convenient to observe them. The Embassy, however, was not a fruitless one, even if the only estimated produce were the stores of information it amassed.

Before the mission of Captain Malcolm to the West, but little was known in India, and nothing in Great Britain, about the Douranee Empire, the nature and extent of its resources, the quality of its soldiers, and the character of its ruler. The information which that officer acquired was not of a very alarming description. The Douranee Empire which has since been shorn of some of its fairest provinces, then consisted of Afghanistan, part of Khorassan, Cashmere, and the Derajat. The Sikh nation had not then acquired the strength which a few years later enabled it, under the military directorship of Runjeet Singh, to curb the pretensions and to mutilate the empire of its dominant neighbour. That empire extended from

---

* These treaties, which have never been officially published, are printed for the first time I believe in the appendix to Vol. I., "Life of Sir John Malcolm."

Herat in the west, to Cashmere in the east; from northern Balkh to southern Shikarpoor. Bounded on the north and east by immense mountain ranges, and on the south and west by vast tracts of sandy desert, it opposed to external hostility natural defences of a formidable character. The general aspect of the country was wild and forbidding; in the imagination of the people haunted by goules and genii; but not unvaried by spots of gentler beauty in the valleys and on the plains, where the fields were smiling with cultivation, and the husbandman might be seen busy at his work.

Few and far between as were the towns, the kingdom was thinly populated. The people were a race—or a group of races—of hardy, vigorous mountaineers. The physical character of the country had stamped itself on the moral conformation of its inhabitants Brave, independent, but of a turbulent vindictive character, their very existence seemed to depend upon a constant succession of internal feuds. The wisest among them would probably have shaken their heads in negation of the adage—"Happy the country whose annals are a blank." They knew no happiness in anything but strife. It was their delight to live in a state of chronic warfare. Among such a people civil war has a natural tendency to perpetuate itself Blood is always crying aloud for blood. Revenge was a virtue among them; the heritage of retribution passed from father to son; and murder became a solemn duty. Living under a dry, clear, bracing climate, but one subject to considerable alternations of heat and cold, the people were strong and active, and as navigable rivers were wanting, and the precipitous nature of the country forbade the use of wheeled carriages, they were for the most part good horsemen, and lived much in the saddle. Early trained to the use of arms, compelled constantly to wear and often to use them in the ordinary intercourse of life, every man was more or less a soldier or a bandit. The very shepherds were men of strife. The pastoral and the predatory character were strangely blended; and the tented cantonments of the sheep-drivers often bristled into camps of war.

But there was a brighter side to the picture. Of a cheerful, lively disposition, seemingly but little in accordance with the outward gravity of their long beards and sober garments, they might be seen in their villages, at evening tide, playing or dancing like children in their village squares; or assembling in the Fakir's gardens, to smoke and talk, retailing the news gathered in the shops, reciting stories, and singing their simple Afghan ballads, often expressive of that tender passion which, among them alone of all Oriental nations, is worthy of the name of love. Hospitable and generous, they entertained the stranger without stint, and even his deadliest enemy was safe beneath the Afghan's roof. There was a simple courtesy in their manner which contrasted favourably with the polished insincerity of the Persians on one side, and the arrogant ferocity of the Rohillas on the other. Judged by the strict standard of a Christian people, they were not truthful in word or honest in deed, but, side by side with other Asiatic nations, their truthfulness and honesty were conspicuous. Kindly and considerate to their immediate dependents, the higher classes were followed with loyal zeal and served with devoted fidelity by the lower; and, perhaps, in no eastern country was less of tyranny exercised over either the slaves of the household or the inmates of the zenana. Unlettered were they, but not incurious; and although their more polished brethren of Persia looked upon them as the Bœotians of Central Asia, their Spartan simplicity and manliness more than compensated for the absence of the Attic wit and eloquence of their western neighbours.

Soldiers, husbandmen, and shepherds, they were described as the very antithesis of a nation of shopkeepers. The vocation of the tradesman they despised. To Taujiks, Hindoos, and other aliens, was the business of selling entrusted, except upon that large scale which entitled the dealer to be regarded as a merchant, and generally entailed upon him the necessities of a wandering and adventurous life. The principal commerce of the country was with the Persian and Russian states. In the bazaars of Herat, Candahar, and Caubul the manufactures of Ispahan, Yezd, and Cashan, the spices of India, and the broad-cloths of Russia, brought by Astrakan and Bokhara, found a ready market. Occasionally, when the settled state of the country gave encouragement to commercial enterprise, an adventurous merchant would make his way, through Dera from Bombay, with a cafila of British goods, for the scarlet cloths of England were in especial demand to deck the persons of the body servants of the king. The indigenous products of the country were few, but important; for the rich shawls of Cashmere and the gaudy chintzes of Mooltan, exported in large quantities, were in good repute all over the civilised world.* At Herat some velvets and taffetas of good quality were manufactured, but only for internal consumption; whilst the assafœtida of that place, the madder of Candahar, and the indigo of the Derajat,† found a market in the Persian cities, and the dried fruits of the country were

---

* There was a considerable trade in horses; but rather through than from Afghanistan. The animals were brought from Balkh and Toorkistan, fattened at Caubul, and sold in India.

† "Five or six cafilas of this indigo leave the Derajat annually, which on an average consist of seven hundred camels, each carrying eighty Tabrizee maunds. These come into Persia by the route of Candahar and Herat."—[*Mahomed Sadik's Answers to Captain Malcolm*, 1800-1 (*MS.*).]

in request in all neighbouring parts. These, a few other drugs of little note, and some iron from the Hindoo Koosh and the Solimanee range, formed the main staple of Afghan commerce. Between the large towns there was a constant interchange of commodities; and long cafilas, or caravans, were ever in motion, from east to west, and from north to south, toiling across the sandy plains or struggling through the precipitous defiles, exposed to the attacks of predatory tribes, who levied their contributions often not without strife and bloodshed.

Such was the not very flattering picture of the commercial wealth of the Douranee Empire, which was painted by Captain Malcolm's informants. Nor was the military strength of the Empire set forth in any more striking colours. Distance and ignorance had vastly magnified the true proportions of that famous military power, which was to have overrun Hindostan, and driven the white men into the sea. The main strength of the Afghan army was in the Douranee horse. The Douranee tribes had been settled in Western Afghanistan by Nadir Shah. He had first conquered, then taken them into his service, and then parcelled out amongst them, as his military dependents, the lands which had before been held by a motley race of native cultivators. It was the policy of Ahmed Shah and his successors—a policy which was subsequently reversed by the Barukzye sirdars—to aggrandise and elevate these powerful tribes, by heaping upon them privileges and immunities at the expense of their less favoured countrymen. Upon the misery and humiliation of others, the Douranee tribes throve and flourished. The chief offices of the state were divided amongst them; they held their lands exempt from taxation. The only demand made upon them, in return for the privileges they enjoyed, was that they should furnish a certain contingent of troops.* It was said to be the principle of the military tenure by which they held their lands, that for every plough used in cultivation † they should contribute a horseman for the service of the state. But it does not appear that the integrity of this system was long preserved. In a little time there ceased to be any just proportion between the ploughs and the horsemen; and it became difficult to account for the arbitrary manner in which each of the different Douranee clans furnished its respective quota of troops ‡

In the time of Ahmed Shah the Douranee horsemen mustered about 6000 strong. The other western tribes and the Persian stipendiaries together reached about the same number. In the reign of Timour Shah, the army was computed at some 40,000 soldiers, almost entirely horsemen, § but no such force had served under Zemaun

---

* And even this obligation ceased to be recognised by Ahmed Shah, who paid the Douranee horsemen for their services, alleging that their lands had been bestowed upon them as a free and unencumbered gift. In Zemaun Shah's time they held pay-certificates, available when they were called out on active service, and realised, if they could, the amount due to them by means of orders on Cashmere, Mooltan, and other outlying provinces.—[*MS. Records—Rawlinson and Malcolm.*]

† Or, more strictly, for every parcel of land demanding the services of a single *kulba*, or plough; from which the division of land, and the assessment founded upon it, took its name.

‡ To an elaborate report on the revenue system of Western Afghanistan, especially as affecting the Douranee tribes, drawn up by Major Rawlinson in 1842, I am indebted for much valuable information, which will be found incorporated with subsequent portions of the narrative.

§ The authority for this, according to Malcolm's informant, was the Caubul records. Forster, who travelled in Afghanistan in the reign of Timour Shah, says that his entire army did not exceed 30,000 men, nor his revenue a million of our money. How these men contrived to pay themselves, may be gathered from a passage in Forster's Travels, which is worth transcribing · "This day a body of Afghan cavalry encamped in the environs of Akorah, and overspread the country like a swarm of locusts,

Shah, and they who had seen in 1799-1800, the muster of his troops near Caubul, and had access to the returns of the muster-masters, reported that he then assembled only some ten or twelve thousand men, and all, with the exception of a few Persian stipendiaries, in the immediate service of the Wuzeer, very miserably equipped. Even the Kuzzilbashes, when Shah Zemaun took the field in 1799, refused to accompany the projected expedition, on the plea that they wanted arms to fight their battles, and money to support their wives.

Fighting men, indeed, were never wanting in Afghanistan, but money was wanting to induce them to leave their homes. It was said that Shah Zemaun might, on any great national enterprise, have led 200,000 men into the field, if he had had money to pay them. But his entire revenues were not equal to the payment of a very much smaller force. He was continually being deserted by his soldiery, at critical times, for want of the sinews of war to retain them. The emptiness of his treasury, indeed, reduced him to all kinds of shifts and expedients, such as that of raising the value of the current coin of the realm. But no devices of this character could confer upon him a really formidable army. In one important branch he was miserably deficient. The Douranee artillery consisted of some twelve brass field-pieces and five hundred zumboorucks, or camel guns. Even these were miserably

devouring and destroying wherever they went. It seemed as if the land was invaded ; they entered in a violent manner every village within their scope, and fed themselves and horses at the expense of the inhabitants. Such expeditions afford these hungry creatures almost the only means of subsistence ; for when inactive, they are often reduced to such distress by the blind parsimony of their prince, that their horses, arms, and clothes, are sold for a livelihood." The same writer, speaking generally of the Afghan army, says that he "felt a sensible disappointment at seeing it composed of a tumultuous body, without order or common discipline."

equipped; the camels wanted drivers, and the guns were often unserviceable. It was said by one who visited the encampment of the grand army, under Zemaun Shah, in 1799-1800, that there were not above 500 good horses in camp, and that these belonged principally to the King and the Wuzeer. The men were mounted for the most part on yaboos, or ponies, few of which, at a liberal valuation, were worth a hundred rupees.

Such was the army with which Zemaun Shah meditated the invasion of Hindostan. The personal character of the monarch was not more formidable than the army which he commanded. A scholar more than a soldier, very strict in the observances of his religion, and an assiduous reader of the Koran, his way of life, judged by the princely standard of Central Asia, was sufficiently moral and decorous. Humane and generous, of a gentle, plastic disposition; very prone to take for granted the truth of all that was told him; by no means remarkable for personal activity, and somewhat wanting in courage, he was designed by nature for a facile puppet in the hands of a crafty Wuzeer. And such was Zemaun Shah in the expert hands of Wuffadar Khan. It was reported of him that he took no active part in the management of public affairs; and that when it was politic that he should make a show of government and appear at Durbar, what he said was little more than a public recital of a lesson well learnt in private. He was, indeed, the mere mouth-piece of the minister—of a worse and more designing man. Content with the gilded externals of majesty, he went abroad sumptuously arrayed and magnificently attended; and mighty in all the state papers of the time was the name of Zemaun Shah. But it was shrewdly suspected that, had the state of his domestic relations and the military resources at his command enabled him to take the field, as the invader of Hindostan, a bribe any day offered to the Wuzeer might have broken up the Douranee army, and kept the invader quietly at home.

On the whole, he was a popular ruler. The cultivating classes were happy under his government. It recognised their claims to remuneration for whatever was taken from them for the service of the state, and no acts of fraud and oppression were ever committed in his name. The merchants and traders were secure under his rule. In the midst of much that was base and unworthy in the character and conduct of the minister, he had a reputation for fair dealing with these classes, and they looked up to him for protection. But far otherwise were his relations with the warlike tribes and the chief people of the empire. They were not without feelings of loyalty towards the king; but it was rather affection for his person, than satisfaction with the government of which he was the head. The grasping character of the minister, who engrossed to himself all the patronage of the state, rendered him, in spite of his courteous manners and affable demeanour, obnoxious to the principal Sirdars; and something of this disaffection began in time to be directed against the monarch himself, who had too long abandoned his own better nature to the sinister guidance of the unprincipled and unpopular Wuzeer.

Like many a monarch, abler and better than himself, Zemaun Shah had chosen his minister unwisely, and was undone by the choice. When he entrusted the affairs of his empire to the administration of Wuffadar Khan, he made the great mistake of his life. A base and designing man, without any of those commanding qualities which impart something of dignity and heroism to crime, the Wuzeer bent his sovereign, but could not bend circumstances to his will. The loyalty of the Douranee sirdars he could extinguish, but their power he could not break by his oppressions. Alarmed at their increasing influence,

Wuffadar Khan sought to encompass them in the toils of destruction; but he destroyed himself and involved his sovereign in the ruin. Prince Mahmoud was in arms against his royal brother. Exasperated by the conduct of the minister, the Douranees threw all the weight of their influence into the scales in favour of the prince. The rebellion which they headed acquired strength and swelled into a revolution. And then began that great strife between the royal princes and the Douranee sirdars, which half a century of continued conflict, now witnessing the supremacy of the one, now of the other, has scarcely even yet extinguished.

The two principal clans or tribes of the Douranees were the Populzyes and the Barukzyes. The Suddozye, or Royal race, was one of the branches of the former. The Bamezye, in which the Wuzeership was vested, but not by inalienable right, was another branch of the same tribe. Second in influence to the Populzyes, and greater in extent, was the tribe of the Barukzyes. To this tribe belonged Futteh Khan. He was the son of Poyndah Khan, an able statesman and a gallant soldier, whose wisdom in council and experience in war had long sustained the tottering fortunes of Timour Shah. On the death of that feeble monarch he had supported the claims of Zemaun Shah. With as little wisdom as gratitude, that prince, it has been seen, suffered himself to be cajoled by a man of less honesty and less ability, and became a tool in the hands of Wuffadar Khan. The favourite of two monarchs was disgraced; and, from a powerful friend, became the resolute enemy of the reigning family. He conspired against the King and the Wuzeer; his designs were detected; and he perished miserably with his associates in the enterprise of treason.

Poyndah Khan died, leaving twenty-one sons, of whom Futteh Khan was the eldest. They are said, after the death of their father, to have stooped into a cloud of poverty and humiliation, and to have wandered about begging their bread. But their trials were only for a season. The Barukzye brothers soon emerged from the night of suffering that surrounded them. There was no power in the Douranee Empire which could successfully cope with these resolute, enterprising spirits. In Afghanistan revenge is a virtue. The sons of Poyndah Khan had the murder of their father to avenge; and they rested not till the bloody obligation had been faithfully fulfilled. Futteh Khan had fled into Persia, and there leagued himself with Prince Mahmoud. Repeated failure had extinguished the ambition of this restless prince. The accession of the Barukzye sirdar now inspired him with new courage. Upheld by the strong arm of the "king-maker," he determined to strike another blow for the sovereignty of Caubul. With a few horsemen they entered Afghanistan, and, raising the standard of revolt, pushed on to unexpected conquest.

There were not many in Afghanistan, nor many among the disinterested lookers-on at that fraternal strife, who were inclined to jeopardise their character for sagacity by predicting the success of the prince. Everything, indeed, was against him. His treasury was always empty. His friends were not men of note. With the exception of the Barukzye sirdars,* no chiefs of influence espoused his cause. His followers were described to Captain Malcolm as men "of low condition and mean extraction." But in

* And even the character of Futteh Khan was at that time very little understood and appreciated. He was described to Captain Malcolm as a man of influence, but of low, dissipated habits, who spent all his time in drinking wine and in smoking bang. It should be mentioned that Prince Ferooz, Mahmoud's brother, was associated in this enterprise. He became master of Herat, whilst Mahmoud pushed on to Candahar.

spite of the slender support which he received, and the strenuous efforts which were made to destroy him, the successes which from time to time he achieved, seemed to show that there was some vitality in his cause. A divinity seemed to hedge him in, and to protect him from the knife of the assassin. He escaped as though by a miracle the snares of his enemies, and from every new deliverance seemed to gather something of prosperity and strength. It was after one of these marvellous escapes, when the weapons of the Kuzzilbashes * had fallen from their hands, palsied by the mysterious presence of the blood royal, that Candahar fell before the insurgents. With two or three thousand horsemen, Mahmoud invested the place for thirty-three days, at the end of which Futteh Khan, with a handful of resolute men, escaladed the fort near the Shikarpoor gate, and put the panic-struck garrison to flight. The Meer Akhoor, or Master of the Horse, fled for his life. The Shah-zadah Hyder sought sanctuary at the tomb of Ahmed Shah; and Prince Mahmoud became master of the place.

It is not a peculiarity of Eastern princes alone to shine with a brighter and steadier light in the hour of adversity than in the hour of success. The trials of prosperity were too great for Prince Mahmoud, as they have been for greater men; and he soon began to lose ground at Candahar. The marvel is, that his fortunes were not utterly marred by his own folly. It was only by the concurrence of greater folly elsewhere, that in this conjecture he was saved from ruin. His impolitic and haughty conduct towards the sirdars early demonstrated his unfitness for rule, and well-nigh precipitated the enterprise in which he was engaged into a sea of disastrous

* The Kuzzilbashes, of whom frequent mention will be made in the course of this narrative, are Persian settlers in Afghanistan; many of whom are retained in the military service of the state.

failure. There seemed, indeed, to be only one thing that could sustain him, and that one thing was wanting. He was as poor as he was unpopular. But the days of Shah Zemaun's sovereignty were numbered, and no folly on the part of his antagonist could arrest the doom that was brooding over him.

At this time Zemaun Shah was on his way towards the borders of Hindostan. He had advanced as far as Peshawur, when intelligence of the fall of Candahar reached his camp. It was believed that he had little actual design of advancing beyond the Sutlej. Partly with a view of enforcing the payment of the Sindh tribute —partly to overawe the Sikhs, and partly to abstract his own army from the dangerous vicinity of Candahar and the corrupting influences to which in such a neighbourhood it was exposed, he had made this move to the southward. It was very obvious that, in such a condition of his own empire, all idea of invading Hindostan was utterly wild and chimerical. If such an idea had ever been formed, it was now speedily abandoned. All other considerations gave place to the one necessity of saving his kingdom from the grasp of his brother. He hastened back to Western Afghanistan; but an impolitic expedition under the prince Soojah-ool-Moolk, who was soon destined to play a conspicuous part in the great Central-Asian drama, had crippled his military resources, and when he retraced his steps, he found that the strength of Prince Mahmoud had increased as his own had diminished. He marched against the rebels only to be defeated. The main body of the royal troops was under the command of one Ahmed Khan, a chief of the Noorzye tribe. Watching his opportunity, Futteh Khan seized the person of the Sirdar's brother, and threatened to destroy him if the chief refused to come over bodily with his troops and swell the ranks of the insurgents.

The character of the Barukzye leader certified that this was no idle threat. Ahmed Khan, already wavering in his loyalty, for the conduct of the Wuzeer had alienated his heart from the royal cause, at once made his election. When the troops of Shah Zemaun came up with the advance of the rebel army, he joined the insurgent force. From that time the cause of the royalists became hopeless. Disaster followed disaster till its ruin was complete. The minister and his master fell into the hands of the enemy. Wuffadar Khan, with his brothers, was put to death. Death, too, awaited the king—but the man was suffered to live. They doomed him only to political extinction. There is a cruel, but a sure way of achieving this in all Mahomedan countries. Between a blind king and a dead king there is no political difference. The eyes of a conquered monarch are punctured with a lancet, and he *de facto* ceases to reign. They blinded Shah Zemaun, and cast him into prison; and the Douranee Empire owned Shah Mahmoud as its head.

So fell Zemaun Shah, the once dreaded Afghan monarch, whose threatened invasion of Hindostan had for years been a ghastly phantom haunting the Council-Chamber of the British-Indian Government. He survived the loss of his sight nearly half a century; and as the neglected pensioner of Loodhianah, to the very few who could rememberer the awe which his name once inspired, must have presented a curious spectacle of fallen greatness—an illustration of the mutability of human affairs scarcely paralleled in the history of the world. He died at last full of years, empty of honours, his death barely worth a newspaper-record or a paragraph in a state paper. Scarcely identified in men's minds with the Zemaun Shah of the reigns of Sir John Shore and Lord Wellesley, he lived an appendage, alike in prosperity and adversity, to his younger brother, Soojah-ool-Moolk. That Soojah had once been reputed and described as an appendage to Shah Zemaun—"his constant companion at all times." They soon came to change places, and in a country where fraternal strife is the rule and not the exception, it is worthy of record that those brothers were true to each other to the last.*

* Since this passage was written, I have had reason to think that it ought to be accepted with some qualification. In October, 1840, when Dost Mahomed was flitting about the Kohistan, and the greatest anxiety prevailed among our political officers at Caubul, Shah Soojah said to Sir William Macnaghten, just as he was taking leave after an excited conference, "You know I have from the first expressed to you a mean opinion of my own countrymen. If you want further proof, look at that from my own brother." The Shah then showed Macnaghten an intercepted letter, bearing the seal of Shah Zemaun, to the address of Sultan Mahomed Barukzye, purposing that, as Shah Soojah had made over the country to the infidels, the Barukzyes and the Sikhs united should make him (Shah Zemaun) King of Afghanistan.—[*Unpublished Correspondence of Sir W. H. Macnaghten.*] This story may seem to be at variance with the statement in the preceding page, —that "between a blind king and a dead king there is no political difference;" but I am acquainted with no Mahomedan law that excludes a blind prince from the throne. The exclusion is based upon the popular assumption that blindness disqualifies a man from managing the affairs of an empire. If, however, in Mahomedan countries, there have been no exceptions to this rule—of which I am doubtful—in the regal line, it is certain that many provincial governments have been in the hands of men who have been deprived of their sight. The case of Shah Allum, the blind King of Delhi, is hardly to the point; for during the years of his darkness, his royalty was only a name.

CHAPTER II.

[1801—1808.]

The Early Days of Soojah-ool-Moolk—Disastrous Commencement of his Career—Defeat of Shah Mahmoud—Reign of Shah Soojah—The Insurrection of Prince Kaysur—Tidings of the British Mission.

FROM the fall of Zemaun Shah we are to date the rise of Soojah-ool-Moolk. They were brothers by the same father and mother. At the time of the political extinction of the elder, the younger was about twenty years of age. He had taken no part in the government; was but lightly esteemed for courage; and had little place in the thoughts of the people, except as an appendage of the reigning monarch. In command of the royal troops, and in charge of the family and property of the king, whilst Zemaun Shah was striking a last blow for empire in the West, he had held his post at Peshawur. There he received the disastrous tidings of the fate that had descended upon his brother and his prince. He at once proclaimed himself king, began to levy troops, and in September, 1801, marched upon Caubul with an army of 10,000 men. Victorious at the outset, he did not improve his successes, and was eventually defeated by the Douranees under Futteh Khan. The destinies of princes were in the hands of the powerful Barukzye sirdar. His energies and his influence alone upheld the drooping sovereignty of Shah Mahmoud. Weak and unprincipled, indolent and rapacious, that prince had been raised to the throne by Futteh Khan; and, though it was not in the nature of things that a ruler so feeble and so corrupt should long retain his hold of the empire, for a while the strong hand of the minister sustained him in his place.

Soojah-ool-Moolk fled to the fastnesses of the Khybur Pass. In the winter of 1801 the Ghilzyes broke out into open rebellion against the Douranee power; but were defeated with great slaughter. The Douranees returned to Caubul, and erected from the heads of the conquered, a pyramid of human skulls. In the spring of the following year the same restless tribe was again in rebellion; and again the energies of Futteh Khan were put forth for the suppression of the dangerous spirit of Ghilzye revolt. In March, 1802, the insurgents were a second time chastised; and, it is said, on the same day, Soojah-ool-Moolk, who had raised an army in the Khybur and marched upon Peshawur, sustained a severe defeat at the hands of the Douranee garrison, and was driven back into the obscurity from which he had fruitlessly emerged.

Thus for a while was tranquillity restored to the Douranee Empire. Reading and conversing with learned men, and taking council with his military adherents, Soojah-ool-Moolk, from the time of his defeat, remained inactive in the Afreedi country. Even there the vigilant enmity of the Wuzeer tracked the unhappy prince. There was no security in such retirement. The shadow of Futteh Khan darkened his resting-place and disturbed his repose. He fled to Shawl; and there, in the depth of winter and on the verge of starvation, wandered about, making vain endeavours to subsist himself and a few followers by the sale of the royal jewels. Among a people little understanding the worth of such costly articles, purchasers were with difficulty to be found. In the extremity which then beset him he changed the character of the pedlar for that of the bandit, and levied money by plundering caravans, and giving notes of hand for the amount that he raised. In this manner he collected three lakhs of rupees, and was enabled to levy troops for an attack upon Candahar. But Providence did not smile upon his endeavours. He was again repulsed. Again was he involved in a great ruin; with little hope of extrication by the energy of his own struggles, or the inherent vitality of his cause.

But in the mean while the sovereignty of Shah Mahmoud was falling to pieces by itself. He had risen upon the weakness of his predecessor, and now by his own weakness was he to be cast down. What Shah Zemaun had done for him, was he now doing for Soojah-ool-Moolk. In the absence of Futteh Khan, the Kuzzilbashes were suffered to ride roughshod over the people. The excesses which they committed at Caubul, scattered the last remnant of popularity which still adhered to the person of the king. At last an open outbreak occurred between the Sheeas and the Soonees. The king identified himself with the former, some of his chief ministers with the latter. In this conjuncture Soojah-ool-Moolk was sent for to strengthen the hands of the Shah's opponents. When he arrived, he found Caubul in a state of siege. Futteh Khan had by this time returned to aid the royal cause, but too late to regain the ground that had been lost in his absence. There was an engagement, which lasted from morning to evening prayer, and at the end of which Mahmoud was defeated. Futteh Khan fled. Soojah-ool-Moolk entered Caubul in triumph; and Mahmoud threw himself at his feet.[*] To him, who in the

[*] This was in July, 1803. Shah Soojah's own account of these transactions, which forms part of the autobiography written by him at Loodhianah in 1826-27, is contained in the following words:—"After our arrival at Kazee, we had scarcely prepared our force, when Futteh

hour of victory had shown no mercy, mercy was shown in the hour of defeat. It is to the honour of Shah Soojah that he forbore to secure the future tranquillity of his empire, by committing the act of cruelty which had disgraced the accession of the now prostrate Mahmoud. The eyes of the fallen prince were spared: and years of continued intestine strife declared how impolitic was the act of mercy.

For from this time, throughout many years, the strife between the royal brothers was fierce and incessant. In his son Kamran, the ex-King Mahmoud found a willing ally and an active auxiliary. To the reigning monarch it was a period of endless inquietude. His resources were limited, and his qualities were of too negative a character to render him equal to the demands of such

Khan's army appeared; our troops immediately were drawn up in battle array, and an attack made upon them. The battle lasted from the morning to the evening prayer, when the enemy gave way, and retreated in great disorder to the valley Advaz, and then to Kamran's camp in Candahar, where the drunkenness of the Kuzzilbash soldiery, and the ill-treatment which the Soonee doctors received, soon disgusted all our subjects, who entirely refused to give Kamran assistance. On hearing this we immediately returned to our capital. Shah Mahmoud was so disheartened by the news of our victory, that after swearing on the Koran he would not again be guilty of treachery, he sent some of his principal attendants to request the royal pardon, which we granted; and had him conveyed from the outer to the inner fort with all due respect to his rank. We then entered the Balla Hissar with regal pomp, and seated ourselves on the throne of Caubul." Mr. Elphinstone says of this "victory," that "Futteh Khan was at first successful; he routed the party of the enemy which was immediately opposed to him, and was advancing to the city, when the desertion of a great lord to Soojah threw the whole into confusion: his own party then fell off by degrees, till he found himself almost alone, and was compelled to provide for his safety by a precipitate flight. Next morning Shah Soojah entered Caubul in triumph. Mooktor-ood-Dowlah walked on foot by the side of his horse, and many other Douranee ameers followed in his train."—[*Elphinstone's* "*Caubul*"—*Appendix.*]

stirring times. He wanted vigour; he wanted activity; he wanted judgment; and above all, he wanted money. It is ever the fate of those who have risen, as Soojah rose to monarchy, to be dragged down by the weight of the obligations incurred and the promises made in the hour of adversity. The day of reckoning comes and the dangers of success are as great as the perils of failure. The Douranee monarch could not meet his engagements without weakening himself, by making large assignments upon the revenues of different provinces; and even then many interested friends were turned by disappointment into open enemies. This was one element of weakness. But the error of his life was committed when he failed to propitiate the loyalty of the great Barukzye, Futteh Khan. Upon the accession of Shah Soojah, that chief had been freely pardoned, and "allowed to salute the step of the throne." But the king did not estimate the real value of the alliance, and, elevating his rival Akrum Khan, refused the moderate demands of the Barukzye chief. Disappointed and chagrined, Futteh Khan then deserted the royal standard. He chose his time wisely and well. The king had set out with an army to overawe Peshawur and Cashmere. When they had proceeded some way, Futteh Khan, who accompanied him, excused himself on the plea of some physical infirmity which disabled him from keeping pace with the royal cortège, and said that he would join the army, following it by easy stages. Thus, disguising his defection, he fell in the rear, and as the royal party advanced, returned to foment a rebellion.

In this distracted country there was at that time another aspirant to the throne. The son of Zemaun Shah, Prince Kaysur, had set up his claims to the sovereignty of Caubul. He had been appointed governor of Candahar by Shah Soojah; and probably would have been satisfied with this extent of power, if Futteh Khan had not incited him to revolt, and offered to aid him in his attempts upon the crown. The prince lent a willing ear to the charmings of the Sirdar; and so it happened that whilst Shah Soojah was amusing himself on the way to Peshawur—"enjoying the beautiful scenery and the diversion of hunting,"—his nephew and the Barukzye chief were raising a large army at Candahar, intent upon establishing, by force of arms, the claims of the family of his sightless brother.

This ill-omened intelligence brought the Shah back in haste to his capital, whence he soon marched towards Candahar to meet the advancing troops of the prince. And here again, to the treachery of his opponents, rather than to the valour of his own troops, the Shah owed his success. On the eve of the expected conflict, the son of Ahmed Khan, with other Douranee chiefs, deserted to the royal standard. Disheartened and dismayed, the prince broke up his army, and fled to Candahar. In the meanwhile, Shah Soojah returned to Caubul to find it occupied by an insurgent force. According to his own confession, he was employed for a month in repossessing himself of the capital. The insurgent prince and the Barukzye chief, during this time, had in some measure recovered themselves at Candahar, and the king marched again to the westward. Kaysur fled at his approach; and Futteh Khan betook himself to Herat, to offer his services to the son of his old master. The prince was brought back and conducted to the royal presence by Shah Zemaun and the Mooktor-ood-Dowlah, who besought the forgiveness of the king on the plea of the youth and inexperience of the offender, and the evil counsel of the Barukzye sirdar Against his better judgment, Shah Soojah forgave him and restored him to the government of Candahar.*

* "Wh le in Candahar," writes Shah Soojah, "we received letters from our b loved brother Shah-zadah Mooktor-ood-Dowlah, requesting

The affairs of Candahar being thus settled for a time, Shah Soojah marched into Sindh to enforce the payment of tribute which had been due for some years to Caubul. He then returned to his capital, and after giving his troops a three months' furlough, began to think of commencing operations against Kamran, who was again disturbing the country to the west. In the meanwhile, this prince had marched upon Candahar, and Kaysur had fled at his approach. This was the second time the two princes had met as enemies—the second time that the scale had been turned by the weight of the chief of the Barukzyes. On one occasion, Futteh Khan had invited Kamran to Candahar, and engaged to deliver up the city —then suddenly formed an alliance with Kaysur, and, sword in hand at the head of a small body of Douranees, driven back the prince with whom he had just before been in close alliance. Now he forsook the son of Shah

Prince Kaysur's pardon, as his inexperience and the advice of Futteh Khan and other rebels had led him from his duty. Out of respect to our brother we agreed to this. Prince Kaysur being in Dehleh, Shah Zemaun and Mooktor-ood-Dowlah went there and brought him into the presence. Shah Zemaun then requested that we would give him Candahar once more, and became security for his good behaviour in future. We agreed to this in spite of our good judgment." It was whilst still engaged with the settlement of affairs at Candahar, not after their complete adjustment, and Soojah's subsequent expedition to Sindh (as stated by Mr. Elphinstone), that ambassadors arrived at Bokhara to negotiate a marriage between the Khan's daughter and the Shah. "A suitable answer," says the Shah, "being given to the royal letter, and dresses of honour being given to the ambassadors, we dismissed them with gifts. *Our thoughts were then directed to the state of Candahar.*" The point is of little importance in Afghan history; and only worth noticing in illustration of the difficulty of determining with precision, the dates of different events, and the order in which they occurred. No two narratives altogether agree—but except where Shah Soojah speaks of his "victories," we may regard him as a tolerably good authority in all that relates to himself.

Zemaun to unite himself with the heir of Mahmoud. Forgetful of past treachery, Kamran received the powerful Barukzye; and they marched together upon Candahar. Kaysur, as I have said, fled at his approach; and the insurgents took possession of the city. In the meanwhile, the Persians were advancing upon Herat, and Shah Soojah was moving up to Candahar. In this critical conjuncture, Kamran returned in alarm to the former place, and Kaysur joined the king at the latter. "We again," says Shah Soojah, "gave him charge of Candahar, at the request of our queen-mother, and our brother, Shah Zemaun. On our return to Caubul, Akrum Khan and the other Khans petitioned us to pardon Futteh Khan, who was now reduced to poverty. We assented. He was then brought into the presence by Akrum Khan. We remained some time in Candahar, in the charge of which we left Prince Zemaun, and sent Kaysur to Caubul."

Again was it in the power of Shah Soojah to conciliate the great Barukzye. Again was the opportunity lost. There was something in the temper of the monarch adverse to the formation of new, and the retention of old, friendships. Whilst Futteh Khan was again made to feel the impossibility of any lasting alliance with a prince who could not appreciate the value of his services, and who neither invited nor inspired confidence, the chain which bound the Mooktor-ood-Dowlah to the sovereign was gradually relaxing, and a new danger began to threaten the latter. When the Shah was absent in the Sindh territory, the minister flung himself into the arms of Prince Kaysur, and publicly proclaimed him king. The rebels moved down upon Peshawur, and took possession of the city. Shah Soojah immediately began to direct his operations against that place. It was on the 3rd of March, 1808, that the two armies came into collision. "The sun rising," says Shah Soojah, who had halted for six days in the vicinity of Peshawur, hoping that the rebellious minister might perhaps repent, "we saw the opposite armies in battle-array. Khojan Mahommed Khan, with a few Khans, followers from Mooktor-ood-Dowlah's army, did great deeds of valour, and at last dispersed our raw soldiers, leaving us alone in the field, protected by a few faithful Douranees. We still remained on our guard, when our attendants warned us of the approach of Khojan Mahommed Khan. We rushed on the traitor sword in hand, and cut through four of the iron plates of his cuirass. Our chief eunuch, Nekoo Khan, brought his horse and accoutrements Mooktor-ood-Dowlah then attacked our force, but he and his whole race perished. Prince Kaysur fled to Caubul We then marched in triumphant pomp to the Balla Hissar of Peshawur." The gory head of the minister, borne aloft on a spear, and carried behind the conqueror, gave *éclat* to the procession, and declared the completeness of his victory.

Prince Kaysur, after a single night spent at Caubul, fled into the hill country; but was brought back to the capital by the emissaries of the Shah. The experience of past treachery and past ingratitude had not hardened the monarch's heart: and he again "pardoned the manifold offences of his nephew." In the meanwhile Mahmoud, who had been joined by Futteh Khan, and had been endeavouring to raise the sinews of war by plundering caravans, obtained, by the usual process of treachery, possession of Candahar, and then marched upon Caubul. Shah Soojah went out to meet him, and Mahmoud, rendered hopeless by disaffection in his ranks, broke up his camp and fled. The king then turned his face towards the west, and ordered his camp to be pitched on the road to Herat. "Hearing of our approach," he says, "our brother, Feroz-ood-Deen, then in charge of the fort of

Herat, sent a petition, requesting our orders, proffering the tribute due, and offering to become security for Mahmoud's future behaviour. The same blood flowed in our veins, and we ordered one lakh of rupees to be paid him yearly from the tribute of Sindh, and conferred on him the government of Herat." This done, he proceeded to Caubul, and thence to Peshawur, where he "received petitions from the Khan of Bahwulpore and Moozuffur Khan, Suddozye, stating that ambassadors from the Company's territories, by name Elphinstone and Strachey, had arrived, and requested orders." "We wrote to the ambassadors," says the Shah, "and ordered our chiefs to pay them every attention."

The history of this mission will be embraced in a subsequent chapter. It is not without some misgivings that I have traced these early annals of the Douranee Empire.* But the chronicle is not without its uses. It illustrates, in a remarkable manner, both the general character of Afghan politics, and the extraordinary vicissitudes of the early career of the man whom thirty years afterwards the British raised from the dust of exile, and reseated on the throne of his fathers. The history of the Afghan monarchy is a history of a long series of revolutions. Seldom has the country rested from strife—seldom has the sword reposed in the scabbard. The temper of the people has never been attuned to peace. They are

* The number of Oriental names which it is necessary to introduce—the repetition of incidents, greatly resembling each other, of conquest and re-conquest, of treachery and counter-treachery, of rebellions raised and suppressed—creates a confusion in the mind of the European reader. It is difficult to interest him in these indistinct phantasmagoric transitions. The events, too, which I have narrated have been chronicled before. I have endeavoured, however, to impart some novelty to the recital by following, and sometimes quoting, Shah Soojah's autobiography, which was not accessible to preceding historians.

impatient of the restraints of a settled government, and are continually panting after change. Half-a-century of turbulance and anarchy has witnessed but little variation in the national character; and the Afghan of the present day is the same strange mixture of impetuosity and cunning—of boldness and treachery—of generosity and selfishness—of kindness and cruelty—as he was when Zemaun Shah haunted the Council-Chamber of Calcutta with a phantom of invasion, and the vision was all the more terrible because "the shape thereof" no one could discern.

CHAPTER III.

[1801—1808.]

France and Russia in the East—Death of Hadjee Khalil Khan—The Mission of Condolence—Aga Nebee Khan—Extension of Russian Dominion in the East—French Diplomacy in Persia—The pacification of Tilsit—Decline of French influence in Teheran.

THE intestine wars, which rent and convulsed the Afghan Empire, were a source of acknowledged security to the British power in the East. From the time when in the first year of the present century Captain Malcolm dictated at the Court of Teheran the terms of that early treaty, which French writers freely condemn, and Englishmen are slow to vindicate, to the date of the romantic pacification of Tilsit, the politics of Central Asia excited little interest or alarm in the Council-Chamber of Calcutta. India had ceased to bestir itself about an Afghan invasion. Instead of a shadowy enemy from beyond the Indus, the British had now to face, on the banks of the Jumna, a real and formidable foe. The genius of the two Wellesleys was called into action to curb the insolence and crush the power of the Mahrattas; and whilst we were alternately fighting and negotiating with Scindiah and Holkar, we scarcely cared to ask who reigned in Afghanistan; or if accident made us acquainted with the progress of events, viewed with philosophic unconcern the vicissitudes of the Douranee Empire.

Engaged in the solution of more pressing political questions at home, Lord Wellesley and his immediate successors bestowed little thought upon the Persian alliance. Throughout the remaining years of that nobleman's administration, one event alone occurred to rouse the Governor-General to a consideration of the temper of the Court of Teheran. That event filled him with apprehensions of danger preposterously incommensurate with its own importance, and ridiculously falsified by the result. An accident, and a very untoward one, it occurred at a time when the Indian Government had not yet recovered from the inquietude engendered by their disturbing dreams of French and Afghan invasion. The story may be briefly told. On the return of Captain Malcolm from Persia, one Hadjee Khalil Khan had been despatched to India to reciprocate assurances of friendship, and to ratify and interchange the treaty. The mission cost the Hadjee his life. He had not been long resident in Bombay,* when the Persian attendants of the ambassador and the detachment of Company's sepoys forming his escort quarrelled with each other in the court-yard before his house, and came into deadly collision. The Hadjee went out to quell the riot, and was struck dead by a chance shot. The intelligence of this unhappy disaster was brought round to Calcutta by a king's frigate. The sensation it created at the Presidency was intense. Every possible demonstration of sorrow was made by the Supreme Government. Minute guns were fired from the ramparts of Fort William. All levees and public dinners at Government-House were suspended. Distant stations caught the alarm from the Council-Chamber of Calcutta The minor presidencies were scarcely less convulsed Bombay having previously thrown itself into mourning instructions for similar observances were sent round to

* Hadjee Khalil Khan reached Bombay on the 21st of May, 1802 and was killed on the 20th of July.

Madras; and two days after the arrival of the *Chiffone* it was announced in the Gazette that Major Malcolm, who was at that time acting as private secretary to Lord Wellesley, had been directed to proceed to Bombay, for the purpose of communicating with the relations of the late Hadjee Khalil Khan, taking with him, as secretary, his young friend and relative, Lieutenant Pasley, who had accompanied him on his first mission to Persia. At the same time Mr. Lovett, a civilian of no long standing, was ordered to proceed immediately to Bushire, charged with an explanatory letter from Lord Wellesley to the Persian king, and instructed to offer such verbal explanations as might be called for by the outraged monarch. For some days nothing was thought of in Calcutta beyond the circle of this calamitous affair. In other directions a complete paralysis descended upon the Governor-General and his advisers. The paramount emergency bewildered the strongest understandings, and dismayed the stoutest hearts at the Presidency. And yet it was said, not long afterwards, by the minister of Shiraz, that "the English might kill ten ambassadors, if they would pay for them at the same rate."

Major Malcolm left Calcutta on the 30th of August, and beating down the Bay of Bengal against the south-west monsoon, reached Masulipatam on the 19th of September. Taking dawk across the country, he spent a few days at Hyderabad in the Deccan, transacted some business there, and then pushed on to Bombay. Reaching that Presidency on the 10th of October, he flung himself into his work with characteristic energy and self-reliance. Mr. Lovett, who had none of his activity, followed slowly behind, and fell sick upon the road. Jonathan Duncan, the most benevolent of men, was at that time Governor of Bombay, and some members of the Persian embassy had presumed upon his good-nature to assume an arrogance of demeanour which it now became Malcolm's duty to check. He soon reduced them to reason. Before the end of the month every difficulty had vanished. Many of the Persians were personally acquainted with the English diplomatist. All were acquainted with his character. But above all, it was known that he was the bearer of the public purse. He came to offer the mourners large presents and handsome pensions from the Supreme Government, and it is no matter of surprise, therefore, that he had soon, in his own words, " obtained from them a confidence which enabled him to set aside all intermediate agents, and consequently freed him from all intrigues."*

It was arranged that the body of the deceased ambassador should be put on board at the end of October, and that, a day or two later, the vessel should set sail for the Persian Gulf. Mr. Pasley was directed to attend the Hadjee's remains, and was charged with the immediate duties of the mission.† When the vessel reached Bushire,

* *MS. Correspondence.*
† "I shall send," wrote Major Malcolm, "Mr. Pasley with the Hadjee's body, which will not only be considered a high compliment, but be useful in a thousand ways. It will preserve this transaction from the *touch* of Mr. Manesty and Mr. Jones. It will enable me to convey a correct state of the feeling here on the subject to many respectable Persians, and I shall obtain from Mr. P. a true account of the manner in which the transaction is received in Persia. He will give Lovett information which will secure him from error at the outset, and be of the highest utility to him during his residence in India."—[*MS. Correspondence.*] It is not certain, however, that the high compliment here designed was duly appreciated by the Persians. Sir Harford Jones (from whose "touch" the transaction was to be preserved) says that "it seems to have escaped Marquis Wellesley that that which might be considered a compliment at Calcutta, might in Arabia, Turkey, and Persia, be regarded as so improper as almost to become an insult. . . . . The Persian moollahs as well as the Persian merchants at Bagdad, were shocked, and on my applying to old Sulemein Pacha for certain honours

it was found that the death of the Hadjee had created little sensation in the Persian territories, and that before the intelligence was ten days old it had been well-nigh forgotten. The Resident at Bushire, a Persian of good family, naturalised in India, and employed by the Company—an astute diplomatist and a great liar—had thought it necessary to testify his zeal by circulating a false version of the circumstances attending the death of the Hadjee, and calumniating the memory of the deceased.

to be paid to the corpse, when removed from Bagdad to be carried to Nejeef, he said, 'Very well : as you desire it to be done, it shall be done : but Hadjee Khalil Khan lived an infidel, and with infidels, and was, therefore, destined to hell; he was, however, murdered by infidels, and so became a *shahyde* (martyr) ; but his former friends have robbed him of this chance, by deputing an infidel to attend his corpse to the grave ; his fate, therefore, is now fixed, and you may carry him to the devil in any manner you like best.'"—[*Sir Harford Jones's account of the transactions of H. M.'s mission to the Court of Persia, &c. Note* vii.] It is curious, but somewhat humiliating, to read the different versions of the same transactions put forth by Jones and Malcolm, and their respective adherents. For example, Sir Harford Jones says that when the Hadjee's body reached Bagdad, Mr. Day, a Bombay civilian, who had been deputed to accompany it into the interior, took fright at the plague, and abandoned his charge. "Mr. Day's alarm was so great," he says, "as to become most tormenting to himself, and most ridiculous and troublesome to us, who had stood the plague the preceding year. I, therefore, re-shipped him for Bussorah as soon as possible, and undertook to receive and execute such wishes as the Khan's relatives expressed to me." Now the account given of this matter by one of the gentlemen of Malcolm's mission, sets forth that "Jones had frightened away Mr. Day by alarming accounts of the plague."— "On this subject," it was added, "I need make no remarks to you, who know him so well. This might be improper, and would, I imagine, be perfectly unnecessary." I have dwelt upon these personal matters at greater length than they deserve, because they illustrate the feelings, on either side, with which Jones and Malcolm, at a later and more important period, were likely each to have regarded the parallel but antagonistic mission of the other to the Persian Court. The bitterness which then overflowed was the accumulated gall of years.

There was no need, indeed, of this The Persian Government seems to have regarded the death of the Hadjee with exemplary unconcern; and marvelled why the English should have made so great a stir about so small a matter. If a costly British mission could have been extracted out of the disaster, the Court would have been more than satisfied; whilst they who were most deeply interested in the event, moved by the same *sacra fames*, thought rather of turning it to profitable account than of bewailing the death of their relative and friend.

The brother-in-law of the late envoy lost no time in offering his services to fill the place of the deceased. The name of this man was Aga Nebee Khan. He was the son, by a second connexion, of the mistress of Mr. Douglas, chief of the Bussorah factory, and had been Mr. Jones's moonshee, on a monthly salary of thirty rupees. The Hadjee himself had been a person of no consideration. Half-minister and half-merchant, he had thought more of trading upon his appointment than of advancing the interests of the state; and Nebee Khan, who had embarked with him in his commercial speculations, now lusted to succeed his murdered relative in his diplomatic office, as well as in the senior partnership of the mercantile concern. And he succeeded at last. It cost him time, and it cost him money to accomplish his purpose; but partly by bribery, partly by cajolery, he eventually secured the object of his ambition.* It was not, however,

* Especial instructions having been given to the British mission to secure the appointment of a man of rank as successor to Khalil Khan, the intrigues of Aga Nebee to obtain the appointment greatly embarrassed our diplomatists in Persia. But it was acknowledged that the aspirant was a man of good temper, good abilities, and more than average respectability. He professed himself to be heart and soul the friend of the English, and, doubtless, was perfectly sincere in his attachment to their wealth and profusion. Like all his countrymen, he was capable of profound dissimulation, and lied without the slightest

till three full years had passed away since the death of the Hadjee, that his brother-in-law reached Calcutta, "not exactly to fill his relative's place, but to exercise the triple functions of minister, merchant, and claimant of blood-money, which he roundly assessed at twenty lakhs of rupees."

And in those three years a great change had come over the Supreme Government of India. A long war, prosecuted with extraordinary vigour, had exhausted the financial resources of the state. The reign of India's most magnificent satrap—the "sultanised" Governor-General—was at an end. A new ruler had been sent from England to carry out a new policy; and that policy was fatal to the pretensions of such a man as Nebee Khan.

He had fallen, indeed, upon evil times. Those were not days when moneyed compensations were likely to

remorse. Knowing the views of the British functionaries with regard to the succession, he sent through his brother to Mr. Lovett an account of an interview he had had with the Shah, representing that he had urged upon his majesty the propriety of appointing an elchee of high rank as successor to Hadjee Khalil Khan, but that the king had insisted upon appointing him. In the same letter an amusing attempt is made to persuade Mr. Lovett to proceed to Teheran as an ambassador from the British-Indian Government, "with handsome and splendid equipments, so as to exceed by many degrees those with which Major Malcolm travelled: for this is the particular wish of the king and his ministers, in order that it may get abroad universally that the English had, for the sake of apologising, made these new preparations far exceeding the former, and that it is evident they highly regard the friendship of the king, and were not to blame for the death of Hadjee Khalil Khan. His majesty, too, when he hears of the splendour and greatness of your retinue, will be much pleased, and most favourably inclined. . . . . *Do not be sparing in expenditure, or presents, or largesses. Every country has its customs; and every nation may be won somehow or other. The people of Persia in the manner above stated.*" It is hard to say which is to be most admired, the candour or the craft of this.—[*MS. Records.*]

be granted even to ambassadors, or when there was any greater likelihood of an Indian statesman embarrassing himself with distant engagements which might compel him to advance an army into unknown regions, or send a fleet into foreign seas. So there was nothing but disappointment in store for Nebee Khan. In the month of October, 1805, the vessel bearing the ambassador sailed into the harbour of Bombay. He was welcomed with all the formalities befitting his station, and with every demonstration of respect. But a series of untoward circumstances, like those which, in the reign of our second James, delayed the public audience of Lord Castlemaine at Rome, postponed, for the space of many months, the reception of Nebee Khan at Calcutta. At length, on the 28th of April, 1806, the ceremony of presentation took place. Sir George Barlow was then at the head of the Indian Government. The Governor-General lined the public way with soldiers, and sent the leading officers of the state to conduct the merchant-minister to his presence. It was an imposing spectacle, and a solemn farce. The Persian elchee knew that he had come to Calcutta not to treat of politics, but of pice; and the English governor, while publicly honouring the Persian, secretly despised him as a sordid adventurer, and was bent upon baffling his schemes. At the private interviews which took place between the British functionaries and Nebee Khan, there was little mention of political affairs. There was a long outstanding money account between the parties, and the settlement of the account-current was the grand object of the mission. The Persian, who thought that he had only to ask, found that times had changed since the commencement of the century, and was overwhelmed with dismay when the British secretary demonstrated to him that he was a debtor to our government of more than a lakh of rupees.

Satisfied with existing relations of friendship between Persia and Great Britain, and never at any time disposed to embarrass himself with unnecessary treaties, Barlow declined to enter into new political negotiations, or to satisfy the exorbitant personal claims of the representative of the Persian Court. Nebee Khan left Calcutta a disappointed man. The speculation had not answered. The investment had been a bad one. He had toiled for four long years; he had wasted his time and wasted his money only to be told at last, by an officious secretary, that he owed the British-Indian Government a lakh and seven thousand rupees. In January, 1807, carrying back a portfolio, not more full of political than his purse of financial results, the ambassador left Calcutta. Neither the merchant nor the minister had played a winning game. Compensation and treaties were alike refused him; and he went back with empty hands.

In the mean while, the French had succeeded in establishing their influence at the Court of Teheran.* They had long been pushing their intrigues in that quarter, and now at last were beginning to overcome the difficulties which had formerly beset them. The Malcolm treaty of 1800 bound the contracting parties to a defensive alliance against France; but the terms of the treaty had been

* Some French agents, under the feigned character of botanists, had visited Teheran before Buonaparte invaded Egypt, and wished Aga Mahomed Khan, the then ruler of Persia, to seize Bussorah and Bagdad. They also endeavoured to stimulate the Shah to assist Tippoo Sultan against the British, and endeavoured to obtain permission to re-establish their footing at Gombroon. Had the emissaries appeared in a more openly diplomatic character, they might have succeeded, for Aga Mahomed Khan coveted the territory named, and might have been induced to co-operate in an attack upon the Turkish dominions; but the doubtful character of the agents thwarted their schemes, and he gave little heed to the representations of the *savans.*—[See *Brigadier Malcolm to Lord Minto: MS. Records.*]

scarcely adjusted, when French emissaries endeavoured to shake the fidelity of Persia by large offers of assistance. The offers were rejected. The French were told, in emphatic language, that "if Napoleon appeared in person at Teheran, he would be denied admission to the centre of the universe." But, undaunted by these failures, they again returned to tempt the embarrassed Persians. Every year increased the difficulties of the Shah, and weakened his reliance on the British. He was beset with danger, and he wanted aid. The British-Indian Government was either too busy or too indifferent to aid him. The energetic liberality of the French contrasted favourably with our supineness; and before the year 1805 had worn to a close, Persia had sought the very alliance and asked the very aid, which before had been offered and rejected.

The assistance that was sought was assistance against Russia. In 1805, the Shah addressed a letter to Napoleon, then in the very zenith of his triumphant career, seeking the aid of the great western conqueror to stem the tide of Russian encroachment. For years had that formidable northern power been extending its conquests to the eastwards. Before the English trader had begun to organise armies in Hindostan, and to swallow up ancient principalities, the grand idea of founding an Eastern empire had been grasped by the capacious mind of Peter the Great. Over the space of a century, under emperors and empresses of varying shades of character, had the same undeviating course of aggressive policy been pursued by Russia towards her eastern neighbours. The country which lies between the Black Sea and the Caspian was the especial object of Muscovite ambition. A portion of it, occupied by a race of hardy, vigorous mountaineers, still defies the tyranny of the Czar, and still from time to time, as new efforts are made to subjugate it, new detachments of Russian troops are buried in its formidable defiles. But Georgia, after a series of wars, notorious for the magnitude of the atrocities which disgraced them, had been wrested from the Persians before the close of the last century, and in 1800 was formally incorporated with the Russian Empire by the Autocrat Paul.

These encroachments beyond the Caucasus brought Russia and Persia into a proximity as tempting to the one as it was perilous to the other. The first few years of the present century were years of incessant and sanguinary strife. In the Russian Governor-General, Zizianoff, were combined great personal energy and considerable military skill, with a certain ferocity of character which seldom allowed him to display much clemency towards the vanquished. A Georgian by extraction, and connected by marriage with the princes of that country, he never forgot the cruelties which had alienated for ever the hearts of the Georgian people from their old Mahomedan masters. The restless aggressive spirit of the great Muscovite power was fitly represented by this man. He was soon actively at work. He entered Daghistan— defeated the Lesghees with great slaughter—carried Ganja by assault, and massacred the garrison—a second time defeated the Lesghees, after a sanguinary engagement; and then returning to Tiflis, addressed the governors of Shamakhee, Sheesha, and other fortresses to the north of the Aras, threatening them with the fate of Ganja if they did not make instant submission in compliance with the orders of the Russian monarch, who had instructed him not to pause in his career of conquest until he had encamped his army on the borders of that river.

In the spring of 1804, Abbas Mirza, the heir-apparent to the throne of Persia, took the field at the head of a formidable army, and marched down upon Erivan, the capital of Armenia. The governor refused to abandon his charge, and when the prince prepared to attack him, called the Russian general to his aid. The result was fatal to the Persian cause. In the month of July, the army of the Crown-Prince of Persia and the Russian and Georgian force under Zizianoff, twice encountered each other, and twice the Persian army was driven back with terrible loss. On the second occasion the rout was complete. Abbas Mirza lost everything. Taking refuge in a small fort, he endeavoured to negotiate terms with Zizianoff; but the Russian general told him haughtily, that the orders of his sovereign were, that he should occupy all the country along the Aras River, from Erivan to the borders of the Caspian, and that he chafed under the instructions which confined his conquests to a limit so far within the boundaries of his own ambition

The disasters of the heir-apparent brought the king himself into the field. Moving down with a large army to the succour of the prince, he again encountered the Russian forces, but only to see his troops sustain another defeat. Disheartened by these repeated failures, the Persians then changed their tactics, and adopting a more predatory style of warfare, harassed their northern enemy by cutting off his supplies. The year being then far advanced, Zizianoff drew off his forces, and prepared to prosecute the war with renewed energy in the following spring. That spring was his last. An act of the blackest treachery cut short his victorious career. He was conducting in person the siege of Badkoo, when the garrison, making overtures of capitulation, invited the Russian general to a conference for the settlement of the terms. He went unattended to a tent that had been pitched for his reception, and was deliberately set upon and slain by a party of assassins stationed there for the bloody purpose.

The King of Persia, when the tidings reached him, grew wild with delight. In an ecstasy of joy he published an inflated proclamation, setting forth that he had achieved a great victory, and slain the celebrated Russian commander. But other thoughts soon forced themselves upon the king and his ministers. A black cloud was brooding over them—the retribution of an outraged nation. A signal chastisement was expected. New armies were looked for; new encroachments anticipated from the North; new forfeitures of dominion seemed inevitable—the righteous result of an act of such atrocious perfidy. Persia felt her weakness, and, in an extremity which seemed to threaten her very existence, trusted to foreign European aid to rescue her from the jaws of death.

It was at this time, when threatened with the vengeance of Russia, that the Persian Court addressed a letter to Napoleon, then in the full flush of unbroken success, seeking the aid of that powerful chief. It was at this time, too, that Aga Nebee Khan commenced his journey to India, and it is probable that if the Indian Government had shown any disposition to aid the Persian monarch in his efforts to repel the aggressions of the Muscovite, the French alliance would have been quietly but effectually relinquished. But the supineness of England was the opportunity of France. The Indian Government had left the settlement of the Persian question to the Cabinet of St. James's, and the Cabinet had dawdled over it as a matter that might be left to take care of itself. In this extremity, the Persian monarch forgot the treaty with the British, or thought that the British, by deserting him in his need, had absolved him from all obligations to observe it, and openly flung himself into the arms of the very enemy which that treaty so truculently proscribed.

In the autumn of 1805, an accredited French agent arrived at Teheran. The result of the Indian mission was then unknown; and Colonel Romieu was received with that barren courtesy which almost amounts to discouragement. It would probably, too, have been so regarded by the French envoy, had not death cut short his diplomatic career, after a few days spent at Teheran, and a single audience of the king. But the following spring beamed more favourably on the diplomacy of France. The cold indifference of England had been ascertained beyond a doubt, and the danger of Russian aggressiveness, now sharpened by revenge, was becoming more and more imminent. All things conspired to favour the machinations of the French; and they seized the opportunity with vigour and address. Another envoy appeared upon the scene. Monsieur Jaubert was received with marked attention and respect. He came to pave the way for a splendid embassy, which Napoleon proposed to despatch to the Persian Court. Overjoyed at these assurances of friendship, the king eagerly grasped the proffered alliance. He was prepared to listen to any proposal, so that his new allies undertook to co-operate against his Russian enemies. He would join in an invasion of Hindostan, or, in concert with the French, amputate any given limb from the body of the Turkish Empire. There was much promise of aid on either side, and for a time French counsels were dominant at the Persian capital. Two years passed away, during which the emissaries of Napoleon, in spite of accidental hindrances, contrived to gain the confidence of the Court of Teheran. They declared that England was a fallen country—that although protected for a time by its insular position, it must fall a prey to the irresistible power of Napoleon—that, as nothing was to be expected from its friendship, nothing was to be apprehended from its enmity; and so.

industriously propagating reports to our discredit, they established themselves on the ruins of British influence, and for a time their success was complete.

And so it happened, that when the British Governments in London and Calcutta awoke almost simultaneously to the necessity of "doing something," they found a well-appointed French embassy established at Teheran, under General Gardanne, an officer of high reputation, whom even hostile diplomatists have delighted to commend; they found a numerous staff of officers,* civil and military, with engineers and artificers, prepared to instruct and drill the native troops, to cast cannon, and to strengthen the defences of the Persian cities; they found French agents, under the protection of duly constituted *mehmendars*, visiting Gombroon, Bushire, and other places, surveying the harbours of the gulf, and intriguing with the ambassadors of the Ameers of Sindh. And it was pretty well ascertained that the invasion of India by a French and Persian army was one of the objects of the treaty, which, soon after the arrival of Gardanne at Teheran, was sent home for the approval of Napoleon.

But a mighty change had, by this time, passed over the politics of Europe. It was in July, 1807, that on a raft floating upon the bosom of the River Niemen, near the city of Tilsit, in the kingdom of Prussia, the Emperor Alexander and Napoleon Buonaparte, after a brief and bloody campaign, embraced each other like brothers. In the short space of ten days, fifty thousand of the best French and Russian troops had been killed or disabled on the field of battle. Yet so little had been the vantage

* General Gardanne's suite, according to Colonel Malcolm, consisted of "twenty-five officers, two clergymen, a physician, some artillery and engineer officers, thirty European sub-officers, and a number of artificers."—[*MS. Records.*]

gained by either party, that it is even to this day a moot point in history, as it was in the contemporary records of the war, whether the first peaceful overture was made by the Russian monarch or the Corsican invader. Both powers eagerly embraced the opportunity of repose ; and in a few days the scene was changed, as by magic, from one of sanguinary war and overwhelming misery to one of general cordiality and rejoicing. The French and Russian soldiers, who a few days before had broken each other's ranks on the bloody plains of Eylau and Friedland, now feasted each other with overflowing hospitality, and toasted each other with noisy delight. Such, indeed, on both sides was the paroxysm of friendship, that they exchanged uniforms one with the other, and paraded the public streets of Tilsit in motley costume, as though the reign of international fraternity had commenced in that happy July. And whilst the followers of Alexander and Napoleon were abandoning themselves to convivial pleasures, and the social affections and kindly charities were in full play, those monarchs were spending quiet evenings together, discussing their future plans, and projecting joint schemes of conquest. It was then that they meditated the invasion of Hindostan by a confederate army uniting on the plains of Persia. Lucien Buonaparte, the brother of the newly-styled emperor, was destined for the Teheran mission ; and no secret was made of the intention of the two great European potentates to commence, in the following spring, a hostile demonstration "contre les possessions de la Compagnie des Indes."

But by this time both the British and the Indian Governments had awakened from the slumbers of indifference in which they had so long been lulled. They could no longer encourage theories of non-interference whilst the most formidable powers in Europe were pushing their conquests and insinuating their intrigues over the countries and into the courts of Asia. Lord Minto had succeeded Sir George Barlow as head of the Supreme Government of India. Naturally inclined, as he was instructed, to carry out a moderate policy, and to abstain as much as possible from entanglements with native rulers, he would fain have devoted himself to the details of domestic policy, and the replenishment of an exhausted exchequer. But the unsettled state of our European relations compelled him to look beyond the frontier. What he saw there roused him into action. It is observable that statesmen trained in the cabinets and courts of Europe have ever been more sensitively alive to the dangers of invasion from the North than those whose experience has been gathered in the fields of Indian diplomacy. Lord Wellesley and Lord Minto were ever tremulous with intense apprehension of danger from without, whilst Sir John Shore and Sir George Barlow possessed themselves in comparative confidence and tranquillity, and, if they were not wholly blind to the peril, at all events did not exaggerate it. There is a sense of security engendered by long habit and familiarity with apparent danger, which renders a man mistrustful of the reality of that which has so often been shown to be a counterfeit. The inexperience of English statesmen suddenly transplanted to a new sphere of action, often sees in the most ordinary political phenomena strange and alarming portents. It is easy to be wise after the event. We know now that India has never been in any real danger from French intrigue or French aggressiveness; but Lord Wellesley and Lord Minto saw with different eyes, and grappled the shadowy danger as though it were a substantial fact. In those days such extraordinary events were passing around us, that to assign the limits of political probability was beyond the reach of human wisdom. The attrition of great events had rubbed out the line which separates fact from fiction, and the march of a grand army under one of Napoleon's marshals from the banks of the Seine to the banks of the Ganges did not seem a feat much above the level of the Corsican's towering career

Rightly understood, the alliance between the two great continental powers which seemed to threaten the destruction of the British Empire in the East, was a source of security to the latter. But in 1807 it was not so clearly seen that Persia was more easily to be conciliated by the enemies, than by the friends, of the Russian Autocrat— that the confederacy of Alexander and Napoleon was fatal to the Persian monarch's cherished hopes of the restitution of Georgia, and the general retrogression of the Russian army; and that, therefore, there was little prospect of the permanency of French influence at the Court of Teheran. Forgetful as we were of this, the danger seemed imminent, and only to be met by the most active measures of defence. To baffle European intrigue, and to stem the tide of European invasion, it then appeared to the British Indian Government expedient to enlace in one great network of diplomacy all the states lying between the frontier of India and the eastern points of the Russian Empire. Since India had been threatened with invasion at the close of the last century, the Afghan power had by disruption ceased to be formidable. We had formerly endeavoured to protect ourselves against France on the one side, and Afghanistan on the other, by cementing a friendly alliance with Persia. It now became our policy, whilst endeavouring to re-establish our influence in that country, to prepare ourselves for its hostility, and to employ Afghanistan and Sindh as barriers against encroachments from the West; and at the same time to increase our security by enlisting against the French and Persian confederacy the friendly offices of the

Sikhs. That strange new race of men had by this time erected a formidable power on the banks of the Sutlej, by the mutilation of the Douranee Empire; and it was seen at once that the friendship of a people occupying a tract of country so situated, and inspired with a strong hatred of the Mahomedan faith, must, in such a crisis as had now arrived, be an object of desirable attainment. Whilst, therefore, every effort was to be made to wean the Court of Teheran from the French alliance, preparations were commenced, in anticipation of the possible failure of the Persian mission, for the despatch of British embassies to the intervening countries.

The duty of negotiating with the Sikh ruler was entrusted to Mr. Metcalfe, a civil servant of the Company, who subsequently rose to the highest place in the government of India, and consummated a life of public utility in a new sphere of action, as Governor-General of our North American colonies. Mr. Elphinstone, another civil servant of the Company, who still lives, amidst the fair hills of Surrey, to look back with pride and contentment upon a career little less distinguished than that of his contemporary, was selected to conduct the embassy to the Court of the Douranee monarch. Captain Seton had been previously despatched to Sindh; and Colonel Malcolm, who was at that time Resident at Mysore, was now again ordered to proceed to the Persian Court, charged with duties which had been rendered doubly difficult by our own supineness, and the contrasted activity of our more restless Gallic neighbours.

CHAPTER IV.

[1808—1809.]

The Second Mission to Persia—Malcolm's Visit to Bushire—Failure of the Embassy—His Return to Calcutta—Mission of Sir Harford Jones—His Progress and Success.

WHEN, in the spring of 1808, Colonel Malcolm a second time steered his course towards the Persian Gulf, another British diplomatist had started, from another point, upon the same mission. Moved as it were by one common impulse, the Cabinet of England and the Supreme Council of India had determined each to despatch an embassy to the Court of Teheran. A curious and unseemly spectacle was then presented to the eyes of the world. Two missions, in spirit scarcely less antagonistic than if they had been despatched by contending powers, started for the Persian Court; the one from London—the other from Calcutta. The Court of St. James's had proposed to assist Persia by mediating with St. Petersburgh, and Mr. Harford Jones, a civil servant of the Company, who was made a baronet for the occasion, was deputed to Teheran to negotiate with the ministers of the Shah. It was originally intended that he should proceed to Persia, taking the Russian capital in his route; but the pacification of Tilsit caused a departure from this design, and Sir Harford Jones sailed for Bombay with the mission on board one of his Majesty's ships. He reached that port in the month of April, 1808, just as the embassy under Brigadier-General Malcolm, despatched by the Governor-

General to the Court of Teheran, was putting out to sea on its way to the Persian Gulf.*

Sir Harford Jones, therefore, rested at Bombay, awaiting the result of Malcolm's proceedings. On the 10th of May, the latter reached Bushire, and on the 18th wrote to Sir George Barlow, who had succeeded to the governorship of Madras, "I have not only received the most uncommon attention from all here, but learnt from the best authority that the accounts of my mission have been received with the greatest satisfaction at Court. The great progress which the French have made and are daily making here satisfied me of the necessity of bringing matters to an early issue. I have a chance of complete victory. I shall, at all events, ascertain exactly how we stand, and know what we ought to do; and if I do not awaken the Persian Court from their delusion, I shall at least excite the jealousy of their new friends. I send Captain Pasley off to-morrow for Court—ostensibly, with a letter for the king; but he has secret instructions, and will be able to make important observations. He is charged with a full declaration of my sentiments and instructions in an official form, and you will, I think, when you see that declaration of the whole proceeding, think it calculated for the object. I have endeavoured to combine moderation with spirit, and to inform the Persian Court, in language that cannot irritate, of all the danger

* Malcolm wrote from Bombay on the 15th of April, stating the course of policy he intended to pursue, and the tone of remonstrance he purposed to adopt, at the same time urging the Governor-General to suspend the mission of Sir Harford Jones. In this letter he says that he should despair, "from his knowledge of Sir Harford's character and former petty animosities on the same scene, of maintaining concord and unanimity in the gulf one hour after his arrival. Sir Harford," he added, "is not in possession of that high local respect and consideration in the countries to which he is deputed that should attach to a national representative."

of their French connexion. Captain Pasley will reach Court on the 20th of June, and on the 15th of July I may expect to be able to give you some satisfactory account of his success."*

But in this he was over-sanguine. The French envoy had established himself too securely at Teheran to be driven thence by the appearance of Malcolm at Bushire. A little too impetuous, perhaps—a little too dictatorial, that energetic military diplomatist commenced at the wrong end of his work He erred in dictating to the Persian Court the dismissal of the French embassy as a preliminary to further negotiations, when in reality it was the end and object of his negotiations. He erred in blurting out all his designs, in unfolding the scheme of policy he intended to adopt, and so committing himself to a line of conduct which after-events might have rendered it expedient to modify or reject. He erred in using the language of intimidation at a time when he should have sought to inspire confidence and diffuse goodwill among the officers of the Persian Court. These may not have been the causes of his want of success; but it is certain that he was completely unsuccessful. The large promises and the prompt movements of the French contrasted favourably with our more scanty offers and more dilatory action; and although Malcolm now came laden with presents, and intending to pave his way to the Persian capital with gold, the British mission was received with frigid indifference, if not with absolute disrespect. The despatch of Captain Pasley to the capital was negatived by the Persian Government. His progress was arrested at Shiraz ; and there, at that provincial town, whilst a French and a Russian agent were basking in the royal sunshine at Teheran, and were entertained as guests

* *MS. Correspondence of Sir John Malcolm.*

of the prime minister, the representative of Great Britain was told that he must conduct his negotiations and content himself with the countenance of lesser dignitaries of state. Persian officers were instructed to amuse the British envoys, and to gain time. "The earnest desire of the king," wrote the prime minister to Nussur-ood-Dowlah, at Shiraz, "is to procrastinate, and to avoid all decided measures. You must, therefore, amuse General Malcolm by offering your assistance;" and in this and other letters the local officers at Shiraz were instructed by every means in their power to detain Captain Pasley at that place; but he had departed before they were received, or it is difficult to say in what manner the imperial mandate might not have been obeyed.* "A consideration of all these things," wrote Captain Pasley to Government, "induces me to conclude that the subsisting alliance between the Government of France and Persia is more intimate than we have yet imagined—that its nature is more actively and decidedly hostile to our interests than has hitherto been suspected, and that the reliance of the king on the promises and assurances of the French agents must be founded on better grounds than have yet come to our knowledge."†

Chafed and indignant at the conduct of the Persian Court, General Malcolm at once came to the determination to return immediately to Calcutta, and to report to the Supreme Government the mortifying result of his

---

* *MS. Records.*—Copies of these letters were obtained by the Mission, and are now before me. I do not find in them anything to give colour to the suspicion that it was intended forcibly to detain Pasley at Shiraz. But such appears to have been the impression at the time, and may have been the case. Sir James Mackintosh, writing from Bombay to his son-in-law, Mr. Rich, at Bagdad, counsels him to be prepared for a rapid retreat, and adds, "Pasley was very nearly made prisoner at Shiraz."

† *MS. Records.*

mission. On the 12th of July he sailed from Bushire, leaving the charge of the embassy in the hands of Captain Pasley, who remained at his post only to be insulted, and at last narrowly escaped being made prisoner by a precipitate retreat from the Persian dominions.* The failure of the mission, indeed, was complete. Persia continued to make professions of friendship to the British Government; but it was obvious that at that moment neither British diplomacy nor British gold, which was liberally offered, could make any way against the dominant influence of the French mission. Napoleon's officers were drilling the Persian army, casting cannon, and strengthening the Persian fortresses by the application, for the first time, to their barbaric defences, of that science which the French engineers had learnt in such perfection from the lessons of Vauban and Cormontague.

Of the wisdom of Malcolm's abrupt departure from Bushire, different opinions may be entertained. On the day after he embarked for Calcutta, one of the most sagacious men then in India was seated at his writing-table discoursing, for Malcolm's especial benefit, on the advantages of delay. "As to the real question," wrote Sir James Mackintosh to the Brigadier-General, "which you have to decide in the cabinet council of your own understanding, whether delay in Persia be necessarily and universally against the interests of Great Britain, it is a question on which you have infinitely greater means of correct decision than I can pretend to, even if I were foolish enough, on such matters, to aspire to any rivalship

* "General Malcolm came round to Calcutta in August to communicate the information he had been able to collect, leaving his secretary at Abushire, who was obliged subsequently to quit the place to prevent his person being seized by the Persian Government, instigated by the French agents."—[*From letter of Instructions sent by Supreme Government to Mountstuart Elphinstone, in* 1809.—*MS. Records.*]

with a man of your tried and exercised sagacity. I should just venture in general to observe, that delay is commonly the interest of the power which is on the defensive. As long as the delay lasts, it answers the purpose of victory, which, in that case, is only preservation. It wears out the spirit of enterprise necessary for assailants, especially such as embark in very distant and perilous attempts. It familiarises those who are to be attacked with the danger, and allows the first panic time to subside. It affords a chance that circumstances may become more favourable; and to those who have nothing else in their favour, it leaves at least the 'chapter of accidents.'"* The 'chapter of accidents' is everything in Oriental diplomacy. Malcolm, too impetuous to profit by it, left his successor to reap the harvest of altered circumstances. Sir Harford Jones, who had been waiting his opportunity at Bombay, entered the arena of diplomacy a few months later than Malcolm, and his progress was a long ovation. It was the 'chapter of accidents' that secured his success.

On the first receipt of intelligence of General Malcolm's withdrawal, Lord Minto despatched a letter to Sir Harford Jones, urging him to proceed to Persia with the

* Another passage from this letter is worth quoting in the margin:
—"What I doubt (for I presume to go no further), is, whether it be for our interest to force on the course of events in the present circumstances. You are a man of frank character and high spirit, accustomed to represent a successful and triumphant government. You must from nature and habit be averse to temporise. But you have much too powerful an understanding to need to be told, that to temporise is sometimes absolutely necessary, and that men of your character only can temporise with effect. When Gentz was in England, in 1803 (during the peace), he said to me, that 'it required the present system, and the late ministers;' for nothing required the reality and the reputation of vigour so much as temporising."—[*Mackintosh to Malcolm, July* 13, 1808.]

least possible delay. But he very soon revoked those orders, and addressed to the English envoy stringent communications, desiring him to remain at Bombay.* Malcolm had reached Calcutta in the interval; and set forth, in strong colours, the nature of the influence that had been opposed to his advance, and mapped out a plan of action which, in his estimation, it would now be expedient to adopt. Lord Minto appears to have fallen readily into the views of the military diplomatist; but he failed altogether to cut short the career of Sir Harford Jones. Letters travelled slowly in those days; and before the missive of the Governor-General, ordering his detention, had reached Bombay, the vessel which was to bear the representative of the Court of London to the Persian Gulf had shaken out its sails to the wind.

On the 14th of October the Mission reached Bushire. Sir Harford Jones set about his work earnestly and conscientiously. He had difficulties to contend against of no common order, and it must be admitted that he faced them manfully. He found the Persian authorities but too well disposed to arrogance and insolence; and he

* The first letter appears to have been written on the 10th of August. On the 22nd, Brigadier Malcolm landed at Calcutta. On the same day a letter was sent to Sir Harford Jones, directing him to wait for further orders, and on the 29th another and more urgent communication was addressed to him, with the intent of annulling his mission. It appears that in those days a letter took more than three weeks to accomplish the journey between Calcutta and Bombay. The Governor-General's letter of the 10th of August must have reached the latter place about the 5th of September. Jones says, "In seven days from receiving Lord Minto's letter, I embarked on board *La Nereide*, and she, with the *Sapphire*, and a very small vessel belonging to the Company, called the *Sylph*, sailed out of Bombay harbour for Persia on the 12th of September, 1808." Malcolm had calculated that the letter of August 22nd would reach Bombay by September 13th; and that in all probability Jones would not embark before that date. But, as usual, he was over-sanguine.

met their pompous impertinence with a blustering bravery, which may have been wanting in dignity, but was not without effect. He bullied and blasphemed, and, after a series of not very becoming scenes, made his way to Teheran, where he was graciously received by the Shah. The 'chapter of accidents' had worked mightily in his favour. The reign of Gallic influence was at an end. Our enemies had overreached themselves, and been caught in their own toils. Before Napoleon and the Czar had thrown themselves into each other's arms at Tilsit, it had been the policy of the French to persuade the Persian Court that the aggressive designs of Russia could be successfully counteracted only by a power at enmity with that state; and now Napoleon boasted that he and the Emperor were "invariablement unis pour la paix comme pour la guerre."

Skilfully taking advantage of this, Sir Harford Jones ever as he advanced inculcated the doctrine which had emanated in the first instance from the French embassy, and found every one he addressed most willing to accept it. There was, fortunately for us, a galling fact ever present to the minds of the Persian ministers to convince them of the truth of the assertion that it was not by the friends, but by the enemies of Russia that their interests were to be best promoted. The French had undertaken to secure the evacuation of Georgia; but still the Russian eagles were planted on Georgian soil. The star of Napoleon's destiny was no longer on the ascendant. The "Sepoy General," whom he had once derided, was tearing his battalions to pieces in the Spanish peninsula. Moreover, the French had lost ground at Teheran, in their personal as in their political relations. They had not accommodated themselves to the manners of the Persian Court, nor conciliated, by a courteous and considerate demeanour, the good-will of their new allies. They were many degrees less popular than the English, and their influence melted away at the approach of the British envoy. The Shah, too, had by this time, not improbably, become suspicious of the designs of the French. It was urged with some force that if the French invaded India they would not leave Persia alone. Mahomed Shereef Khan, who was sent by Nussur-oolah-Khan to General Malcolm just before his departure from Bushire, to repeat the friendly assurances of the Persian Government, very sagaciously observed, "If the French march an army to India, will they not make themselves masters of Persia as a necessary prelude to further conquests, and who is to oppose them after they have been received as friends? But our king," continued the old man, "dreams of the Russians. He sees them in Aderbijan, and within a short distance of the capital, and, despairing of his own strength, he is ready to make any sacrifice to obtain a temporary relief from his excessive fear. In short," he concluded, whilst strong emotion proved his sincerity, "affairs have come to that state that I thank my God I am an old man, and have a chance of dying before I see the disgrace and ruin of my country."* Had Malcolm remained a little longer at Bushire, he would have seen all these dreams of French assistance pass away from the imaginations of the Persian Court, and might, under the force of altered circumstances, have carried everything before him.

When Sir Harford Jones reached the Persian capital, General Gardanne had withdrawn; and there was little difficulty in arranging preliminaries of a treaty satisfactory alike to the Courts of Teheran and St. James's The work was not done in a very seemly manner; but it

* *MS. Correspondence.*

was not less serviceable when done, for the manner of its doing. Perhaps there is not another such chapter as this in the entire history of English diplomacy. Jones had left Bombay under the impression that he was acting in accordance with the wishes of Lord Minto; but he had not been long in Persia before he found that the Indian Government were bent upon suspending his operations, and, failing in this, were resolute to thwart him at every turn. They dishonoured his bills and ignored his proceedings. A totally opposite course of policy had been determined upon in the Council-Chamber of Calcutta. The proceedings of Brigadier Malcolm at Bushire had not been viewed with unmixed approbation by Lord Minto and his council; but he was the employé of the Indian Government; they had confidence in the general soundness of his views; and they felt that in the maintenance of their dignity it was expedient to support him. In no very conciliatory mood of mind had that eager, energetic officer returned to Calcutta. Chewing the cud of bitter fancies as he sailed up the Bay of Bengal, he prepared a plan for the intimidation of Persia, and was prepared with all the details of it when, on the 22nd of August, he disembarked at Calcutta. There was no unwillingness in the Council-Chamber to endorse his schemes. It was agreed that an armament should be fitted out to take possession of Karrack, an island in the Persian Gulf, or, in the delicate language of diplomacy, "to form an establishment" there, as "a central position equally well adapted so obstruct the designs of France against India, as to assist the King of Persia (in the event of a renewal of the alliance) against his European enemies."

These measures were described as "entirely defensive, and intended even to be amicable." The command of the force was of course conferred on Brigadier Malcolm. "I am vested," he wrote to his friends at Madras, "with supreme military and political authority and control in the Gulf, to which, however threatening appearances may be, I proceed with that species of hope which fills the mind of a man who sees a great and unexpected opportunity afforded him of proving the extent of his devotion to the country."* It was to be a very pretty little army, with a compact little staff, all the details of which, even to the allowances of its members, were soon drawn up and recorded. An engineer officer was called in and consulted about the plan of a fort, with a house for the commandant, quarters for the officers, barracks for the men, a magazine to contain five hundred barrels of gunpowder, and everything else complete. The activity of the Brigadier himself at this time was truly surprising. He drew up elaborate papers of instructions to himself, to be adopted by the Governor-General. One of these, covering twenty-six sheets of foolscap, so bewildered Lord Minto in his pleasant country retreat at Barrackpore, that he could come to no other conclusion about it than that the greater part had better be omitted. Every conceivable contingency that could arise out of the movements of France or Russia, or dispensations of Providence in Persia, was contemplated and discussed, and instructions were sought or suggested; but a new series of contingencies occurred to the Brigadier after he had embarked, and a new shower of *ifs* was poured forth from the Sand-heads still further to perplex the government. Lord Minto had by this time fully made up his mind that the French were coming; wrote of it, not as a possible event, but as a question merely of time; and contemplated the probability of contending in Turkey for the sovereignty of Hindostan.† But the French had too much work to do

* *MS. Correspondence.*

† For example, in one of his minutes written about this time, he says: "It appears doubtful whether the partition of European Turkey

in Europe to trouble themselves about operations in the remote Asiatic world.

At the beginning of October, Malcolm started for Bombay, from which Presidency the details of his army were to be drawn. But before the vessel on which he had embarked had steered into the black water, he was recalled, in consequence of the receipt of intelligence of Sir Harford Jones's intended departure for Bushire. This was, doubtless, very perplexing; but Malcolm did not despair. "I am this instant," he wrote, on the 5th of October, "recalled to Calcutta in consequence of advices from Sir Harford, stating his intention of leaving Bombay on the 11th of September. As it appears possible that he may not be ready to sail before the 13th, he will, I think, receive a letter from this government of the 22nd, desiring him to stay; and if that has the effect of stopping him, the letter of the Supreme Government, dated the 29th, will probably put an end to the mission."* Vain hope! Sir Harford Jones was at that time not many days' sail from Bushire; and before Malcolm finally quitted Calcutta, had started fairly on his race to Teheran.

The Supreme Government now more urgently than before addressed instructions to the nominee of the British Cabinet, ordering him to retire from Persia. The Council were all agreed upon the subject. Mr. Lumsden and Mr. Colebrooke, who were Members of Council at the time,

will precede the French expedition to India. There appears to be reason, by the late advices, to suppose that the consent of the Porte may have been obtained to the passage of the French army. In this case, the approach of the army may be earlier than on the former supposition, and it will have less difficulty to encounter. The route of our divisions must in this event be through the territory of Bagdad. . . . I incline, under all the circumstances now known to me, to think that the force stationed at Karrack should be greater than we before looked to."—[*MS. Records.*]

* *MS. Correspondence of Sir John Malcolm.*

expressed themselves even more strongly on the subject than the Governor-General. All were certain that Sir Harford Jones must either fail signally, or disgrace and embarrass the government by a delusive success. He might be repulsed at Bushire—or baffled at Shiraz—or drawn into a treaty favourable to the French. In any case, it was assumed that he was sure to bring discredit on the British Government and the East India Company. Without asserting that the conduct of the Persian Court had been such as to call for a declaration of war from the rulers of British India, it was contended, and not, perhaps, without some show of reason, that any advances made at such a time would compromise its dignity, and that the attitude to be assumed should be rather one of reserve than of solicitation. Both parties were in an embarrassing position. Whilst Lord Minto was writing letters to Sir Harford Jones, telling him that if he did not immediately close his mission, all his proceedings would be publicly repudiated,* Sir Harford Jones, as representative of the sovereign, was repudiating the proceedings of the Supreme Government of India, and offering to answer with his fortune and his life for any hostile proceedings on the part of the British, not provoked by the Persians themselves. The government did its best to disgrace Sir Harford Jones by dishonouring his bills and ignoring his proceedings , and Sir Harford Jones lowered the character of the Indian Government by declaring that it had no authority to revoke his measures or to nullify his engagements with the Persian Court.

* In one of these letters, written in February, 1809, it is said: "I cannot venture to omit acquainting you that, in the event of your not complying, without further reference or delay, with the instructions conveyed in this letter, by closing your mission and retiring from Persia, it has been determined, and measures have been taken accordingly, to disavow your public character in that country subsequent to your receipt of my letter of 31st of October."—[*MS. Records.*]

In the mean while, Brigadier Malcolm had sailed down the Bay of Bengal, and reached Bombay by the first day of December. His instructions had preceded him; a select force of some two thousand men was ready to receive his orders; and by the 18th of January the expedition was prepared, at all points, to take ship for the Gulf, to pounce upon Karrack, and to strike a great panic into the rebellious heart of the Persian nation. "But," says Malcolm, in one of his voluminous narratives, "the accounts I heard of the great change caused in the affairs of Europe by the general insurrection of Spain, and the consequent improbability of Buonaparte making an early attack upon India, combined with the advance of Sir Harford Jones into Persia, led me to suspend the sailing of the expedition. My conduct on that occasion was honoured by approbation, and the expedition countermanded." But though the military expedition was countermanded, the Mission was not. Malcolm, confident that the proceedings of such a man as Jones, for whom he entertained the profoundest possible contempt, could be attended only with disastrous failure, determined to proceed to Persia, in spite of the civilian's accounts of his favourable reception. " I have private accounts from Bushire," he wrote on Christmas-eve, "which state that Sir Harford Jones is, or pretends to be, completely confident of a success which every child with him sees is unattainable through the means he uses. His friends now believe he will go on in spite of any orders he may receive from the Governor-General. *I mean to go on too* (there is, indeed, nothing in these despatches that can stop me for a moment), so we shall have a *fine mess* (as the sailors say) in the Gulf."* Such, indeed, was the feeling between the two diplomatists, and so little was it dis-

* *MS. Correspondence of Sir John Malcolm—December* 24, 1808.

guised, that the Shah, perceiving plainly the true state of the case, abused Malcolm before Jones, and Jones before Malcolm, as the best means, in his opinion, of ingratiating himself with them both.

In March, 1809, the preliminary treaty was interchanged, on the part of their respective sovereigns, by Sir Harford Jones and Meerza Sheffee. No treaty before or since was ever interchanged under such extraordinary and unbecoming circumstances. Meerze Sheffee, the prime minister of Persia, was an old and infirm man. His age and rank among his own people had given him a sort of license to speak with an amount of freedom such as is not tolerated among Europeans in social, much less in diplomatic converse. There was an intentional indefiniteness in one of the articles of the treaty, which was to be referred to the British Government for specific adjustment, and Meerza Sheffee, not understanding or approving of this, blurted out that the British envoy designed to "cheat" him. The figure used in the Persian language is gross and offensive, and the word I have employed but faintly expresses the force of the insult. Jones had not patience to bear it. He started up, seized the counterpart treaty lying signed on the carpet before him, gave it to Mr. Morier, and then turning to the astonished Wuzeer, told him that he was a stupid old blockhead to dare to use such words to the representative of the King of England, and that nothing but respect for the Persian monarch restrained him from knocking out the old man's brains against the wall. "Suiting the action to the word, I then," says Jones, in his own narrative of his mission, "pushed him with a slight degree of violence against the wall which was behind him, kicked over the candles on the floor, left the room in darkness, and rode home without any one of the Persians daring to impede my passage." It is not surprising that, after such a scene as this, the Persians should have shaken their heads, and said, "By Allah! this Feringhee is either drunk or mad."

But, in spite of this and other untoward occurrences, the preliminary treaty was duly interchanged. It bears date the 12th of March, 1809. By this treaty, the Shah of Persia, declaring all other engagements void, covenanting "not to permit any European force whatever to pass through Persia, either towards India, or towards the ports of that country." He further undertook, in the event of the British dominions in India being attacked or invaded by the Afghans or any other power, "to afford a force for the protection of the said dominions." On the part of the British Government, it was stipulated that, in case any European force had invaded, or should invade, the territories of the King of Persia, his Britannic Majesty should afford to the Shah a force, or, in lieu of it, a subsidy, with warlike ammunition, such as guns, muskets, &c., and officers, to the amount that might be to the advantage of both parties, for the expulsion of the force so invading." The general provisions of the treaty were included in this, but the anticipated arrival of Brigadier Malcolm with a military expedition in the Persian Gulf rendered it necessary that certain specific articles should be inserted with especial reference to this movement. It was provided that the force should on no account possess itself of Karrack or any other places in the Persian Gulf; but that, unless required by the Governor-General for the defence of India, it should be held at the disposal of the Persian shah, the Shah undertaking to receive it in a friendly manner, and to direct his governors to supply it with provisions "at the fair prices of the day." This preliminary treaty was conveyed by Mr. Morier, accompanied by a Persian ambassador, to England, where it was duly ratified and exchanged; and Sir Harford Jones was confirmed in the post of Resident Minister at the Court of Teheran.

The success of Sir Harford Jones embarrassed the British-Indian Government even more than did the apprehension of his failure. Lord Minto and his councillors were sorely perplexed. It was desirable, as they all acknowledged, that the engagements entered into by the representative of the Court of England should be completed, but it was not desirable that the Indian Government should be degraded in the eyes of the Persian Court. Between their anxiety to accept the thing done and to disgrace the doer, they were thrown into a state of ludicrous embarrassment.* The resolution, however, at which they arrived was, under all the circumstances of the case, as reasonable as could be expected. It was determined to accept Sir Harford Jones's treaty, and to leave the dignity of the British-Indian Government to be vindicated on a

* Mr. Lumsden wrote a minute (July 10, 1809), in which he says "We must either continue to employ at the Court of Persia an agent in whom we have no confidence, who has studiously endeavoured to degrade the authority of the Government of India, under whose orders he was placed; or by deputing an agent of our own to Teheran, whilst he continues there acknowledged by the Persian Government as the representative of his Britannic Majesty, we may expose the public interest to danger from the presence in Persia of two distinct authorities, who cannot act in concert, but will, it is to be feared, necessarily counteract each other, and occasion great perplexity to the Persian minister." At the same time, Mr. Colebrooke wrote. "Our situation as regards Sir H Jones is certainly difficult and embarrassing in the extreme We are desirous of fulfilling the engagements he has contracted, and of maintaining the alliance concluded by him. And we are glad that he should continue at the Court of Persia to watch the wavering counsels of that Court, and to oppose the revival of French influence at it, until he can be replaced by our own envoy; but by either re-accrediting him with the Court, or silently executing his engagements, we acquiesce in the continued degradation of this government."—[*MS Records.*]

future occasion. Perhaps it would have been even better quietly to have lived down the slight; for it cost a large sum of money to satisfy the British-Indian Government that it had re-established its name at the Court of the Persian, and confounded the malignity of Jones.*

This is a curious chapter of diplomatic history. It is one, too, which has evoked from the partisans of both parties an extraordinary amount of bitterness. It hardly comes within the proper compass of this history to narrate the incidents of the ambassadorial war, still less to comment upon them. But it may be briefly remarked that all parties were wrong. Mistakes were unquestionably committed by Malcolm, by Jones, and by the Indian Government. There was an old feud between the two former, which certainly did not tend to smooth down the difficulties which had arisen; and the Government of India was not very patient of the home-born interference with what it conceived to be its rightful diplomatic prerogative. Jones, though receiving his credentials from the Crown, was placed in subordination to the local government, and ought to have obeyed its mandates. That he would have done so, had he received instructions to withdraw before he had fairly entered upon his work, it is only just to assume; but having once made his appearance in Persia as the representative of his sovereign, he thought that he could not abandon his mission under orders from

* On the details of Malcolm's supplementary mission it is unnecessary to dwell. Its political results are compressible into the smallest possible space. It was, indeed, a mere pageant; and a very costly, but not wholly a profitless one. It yielded a considerable harvest of literary and scientific results, among the most important of which may be mentioned Malcolm's elaborate and valuable "History of Persia" and the present Sir Henry Pottinger's admirable "Account of Beluchistan;" works which, it has been well said, "not only filled up an important blank in our knowledge of the East, but which materially helped to fix the literary character of the Indian services"

the Indian Government without lowering the dignity of the Crown.

He did not commence his expedition to Persia until some time after Malcolm had retired; and when he went at last, it was under urgent solicitations from the Governor-General to proceed there without delay. He cannot, therefore, be charged with indelicacy or precipitancy. He went only when the coast was clear. That he succeeded better than Malcolm must be attributed mainly to the "chapter of accidents," for he was a man of vastly inferior parts. Malcolm says that it was owing to his measures that Jones was enabled to advance—that the rumour of his military preparations overawed the Persian Court—and that all the rest was done by bribery. That there was at that time little hope of any mission succeeding without bribery, no man know better than Malcolm.* But Malcolm could not bribe his way to Teheran in the spring, because the French were then dominant at Court. Had he waited till the autumn, the

* It is just to Sir John Malcolm that his views of this question of bribery, with reference to his proceedings and those of Sir H. Jones, should be given in his own words: "Everything then," he wrote, "with Jones is a question of money. By cash alone all political questions are decided—one article of a treaty he values at so much, another has its price also. Is a French agent to be removed? the price of his dismissal is as regularly settled as the price of a horse. The dismissal of one (Monsieur Jouanin) has been purchased four times—three times by advances of subsidy, and once with 50,000 piastres to monsieur himself; and I suspect the convenient instrument of extortion is not yet far from Tabruz. This is a country in which one cannot go on without a large expenditure of money; but it should never form the basis of our connection, as it now does; and if we add to our large annual bribe (for a pecuniary subsidy over the application or which we have no control, must be considered such) disbursements on every occasion where Persia shows an inclination towards our enemies, we shall lose both our money and our reputation."—[*Brigadier Malcolm to Mr. Manesty, Feb.* 23, 1810. *MS.*]

road would have been lubricated for him. One thing at least is certain. Nothing could have been more fortunate than the miscarriage of Malcolm's military expedition. It would have embarrassed our future proceedings, and entailed a large waste of public money. As to the question of prerogative, it would be little use to discuss it. It has been settled long ago. The Crown ministers have taken into their own hands the appointment of our Persian ambassadors, and the conduct of all subsequent negotiations with the Persian Court. Henceforth we shall have to regard the relations subsisting between Persia and Great Britain as affairs beyond the control of the East India Company and their representatives, and to look upon the ministers of the Crown as responsible for all that we have to contemplate in that quarter of the world.*

* From 1826 to 1835, however, the nomination of the Persian envoy was again vested in the Indian Government; but the diplomatic control was not relinquished by the Foreign-office.

Note to New Edition (1856).—The arguments with which Malcolm supported the proposal for the occupation of the island of Karrack, may be advantageously given in this place, as they are set forth in his own words in his "Life and Correspondence":—

First. That in the event of an attempt to invade India being made by an European State, it was impossible to place any dependence on the efforts of the King of Persia or the Pacha of Baghdad, unless we possessed the immediate power of punishing their hostility and treachery.

Secondly. That the States of Persia, Eastern Turkey, and Arabia were, from their actual condition, to be considered less in the light of regular Governments than as countries full of combustible materials, which any nation whose interests it promoted, might throw into a flame.

Thirdly. That though the French and Russians might, no doubt, in their advance, easily conquer those States, in the event of their opposing their progress, it was their obvious policy to avoid any contest with the inhabitants of the country through which they passed, as such must, in its progress, inevitably diminish the resources of those countries, and thereby increase the difficulty of supporting their armies—which difficulty formed the chief, if not the sole, obstacle to their advance.

Fourthly. That though it was not to be conceived that the King of Persia or Pacha of Baghdad would willingly allow any European army to pass through his country, but there was every ground to expect that the fear of a greater evil was likely not only to make these rulers observe a neutrality, but to dispose them to aid the execution of a plan which they could not resist, and make them desire to indemnify themselves for submission to a power they dreaded by agreeing to share in the plunder of weaker States—a line of policy to which it was too obvious they would be united, and to which their fear, weakness, and avarice made it probable that they would accede.

Fifthly. That under a contemplation of such occurrences, it appeared of ultimate importance that the English Government should instantly possess itself of means to throw those States that favoured the approach of its enemies, into complete confusion and destruction, in order that it might, by diminishing their resources, increase the principal natural obstacle that opposed the advance of an European army, and this system, when that Government had once established a firm footing and a position situated on the confines of Persia and Turkey, it could easily pursue, with a very moderate force, and without any great risk or expenditure.

Sixthly. That with an established footing in the Gulf of Persia, which must soon become the emporium of our commerce, the seat of our political negotiations, and a dépôt for our military stores, we should be able to establish a local influence and strength that would not only exclude other European nations from that quarter, but enable us to carry on negotiations and military operations with honour and security to any extent we desired; whereas, without it, we must continue at the mercy of the fluctuating policy of unsteady, impotent, and faithless Courts, adopting expensive and useless measures of defence at every uncertain alarm, and being ultimately obliged either to abandon the scene altogether, or, when danger actually came, to incur the most desperate hazard of complete failure by sending a military expedition which must trust for its subsistence and safety, to States who were known, not only from the individual character of their rulers, but from their actual condition and character, to be undeserving of a moment's confidence.

Seventhly. That there was great danger in any delay, as the plan recommended could only be expected to be beneficial if adopted when there was a time to mature it and to organise all our means of defence before the enemy were too far advanced; otherwise that momentary irritation which must be excited by its adoption, would only add to the many other advantages which our want of foresight and attention to our interests in that quarter had already given to our enemies.

CHAPTER V.

[1808—1809.]

The Missions to Lahore and Caubul—The Aggressions of Runjeet Singh —Mr. Metcalfe at Umritsur—Treaty of 1809—Mr. Elphinstone's Mission—Arrival at Peshawur—Reception by Shah Soojah—Withdrawal of the Mission—Negotiations with the Ameers of Sindh.

IT was while Sir Harford Jones was making his way from Bombay to Bushire, in the months of September and October, 1808, that the Missions to Caubul and Lahore set out for their respective destinations. Since the time when the rumoured approach of an army of invasion under Zemaun Shah had troubled the hearts of the English in India, the might of the Douranee rulers had been gradually declining, as a new power, threatening the integrity of the Afghan dominions, swelled into bulk and significance, and spread itself over the country between the Sutlej and the Indus. It was no longer possible to regard with indifference the growth of this new empire. We had supplanted the Mahrattas on the banks of the Jumna, and brought ourselves into proximity with the Sikhs. A group of petty principalities were being rapidly consolidated into a great empire by the strong hand and capacious intellect of Runjeet Singh, and it had become apparent to the British that thenceforth, for good or for evil, the will of the Sikh ruler must exercise an influence over the councils of the rulers of Hindostan.

It was part of Lord Minto's policy at this time, as we

have seen, to include the Lahore chief in the great Anti-Gallican confederacy with which he had determined to frustrate the magnificent designs of Napoleon. But the posture of affairs on our northern frontier was such as to occasion some embarassment in the Council-Chamber of Calcutta. The military power of the Sikh rajah had been put forth, with almost unvarying success, for the subjection of the petty principalities within his reach; and now it appeared that he was desirous of reducing to a state of vassalage all the chiefs holding the tract of country which lies between the Sutlej and the Jumna. There was much in this to perplex and embarrass Lord Minto and his colleagues. It was desirable, above all things, to maintain a friendly power beyond the frontier; but whether this were to be done by supporting the Sikh chiefs in the Cis-Sutlej territories, even at the risk of actual hostilities with Runjeet Singh, or whether, on the other hand, it were expedient to sacrifice the petty chieftains to Runjeet's ambition, and enter into an offensive and defensive alliance against the Persians and the French with that prince, were questions which agitated the minds of our Indian statesmen, and found no very satisfactory solution in the elaborate minutes which they provoked. Lord Minto, whilst expressing his natural inclination to assist a weak country against the usurpation of a powerful neighbour, and fully recognising the principle of non-interference, so consistently inculcated by the Government at home, maintained that the emergency of the case was such as to justify a departure from ordinary rules of conduct, and a violation of general maxims of policy. The defence of India against the dangers of French invasion was stated to be the most pressing object of attention, and entitled to most weight in the deliberations of the state; but it was doubted whether the alliance with Runjeet Singh would effectually secure that desirable end,* whilst it was certain that the gradual extension of his dominions would be permanently injurious to British interests in the East. It was desirable, in a word, to secure his alliance and to check his presumption at the same time. Any act of hostility and discourtesy on our part might throw him into the arms of Holkar and Scindiah, and other native princes; and a confederacy might be formed against us, that would disturb the peace of India for years Starting, however, with the assumption that the French were undeniably about to invade Hindostan, it was contended by the Governor-General, that whilst the native princes would be inclined to wait the coming of the great western liberator, it was our policy to husband our strength for the grand struggle with our terrible European opponent. "We are, in reality," wrote Lord Minto, "only waiting on both sides for a more convenient time to strike We know that Holkar and Scindiah, the Rajah of Bhurtpore, and probably other chiefs, have taken their part, and are sharpening their weapons in expectation of a concerted signal."

Thus, oscillating between two courses of policy, and considering the question solely as one of expediency—that kind of expediency, however, to which something of dignity is imparted by a great national crisis, real or supposed—the Governor-General at last came to favour an opinion that sound policy dictated a strenuous effort on the part of the British Government to curb the aggressive spirit of the Sikh conqueror, and to set a limit to his dominions.

* "I doubt," wrote Lord Minto, "whether his jealousy would permit him to admit, by treaty, our troops freely into his country, and to consent that we should establish such posts both in front against the enemy and elsewhere for the purpose of communication, as should render us independent of his fidelity. If he does not accede to this, we shall derive little benefit from his alliance."—[*Minute of Lord Minto: MS. Records.*]

It was seriously debated by Lord Minto whether Runjeet should not at once be deprived of all power to work us mischief; but the recollection of the advantages of maintaining, if possible, a longer peace, and of the non-interference system so strenuously enforced upon him by the home authorities, suggested the expediency of following a more cautious line of policy, and merely simulating, in the first instance, an intention to oppose a hostile front to the aggressiveness of the Sikhs. "If it were not found expedient," wrote Lord Minto, "ultimately to pursue or to favour these views, the apprehension alone of so great danger brought home to him, may be expected to render Runjeet Singh more subservient to our wishes than any concessions or compliances will ever make him."

In this conjuncture the Governor-General, harassed and perplexed by doubts, was fortunate in the personal character of the officer to whom had been entrusted the conduct of the mission to the Sikh ruler. Mr. Charles Metcalfe had early recommended himself to the favourable consideration of Lord Wellesley, who was never slow to recognise in the junior officers of the state the promise of future eminence.* He had been but a short time in the service, when the Governor-General placed him in his own Office—that best nursery of Indian statesmen—and he soon confirmed the expectations that had been formed of his judgment and intelligence by proving himself, in

* A remarkably able paper, on the disposal of the subsidiary force which, under the provisions of the defensive alliance with Scindiah, that prince had agreed to receive, drawn up by Mr. Metcalfe, in 1804, conduced more, perhaps, than anything else to confirm Lord Wellesley's high opinion of the young civilian's talents. On a copy of it now before me is the following marginal note, written in the Governor-General's fine, bold, characteristic hand:—"This paper is highly creditable to Mr. Metcalfe's character and talents. It may become very useful. A copy of it should be sent to the Commander-in-Chief, and another to Major Malcolm.—W."

CONDUCT OF RUNJEET SINGH.

the camp of the Commander-in-Chief, and at the Court of Delhi, an officer of equal courage and sagacity. The estimate which Lord Wellesley had formed of his talents was accepted by Lord Minto; and in the whole range of the civil service—a service never wanting in administrative and diplomatic ability of the highest order—it is probable that he could not now have found a fitter agent to carry out his policy at Lahore.

On the 1st of September, 1808, Mr. Metcalfe crossed the Sutlej, and on the 11th of the same month met the Sikh ruler at Kussoor. The conduct of the Rajah was arbitrary and capricious. At one time courteous and friendly, at another querulous and arrogant, he now seemed disposed to enter into our views and to aid our designs; and then, complaining bitterly of the interference of the British Government, insisted on his right to occupy the country beyond the Jumna. Nor did he confine his opposition to mere verbal argument, for whilst the British envoy was still in his camp, he set out to illustrate his views by crossing the river, seizing Furreedkote and Umballah, and otherwise overawing the petty Sikh chiefs between the Sutlej and the Jumna.*

* "The Rajah coupled his acquiescence in the proposed arrangements of defence against an invading European army with the condition of being permitted to extend his dominions over all the Sikh territories between the Sutlej and the Jumna. He also provisionally demanded that the British Government should not interfere in favour of the King of Caubul in his aggressions against that monarch's dominions—at the same time shackling the advance of the British troops into his country, and the establishment of the necessary depôts, with conditions which would render any engagements with him for that purpose entirely inefficient and nugatory. Even during the reference he made to government on these demands, he crossed the Sutlej to attack the Sikh territories. The extreme jealousy and suspicion of us evinced by the Rajah, together with his own conduct and ambitious character, rendered it indispensably necessary to resist his pretensions to sovereignty over the territories on this side of the Sutlej, and the Rajah

On the receipt of this intelligence by the Calcutta Council, it was debated whether it would be expedient to adopt the more dignified course of ordering Mr. Metcalfe to withdraw at once from the Sikh camp, and, regarding the conduct of Runjeet Singh as an outrage against the British Government, to take measures at once to chastise him;—whether, as recommended by Mr. Edmonstone, who always brought a sound judgment to bear upon such questions, and whose opinions were seldom disregarded by the Governor-General, to limit the negotiations with Runjeet Singh to defensive measures against the French, leaving the question of the subjugation of the Cis-Sutlej states for future adjustment;—or whether it would not be more prudent to direct Mr. Metcalfe to encumber himself as little as possible with engagements of any kind—to adopt a cautious and temporising line of policy, so as to admit of frequent references to Calcutta in the course of his negotiations, and to wait for anything that might chance to be written down in our favour in that great "chapter of accidents," which so often enabled us to solve the most perplexing questions, and to overcome the most pressing difficulties.*

This was the course finally adopted. On one point, however, the tone of Government was decided. Runjeet Singh had required the British Government to pledge itself not to interfere with his aggressions against Caubul; and Mr. Metcalfe was now informed, that "were the Rajah to conclude engagements with the British Govern-

was required to withdraw his army."—[*Statement in Instructions to Mr Elphinstone: MS. Records.*]

* "The point to aim at in our present transactions with the Rajah of Lahore," wrote Lord Minto, "appears to be that we should keep ourselves as free as can be done without a rupture. I should, on this principle, rather wish to protract than to accelerate the treaty."—[*Minute of Lord Minto: MS. Records.*]

ment in the true spirit of unanimity and confidence, we could not accede to any proposition upon the part of Caubul injurious to his interests: uncombined with such engagements, that question (of his aggressions against the Caubul territories) cannot possibly form an article of agreement between this government and the Rajah of Lahore; and on this ground the discussion of it may be properly rejected. At the same time, if the occasion should arise, you may inform the Rajah that Mr. Elphinstone is not authorised to conclude with the State of Caubul any engagements injurious to his interests. You will be careful, however, as you have hitherto been, to avoid any pledge on the part of government which might preclude any future engagements with the State of Caubul on that subject." And whilst Mr. Metcalfe was carrying out this temporising policy inculcated by the Calcutta council, troops were pushed forward to the frontier to watch the movements of the Punjabee chief. A body of King's and Company's troops, under General St. Leger, and another under Colonel Ochterlony, composed entirely of native regiments, were posted in the neighbourhood of Loodhianah, ready, at a moment's notice, to take the field against the followers of Nanuk. Vested with political authority, the latter officer, on the 9th of February, 1809, issued a proclamation calling upon the Sikh ruler to withdraw his troops to the further side of the Sutlej, and placing all the Cis-Sutlej principalities under the protection of the British Government. It was plain that we were no longer to be tampered with, and that there was nothing left to Runjeet Singh but to yield a reluctant compliance to our terms.

Up to this time the primary object of the British Government had been the establishment of such an alliance with the rulers of the Punjab, as might ensure a strenuous conjoint opposition to an European army advancing from the West. But those were days when a constant succession of great changes in the European world necessarily induced a shifting policy on the part of our Indian statesmen. It was difficult to keep pace with the mutations which were passing over the political horizon—difficult to keep a distant mission supplied with instructions which were not likely to become totally useless before they could be brought into effective operation. With Mr. Metcalfe at Umritsur it was comparatively easy to communicate. He had been ordered to temporise—to do nothing in a hurry; and he had succeeded so well as to protract his negotiations until the spring of 1809. The delay was most advantageous to British interests. The "chapter of accidents" worked mightily in our favour. The war with Napoleon had now been carried into the Spanish peninsula, and it demanded all the energies of the Emperor to maintain his position in Europe. The necessity of anti-Gallican alliances in India became less and less urgent. The value of Sikh friendship dwindled rapidly down, and the pretensions of the Sikh ruler naturally descended with it. The sight of a formidable British force on the frontier—the intelligence of the European successes of the great "Sepoy General" who, a few years before, on the plains of Berar, had given the Mahrattas a foretaste of the quality of his military skill*—the

* "At the time when the proposal was made for the adjustment of differences, the forces on both sides remained quiet in sight of each other, when the news of the defeat of Junot (Duke of Abrantes) at Vimiera, by the British army, under Sir Arthur Wellesley, was received in the camps of General St. Leger and Colonel Ochterlony, and, as usual, celebrated by royal salutes. The cause of this firing being made known to Runjeet Singh, the salute was, by his special command, repeated from all the artillery in his camp—a circumstance which, whether it be attributed to politeness towards the British commanders, with whom he was in treaty, or to a general condemnation of the system of Buonaparte, was felt equally agreeable."—[*Asiatic Annual Register.*]

declining influence of the French in Central Asia,—and more than all, perhaps, the wonderful firmness and courage of the young English diplomatist—suggested to the wily Sikh Rajah the expediency of ceasing to tamper with us, and of forming at once a friendly alliance with the British.* He was now in a temper to accede to the terms proposed to him by the British diplomatist; and accordingly, on the 25th of April, 1809, a treaty was executed by Runjeet Singh in person, and by Mr. Metcalfe on the part of the British Government, in which there was no more mention of the French than if the eagles of Napoleon had never threatened the eastern world. It was stipulated that the Rajah should retain possession of the territories to the north of the Sutlej, but should abstain from all encroachments on the possessions or rights of the chiefs on the left bank of the river. This limitation was merely a prospective one. It had been intended to deprive Runjeet of the tracts of country which he had previously occupied to the south of the Sutlej; and the rough draft of the treaty contained, as a part of the first article as it now stands, the words, "And on the other hand, the Rajah renounces all claim to sovereignty over the Sikh chiefs to the southward of that river, and all right of interference in their affairs;"† but this passage had been subsequently erased by Lord Minto, and Runjeet Singh was now left in possession of the tracts he had originally occupied, though restrained from all further encroachments. The Sikh chiefs between the Sutlej and the Jumna, not already under the yoke of Runjeet Singh, were taken under

* An accidental collision between some of the Mahomedan sepoys of Mr. Metcalfe's mission, and a far superior body of Sikhs, in which the inferiority of the latter was most unmistakeably demonstrated, had no inconsiderable effect upon the mind of Runjeet Singh, who was a spectator of the discomfiture of his countrymen.

† *MS. Records.*

British protection, and on the 5th of May a proclamation was issued declaring the nature of the connection which was thenceforth to exist between them and the dominant power on the south of the Jumna,

In the meanwhile, Mr. Elphinstone's Mission was making its way to the Court of Shah Soojah-ool-Moolk. The envoy had been originally instructed that he was empowered to receive from the King of Caubul proposals having for their basis the employment of the power and resources of that state against the advance of any European army. He was authorised to express a conviction, as regarded offensive operations, that in the event of Persia being found decidedly confederated with the French in their projected expedition to India, the British Government "would not hesitate to adopt any plan of hostility against Persia consonant to the views of the King of Caubul." But he was cautioned against entering into any permanent arrangement, or pledging his government to any ulterior line of conduct. Everything was to be limited to the occasion. It was to be the policy of the envoy rather to draw the Court of Caubul into solicitations to the British Government, than to make any spontaneous offers of assistance. And he was instructed especially to impress upon the mind of the King, that both as regarded security from without, and the internal safety and tranquillity of his own dominions, it was above all things the interest of the Douranee monarch to break up the alliance existing between the Court of Teheran and those of St. Petersburgh and Paris.

But this alliance was already in a state of dissolution. The spring of 1809 brought, as we have seen, glad tidings from Europe to the Anglo-Indian capital, and all fear of a French invasion passed away from the minds of our rulers. Whilst Mr. Metcalfe was bringing to a conclusion, irrespective of all reference to the French, his long-pending negotiations with Lahore, Mr. Elphinstone was instructed* that the important events which had occurred in Europe would necessarily induce a modification of the course of policy to be pursued at the Court of Caubul. He was told that it was no longer necessary to entertain a thought of offensive operations against Persia, but that the British Government would accede to engagements of a nature purely defensive against that state, should such a stipulation appear to be an object of solicitude to the Afghan monarch. This was merely stated as an admissible course. The Governor-General declared that he would wish, if possible, to avoid contracting even defensive engagements with the Court of Caubul; and added, "Should the contracting those engagements be absolutely required by the King, the eventual aid to be afforded by us ought to be limited to supplies of arms, ordnance, and military stores, *rather than of troops*." †

The Mission proceeded through Bekanier, Bahwulpore,‡ and Mooltan; and ever as they went the most marked civility was shown to the British ambassadors. But one

* Under date March 6, 1809.

† *MS. Records.* Another paragraph of these instructions is worth quoting. "Although there is not now the same immediate exigency for forming a friendly connexion with the Court of Caubul, yet that measure is of importance, and contains an object of sound policy, in the event, however remote, of either the French or any other European power endeavouring to approach India by that route."

‡ It is worthy of remark in this place, that Mr. Strachey, who accompanied Mr. Elphinstone's Mission in the capacity of secretary, and who on this as on other occasions evinced the possession of a high order of intellect, drew up a very able memorandum on the advantages of forming a connexion with Bahwul Khan. In this paper there occurs the following prescient passage:—"Bahwul Khan might also be induced, in the event of actual hostilities, to invade the territories of Runjeet Singh at any point we might suggest, and thereby form an important diversion, whilst the British army would be advancing from another quarter of the Sikh territory."—[*MS. Records.*]

thing was wanting to render the feeling towards them a pervading sentiment of universal respect. They had not long crossed the frontier before they discovered that a more liberal display of the facial characteristics of manhood would elevate them greatly in the eyes of a people who are uniformly bearded and moustached.* Our officers have ever since carefully abstained from incurring this reproach; and it may be doubted whether, ever again, any hint will be required to stimulate them to

* It is said that Mr. Elphinstone's Mission received this hint from an European deserter, named Pensley, who had been entertained, in a military capacity, by Shah Soojah. They might have learnt the lesson from Mr. Forster, who, twenty years before, had travelled in Afghanistan. That enterprising gentleman, a civil servant of the Company, found his beard of the greatest service. He suffered it to grow for fifteen months, and had reason to regret that before he had wholly shaken off Eastern associations, he allowed the razor to profane it. Putting himself on board a Russian frigate in the Caspian, he thought that he might reduce his face to its old European aspect; but he tells us that "the Ghilan envoy, then proceeding on the frigate, expressed a surprise to see me, whom he thought a Mahomedan, eating at the same board with the Russian gentlemen; but when he saw a barber commencing an operation on my beard, which I took the opportunity of having shaved, he evinced great amazement and indignation; nor did he, until repeatedly informed of my real character, cease his reprehension of the act; during the process of which he threw on me many a look of contempt. When the barber began to cut off the moustachios, he several times, in a peremptory manner, required him to desist, and, seeing them gone, 'Now,' said he, 'of whatever country or sect you may be, your disgrace is complete, and you look like a woman.' Thus, after a growth of fifteen months fell my beard, which in that period had increased to a great magnitude, both in length and breadth, though it had been somewhat shrivelled by the severity of the late winter. When you advert to the general importance of an Asiatic beard, to the essential services which mine had rendered, and to our long and intimate association, I trust that this brief introduction of it to your notice will not be deemed impertinent. This operation of cutting it ought, however, to have been postponed till my arrival at Astracan."

encourage an Asiatic development of hair on the lower part of the face

I do not intend to trace the progress of the Mission The story has been told with historical fidelity and graphic distinctness in a book which is still, after the lapse of nearly forty years, the delight of Anglo-Indian readers, and which future generations of writers and cadets will turn to with undiminished interest. On the 25th of February, the Mission entered Peshawur. Crowds of wondering inhabitants came out to gaze at the representatives of the nation which had reduced the great Mogul to a shadow, and seated itself on the throne of Tippoo. Pushing forward with the outstretched neck of eager curiosity, they blocked up the public ways The royal body-guards rode among the foot passengers; lashed at them with their whips; tilted with their lances at grave spectators sitting quietly in their own balconies; and cleared the way as best they could. But fast as they dispersed the thronging multitude, it closed again around the novel cavalcade. Through this motley crowd of excited inhabitants, the British Mission was with difficulty conducted to a house prepared for them by royal mandate. Seated on rich carpets, fed with sweetmeats, and regaled with sherbet, every attention was paid to the European strangers. The hospitality of the King was profuse. His fortunes were then at a low ebb; but he sent provisions to the Mission for two thousand men, with food for beasts of burden in proportion, and was with difficulty persuaded to adopt a less costly method of testifying his regal cordiality and respect.

Some dispute about forms of presentation delayed the reception of the English ambassadors. But in a few days everything was arranged for the grand ceremonial to take place on the 5th of March. When the eventful day arrived, they found the King, with that love of outward pomp which clung to him to the last, sitting on a gilded throne, crowned, plumed, and arrayed in costly apparel. The royal person was a blaze of jewellery, conspicuous among which the mighty diamond, the Koh-i-noor, destined in after days to undergo such romantic vicissitudes, glittered in a gorgeous bracelet upon the arm of the Shah. Welcoming the English gentlemen with a graceful cordiality; he expressed a hope that the King of England and all the English nation were well, presented the officers of the embassy with dresses of honour, and then, dismissing all but Mr. Elphinstone and his secretary, proceeded to the business of the interview. Listening attentively to all that was advanced by the British envoy, he professed himself eager to accede to his proposals, and declared that England and Caubul were designed by the Creator to be united by bonds of everlasting friendship. The presents which Mr. Elphinstone had taken with him to Afghanistan were curious and costly; and now that they were exposed to the view of the Shah, he turned upon them a face scintillating with pleasure, and eagerly expressed his delight. His attendants, with a cupidity that there was no attempt to conceal, laid their rapacious hands upon everything that came in their way, and scrambled for the articles which were not especially appropriated by their royal master. Thirty years afterwards, the memory of these splendid gifts raised longing expectations in the minds of the courtiers of Caubul, and caused bitter disappointment and disgust, when Captain Burnes appeared with his pins and needles, and little articles of hardware, such as would have disgraced the wallet of a pedlar of low repute.*

* It was the very costliness of these presents, and the lavish expenditure of the entire Mission, that gave the deathblow to the old system of diplomatic profusion. When the accounts of the Afghan and Persian Missions came before the Governor-General in Council, Lord

At subsequent interviews the impression made by the Shah upon the minds of the English diplomatists was of a description very favourable to the character of the Afghan ruler. Mr. Elphinstone was surprised to find that the Douranee monarch had so much of the "manners of a gentleman," and that he could be affable and dignified at the same time. But he had much domestic care to distract him at this epoch, and could not fix his mind intently on foreign politics. His country was in a most unsettled condition. His throne seemed to totter under him. He was endeavouring to collect an army, and was projecting a great military expedition. He hoped to see more of the English gentlemen, he said, in more prosperous times. At present, the best advice that he could give them was that they should retire beyond the frontier. So on the 14th of June the Mission turned its back upon Peshawur, and set out for the provinces of Hindostan.*

Minto stood aghast at the enormous expenditure, and, in a stringent minute, recorded "his deliberate opinion, that the actual expenditure has far exceeded the necessity of the occasion—that the personal expenses of the envoys might have been limited with respect both to the nature and extent of the items composing them, and that the provision of articles for presents to an extent so enormous as that exhibited in the accounts of these Missions has been regulated by a principle of distribution unnecessarily profuse."—[*MS. Records.*]

* It is to be regretted that Shah Soojah's own notices of the British Mission are very scanty. He says, in his autobiographical narrative, "On receiving intelligence that the English ambassadors had arrived at Kohat, we sent an appropriate party to meet and do them honour. On their arrival, we gave them suitable dwellings, and ordered their wants and wishes to be attended to. After a few days' rest the ambassadors came to the presence, and presented various articles of European and Hindostanee workmanship, also many elephants with superb accoutrements. Dresses of honour were conferred on all. We gave strict orders that the Mission should be treated with every dignity, and our most confidential Ameers waited on them. . . . We learned that Shah Mahmoud had left Caubul, and halted at Chuk-Dilah. Hearing this, we immediately reflected on the state of the

Three days after the Mission commenced its homeward journey, the treaty which had been arranged by Mr. Elphinstone was formally signed at Calcutta by Lord Minto. The first article set out with a mis-statement, to the effect that the French and Persians had entered into a confederacy against the State of Caubul. The two contracting parties bound themselves to take active measures to repel this confederacy, the British "holding themselves liable to afford the expenses necessary for the above-mentioned service, to *the extent of their ability.*" The remaining article decreed eternal friendship between the two States: "The veil of separation shall be lifted up from between them; and they shall in no manner interfere in each other's countries; and the King of Caubul shall permit no individual of the French to enter his territories." Three months before these articles were signed Sir Harford Jones had entered into a preliminary treaty with the Persian Court, stipulating that in case of war between Persia and Afghanistan, his Majesty the King of Great Britain should not take any part therein, unless at the desire of both parties. The confederacy of the French and Persians had been entirely broken up, and all the essentials of the Caubul treaty rendered utterly null and useless.

But before this rapid sketch of the diplomacy of 1808-9 is brought to a close, some mention must be made of another subordinate measure of defence against the possibility of a foreign invasion. The low countries lying on the banks of the river Indus, from its junction with the Punjabee tributaries to the sea, were known as Upper and Lower Sindh. The people inhabiting the former were

Company's ambassadors. We resolved, first, to place them in a state and place of safety; and proceed to punish the rebels; and then, if God would grant a victory, we intended to return to treat them in a proper manner."

for the most part Beloochees—a warlike and turbulent race, of far greater physical power and mental energy than their feeble, degraded neighbours, the Sindhians, who occupied the country from Shikarpoor to the mouths of the Indus The nominal rulers of these provinces were the Talpoor Ameers, but they were either tributary to, or actually dependent upon the Court of Caubul. The dependence, however, was in effect but scantily acknowledged. Often was the tribute to be extracted only by the approach of an army sent for its collection by the Douranee monarch. There was constant strife, indeed, between Sindh and Caubul—the one ever plotting to cast off its allegiance, and the other ever putting forth its strength more closely to rivet the chains.

In July, 1808, Captain Seton was despatched by the Bombay Government to the Court of the Ameers at Hyderabad. Misunderstanding and exceeding his instructions, he hastily executed a treaty with the State of Sindh, imposing, generally and unconditionally, upon each party an obligation to furnish military aid on the requisition of the other. The mind of the envoy was heavy with thoughts of a French invasion, which seem to have excluded all considerations of internal warfare and intrigue in Central Asia. But the Ameers were at that time intent upon emancipating themselves from the yoke of Caubul, and Captain Seton found that he had committed the British Government to assist the tributary State of Sindh against the Lord Paramount of the country, thereby placing us in direct hostility with the very power whose good offices we were so anxious to conciliate. There was, indeed, a Persian ambassador at that very time resident at the Sindh capital. charged with overtures for the formation of a close alliance between Persia and Sindh subversive of the tributary relations of the latter to the State of Caubul.* He was acting,

* The Ameers had sent vakeels to Persia, seeking assistance against

too, as the secret agent of the French; and the Ameers made no secret of the fact, that but for the friendly overtures of the British they would have allied themselves with the Persians and French. They now grasped at the proffered connexion with the Indian Government, believing, or professing to believe, that it entitled them to assistance against the State of Caubul, and industriously propagated a report of the military strength which they had thus acquired. The danger of all this was obvious.[*] Captain Seton's treaty was accordingly ignored; and Mr. Elphinstone was instructed that, in the event of Shah Soojah remonstrating against Captain Seton's treaty, he might, without hesitation, apprise the Court of Caubul that the engagements entered into were "totally unauthorised and contrary to the terms of the instructions given him;" and that, in consequence of these errors, Captain Seton had been officially recalled, and another envoy despatched to Sindh to negotiate the terms of a new treaty.

The agent then appointed was Mr. N. H. Smith, who had been filling, with credit to himself, the office of Resident at Bushire. He was instructed to annul the former treaty, and to "endeavour to establish such an intercourse with the chiefs of Sindh as would afford the means of watching and counteracting the intrigues of the French in that and the neighbouring States." It was no easy thing to establish on a secure basis friendly relations with so many different powers, if not at open war with one

Caubul; and the Persian ambassador had accompanied them on their return to Sindh.

[*] Nor was this the only error into which Captain Seton had fallen. That officer was instructed, before Mr. Elphinstone's Mission had been determined upon, to ascertain the practicability of sending an embassy to Candahar or Caubul, by the route of Sindh; and upon the strength of these instructions, had taken upon himself to address a letter to the King of Caubul, expressing the desire of the British Government to form an alliance with that monarch.

another, in that antagonistic state of conflicting interests which rendered each principality eager to obtain the assistance of the British to promote some hostile design against its neighbour. But partly by open promises, and partly by disguised threats, our agents at this time succeeded in casting one great network of diplomacy over all the states from the Jumna to the Caspian Sea The Ameers of Sindh coveted nothing so much as assistance against the Douranee monarch. The British envoy was instructed to refuse all promises of assistance, but to hint at the possibility of assistance being given to the paramount State in the event of the tributary exhibiting any hostility to the British Government. It was distinctly stated that the object of Mr Elphinstone's Mission to Caubul was exclusively connected with the apprehended invasion of the Persians and the French; that the affairs of Sindh would not be touched upon by the Caubul embassy, and that, therefore, the affairs of Caubul could not with propriety be discussed by the ambassador to Sindh; and it was adroitly added, that the relations between Caubul and Sindh could only be taken into consideration by the British Government in the event of the latter state exhibiting a decided disposition to encourage and assist the projects of our enemies.

Nor was this the only use made of the conflicting claims of Caubul and Sindh. It happened, as has been said, that Persia had been intriguing with the Ameers, and had promised to assist them in the efforts to cast off the Douranee yoke. The French had favoured and assisted these intrigues; and Mr. Elphinstone was accordingly instructed to instigate the resentment of the Afghan monarch against the French and Persian allies, and to demonstrate to him that the very integrity of his empire was threatened by the confederacy. It was the policy of the British-Indian Government to keep Sindh in check by hinting at the possibility of British assistance rendered to Caubul for its coercion; and, at the same time, to alarm Caubul by demonstrating the probability of Sindh being assisted by Persia to shake off the Douranee yoke. Operating upon the fears of both parties, our diplomatists found little difficulty in bringing their negotiations to a successful termination. The Ameers of Sindh entered readily into engagements of general amity, and especially stipulated never to allow the tribe of the French to settle in their country. But before these treaties were executed, France had ceased to be formidable, and Persia had become a friend. The Sindh and Caubul treaties were directed against exigencies which had ceased to exist; but they were not without their uses. If the embassies resulted in nothing else, they gave birth to two standard works on the countries to which they were despatched; and brought prominently before the world the names of two servants of the Company, who have lived to occupy no small space in the world's regard, and to prove themselves as well fitted, by nature and education, to act history as to write it.*

* I need scarcely write the names of Elphinstone and Pottinger—or allude to their respective works. Of the former statesman I have already spoken. The Lieutenant Henry Pottinger, who, early in the century, accompanied the Sindh Mission, and was attached to General Malcolm's staff on his second visit to Persia, after passing, at a later stage of his career, from the management of the wild tribes of Beloochistan to play an intricate game of diplomacy with the flowery courtiers of the Celestial Empire, and thence to the control of the Caffre savages of Southern Africa, closed his public life in the more commonplace government of Madras.

CHAPTER VI.

[1809—1816]

The Mid-Career of Shah Soojah—His Wanderings and Misfortunes—Captivity in Cashmere—Imprisonment at Lahore—Robbery of the Koh-i-noor—Reception of the Shah by the Rajah of Kistawar—His Escape to the British Territories.

BEFORE Mr. Elphinstone's Mission had cleared the limits of the Douranee Empire, Shah Soojah had given battle to his enemies, and been disastrously defeated. The month of June, 1809, had not worn to a close, before it was evident that his cause was hopeless. Still he did not abandon the contest Despatching his Zenana, with which was his blind brother, to Rawul Pindee, he made new efforts to splinter up his broken fortunes. But sustaining several defeats, and narrowly escaping, on more than one occasion, with his life, he desisted for a time from operations, of which every new struggle demonstrated more painfully the utter fruitlessness. He wanted military genius, and he wanted the art to inspire confidence and to win affection. Deserted by the chiefs and the people, he withdrew beyond the frontier, and there entered upon new preparations for the renewal of the contest under circumstances more favourable to success. Entertaining and drilling troops, he spent a year at Rawul Pindee. Some defections from his brother's party inspiring him with new hopes, he marched thence to Peshawur, and took possession of the Balla Hissar, or royal fortress. But here the treachery of his friends was likely to have proved more fatal to him than the malice of his enemies. The chiefs on whom he most relied were bribed over by the Governor of Cashmere to seize the person of the King. Persuading him, before he commenced the expedition to Caubul, to send out the horses of his troopers to graze in the neighbouring villages, and thus stripping him of his only defence, they escaladed the Balla Hissar, seized the royal person, and carried the unfortunate monarch to the valley of Cashmere. Here he was offered his release at the price of the Koh-i-noor; but he refused to surrender this magnificent appendage to the Crown of Caubul, and rescued it from the hands of one plunderer only to suffer it to fall into the gripe of another.

It was in 1812 that Shah Soojah was carried off a prisoner to Cashmere. He appears to have remained there about a year, and, during that time, to have been treated with little kindness and respect. Mahmoud was then in comparative quiet and security at Caubul, and, in his good fortune, seems to have regarded with compassion the fate of his unhappy brother. "When Shah Mahmoud heard of the way in which we were treated," writes the royal autobiographer, "the latent feelings of fraternal affection were aroused within him, and he immediately sent a force into the Barukzye country. After plundering the whole tribe of Atta Mahmoud Khan, he carried men, women, and children into captivity. Finding that this had not the desired effect, viz., our release from bondage, he sent a force to Cashmere, under Futteh Khan." Atta Mahmoud advanced to give him battle; but his followers deserted to the standard of the Barukzye Wuzeer, and he fled homewards to Cashmere. Here, threatened by Futteh Khan, he implored the assistance of his captive. "Seeing his escape could not be effected without our aid, he came," says Shah Soojah, "to our place of confinement, bare-headed, with the Koran in one hand, a naked sword in the other, and a rope about his neck, and requested our forgiveness for the sake of the sacred volume." The Shah, who, according to his own statements, was never wanting in that most kingly quality of forgiveness, forgave him on his own account, and recommended him to make submission to Futteh Khan. The Wuzeer was advancing upon Cashmere from one direction, and the Sikhs from another; and it was plain that the rebellious Nazim had nothing before him but to submit.

I wish to believe Shah Soojah's history of the amiable fraternal impulses which dictated the expedition to Cashmere. But it is difficult to entertain a conviction that it was not directed towards other objects than the release of the exiled monarch. The result was, that Atta Mahmoud, the rebellious Nazim, made submission to Futteh Khan; —that Mokhum Chund, the leader of the Sikh expedition, met the Douranee minister about the same time, and that both recommended Shah Soojah to proceed on a visit to Runjeet Singh.* The Maharajah, it soon became very clear, coveted the possession of the great Douranee diamond. On the second day after Shah Soojah entered Lahore, he was waited on by an emissary from Runjeet, who demanded the jewel in the name of his master. The fugitive monarch asked for time to consider the request, and hinted that, after he had partaken of Runjeet's hospitality, he might be in a temper to grant it. On the following day, the same messenger presented him-

* The Shah says: "Mokhum Chund, on the part of Runjeet Singh, informed us, that his master was anxious that we should proceed to Lahore as soon as at liberty, and visit the residence of our seraglio in that city; he also mentioned that his master's fame would be increased by our going. According to Futteh Khan's petition, we agreed to this, and marched towards Lahore with Mokhum Chund and other Singhs, whilst Futteh Khan returned to Shah Mahmoud in Caubul."

self again, and received a similar rep_y. Runjeet Singh was in no mood to brook this delay. Determined to possess himself of the Koh-i-noor, he now resorted to other measures to extort it from the luckless owner. "We then," says Shah Soojah, "experienced privations of the necessaries of life, and sentinels were placed over our dwelling. A month passed in this way. Confidential servants of Runjeet Singh then waited on us, and inquired if we wanted ready cash, and would enter into an agreement and treaty for the above-mentioned jewel. We answered in the affirmative, and next day, Ram Singh brought 40,000 or 50,000 rupees, and asked again for the Koh-i-noor, which we promised to procure when some treaty was agreed upon. Two days after this, Runjeet Singh came in person, and, after friendly protestations, he stained a paper with safflower, and swearing by the Grunth of Baba Nanuck and his own sword, he wrote the following security and compact:—That he delivered over the provinces of Kote Cumaleeh, Jung Shawl, and Khuleh Noor, to us and our heirs for ever; also offering assistance in troops and treasure for the purpose of again recovering our throne. We also agreed, if we should ever ascend the throne, to consider Runjeet Singh always in the light of an ally. He then proposed himself that we should exchange turbans, which is among the Sikhs a pledge of eternal friendship, and we then gave him the Koh-i-noor."

Having thus obtained possession of the great diamond, Runjeet Singh, who at no time of his life had very high ideas of honour, was unwilling to give up the jagheer which he had promised as the price of it. Whilst Shah Soojah was still thinking over the non-performance of the contract, Runjeet invited him to accompany an expedition which was proceeding under the Maharajah to Peshawur, and held out to him hopes of the recovery of his lost dominions. The Shah joined Runjeet at Rotas, and they proceeded together to Rawul Pindee. There the Maharajah, seeing little chance of success, abandoned the expedition, and, according to the account given by Shah Soojah, desired him to proceed onward in the company of Ram Singh. Left alone with that chief, he was shamelessly plundered by robbers of higher note than the Sikh chiefs would willingly admit. All thought of proceeding to Peshawur was now abandoned, and, accompanied by Ram Singh and the heir-apparent, Shah Soojah returned to Lahore

At the capital his property was not more secure than on the line of march There was something yet left to be plundered, and the plunderers were of still higher rank. Runjeet Singh stripped the wretched monarch of everything that was worth taking, and "even after this," says Shah Soojah, "he did not perform one of his promises" Instead of bestowing new favours upon the man who had yielded up his treasures so unsparingly, the Maharajah began to heap new indignities upon him. Spies were set over him, and guards surrounded his dwelling Five months passed in this way; and as time advanced, the condition of the wretched Douranee Prince became more hopeless, his escape from this wretched thraldom more to be coveted, and yet more difficult to encompass. He remembered the friendly overtures of the British Government, and sighed for a peaceful asylum under the shelter of the wings of the great power beyond the Sutlej. "We thought," he says, "of the proffered friendship of the British Government, and hoped for an asylum in Loodhianah. Several Mussulmans and Hindoos had formerly offered their services, and we now engaged them and purchased several of the covered hackeries of the country. Every stratagem was defeated by the spies, until at last we found that Abdool Hussan had disclosed our plans to Runjeet Singh. At last, being hopeless, we called Abdool Hussan and Moollah Jaffier into the presence, and after offering them bribes, and giving expectations of reward, we bought them to our purpose; and the members of the seraglio, with their attendants, all dressed in the costume of the country, found a safe conveyance in the hackeries above mentioned to the cantonments of Loodhianah. When we received accounts of their safe arrival, we gave sincere thanks to Almighty God!"

But his own escape was yet to be effected. Outwitted to this extent, Runjeet Singh redoubled his precautions, and in no very conciliatory mood of mind hemmed in the ex-King with guards, and watched him day and night with the keenest vigilance. "Seven ranges of guards," says the royal autobiographer, "were put upon our person, and armed men with lighted torches watched our bed. When we went as far as the banks of the river at night, the sentinels upon the ramparts lighted flambeaux until we returned. Several months passed in this manner, and our own attendants were with difficulty allowed to come into the presence. No relief was left but that of our holy religion, and God alone could give us assistance." And assistance was given, in the shape of unwonted resolution and ingenuity. In this critical hour the resources of the Shah seem to have developed themselves in an unexampled manner. He foiled all Runjeet's efforts to secure his prisoner, and baffled the vigilance of his guards. A few faithful attendants aided his endeavours, and he escaped from the cruel walls of Lahore. "We ordered," he says, "the roof of the apartment containing our camp equipage to be opened, so as to admit of a person passing through; apertures were formed by mining through seven other chambers to the outside of the building." Everything being thus prepared, the unhappy King disguised himself as a mendicant, and leaving one of his attendants to simulate the royal person on his bed, crept through the fissures in the walls, escaped with two followers into the street, and emerged thence through the main sewer which ran beneath the city wall.

Outside Lahore he was joined by his remaining followers. He had been thinking, in confinement, of the blessings of a safe retreat at Loodhianah ; but no sooner did he find himself abroad than he courted new adventures, and meditated new enterprises. Instead of hastening to the British provinces, he turned his face towards the hills of Jummoo. Wandering about in this direction without seemingly any fixed object, he received friendly overtures from the Rajah of Kistawar, and was easily persuaded to enter his dominions.

The Rajah went out to meet him, loaded him with kindness, conducted him to his capital, and made the kingly fugitive happy with rich gifts and public honours. Offering up sacrifices, and distributing large sums of money in honour of his royal guest, the Rajah spared nothing that could soothe the grief or pamper the vanity of the exiled monarch. But the novelty of this pleasant hospitality soon began to wear away, and the restless wanderer sighed for a life of more enterprise and excitement. "Tired of an idle life," he says, "we laid plans for an attack on Cashmere." The Rajah of Kistawar was well pleased with the project, and placed his troops and his treasury at the command of his royal guest. The Shah himself, though robbed of all his jewels, had a lakh of rupees remaining at Lahore, but as soon as he began to possess himself of it, the Maharajah stretched out his hand, and swept it into his own treasury. Nothing daunted by this accident, the Kistawar chief, who was "ready to sacrifice his territory for the weal" of the Shah, freely supplied the sinews of war ; troops were levied, and operations commenced.

But it was not written in the Shah's book of life that his enterprises should result in anything but failure. The outset of the expedition was marked by some temporary successes; but it closed in disaster and defeat. The Shah's levies charged the stockaded positions of the enemy sword in hand, and were pushing into the heart of the country, when the same inexorable enemy that has baffled the efforts of the greatest European states raised its barriers against the advance of the invading army. "We were only three coss," relates Shah Soojah, "from Azim Khan's camp, with the picturesque city of Cashmere full in view, when the snow began again to fall, and the storm continued with violence, and without intermission, for two days. Our Hindostanees were benumbed with a cold unfelt in their sultry regions; the road to our rear was blocked up with snow, and the supplies still far distant. For three days our troops were almost famished, and many Hindostanees died. We could not advance, and retreat was hazardous. Many lost their hands and feet from being frost-bitten, before we determined to retreat."

These calamities, which seemed to strengthen the devotion of the Rajah of Kistawar to the unfortunate Shah, and which were borne by him with the most manly fortitude, sobered the fugitive Afghan monarch, and made him again turn his thoughts longingly towards a tranquil asylum in the Company's dominions. At the earnest request of his new friend, he remained during nine months beneath the hospitable roof of the Rajah, and then prepared for a journey to Loodhianah.* Avoiding the Lahore

* Shah Soojah records that the faithful Rajah, on the King announcing his determination to depart, "burst into tears. He urged the dangers of the road, his wish to sacrifice his wealth for us, and every excuse which affection could dictate, to prolong our stay." "The Rajah," he adds, "accompanied us two marches, and at parting, which took place in silence, tears stood in the eyes of both parties. We had

territory, lest he should fall into the hands of Runjeet Singh, willing rather to encounter the eternal snows of the hill regions than his ruthless enemies on the plains, he tracked along the inhospitable mountains of Thibet, where for days and days no signs of human life or vegetation appeared to cheer his heart and encourage his efforts. "The depth of the eternal snows," he says, "was immense. Underneath the large bodies of ice the mountain torrents had formed themselves channels. The five rivers watering the Punjaub have their rise here from fountains amid the snows of ages. We passed mountains, the snows of which varied in colour, and at last reached the confines of Thibet, after experiencing the extremes of cold, hunger, and fatigue."

His trials were not yet over. He had still to encounter dangers and difficulties among the hill tribes. The people of Kulloo insulted and ill-treated him; but the Rajah came to his relief, and, after a few days of onward travelling, to the inexpressible joy of the fugitive monarch the red houses of the British residents at one of our hill stations appeared in sight. " Our cares and fatigues were now," says the Shah, " forgotten, and giving thanks to

no dress of honour, no khillaut worth his acceptance, but he accepted our thanks and blessing, and departed with every mark of grief." Amidst so much of selfish rapacity and dark ingratitude as marks these annals of the Douranee Empire, it is a pleasure to chronicle such an episode as this in the history of Shah Soojah's fortunes. I am too willing to believe the whole story to encourage any doubt of its authenticity. The free use, indeed, which I have made of Shah Soojah's autobiography is sufficient proof of my belief in the general fidelity of the narrative It was written by the Shah's Moonshee, under his Majesty's superintendence. I have quoted Lieutenant Bennett's translation, as published in the *Calcutta Monthly Journal*. It supplies, at the same time, more interesting and more authentic materials of Afghan history than are to be found elsewhere, and to the majority of readers is probably as fresh as manuscript.

Almighty God, who, having freed us from the hands of our enemies, and led us through the snows and over the trackless mountains, had now safely conducted us to the land of friends, we passed a night, for the first time, with comfort and without dread. Signs of civilisation showed themselves as we proceeded, and we soon entered a fine broad road. A chuprassie from Captain Ross attended us; the hill ranas paid us every attention; and we soon reached Loodhianah, where we found our family treated with marked respect, and enjoying every comfort after their perilous march from Lahore."

It was in the month of September, 1816, that Shah Soojah joined his family at Loodhianah. He sought a resting-place, and he found one in the British dominions. Two years of quietude and peace were his. But quietude and peace are afflictions grievous and intolerable to an Afghan nature. The Shah gratefully acknowledged the friendly hospitality of the British, but the burden of a life of inactivity was not to be borne. The Douranee Empire was still rent by intestine convulsions. The Barukzye sirdars were dominant at Caubul; but their sovereignty was threatened by Shah Mahmoud and the Princes of Herat, and not, at that time, professing to conquer for themselves, for the spirit of legitimacy was not extinct in Afghanistan, they looked abroad for a royal puppet, and found one at Loodhianah. Azim Khan invited Shah Soojah to re-assert his claims to the throne; and the Shah, weary of repose, unwarned by past experience, flung himself into this new enterprise, only to add another to that long list of failures which it took nearly a quarter of a century more to render complete.

CHAPTER VII.

[1816—1837.]

Dost Mahomed and the Barukzyes—Early days of Dost Mahomed—The fall of Futteh Khan—Defeat of Shah Mahmoud—Supremacy of the Barukzyes—Position of the Empire—Dost Mahomed at Caubul—Expedition of Shah Soojah—His Defeat—Capture of Peshawur by the Sikhs.

AMONG the twenty brothers of Futteh Khan was one many years his junior, whose infancy was wholly disregarded by the great Barukzye Sirdar. The son of a woman of the Kuzzilbash tribe, looked down upon by the high-bred Douranee ladies of his father's household, the boy had begun life in the degrading office of a sweeper at the sacred cenotaph of Lamech.* Permitted, at a later period, to hold a menial office about the person of the powerful Wuzeer, he served the great man with water, or bore his pipe; was very zealous in his ministrations; kept long and painful vigils; saw everything, heard everything

---

* "By an honorary or devotional vow of his mother he was consecrated to the lowest menial service of the sacred cenotaph of Lamech. . . . . This cenotaph is known in the colloquial dialect of the country by the appellation of Meiter Lam. In conformity with the maternal vow, when the young aspirant became capable of wielding a brush, he was carried to Meiter Lam by his mother, and instructed to exonerate her from the consequences of a sacred obligation, by sweeping, for the period of a whole day, the votive area included within the precincts of the holy place inclosing the alleged tomb of the antediluvian, the father as he is termed of the prophet Noah."—[*General Halan.*]

in silence; bided his time patiently, and when the hour came, trod the stage of active life as no irresolute novice. A stripling of fourteen, in the crowded streets of Peshawur in broad day, as the buyers and the sellers thronged the thoroughfares of the city, he slew one of the enemies of Futteh Khan, and galloped home to report the achievement to the Wuzeer. From that time his rise was rapid. The neglected younger brother of Futteh Khan became the favourite of the powerful chief, and following the fortunes of the warlike minister, soon took his place among the chivalry of the Dourance Empire.

The name of this young warrior was Dost Mahomed Khan. Nature seems to have designed him for a hero of the true Afghan stamp and character. Of a graceful person, a prepossessing countenance, a bold frank manner, he was outwardly endowed with all those gifts which most inspire confidence and attract affection; whilst undoubted courage, enterprise, activity, somewhat of the recklessness and unscrupulousness of his race, combined with a more than common measure of intelligence and sagacity, gave him a command over his fellows and a mastery over circumstances, which raised him at length to the chief seat in the empire. His youth was stained with many crimes, which he lived to deplore. It is the glory of Dost Mahomed that in the vigour of his years he looked back with contrition upon the excesses of his early life, and lived down many of the besetting infirmities which had overshadowed the dawn of his career. The waste of a deserted childhood and the deficiencies of a neglected education he struggled manfully to remedy and repair. At the zenith of his reputation there was not, perhaps, in all Central Asia a chief so remarkable for the exercise of self-discipline and self-control; but he emerged out of a cloudy morn of vice, and sunk into a gloomy night of folly.

As the lieutenant of his able and powerful brother, the

young Dost Mahomed Khan displayed in all the contests which rent the Douranee Empire a daring and heroic spirit, and considerable military address. Early acquiring the power of handling large bodies of troops, he was regarded, whilst yet scarcely a man, as a dashing, fearless soldier, and a leader of good repute. But, in those early days, his scruples were few, his excesses were many. It was one of those excesses, it is supposed, which cost the life of Futteh Khan, and built up his own reputation on the ruin of his distinguished brother.

It was shortly after the retirement of Shah Soojah to the British possessions that Futteh Khan set out, at the head of an army, to the western boundary of Afghanistan Persia had long been encroaching upon the limits of the Douranee Empire, and it was now to stem the tide of Kujjar invasion that the Afghan Wuzeer set out for Khorassan. At this time he was the virtual ruler of the country. Weak, indolent, and debauched, Shah Mahmoud, retaining the name and the pomp of royalty, had yielded the actual government of the country into the hands of Futteh Khan and his brothers The Princes of the blood royal quailed before the Barukzye Sirdars. Ferooz-ood-Deen, brother of the reigning monarch, was at that time governor of Herat. Whether actuated by motives of personal resentment or ambition, or instigated by Shah Mahmoud himself, Futteh Khan determined to turn the Persian expedition to other account, and to throw Herat into the hands of the Barukzyes. The execution of this design was entrusted to Dost Mahomed. He entered Herat with his Kohistanee followers as a friend; and when the chiefs of the city were beyond its gates, in attendance upon the Wuzeer, with characteristic Afghan treachery and violence he massacred the palace guards, seized the person of the Prince, spoiled the treasury, and violated the harem. Setting the crown upon this last act of violence, he tore the jewelled waistband from the person of the royal wife of one of the royal Princes.* The outraged lady is said to have sent her profaned garment to Prince Kamran, and to have drawn from him an oath that he would avenge the injury. He was true to his vow. The blow was struck; but it fell not on the perpetrator of the outrage: it fell upon Futteh Khan.

Dost Mahomed had fled for safety to Cashmere. The Wuzeer, returning from the Persian expedition, fell into the hands of Prince Kamran, who punctured his eyes with the point of a dagger.† What followed is well known. Enraged by so gross an outrage on a member of the Suddozye family, alarmed at the growing power of the Barukzyes, and further irritated by the resolute refusal of Futteh Khan to betray his brothers, who had effected their escape from Herat, Kamran and his father, Shah Mahmoud, agreed to put their noble prisoner to death. They were then on their way from Candahar to Caubul. The ex-minister was brought into their presence, and again called upon to write to his brothers, ordering them to surrender themselves to the Shah.

* There are varying accounts respecting the identity of this lady. Mr. Vigne says that she was daughter of Timour Shah, and sister to Shah Mahmoud. Mohun Lall, probably with more correctness, places her in a lower generation—asserting that she was the sister of Prince Kamran, and the wife of Prince Malik Quasim, son of Ferooz-ood-Deen. There is something rather perplexing in these relationships. As Ferooz-ood-Deen was the brother of Shah Mahmoud, if Mr. Vigne's account be correct, his son was the nephew of the lady in question.

† So Shah Soojah—who, however, does not allude to the outrage committed by Dost Mahomed. He merely says, "After the Kujjar campaign, Futteh Khan grew ambitious, and determined to take into his own hands the reins of government, and for this purpose resolved to ensnare Prince Kamran, who, hearing of the plot, seized Futteh Khan, put out his eyes with the point of a sharp dagger, and after performing on him an operation similar to the African mode of scalping, placed him in confinement."—[*Autobiography.*]

Again he refused, alleging that he was but a poor blind captive; that his career was run; that he had no longer any influence; and that he could not consent to betray his brethren. Exasperated by the resolute bearing of his prisoner, Mahmoud Shah ordered the unfortunate minister —the king-maker to whom he owed his crown—to be put to death before him; and there, in the presence of the feeble father and the cruel son, Futteh Khan was by the attendant courtiers literally hacked to pieces. His nose, ears, and lips were cut off; his fingers severed from his hands, his hands from his arms, his arms from his body. Limb followed limb, and long was the horrid butchery continued before the life of the victim was extinct. Futteh Khan raised no cry, offered no prayer for mercy. His fortitude was unshaken to the last. He died as he had lived, the bravest and most resolute of men—like his noble father, a victim to the perfidy and ingratitude of princes. The murder of Poyndah Khan shook the Suddozye dynasty to its base. The assassination of Futteh Khan soon made it a heap of ruins.*

* *Calcutta Review*. This passage, with many others of the present chapter, is taken, with some additions and curtailments, from a biography of Dost Mahomed Khan, written a few years ago by the author of this work. As the article was the result of much research, and written at least with the greatest care, I do not know that I can much improve upon it. Of the circumstances attending the death of Futteh Khan, an elaborate account is given by Captain James Abbott in his "Journey to Khiva." He received the story from Sumund Khan, "who had been much about the person of Shah Kamran." I subjoin the closing scene of this tragic episode :—"Futteh Khan was brought into a tent, pitched between Herat and the river, (?) in which sat a circle of his mortal foes. They commenced by each in turn accusing him of the injuries received at his hands, and heaping upon him the most opprobrious epithets. Atta Mahmoud Khan then stepped up to him, and seizing one of his ears, cut it off with his knife, saying, 'This is for such and such an injury done to such an one of my relatives.' Shahagaussie Newaub cut off the other ear. Each, as he

From this time, the rise of Dost Mahomed was rapid. He had the blood of kindred to avenge. The cruelty and ingratitude of Mahmoud and his son were now to be signally punished by the brother of the illustrious sufferer. Azim Khan, who ruled in Cashmere, counselled a course of forbearance; but Dost Mahomed indignantly rejected the proposal; and declaring that it would be an eternal disgrace to the Barukzyes not to chastise the murderers of their chief, swore that he would march upon Caubul, at the head of an army of retribution. Inclined neither to enter personally upon so perilous an undertaking, nor to appear, in such a juncture, wholly supine, Azim Khan presented his brother with three or four lakhs of rupees to defray the charges of the expedition—a sum which was exhausted long before the Sirdar neared Caubul. But in spite of every obstacle, Dost Mahomed reached Koord-Caubul, two marches from the capital, and there encamped his army.

wreaked this unmanly vengeance upon the victim, whom he would have crouched to the day before, named the wrong of which it was the recompence; thus depriving him of the highest consolation the mind of man can possess under torment—the conscience void of offence. Another of the barbarians cut off his nose; Khana Moolla Khan severed his right hand; Khalook Dad Khan his left hand, the blood gushing copiously from each new wound. Summurdar Khan cut off his beard, saying, 'This is for dishonouring my wife.' Hitherto the high-spirited chief had borne his sufferings without either weakness or any ebullition of his excitable temper. He had only once condescended, in a calm voice, to beg them to hasten his death. The mutilation of ears and nose, a punishment reserved for the meanest offences of slaves, had not been able to shake his fortitude; but the beard of a Mahomedan is a member so sacred, that honour itself becomes confounded with it; and he who had borne with the constancy of a hero the taunts and tortures heaped upon him, seemed to lose his manhood with his beard, and burst into a passion of tears. His torments were now drawing to a close. Gool Mahomed Khan, with a blow of his sabre, cut off his right foot, and a man of the Populzye tribe severed the left. Attah Mahomed Khan finished his torments by cutting his throat."

The youthful son of Kamran, Prince Jehangire, was then the nominal ruler of Caubul. But the actual administration of affairs was in the hands of Atta Mahomed. A Sirdar of the Bamezye tribe, a man of considerable ability, but no match for Dost Mahomed, he was now guilty of the grand error of underrating such an adversary. He had acted a conspicuous part in the recent intestine struggles between the Suddozye brothers; but he had no love for the royal family—none for the Barukzyes. He it was who had instigated Kamran to the cruel murder of Futteh Khan, and had with his own hands commenced the inhuman butchery. Now to advance ambitious projects of his own, he was ready to betray his masters. Simulating a friendship which he did not feel, he leagued himself with their enemies, and covenanted to betray the capital into the hands of the Barukzye Sirdars. But Dost Mahomed and his brethren had not forgotten the terrible tragedy which had cut short the great career of the chief of their tribe. In a garden-house which had once belonged to the murdered minister, they met Atta Mahomed, there to complete the covenant for the surrender of the city. A signal was given, when one—the youngest—of the brothers rushed upon the Bamezye chief, threw him to the ground, and subjected him to the cruel process which had preceded the murder of Futteh Khan. They spared his life; but sent him blind and helpless into the world, with the mark of Barukzye vengeance upon him— an object less of compassion than of scorn.

The seizure of the Balla Hissar was now speedily effected. The Shah-zadah was surrounded by treachery. Young and beautiful, he was the delight of the women of Caubul; but he had few friends among the chivalry of the empire. Too weak to distinguish the true from the false, he was easily betrayed. Persuaded to withdraw himself into the upper citadel, he left the lower fortress at the mercy of Dost Mahomed. The Sirdar made the most of the opportunity; ran a mine under the upper works, and blew up a portion of them. Death stared the Shah-zadah in the face. The women of Caubul offered up prayers for the safety of the beautiful Prince. The night was dark; the rain descended in torrents. To remain in the citadel was to court destruction. Under cover of the pitchy darkness, it was possible that he might effect his escape. Attended by a few followers, he made the effort, and succeeded. He fled so Ghuzni, and was saved.

Dost Mahomed was now in possession of Caubul. But threatened from two different quarters, his tenure was most insecure. Shah Mahmoud and Prince Kamran were marching down from Herat, and Azim Khan was coming from Cashmere to assert his claims, as the representative of the Barukzye family. But the spirit of legitimacy was not wholly extinct in Afghanistan. The Barukzyes, did not profess to conquer for themselves. It was necessary to put forward some scion of the royal family, and to fight and conquer in his name. Dost Mahomed proclaimed Sultan Ali, whilst Azim Khan invited Shah Soojah to emerge from the obscurity of Loodhianah and re-assert his claims to the throne.*

* This was in 1818. See close of the last chapter. "Azim Khan," says Shah Soojah, in his autobiography, "sent us a fawning petition, informing us that he had collected all Futteh Khan's relations, comprehending the whole of the Barukzye tribe, and swearing, by everything sacred, that he and the other chiefs had taken an oath of fidelity to us their lawful king, entreated that we would march immediately to Peshawur, where he would join the royal standard with all the troops and the treasury of Cashmere. We sent for Mr. Murray, and ordered him to make the Resident of Delhi acquainted with this, and inform us of their opinion. This opinion he gave us, some days afterwards, namely, 'That for political reasons no assistance could be given, but that we were at liberty either to depart or remain in the asylum allotted to us.' Two years had been passed in ease, and we now determined to make an attempt to reascend our throne."

Weary of retirement and inactivity, the Shah consented, and an expedition was planned. But the covenant was but of short duration. The contracting parties fell out upon the road, and, instead of fighting a common enemy, got up a battle among themselves. The Shah, who never lived to grow wiser, gave himself such airs, and asserted such ridiculous pretentions, that Azim Khan deserted his new master, and let loose his troops upon the royal cortége. Defeated in the conflict which ensued,* Shah Soojah fled to the Khybur hills, and thence betook himself to Sindh. Another puppet being called for, Prince Ayoob, for want of a better, was elevated to that dignity, and the new friends set out for Caubul.

In the meanwhile the royal army, which had marched from Herat under Shah Mahmoud and Prince Kamran approached the capital of Afghanistan. Unprepared to receive so formidable an enemy, weak in numbers, and ill-supplied with money and materials, Dost Mahomed could not, with any hope of success, have given battle to Mahmoud's forces. The danger was imminent. The royal troops were within six miles of the capital. Dost Mahomed and his followers prepared for flight. With the bridles of their horses in their hands, they stood waiting the approach of the enemy. But their fears were groundless. A flight ensued; but it was not Dost Mahomed's, but Mahmoud's army that fled. At the very threshold of victory, the Suddozye Prince, either believing that

* Shah Soojah attributes his defeat to an accidental explosion of gunpowder. "Our attendants," he says, "only amounted to 300, with two guns, but they had taken up an advantageous position on a bridge, near the garden. The Meer Akhor charged us with his horse; but the first fire from the cannon made him bite the dust, when an unfortunate accident happened. A large quantity of powder had been brought to be divided among the matchlock men. This caught fire, by which fifty men were blown up and others wounded. Resistance was now in vain, and we escaped with difficulty to the Khybur hills."

there was treachery in his ranks, or apprehending that the Barukzyes would seize Herat in his absence, turned suddenly back, and flung himself into the arms of defeat.

The Barukzyes were now dominant throughout Afghanistan. The sovereignty, indeed, of Azim Khan's puppet, Ayoob, was proclaimed; but, Herat alone excepted, the country was in reality parcelled out among the Barukzye brothers. By them the superior claims of Azim Khan were generally acknowledged. Caubul, therefore, fell to his share. Dost Mahomed took possession of Ghuzni Pur Dil Khan, Kohan Dil Khan, and their brothers, occupied Candahar. Jubbar Khan, a brother of Dost Mahomed, was put in charge of the Ghilji country. Sultan Mahomed and his brothers succeeded to the government of Peshawur, and the Shah-zadah Sultan Ali, Dost Mahomed's puppet, sunk quietly into the insignificance of private life.

But this did not last long. Shah Soojah had begun again to dream of sovereignty. He was organising an army at Shikarpoor. Against this force marched Azim Khan, accompanied by the new King, Ayoob. Recalled to the capital by the intrigues of Dost Mahomed, and delayed by one of those complicated plots which display at once the recklessness and the treachery of the Afghan character,* the Wuzeer was compelled for a while to postpone the southern expedition. The internal strife sub-

---

* The story is worth giving in a note, as eminently characteristic of Afghan history. Dost Mahomed, who had proclaimed Sultan Ali king, advised that prince to murder Shah Ayoob; and Azim Khan advised Shah Ayoob to murder Sultan Ali. Sultan Ali indignantly rejected the proposal; Shah Ayoob consented, on condition that Azim Khan would return the compliment, by assassinating Dost Mahomed. This was agreed upon. Sultan Ali was strangled in his sleep. Shah Ayoob then called upon Azim Khan to perform his part of the tragedy; but the minister coolly asked, "How can I slay my brother?" and recommended a renewal of the expedition to Shikarpoor.

sided, the march was renewned, and Azim Khan moved down on Shikarpoor. But the army of Shah Soojah melted away at his approach.

Then Azim Khan planned an expedition against the Sikhs. He had no fear of Runjeet Singh, whom he had once beaten in battle. Dost Mahomed accompanied his brother, and they marched upon the frontier, by Jellalabad and the Karapa Pass. But the watchful eye of Runjeet was upon them, and he at once took measures for their discomfiture. He well knew the character of the Barukzye brothers—knew them to be avaricious, ambitious, treacherous; the hand of each against his brethren. He thought bribery better than battle, and sent agents to tamper with Sultan Mahomed and the other Peshawur chiefs. Hoping to be enabled, in the end, to throw off the supremacy of Azim Khan, they gladly listened to his overtures. Dost Mahomed received intelligence of the plot, and signified his willingness to join the confederacy. His offer was accepted. This important accession to his party communicated new courage to Runjeet Singh. Everything was soon in train. Azim Khan was at Minchini with his treasure and his Harem, neither of which, in so troubled a state of affairs, could he venture to abandon. Sultan Mahomed wrote to him from the Sikh camp that there was a design upon both. The intelligence filled the Sirdar with grief and consternation. He beheld plainly the treachery of his brothers, shed many bitter tears, looked with fear and trembling into the future; saw disgrace on one side, the sacrifice of his armies and treasure on the other; now resolved to march down upon the enemy, now to break up his encampment and retire Night closed in upon him whilst in this state of painful agitation and perplexity. Rumours of a disastrous something soon spread through the whole camp. What it was, few could declare beyond the Sirdar's own tent; but his followers lost confidence in their chief. They knew that some evil had befallen him; that he had lost heart; that his spirit was broken. The nameless fear seized upon the whole army, and morning dawned upon the wreck of a once formidable force. His troops had deserted him, and he prepared to follow, with his treasure and his Harem, to Jellalabad. Runjeet Singh entered Peshawur in triumph; but thought it more prudent to divide the territory between Dost Mahomed and Sultan Mahomed, than to occupy it on his own account, and rule in his own name. The division was accordingly made. In the mean while Azim Khan, disappointed and broken-spirited, was seized with a violent disorder, the effect of anxiety and sorrow, and never quitted the bed of sickness until he was carried to the tomb.*

This was in 1823. The death of Azim Khan precipitated the downfal of the Suddozye monarchy, and raised Dost Mahomed to the chief seat in the Douranee Empire. The last wretched remnant of legitimacy was now about to perish by the innate force of its own corruption. The royal puppet, Ayoob, and his son attempted to seize the property of the deceased minister. Tidings of this design reached Candahar, and Shere Dil Khan, with a party of Barukzye adherents, hastened to Caubul to rescue the wealth of his brother and to chastise the spoliators. The Prince was murdered in the presence of his father, and the unhappy King carried off a prisoner to that ill-omended

* Azim Khan does not appear to have recognised the strength of Dost Mahomed's character.; and to this grand error must be attributed his premature death. Shortly before the expedition to the Sikh frontier, he had not only contemptuously declared that he did not require the services of his brother, but had actually laid siege to Ghuzni. Azim Khan's batteries caused great slaughter; but Dost Mahomed could not be persuaded to open the gates of the fortress. A negotiation took place; and the brothers embraced. But they never forgave each other.

FALL OF HABIB-OOLLAH 119

garden-house of Futteh Khan, which had witnessed the destruction of another who had done still fouler wrong to the great Barukzye brotherhood.*

In the mean while, Habib-oolah-Khan, son of Azim Khan, had succeeded nominally to the power possessed by his deceased parent. But he had inherited none of the late minister's intellect and energy, and none of his personal influence. Beside the deathbed of his father he had been entrusted to the guidance of Jubbar Khan, but he had not the good sense to perceive the advantages of such a connexion. He plunged into a slough of dissipation, and, when he needed advice, betook himself to the counsels of men little better and wiser than himself. The ablest of his advisers was Ameen-oolah-Khan, the Loghur chief—known to a later generation of Englishmen as "the infamous Ameen-oolah" This man's support was worth retaining, but Habib-oolah, having deprived Jubbar Khan of his government, attempted to destroy Ameen-oolah-Khan; and thus, with the most consummate address, paved the way to his own destruction. Dost Mahomed, ever on the alert, appeared on the stage at the fitting moment. Alone, he had not sufficient resources to compete with the son of Azim Khan; but the Newab speedily joined him; and soon afterwards, in the midst

---

* "One Haji Ali," says Mr. Masson, "who is reported to have shot the Prince, despoiled the Shah of his raiments and clad him in his own; then by the Sirdar's orders, placed him behind himself on a horse and carried him off to the Burj Vazir. A singular spectacle was offered to the people of the city as Haji Ali bore the degraded monarch along the streets; but they had become familiar with extraordinary events, and regarded them with apathy. The Sirdars, when they had given the orders consequent on the feat they had performed, returned to their dwellings in the city with the same composure after the deposition of a monarch, as if they had been enjoying a morning ride" The unfortunate puppet subsequently found his way to Lahore, where Runjeet Singh allowed him a monthly pension of 1000 rupees

of an engagement in the near neighbourhood of Caubul, the troops of Ameen-oolah-Khan went over bodily to Dost Mahomed; and the son of Azim Khan sought safety within the walls of the Balla Hissar.

Dost Mahomed, having occupied the city, invested the citadel, and would, in all probability, have carried everything before him, if the Candahar chiefs, alarmed by the successes of their brother, and dreading the growth of a power which threatened their own extinction, had not moved out to the ostensible assistance of their nephew. Dost Mahomed retreated into the Kohistan, but the unfortunate Habib-oolah soon found that he had gained nothing by such an alliance. His uncles enticed him to a meeting outside the city, seized him, carried him off to the Loghur country; then took possession of the Balla Hissar, and appropriated all his treasure. Dost Mahomed, however, was soon in arms again, and the Peshawur brothers were before Caubul. The affairs of the empire were then thrown into a state of terrible confusion. The Barukzye brothers were all fighting among themselves for the largest share of sovereignty; but it is said that "their followers have been engaged in deadly strife when the rival leaders were sitting together over a plate of cherries." To this fraternal cherry-eating, it would appear that Dost Mahomed was not admitted.* Sitting over their fruit, his brothers came to the determination of alluring him to an interview, and then either blinding or murdering him. The plot was laid; everything was arranged for the destruction of the Sirdar; but Hadjee Khan Kakur, who subsequently distinguished himself as a traitor of no slight accomplishments, having discovered in time that Dost Mahomed was backed by the strongest party in Caubul,

* Masson.—Mr. Vigne says, that Dost Mahomed and Shere Dil Khan were the cherry-eaters. We do not pretend to determine the point.

gave him a significant hint, at the proper moment, and the Sirdar escaped with his life. After a few more fraternal schemes of mutual extermination, the brothers entered into a compact by which the government of Ghuzni and the Kohistan was secured to Dost Mahomed, whilst Sultan Mahomed of Peshawur succeeded to the sovereignty of Caubul.

The truce was but of short duration. Shere Dil Khan, the most influential of the Candahar brothers, died. A dangerous rival was thus swept away from the path of Dost Mahomed. The Kuzzilbashes, soon afterwards, gave in their adherence to him; and thus aided, he felt himself in a position to strike another blow for the recovery of Caubul. Sultan Mahomed had done nothing to strengthen himself at the capital. Summoned either to surrender or to defend himself, he deemed it more prudent to negotiate. Consenting to retire on Peshawur, he marched out of one gate of Caubul whilst Dost Mahomed marched in at another, and the followers of the latter shouted out a derisive adieu to the departing chief.

From this time (1826) to the day on which his followers deserted him at Urghandi, after the capture of Ghuzni by the British troops, Dost Mahomed was supreme at Caubul. His brothers saw that it was useless to contest the supremacy; and at last they acknowledged the unequalled power of one whom they had once slighted and despised. And now was it that Dost Mahomed began fully to understand the responsibilities of high command, and the obligations of a ruler both to himself and his subjects. He had hitherto lived the life of a dissolute soldier. His education had been neglected, and in his very boyhood he had been thrown in the way of pollution of the foulest kind. From his youth he had been greatly addicted to wine, and was often to be seen in public reeling along in a state of degrading intoxication, or scarcely able to keep his place in the saddle. All this was now to be reformed. He taught himself to read and to write, accomplishments which he had before, if at all, scantily possessed. He studied the Koran, abandoned the use of strong liquors, became scrupulously abstemious, plain in his attire, assiduous in his attention to business, urbane, and courteous to all. He made a public acknowledgment of his past errors and a profession of reformation, and did not belie by his life the promises which he openly made.*

It is not to be questioned that there was, at this time, in the conduct of Dost Mahomed, as a ruler, much that may be regarded with admiration and respect even by Christian men. Success did not disturb the balance of his mind, nor power harden his heart. Simple in his habits, and remarkably affable in his manner, he was accessible to the meanest of his subjects. Ever ready to listen to

* "The days," says General Harlan—and the truth of the statement is not to be questioned—"That Dost Mahomed ascended the musnud, he performed the 'Toba,' which is a solemn and sacred formula of reformation, in reference to any accustomed moral crime or depravity of habit. He was followed in the Toba by all his chiefs, who found themselves obliged to keep pace with the march of mind—to prepare for the defensive system of policy, this assumption of purity, on the part of the Prince, suggested. The Toba was a sort of declaration of principles; and the chiefs, viewing it in that light, beheld their hopes of supremacy in imminent hazard. . . . In later life the Ameer became sensible of the advantages arising from learning. Although knowledge of literature among Mahomedan nations is confined to a contracted sphere, at least the reputation of theological science was essential to the chief, on whom had been conferred the title of Ameer-ul-Mominin, or Commander of the Faithful. To escape the humility of dependence upon subordinate agents, more especially the secretaries necessarily employed in all revenue and judicial transactions, he tasked his mind with the acquisition of letters, and became worthy, by his industry and success in the pursuit, of the greatest respect of the great, as he commanded the admiration of the vulgar, who are ever accustomed to venerate the divinity of wisdom."

their complaints and to redress their grievances, he seldom rode abroad without being accosted in the public streets or highways by citizen or by peasant waiting to lay before the Sirdar a history of his grievances or his sufferings, and to ask for assistance or redress. And he never passed the petitioner—never rode on, but would rein in his horse, listen patiently to the complaints of the meanest of his subjects, and give directions to his attendants to take the necessary steps to render justice to the injured, or to alleviate the sufferings of the distressed. Such was his love of equity, indeed, that people asked, "Is Dost Mahomed dead that there is no justice?"

He is even said, by those who knew him well, to have been kindly and humane—an assertion which many who have read the history of his early career will receive with an incredulous smile. But no one who fairly estimates the character of Afghan history and Afghan morals, and the necessities, personal and political, of all who take part in such stirring scenes, can fail to perceive that his vices were rather the growth of circumstances than of any extraordinary badness of heart. Dost Mahomed was not by nature cruel; but once embarked in the strife of Afghan politics, a man must fight it out or die. Every man's hand is against him, and he must turn his hand against every man. There is no middle course open to him. If he would save himself, he must cast his scruples to the winds. Even when seated most securely on the musnud, an Afghan ruler must commit many acts abhorrent to our ideas of humanity. He must rule with vigour, or not at all. That Dost Mahomed, during the twelve years of supremacy which he enjoyed at Caubul, often resorted, for the due maintenance of his power, to measures of severity incompatible with the character of a humane ruler, is only to say that for twelve years he retained his place at the head of affairs. Such rigour is inseparable from the government of such a people. We cannot rein wild horses with silken braids.

Upon one particular phase of Barukzye policy it is necessary to speak more in detail. Under the Suddozye Kings, pampered and privileged, the Douranee tribes had waxed arrogant and overbearing, and had, in time, erected themselves into a power capable of shaping the destinies of the empire. With one hand they held down the people, and with the other menaced the throne. Their sudden change of fortune seems to have unhinged and excited them. Bearing their new honours with little meekness, and exercising their new powers with little moderation, they revenged their past sufferings on the unhappy people whom they had supplanted, and, partly by fraud, partly by extortion, stripped the native cultivators of the last remnant of property left to them on the new allocation of the lands. In the revolutions which had rent the country throughout the early years of the century, it had been the weight of Douranee influence which had ever turned the scale. They held, indeed, the crown at their disposal, and, seeking their own aggrandisement, were sure to array themselves on the side of the prince who was most liberal of his promises to the tribes. The danger of nourishing such a power as this was not overlooked by the sagacious minds of the Barukzye rulers. They saw clearly the policy of treading down the Douranees, and soon began to execute it.

In the revolution which had overthrown the Suddozye dynasty, the tribes had taken no active part, and the Barukzye Sirdars had risen to power neither by their aid nor in spite of their opposition. A long succession of sanguinary civil wars, which had deprived them, one by one, of the leaders to whom they looked for guidance and support, had so enfeeble and prostrated them, that but a remnant of their former power was left. No immediate apprehension of danger from such a source darkened the dawn of the Barukzye brethren's career. But to be cast down was not to be broken—to be enfeebled was not to be extinct. There was too much elasticity and vitality in the order for such accidents as this to subject it to more than temporary decline. The Douranees were still a privileged class; still were they fattening upon the immunities granted them by the Suddozye Kings. To curtail these privileges and immunities would be to strike at the source of their dominant influence and commanding strength; and the Barukzye Sirdars, less chivalrous than wise, determined to strike the blow, whilst the Douranees, crippled and exhausted, had little power to resist the attack. Even then they did not venture openly and directly to assail the privileges of the tribes by imposing an assessment on their lands in lieu of the obligation to supply horsemen for the service of the state—an obligation which had for some time past been practically relaxed—but they began cautiously and insidiously to introduce "the small end of the wedge," by taxing the Ryots, or Humsayehs of the Douranees, whose various services, not only as cultivators but as artificers, had rendered them in the estimation of their powerful masters a valuable kind of property, to be protected from foreign tyranny that they might better bear their burdens at home. These taxes were enforced with a rigour intended to offend the Douranee chiefs; but the trials to which they were then subjected but faintly foreshadowed the greater trials to come.

Little by little, the Barukzye Sirdars began to attach such vexatious conditions to the privileges of the Douranees—so to make them run the gauntlet of all kinds of exactions short of the direct assessment of their lands—that in time, harassed, oppressed, impoverished by these more irregular imposts, and anticipating every day the development of some new form of tyranny and extortion, they were glad to exchange them for an assessment of a more fixed and definite character. From a minute detail of the measures adopted by the Barukzye Sirdars, with the double object of raising revenue and breaking down the remaining strength of the Douranees, the reader would turn away with weariness and impatience; but this matter of Douranee taxation has too much to do with the after-history of the war in Afghanistan, for me to pass it by without at least this slight recognition of its importance.

In the heyday of their prosperity, the Douranees had been too arrogant and unscrupulous to claim from us commiseration in the hour of their decline. The Barukzye Sirdars held them down with a strong hand; and the policy was at least successful. It was mainly the humiliation of these once dominant tribes that secured to Dost Mahomed and his brothers so many years of comparative security and rest. Slight disorders, such as are inseparable from the constitution of Afghan society—a rebellion in one part of the country, the necessity of coercing a recusant governor in another—occasionally distracted the mind of the Sirdar from the civil administration of Caubul. But it was not until the year 1834 that he was called upon to face a more pressing danger, and to prepare himself for a more vigorous contest. The exiled Suddozye Prince, Shah Soojah, weary again of inactivity, and undaunted by past failure, was about to make another effort to re-establish himself in the Douranee Empire; and, with this object, was organising an army in Sindh.

Had there been any sort of unanimity among the Barukzye brothers, this invasion might have been laughed to scorn; but Dost Mahomed felt that there was treachery within, no less than hostility without, and that the open enemy was not more dangerous than the concealed one. Jubbar Khan, Zemaun Khan, and others, were known to be intriguing with the Shah. The Newab, indeed, had gone so far as to assure Dost Mahomed that it was useless to oppose the Suddozye invasion, as Soojah-ool-Moolk was assisted by the British Government, and would certainly be victorious. He implored the Sirdar to pause before he brought down upon himself certain destruction, alleging that it would be better to make terms with the Shah—to secure something rather than to lose everything. But Dost Mahomed knew his man— knew that Jubbar Khan had thrown himself into the arms of the Suddozye, laughed significantly, and said, "Lala, it will be time enough to talk about terms when I have been beaten." This was unanswerable. The Newab retired; and preparations for war were carried on with renewed activity.

In the mean while, Shah Soojah was girding himself up for the coming struggle with the Barukzye Sirdars. In 1831 he had sought the assistance of Runjeet Singh towards the recovery of his lost dominions; but the Maharajah had set such an extravagant price upon his alliance, that the negotiations fell to the ground without any results.* The language of the Sikh ruler had been

* Among other stipulations was one, that "the heir-apparent of the Shah shall always attend his highness with a force, having also his family along with him; that he shall be treated with distinction, and expected to accompany the Maharajah in all his journeys" Another demand put forth by Runjeet was for the delivery to him of the sandal-wood gates of Somnauth (or Juggernauth, as the Maharajah called them), destined afterwards to confer such celebrity upon the Indian administration of Lord Ellenborough. Shah Soojah's answer to the demand is worth quoting —"Regarding the demand of the portals of sandal at Ghiznee, a compliance with it is inadmissible in two ways. firstly, a real friend is he who is interested in the good name of his friend. The Maharajah being my friend, how can he find satisfaction

insolent and dictatorial. He had treated the Shah as a fallen prince, and endeavoured, in the event of his restoration, to reduce him to a state of vassalage so complete, that even the prostrate Suddozye resented the humiliating attempt. The idea of making another effort to regain his lost dominions had, however, taken such shape in his mind, that it was not to be lightly abandoned. But empires are not to be won without money, and the Shah was lamentably poor. Jewels he had to the value of two or three lakhs of rupees; and he was eager to pledge them. But the up-country bankers were slow to make the required advances. "If 1000 rupees be required," said the Shah, "these persons will ask a pledge in property of a lakh of rupees." From the obdurate bankers he turned, in his distress, to the British Government; but the British Government was equally obdurate.

In vain the exiled Shah pleaded that the people of Afghanistan were anxious for his arrival; and that those of Khorassan would flock to his standard and acknowledge no other chief. In vain he declared that the Barukzye Sirdars were "not people around whom the Afghans would rally"—that they had no authority beyond the streets and bazaars of Caubul, and no power to resist an enemy advancing from the northward. Neither up-country bankers nor British functionaries would advance him the requisite funds. "My impatience," he said, "exceeds all bounds; and if I can raise a loan of two or three lakhs of rupees from any banker, I entertain every expectation that,

in my eternal disgrace? To desire the disgrace of one's friend is not consistent with the dictates of wisdom. Secondly, there is a tradition among all classes of people that the forefathers of the Sikhs have said that their nation shall, in the attempt to bring away the portals of sandal, advance to Ghiznee; but having arrived there, the foundation of their empire shall be overthrown. I am not desirous of that event. I wish for the permanence of his highness's dominion."

with the favour of God, my object will be accomplished." But although the Persians were at that time pushing their conquests in Khorassan, and the Shah continued to declare that the Douranee, Ghilzye, and other tribes, were sighing for his advent, which was to relieve them from the tyranny and oppression of the Barukzyes, and to secure them against foreign invasion, Lord William Bentinck, too intent upon domestic reforms to busy himself with schemes of distant defence, quietly smiled down the solicitations of the Shah, and told him to do what he liked on his own account, but that the British Government would not help him to do it. "My friend," he wrote, "I deem it my duty to apprise you distinctly, that the British Government religiously abstains from intermeddling with the affairs of its neighbours when this can be avoided. Your Majesty is, of course, master of your own actions; but to afford you assistance for the purpose which you have in contemplation, would not consist with that neutrality which on such occasions is the rule of guidance adopted by the British Government." But, in spite of these discouragements, before the year 1832 had worn to a close, Shah Soojah "had resolved on quitting his asylum at Loodhianah for the purpose of making another attempt to regain his throne."

The British agent on the north-western frontier, Captain Wade, officially reported this to Mr. Macnaghten, who then held the office of Political Secretary; and with the announcement went a request, on the part of the Shah, for three months of his stipend in advance. The request, at a later period, rose to a *six* months' advance; and a compromise was eventually effected for *four*. So, with 16,000 rupees extracted as a forestalment of the allowance granted to his family in his absence, he set out for the reconquest of the Douranee Empire.

On the 28th of January, 1833, he quitted his residence

at Loodhianah, and endeavouring, as he went, to raise money and to enlist troops for his projected expedition, moved his camp slowly to Bahwulpore, and thence, across the Indus, to Shikarpoor, where he had determined to rendezvous.

But having thus entered the territory of the Ameers of Sindh as a friend, he did not quit it before he had shown his quality as an enemy, by fighting a hard battle with the Sindhians, and effectually beating them. The pecuniary demands which he had made upon them they had resisted; and the Shah having a considerable army at his command, deeply interested in the event, thought fit to enforce obedience. Early in January, 1834, an engagement took place near Rori, and the pride of the Ameers having been humbled by defeat, they consented to the terms he demanded, and acknowledged the supremacy of the Shah.*

Having arranged this matter to his satisfaction, Shah Soojah marched upon Candahar, and in the early summer was before the walls of the city. He invested the place, and endeavoured ineffectually to carry it by assault. The Candahar chiefs held out with much resolution, but it was not until the arrival of Dost Mahomed from Caubul that a general action was risked. The Sirdar lost no time in commencing the attack. Akbar Khan, the chief's son, who, at a later period, stood out so prominently from the canvas of his country's history, was at the head of the Barukzye horse; Abdul Samat Khan† commanded the

* "The Sindhians have agreed to pay a contribution of either five or seven lakhs of rupees to farm the Shikarpoor territory for a settled annual sum from Shah Soojah, and to provide him with an auxiliary force, the Shah taking hostages from them for the entire execution of these articles."—[*Captain Wade to Mr. Macnaghten, March 5,* 1834.]

† Not the minister—but a Persian adventurer of the same name, who afterwards obtained service in Bokhara.

foot. No great amount of military skill appears to have been displayed on either side. Akbar Khan's horsemen charged the enemy with a dashing gallantry worthy of their impetuous leader ; but a battalion of the Shah's troops, under an Indo-Briton, named Campbell, fought with such uncommon energy, that at one time the forces of the Barukzye chiefs were driven back, and victory appeared to be in the reach of the Shah. But Dost Mahomed, who had intently watched the conflict, and kept a handful of chosen troops in reserve, now let them slip, rallied the battalions which were falling back, called upon Akbar Khan to make one more struggle, and, well responded to by his gallant son, rolled back the tide of victory. Shah Soojah, who on the first appearance of Dost Mahomed had lost all heart, and actually given orders to prepare for flight, called out in his desperation to Campbell, "Chupao-chupao,"* then ordered his elephant to be wheeled round, and turned his back upon the field of battle. His irresolution and the unsteadfastness of the Douranees proved fatal to his cause.

The Douranee tribes had looked upon the advance of the King with evident satisfaction Trodden down and crushed as they had been by the Barukzyes, they would have rejoiced in the success of the royal cause. But they had not the power to secure it. Depressed and enfeebled by long years of tyranny, they brought only the shadow of their former selves to the standard of the Suddozye monarch. Without horses, without arms, without discipline, without heart to sustain them upon any great enterprise, and without leaders to inspire them with the courage they lacked themselves, the Douranees went into the field a feeble, broken-spirited rabble. Had they been

* Mr. Vigne says that he had this from Campbell himself. The word indicates more properly a plundering attack; but is employed here to signify an irregular descent, or rush, upon the enemy

assured of the success of the enterprise, they would at least have assumed a bold front, and flung all their influence, such as it was, into the scales on the side of the returned Suddozye; but remembering the iron rule and the unsparing vengeance of the Barukzye Sirdars, they dreaded the consequences of failure, and when the crisis arrived, either stood aloof from the contest, or shamefully apostatised at the last.

The few, indeed, who really joined the royal standard contrived to defeat the enterprise; for whilst the Shah's Hindostanees were engaging the enemy in front, the Douranees, moved by an irrepressible avidity for plunder, fell upon the baggage in the rear, and created such a panic in the ranks that the whole army turned and fled. It was not possible to rally them. The battle was lost. The Barukzye troops pushed forward. Campbell, who had fallen like a brave man, covered with wounds, was taken prisoner, with others of the Shah's principal officers; and all the guns, stores, and camp-equippage of the Suddozye Prince fell into the hands of the victors. The scenes of plunder and carnage which ensued are said to have been terrible. The Shah fled to Furrah, and thence by the route of Seistan and Shorawuk to Kelat. The Candahar chiefs urged the pursuit of the fugitive, but Dost Mahomed opposed the measure, and the unfortunate Prince was suffered to escape.

But scarcely had the Sirdar returned to Caubul when he found himself compelled to prepare for a new and more formidable enterprise. Runjeet Singh was in possession of Peshawur. The treachery of Sultan Mahomed Khan and his brothers had rebounded upon themselves, and they had lost the province which had been the object of so much intrigue and contention. In their anxiety to destroy Dost Mahomed, they opened a communication with the Sikhs, who advanced to Peshawur ostensibly as friends, and then took possession of the city.* Sultan Mahomed Khan ignominiously fled. The Sikh army under Hurree Singh consisted only of 9000 men, and had the Afghans been commanded by a competent leader they might have driven back a far stronger force, and retained possession of the place. The Peshawur chiefs were everlastingly disgraced, and Peshawur lost to the Afghans for ever.

But Dost Mahomed could not submit patiently to this. Exasperated against Runjeet Singh, and indignant at the fatuous conduct of his brothers, he determined on declaring a religious war against the Sikhs, and began with characteristic energy to organise a force sufficiently strong to wrest Peshawur from the hands of the usurpers. To strengthen his influence he assumed, at this time, the title of Ameer-al-Mominin (commander of the faithful †), and exerted himself to inflame the breasts of his followers with that burning Mahomedan zeal which has so often impelled the disciples of the Prophet to deeds of the most consummate daring and most heroic self-abandonment. Money was now to be obtained, and to obtain it much extortion was, doubtless, practised. An Afghan chief has a rude and somewhat arbitrary manner of levying rates and taxes. Dost Mahomed made no exception in his conduct to "the good old rule," which had so long, in critical conjunctures,

* Shah Soojah, when on his way to Shikarpoor, in 1833, had entered into a treaty with Runjeet Singh, by one of the articles of which he ceded Peshawur to the Sikhs. But Runjeet Singh was by no means inclined to wait until the Shah had established his title to give away any portion of the Afghan dominions; so he sent his grandson, Nao Nehal Singh, a boy, who then "took the spear into his hand" for the first time, to take possession of the place.

† He had been recommended by some to assume the titles of royalty, but he replied, that as he was too poor to support his dignity as a Sirdar, it would be preposterous to think of converting himself into a King.

been observed in that part of the world. He took all that he could get, raised a very respectable force, coined money in his own name, and then prepared for battle.

At the head of an imposing array of fighting men, the Ameer marched out of Caubul. He had judged wisely. The declaration of war against the infidel—war proclaimed in the name of the Prophet—had brought thousands to his banner; and ever as he marched the great stream of humanity seemed to swell and swell, as new tributaries came pouring in from every part, and the thousands became tens of thousands. From the Kohistan, from the hills beyond, from the regions of the Hindoo-Koosh, from the remoter fastnesses of Toorkistan, multitudes of various tribes and denominations, moved by various impulses, but all noisily boasting their true Mahomedan zeal, came flocking in to the Ameer's standard. Ghilzyes and Kohistanees, sleek Kuzzilbashés and rugged Oosbegs, horsemen and foot-men, all who could wield a sword or lift a matchlock, obeyed the call in the name of the Prophet. "Savages from the remotest recesses of the mountainous districts," wrote one, who saw this strange congeries of Mussulman humanity,* "who were dignified with the profession of the Mahomedan faith, many of them giants in form and strength, promiscuously armed with sword and shield, bows and arrows, matchlocks, rifles, spears and blunderbusses, concentrated themselves around the standard of religion, and were prepared to slay, plunder, and destroy, for the sake of God and the Prophet, the unenlighted infidels of the Punjab."

The Mussulman force reached Peshawur. The brave heart of Runjeet Singh quailed before this immense assemblage, and he at once determined not to meet it openly in the field. There was in his camp a man named

* General Harlan.

Harlan, an American adventurer, now a doctor and now a general, who was ready to take any kind of service with any one disposed to pay him, and to do any kind of work at the instance of his master.* Clever and unscrupulous, he was a fit agent to do the Maharajah's bidding. Runjeet despatched him as an envoy to the Afghan camp. He went ostensibly to negotiate with Dost Mahomed; in reality to corrupt his supporters. "On the occasion," he says, with as little sense of shame as though he had been performing an exploit of the highest merit, "of Dost Mahomed's visit to Peshawur, which occurred during the period of my service with Runjeet Singh, I was despatched by the Prince as ambassador to the Ameer I divided his brothers against him, exciting their jealousy of his growing power, and exasperating the family feuds with which, from my previous acquaintance, I was familiar, and stirred up the feudal lords of his durbar, with the prospects of pecuniary advantages I induced his brother, Sultan Mahomed Khan, the lately deposed chief of Peshawur, with 10,000 retainers, to withdraw suddenly from his camp about nightfall. The chief accompanied me towards the Sikh camp, whilst his followers fled to their mountain fastnesses. So large a body retiring from the Ameer's control, in opposition to his will and without previous intimation, threw the general camp into inextricable confusion, which terminated in the clandestine rout of his forces, without beat of drum, or sound of bugle, or

* Harlan originally went out to China and India as supercargo of a merchant vessel. He left his ship at Calcutta, and obtained service, as a supernumerary, on the medical establishment of the Company. He was posted to the artillery at Dum-Dum, and afterwards accompanied Major (now Sir George) Pollock to Rangoon. He does not appear to have earned a very good name during his connexion with the Company's army, which he soon quitted, and obtained service with Runjeet Singh—afterwards to seek the patronage of Dost Mahomed, whom he had so foully betrayed.

the trumpet's blast, in the quiet stillness of midnight. At daybreak no vestige of the Afghan camp was seen, where six hours before 50,000 men and 10,000 horses, with all the busy host of attendants, were rife with the tumult of wild emotion." *

Thus was this great expedition, so promising at the outset, brought prematurely to a disastrous close. Treachery broke up, in a single night, a vast army which Runjeet Singh had contemplated with dismay. The Ameer, with the *débris* of his force, preserving his guns, but sacrificing much of his camp-equipage, fell back upon Caubul, reseated himself quietly in the Balla Hissar, and, in bitterness of spirit, declaiming against the emptiness of military renown, plunged deeply into the study of the Koran.

From this pleasant abstraction from warlike pursuits, the Ameer was, after a time, aroused by a well grounded report to the effect that Sultan Mahomed had been again intriguing with the Sikhs, and that a plan had been arranged for the passage of a Punjabee force through the

* It would appear that Dost Mahomed, instigated by Meerza Samad Khan, seized Mr. Harlan, as well as the Fakir Azizoodeen, who was also sent as an ambassador into the Ameer's camp. The Ameer endeavoured to throw the odium of the act upon Sultan Mahomed, hoping thereby to ruin him utterly in the opinion of the Sikhs; but Sultan Mahomed, after having taken a number of oaths on the Koran, pledging himself to compliance with the Ameer's wishes, sent back the prisoners (or *hostages*, as Dost Mahomed called them) to the Maharajah's camp. Mr. Harlan himself, however, says nothing about this. Mohun Lal says that "the appalling news (of the treachery of Sultan Mahomed) wounded the feelings of the Ameer most bitterly. There were no bounds to the sweat of shame and folly which flowed over his face, and there was no limit to the laughter of the people at his being deceived and ridiculed. His minister, Meerza Samad Khan, was so much distressed by this sad exposure of his own trick, and still more by the failure of his plan in losing the Fakir, that he hung down his head with great remorse and shame, and then, throwing away his state papers, he exclaimed, that he would avoid all interference in the government affairs hereafter."

Khybur Pass, with the ultimate intention of moving upon Caubul. An expedition was accordingly fitted out, in the spring of 1837; but the Ameer, having sufficient confidence in his sons Afzul Khan and Mahomed Abkar, sent the Sirdars in charge of the troops with Meerza Samad Khan, his minister, as their adviser. The Afghan forces laid siege to Jumrood, and on the 30th of April Hurree Singh came from Peshawur to its relief. An action took place, in which both the young Sirdars greatly distinguished themselves, and Shumshoodeen Khan's conduct was equally conspicuous. The Sikh chieftain, Hurree Singh, was slain, and his disheartened troops fell back and entrenched themselves under the walls of Jumrood. Akbar Khan proposed to follow up the victory by dashing on to Peshawur; but the Meerza, who, according to Mr. Masson, had, during the action, "secreted himself in some cave or sheltered recess, where, in despair, he sobbed, beat his breast, tore his beard, and knocked his head upon the ground," now made his appearance, declaring that his prayers had been accepted, and "entreated the boasting young man to be satisfied with what he had done." The advice was sufficiently sound, whatever may have been the motives which dictated it. Strong Sikh reinforcements soon appeared in sight, and the Afghan army was compelled to retire. The battle of Jumrood was long a theme of national exultation. Akbar Khan plumed himself greatly on the victory, and was unwilling to share the honours of the day with his less boastful brother. But it was not a very glorious achievement, and it may be doubted whether Afzul Khan did not really distinguish himself even more than his associate. In one respect, however, it was a heavy blow to the Maharajah. Runjeet Singh had lost one of his best officers and dearest friends. The death of Hurree Singh was never forgotten or forgiven.

The loss of Peshawur rankled deeply in the mind of

Dost Mahomed. The empire of Ahmed Shah had been rapidly falling to pieces beneath the heavy blows of the Sikh spoliator. The wealthy provinces of Cashmere and Mooltan had been wrested from the Douranees in the time of the Suddozye Princes, and now the same unsparing hand had amputated another tract of country, to the humiliation of the Barukzye Sirdars. The Ameer, in bitterness of spirit, bewailed the loss of territory, and burned to resent the affront. In spite, however, of the boasted victory of Jumrood, he had little inclination to endeavour to wrest the lost territory, by force of arms, from the grasp of the Sikh usurpers. Mistrusting his own strength, in this conjuncture he turned his thoughts towards foreign aid. Willing to form almost any alliance so long as this great end was to be gained, he now looked towards Persia for assistance, and now invited the friendly aid of the British. It was in the autumn of this year, 1837, that two events, which mightily affected the future destinies of Dost Mahomed, were canvassed in the bazaars of Caubul. A British emissary was about to arrive at the Afghan capital; and a Persian army was advancing upon the Afghan frontier. Before the first snows had fallen, Captain Burnes was residing at Caubul, and Mahomed Shah was laying siege to Herat.*

* The authorities consulted in the preparation of this chapter are the published works of Burnes, Conolly, Vigne, Masson, Mohun Lal, Harlan, &c.; the autobiography of Shah Soojah; and the manuscript reports of Colonel Rawlinson. To the latter I am indebted for much valuable information relative to the Douranee tribes.

CHAPTER VIII.

[1810—1837.]

Later Events in Persia—The Treaty of Goolistan—Arrival of Sir Gore Ouseley—Mr. Morier and Mr. Ellis—The Definitive Treaty—The War of 1826-27—The Treaty of Toorkomanchai—Death of Futteh Ali Shah—Accession of Mahomed Shah—His Projects of Ambition—The Expedition against Herat.

IT is necessary now to revert, for a little space, to the progress of affairs in Western Asia. Whilst the Suddozye Princes in Afghanistan had been gradually relaxing their hold of the Douranee Empire, Persia had been still struggling against Russian encroachment—still entangled in the meshes of a long and harassing war. Though enfeebled by the paramount necessity of concentrating the resources of the empire on the great European contest, which demanded the assertion of all her military strength, the aggressive tendencies of the great northern power were not to be entirely controlled. Little could she think of remote acquisitions of territory in Georgia, whilst the eagles of Napoleon were threatening her very existence at the gates of Moscow itself. Still with little intermission, up to the year 1813, the war dragged languidly on. Then the good offices of Great Britain were successfully employed for the re-establishment of friendly relations between the two contending powers;* and a treaty, known as the treaty of Goolistan, was negotiated between

---

* Russia refused to accept the formal mediation of Great Britain; but the good offices of the ambassador were employed with success.

them. By this treaty Persia ceded to Russia all her acquisitions on the south of the Caucasus, and agreed to maintain no naval force on the Caspian sea; whilst Russia entered into a vague engagement to support, in the event of a disputed succession, the claims of the heir-apparent against all competitors for the throne.

During these wars, which were carried on with varying success, the Persian troops upon more than one occasion had been led to the charge by English officers of approved gallantry and skill. Accompanying General Malcolm to Persia in 1810, they were retained in the country by Sir Harford Jones; and were very soon busily employed in drilling and disciplining the infantry and artillery of the Persian Prince.* Of these officers, the most conspicuous were Captain Christie and Lieutenant Lindsay, who led into the field the battalions which they had instructed, and more than once turned the tide of victory against their formidable European opponents.†

* "Poor Captain Christie and Lieutenant Lindsay," says Sir Harford Jones, "by their indefatigable perseverance had brought, when I left Persia, the one, several of the regiments of the Prince's infantry, and the other, the corps of horse artillery, considering the shortness of the time they had been employed, to a state of perfection that was quite astonishing. And what is equally to the credit of these gallant officers, they were both adored by the officers and men under their tuition; though in the beginning they had often been obliged to treat the latter with a degree of severity that could not then have been practised with safety at Constantinople. The Prince Royal, however, had much merit in this respect, for whenever a punishment was inflicted and complained of to him, he invariably gave the offender a double portion of it, and by this means soon put an end to complaint."—[*Sir Harford Jones's Account of the Transactions of His Majesty's Mission to the Court of Persia,* 1807-1811.] Malcolm took with him to Persia, as a present from the Indian Government to the Shah, twelve field-pieces, with harness and all necessary equipments for horse artillery.

† Captain Christie was an officer of the Bombay army, selected for employment in Persia, by General Malcolm, on account of his high

In the mean while, Sir Harford Jones had been succeeded in the Persian embassy by Sir Gore Ouseley, who in the summer of 1811 reached Teheran in the character

reputation for gallantry and personal activity, and his thorough acquaintance with the native character. Associated with Pottinger, on their first entry into Beloochistan, he afterwards diverged to the northward, and, in the guise of a horse-dealer, penetrated through Seistan to Herat, and thence, by the way of Yezd and Ispahan, reached the northern regions of Persia. A great part of the line which he thus traversed had never before, and has never, I believe, since been explored by an European traveller. Stories of Christie's extraordinary personal strength and prowess, are current to the present day in the north of India and in Persia. In the latter country, indeed, he was adored by the soldiery, and his name is still a household word among the old officers of the Azerbijan army. He was killed at the head of his famous Shegaughee brigade, in the night attack which was made by the Russians on the Persian camp at Aslandooz, in November, 1812.

Lieutenant Lindsay was an officer of the Madras Horse Artillery, and, to scientific attainments of no ordinary extent, added the most imposing personal appearance. He was six feet eight inches in height (without his shoes), and thus realised, in the minds of the Persians, their ideas of the old heroes of romance. After many years' service in Persia, he resigned his appointment in the Indian service, and, succeeding to the estate of Kincolquhair, settled in Scotland as Lindsay Bethune In 1834 he was again sent to Persia by the British Government, with a view to his employment in the expected war of the succession, and was thus enabled, in the following year, to add to his former laurels, by leading (on the death of Futteh Ali Shah) the advanced division of the Persian army from Tabreez to Teheran, and subsequently quelling a very serious rebellion against the authority of Mahomed Shah, that was set afoot in the south of Persia by the Prince of Shiraz and his sons. For this service, on his return to England, he was rewarded with a baronetcy, and in 1836 he was a third time sent out with a Major-General's commission, to take command of the Persian army Owing, however, to the misunderstanding which arose out of the advance upon Herat, the Persian Government on this occasion declined to employ him, and he finally retired from military life in 1839 He lived more than ten years after this; and at the close of his life, again travelled in Persia, revisiting the scenes of his former exploits But death overtook him before he could return.

of Ambassador Extraordinary from the King of England. The preliminary treaty which Jones had negotiated, was now to be wrought into a definitive one. It was somewhat modified in the process. The new treaty was more liberal than the old. In the preliminary articles relating to the subsidy, it had been set down that the amount should be regulated in the definitive treaty; but it was understood between the British and the Persian plenipotentiary, that the amount was on no account to exceed 160,000 tomauns, and that the manner in which it was to be afforded should be left to the discretion of the British Government. But in the definitive treaty the amount was fixed at 200,000 tomauns (or about 150,000*l.*); and a special article was introduced, setting forth that "since it is the custom of Persia to pay her troops six months in advance, the English ambassador shall do all in his power to pay the subsidy granted in lieu of troops, in as early instalments as may be convenient and practicable,"—a pleasant fiction, of which it has been said, with truth, that it might "well be taken for a burlesque."

On the 14th of March, 1812, this treaty was signed by Sir Gore Ouseley, Mahomed Shefi, and Mahomed Hassan; and a week afterwards, the British ambassador wrote to inform the Court of Directors of the East India Company that "the good effects of the definitive treaty, and the proofs of the confidence with which it has inspired the Shah, are already manifest." The Persian monarch, having declared his fixed determination to strengthen Abbas Meerza to the utmost of his ability, by raising for him a disciplined army of 50,000 men, requested Sir Gore Ouseley to obtain for him, with the utmost possible despatch, 30,000 stands of English muskets and accoutrements, the price of which was to be deducted from the subsidy. "The Shah," wrote the envoy, "has further promised me, that this large deduction from the subsidy shall be made up, through me, to Abbas Meerza's army from the royal coffers, so that we may congratulate ourselves on having worked a wonderful (and, by many, unexpected) alteration in the Shah's general sentiments."*

Sir Gore Ouseley returned to England, leaving his secretary, Mr. Morier, in charge of the Mission; but before the treaty was finally accepted, it was modified by the British Government, and Mr. Henry Ellis was despatched to Persia, in 1814, to negotiate these alterations at the Persian Court. A comparison of the treaty, signed by Sir Gore Ouseley, with that which was subsequently accepted, will show that the alterations, which were very considerable in respect of words, were less so in respect of substance. The most important conditions of the treaty are to be found in both documents. But the progress of events had rendered it necessary to expunge certain passages from the treaty negotiated by Sir Gore Ouseley. For example, the 7th article of that treaty provided, that "should the King of Persia form magazines of materials for ship-building on the coast of the Caspian Sea, and resolve to establish a naval force, the King of England shall grant permission to naval officers, seamen, shipwrights, carpenters, &c., to proceed to Persia from London and Bombay, and to enter the service of the King of Persia —the pay of such officers, artificers, &c., shall be given by his Persian Majesty at the rates which may be agreed upon with the English ambassador."† But by the treaty of Goolistan, Persia engaged not to maintain a naval

* *Sir Gore Ouseley to the Court of Directors: March 21, 1812.—* [*MS. Records.*]

† *MS. Records.* Sir Gore Ouseley's treaty is not given in the collection of treaties in the published "Papers relating to Persia and Afghanistan." In another article of this, which does not appear in the subsequent treaty, the amount of the allowances to be granted by the Shah to the British officers serving in Persia is laid down.

force on the Caspian. The article, therefore, was necessarily expunged.

On the 25th of November, the definitive treaty, which was finally accepted, was concluded at Teheran by Messrs. Morier and Ellis. It was declared to be strictly defensive. The plan of defence thus marked out was more extensive than practicable. It bound the Persian Government to engage "not to allow any European army to enter the Persian territory, nor to proceed towards India, nor to any of the ports of that country; and also to engage not to allow any individuals of such European nations, entertaining a design of invading India, or being at enmity with Great Britain, whatever, to enter Persia." "Should any European powers," it was added, "wish to invade India by the road of Khorassan, Tartaristan, Bokhara, Samarcand, or other routes, his Persian Majesty engages to induce the kings and governors of those countries to oppose such invasion as much as is in his power, either by the fear of his arms or by conciliatory measures." In the third article it is laid down, that "the limits of the territories of the two states of Russia and Persia shall be determined according to the admission of Great Britain, Persia, and Russia"—a stipulation of an extraordinary and, perhaps, unexampled character, inasmuch as Russia had not consented to this mode of adjudication. The eighth and ninth articles related to Afghanistan, and are contained in the following words:

VIII. "Should the Afghans be at war with the British nation, his Persian Majesty engages to send an army against them, in such manner, and of such force, as may be concerted with the English Government. The expenses of such an army shall be defrayed by the British Government, in such manner as may be agreed upon at the period of its being required.

IX. "If war should be declared between the Afghans

and Persians, the English Government shall not interfere with either party, unless their mediation to effect a peace shall be solicited by both parties." *

One more clause of the definitive treaty calls for notice in this place. In Article VI, it is covenanted that "should any European power be engaged in war with Persia, when at peace with England, his Britannic Majesty engages to use his best endeavours to bring Persia and such European power to a friendly understanding." "If however," it is added, "his Majesty's cordial interference should fail of success, England shall still, if required, in conformity with the stipulations in the preceding articles, send a force from India, or, in lieu thereof, pay an annual subsidy (200,000 tomauns) for the support of a Persian army, so long as a war in the supposed case shall continue, and until Persia shall make peace with such nation." By this article we, in effect, pledged ourselves to support Persia in her wars with Russia, even though we should be at peace with the latter state. By the convention of Goolistan, it is true that amicable relations had been re-established between the Russian and Persian Governments; but these relations were likely at any time to be interrupted; and it was not difficult to perceive, that, before long, the aggressive policy of Russia would again bring that state into collision with its Persian neighbour. The article, in reality, exposed us at least to the probability of a war with Russia; and laid down

* Of this article it has been said by an experienced writer: "The obligation which we contracted in the 9th article, to abstain from interference in the event of a possible contest between the Afghans and Persians, is hardly intelligible. Such a proposal could not have proceeded from Great Britain; and if proceeding from Persia, it indicated that desire of territorial extension which was more fully developed in the sequel, and which, when developed, compelled us on general grounds to repudiate the treaty altogether." — [*Calcutta Review*, vol. xii.]

the doctrine that every future aggression of the latter against the dominions of the Persian Shah was to be regarded in the light of a hostile demonstration against our Indian possessions.

For some time there was little to disturb the even current of affairs, or to change the character of our relations towards the Persian state. It was the policy of Great Britain, by strengthening the military resources of the country, to render Persia an insurmountable barrier against the invasion of India by any European army. But by this time France had ceased to be formidable; and what was ostensibly defence against the powers of Europe, was, in reality, defence against the ambition of the Czar. It is doubtful, however, how far our policy was successful. We supplied the Persian army with English arms and English discipline; our officers drilled the native troops after the newest European fashions, and for some time the Crown Prince, Abbas Meerza, was delighted with his new plaything. But the best-informed authorities concur in opinion that the experiment was a failure; and that the real military strength of the empire was not augmented by this infusion of English discipline into the raw material of the Persian army.* It has been said, indeed, and with

* The explanation of this failure, given by the same experienced writer, is worth quoting:—"If it be remembered that when the system is affected with chronic paralysis, the attempt is vain to restore any particular member to a healthy action, it will be understood that, to a nation devoid of organisation in every other department of government, a regular army was impossible. It thus happened that, notwithstanding the admirable material for soldiery which were offered by the hardy peasantry of Azerbijan, and the still hardier mountaineers of Kermanshah—notwithstanding the aptitude of the officers to receive instruction—notwithstanding that a due portion of physical courage appertained generally to the men—the disciplined forces of Persia, considered as an army, and for the purpose of national defence, were, from the epoch of their first creation, contemptible. Beyond drill and

undeniable truth, by one who was himself for many years among the instructors of the Persian army, that "when Persia again came into collision with Russia in 1826, her means and power as a military nation were positively inferior to those which she possessed at the close of her former struggle."

From the date of the convention of Goolistan, up to the year 1826, there was at least an outward observance of peace between the Russian and Persian states. The peace, however, was but a hollow one, destined soon to be broken. The irritation of a disputed boundary had ever since the ratification of the treaty of Goolistan kept the two states in a restless, unsettled condition of ill-disguised animosity; and now it broke out at last into acts of mutual defiance. It is hard to say whether Russia or Persia struck the first unpardonable blow. The conduct of the former had been insolent and offensive—designed perhaps to goad the weaker state into open resentment, and to furnish a pretext for new wars, to be followed by new

exercise, they never had anything in common with the regular armies of Europe and India. System was entirely wanting, whether in regard to pay, clothing, food, carriage, equipage, commissariat, promotion, or command; and under a lath-and-plaster government like that of Persia, such must have been inevitably the case. At the same time, however, a false confidence arose of a most exaggerated and dangerous character; the resources of the country were lavished on the army to an extent which grievously impoverished it at the time, and which has brought about at the present day a state of affairs that, in any other quarter of the world, would be termed a national bankruptcy; above all, the tribes—the chivalry of the empire, the forces with which Nadir overran the East from Bagdad to Delhi, and which, ever yielding but ever present, surrounded, under Aga Mahomed Khan, the Russian armies with a desert—were destroyed. Truly then it may be said that in presenting Persia with the boon of a so-called regular army, in order to reclaim her from her unlawful loves with France, we clothed her in the robe of Nessus."—[*Calcutta Review*, vol. xii.] See also *Correspondence of Sir John Malcolm*.

acquisitions of Eastern territory. Both parties were prepared, by a long series of mutual provocations, for the now inevitable contest. It needed very little to bring them into open collision.

In Georgia there had been frightful misrule. The officers of the Christian government had wantonly and insanely outraged the religious feelings of its Mussulman subjects; and now an outburst of fierce Mahomedan zeal in the adjoining kingdom declared how dangerous had been the interference. The Moollahs of Persia rose as one man. Under pain of everlasting infamy and everlasting perdition, they called upon the Shah to resent the insults which had been put upon their religion. The mosques rang with excited appeals to the feelings of all true believers; and every effort was made by the excited ecclesiastics to stimulate the temporal authorities to the declaration of a holy war.

The King, however, shrank from the contest. He had no ambition to face again in the field the formidable European enemy who had so often scattered the flower of the Persian army, and trodden over the necks of the vanquished to the acquisition of new dominions. But the importunity of the Moollahs was not to be withstood. He pledged himself that if Gokchah—one of the disputed tracts of country occupied by the Russians—were not restored, he would declare war against the Muscovite power. Convinced that the Russian Government would yield this strip of land, acquired as it was without justice, and retained without profit, the Shah believed that the condition was, in effect, an evasion of the pledge. The error was soon manifest. It was not in the nature of Russia to yield an inch of country righteously or unrighteously acquired—profitably or unprofitably retained. Gokchah was not restored. The Moollahs became more and more clamorous. The Shah was threatened with the forfeiture of all claims to paradisaical bliss : and the war was commenced.

Excited by the appeals of the Moollahs, the Persians flung themselves into the contest with all the ardour and ferocity of men burning to wipe out in the blood of their enemies the insults and indignities that had been heaped upon them. They rose up and massacred all the isolated Russian garrisons and outposts in their reach. Abbas Meerza took the field at the head of an army of 40,000 men ; and at the opening of the campaign the disputed territory of Gokchah, with Balikloo and Aberan, were recovered by their old masters.

These successes, however, were but short-lived. The son of the Prince Royal, Mahomed Meerza, a youth more impetuous than skilful in the field, soon plunged the divisions he commanded into a sea of overwhelming disaster. The Prince himself, not more fortunate, was in the same month of September, 1826, beaten by the Russian General, Paskewitch, in open battle, with a loss of 1200 men. The war was resumed in the following spring, and continued throughout the year with varying success ; but the close of it witnessed the triumph of the Russians. Erivan and Tabreez fell into their hands * Enfeebled and dispirited, the Persians shrunk from the continuance of the struggle.

* The characteristic words of the Russian manifesto, announcing these events, are worth quoting —" Obliged to pursue the enemy through a country without roads, laid waste by the troops which were to have defended it ; often opposed by nature itself, exposed to the burning sun of summer, and the rigour of winter ; our brave army, after unparalleled efforts, succeeded in conquering Erivan, which was reputed impregnable It passed the Araxes, planted its standards on the top of Ararat, and penetrating further and further into the interior of Persia, it occupied Tabreez itself, with the country depending on it The Khanate of Erivan, on both sides of the Araxes, and the Khanate of Nakhichevan, a part of the ancient Armenia, fell into the hands of the conquerors."

The intervention of Great Britain was gladly accepted, and Persia submitted to the terms of a humiliating peace. After some protracted negotiations, a new treaty, superseding that of Goolistan, was signed at Toorkomanchai, in February, 1828, by General Paskewitch and Abbas Meerza. By this treaty, Persia ceded to the Czar the Khanates of Erivan and Nakhichevan; and consented to the recognition of the line of frontier dictated by the Russian Government. The frontier line between the two empires, laid down in the fourth article of the treaty, commenced at the first of the Ottoman States nearest to the little Ararat mountain, which it crossed to the south of the Lower Karasson, following the course of that river till it falls into the Araxes opposite Sherour, and then extending along the latter river as far as Abbas-Abad.* The line of frontier then followed the course of the Araxes to a point twenty-one wersts beyond the ford of Ledl-boulak, when it struck off in a straight line drawn across the plain of Moghan, to the bed of the river Bolgaron, twenty-one wersts above the point of confluence of the two Rivers Adinabazar and Sarakamyshe; then passing over the summit of Ojilkoir and other mountains, it extended to the source of the River Atara, and followed the stream until it falls into the Caspian Sea.

Such was the boundary laid down in the treaty of Toorkomanchai. The other articles granted an indemnity to Russia of eighty millions of roubles for the expenses of the war—yielded to that state the sole right of having armed vessels on the Caspian—recognised the inheritance of Abbas Meerza—and granted an amnesty to the inhabitants of Aderbijan. To Persia this treaty was deeply humiliating; but the manifestoes of the Emperor, with characteristic mendacity, boasted of its moderation, and

* This fortress, together with the surrounding country, to the extent of three wersts and a half, was ceded to Russia.

declared that its ends were merely the preservation of peace and the promotion of commerce. "For us," it was said, "one of the principal results of this peace consists in the security which it gives to one part of our frontiers. It is solely in this light that we consider the utility of the new countries which Russia has just acquired. Every part of our conquests that did not tend to this end was restored by our orders, as soon as the conditions of the treaty were published. Other essential advantages result from the stipulations in favour of commerce, the free development of which we have always considered as one of the most influential causes of industry, and at the same time as the true guarantee of solid peace, founded on an entire reciprocity of wants and interests."

The hypocrisy of all this is too transparent to call for comment. Russia had thus extended her frontier largely to the eastward; and England had not interfered to prevent the completion of an act, by which it has been said that Persia was "delivered, bound hand and foot, to the Court of St. Petersburgh." * How far the British Government was bound to assist Persia in the war of 1826-27, still remains an open question. The treaty of Teheran pledged Great Britain, in the event of a war between Persia and any European State, either to send an army from India to assist the Shah, or to grant an annual subsidy of 200,000 tomauns during the continuance of the war; but this article was saddled with the condition that the war was to be one in nowise provoked by any act of Persian aggression. A question, therefore, arose, as to whether the war of 1826-27 was provoked by the aggressions of Persia or of Russia. Each party pronounced the other the aggressor. The Persian Government maintained that the unjust and violent occupation of Gokchah by a

* Sir Harford Jones.

Russian force furnished a legitimate *casus belli;* but the Russian manifestoes declared that, "in the midst of friendly negotiations, and when positive assurances gave us the hope of preserving the relations of good neighbourhood with Persia, the tranquillity of our people was disturbed on the frontiers of the Caucasus, and a sudden invasion violated the territory of the Emperor in contempt of solemn treaties." Russian statesmen have never been wanting in ability to make the worse appear the better reason. Whatever overt acts may have been committed, it is certain that the real provocation came not from the Mahomedan, but from the Christian State.* The backwardness of England at such a time was of dubious honesty, as it doubtless was of dubious expediency. A more forward policy might have been more successful. Had Russia been as well disposed to neutrality as Great Britain, it would have been to the advantage of the latter to maintain the most friendly relations with the Muscovite State; but the unscrupulousness of Russia placed England at a disadvantage. The game was one in which the more honourable player was sure to be foully beaten. Russia made new acquisitions of Eastern territory, and England remained a passive spectator of the spoliation.

* The Duke of Wellington wrote to Mr. Canning, in Nov., 1826, "It will not answer to allow the Persian monarchy to be destroyed, particularly upon a case of which the injustice and aggression are undoubtedly on the side of the Russians." Sir John Malcolm, to whom the Duke sent a copy of this letter, wrote, "You certainly are right. There is a positive claim in faith for mediation." Mr. Canning, however, affected to doubt whether there had been any aggression against Persia. "Does not the article," he asked, " which defines the *casus fœderis* to be aggression against Persia, limit the effect of the whole treaty, and the aim of the sixth article, which promises our mediation? Are we bound even to mediate in a case in which Persia was the aggressor."—[*Life and Correspondence of Sir John Malcolm,* vol. ii. pp. 452-455.]

It is doubtful whether our statesmen were ever satisfied that, in refusing the subsidy and hesitating to mediate, they acted up to the spirit of the treaty of Teheran.* Certain it is, that the claim of the Persian Government, at this time, awakened our British diplomatists to a re-consideration of those subsidy articles which had involved, and might again involve us in difficulties, not only of an embarrassing, but of a somewhat discreditable, character. It was desirable to get rid of these perplexing stipulations The time was opportune ; the occasion was at hand The large indemnity insisted upon by Russia drove the Persian financiers to extremities, and reduced them to all kinds of petty shifts to meet the extortionate demand. In this conjucture, England, like an expert money-lender, was ready to take advantage of the embarrassments of the Persian State, and to make its own terms with the impoverished creditor of the unyielding Muscovite The bargain was struck. Sir John Macdonald, on the part of the British Government, passed a bond to the Shah for 250,000 tomauns as the price of the amendment of the subsidy articles, and subsequently obtained the required erasures by the payment of four-fifths of the amount.

* A writer in the *Foreign Quarterly Review*, who, if not Sir John M'Neill himself, has unblushingly appropriated, without acknowledgment, a large portion of the pamphlet on the "Progress and present position of Russia in the East," published some three or four years before, says: "Assuredly Prince Abbas Meerza relied strongly upon this (the 4th article of the treaty), and without it would never have engaged in the contest he provoked ; we are bound in justice to say, and we say it on good authority, wantonly and in defiance of the feelings of the Persian Government and King. But though Persia had fairly executed all her share of the treaty in question, the English minister, when called upon to fulfil this condition, hesitated, hung back, negotiated, and delayed under every possible pretext, while he could not deny the faith or the claim of Persia. It was clear, however, to all the parties that Mr. Canning only sought a means of escaping the

A season of outward tranquillity succeeded the completion of the treaty of Toorkomanchai. But the great northern power did not slumber. Though, during those years it added little outwardly to its dominions, it was obtaining more and more that great moral ascendancy which, perhaps, was better calculated to secure its ends than an ostentatious extension of territory. The game of quiet intimidation was now to be tried. The experiment succeeded to the utmost. Obtaining such an ascendancy over its counsels as enabled it to induce Persia to transgress its legitimate boundaries, and adopt an aggressive policy towards the countries on its eastern frontier, the European power overawed its Asiatic neighbour. It was the object of Russia to use the resources of the Persian State in furtherance of its own ends, without overtly taking possession of them, and thus bringing itself into collision with other powers. To secure this ascendancy it was necessary to assume a commanding—indeed, an offensive—attitude of superiority, and, whilst abstaining from acts of aggression, sufficiently momentous to awaken the jealousy of other European States, to keep alive the apprehensions of its Eastern neighbour by an irritating,

fulfilment of the stipulations. He was hard pressed by the reluctance to engaging in a war with Russia, represented as too probable by the minister of that power at the British Court, and by the dexterity of a first-rate female diplomatist, to whom, indeed, the management of the matter was fairly confided by the Russian Court, and whose influence was fatally effective in this and the Turkish questions. In affecting to adhere simply to the policy of his predecessors, Mr. Canning forgot the immense difference and disgrace of refusing the fulfilment only at the time when, and because, the need was urgent. He could not foresee that Persia must become, if further humbled, the tool of Russia against the East; if he had, no earthly power would have balanced against his duty. He did not even perceive that the crisis to Persia had arrived; and contented himself with a double sacrifice to vanity, in assuming to arbitrate against a sovereign prince, and hearing his praises resounded by the lips of successful beauty."

dictatorial demeanour, often implying threats of renewed hostility. Conscious of weakness, Persia yielded to the influence thus sought to be established; and in due course became, as was intended, a facile tool in the hands of the Russian minister.

Such, briefly stated in a few sentences, is the history of the relations subsisting between Russia and Persia since the treaty of Toorkomanchai. It need not be added that, during this time, English influence declined sensibly at the Persian Court. Little pains, indeed, were taken to preserve it, until it became apparent that the encroachments of Persia upon the countries between its frontier and India, instigated as they were by the Russian Government, were calculated to threaten the security of our Indian Empire. In 1831, Abbas Meerza, the Prince Royal, against the advice of the Shah, determined on sending an army into Khorassan; and then projected an expedition against Khiva, for the chastisement of that marauding state, which had so often invaded the Persian frontier, and carried off into slavery so many Persian subjects. The Russian agent encouraged, if he did not actually instigate, these movements. It was said, indeed, that the active co-operation of Russia would soon be apparent in both enterprises—that it was her policy to seek the assistance of Persia in a movement upon Khiva, and to aid that state in the subjugation of Khorassan. Not only in Khorassan itself, in Afghanistan and Toorkistan, but in the bazaars of Bombay,* was the advance of

* "A letter has been received in town from Persia, which has excited a good deal of talk in the bazaar, and the substance of which we give merely as a rumour of the day. It states that Prince Abbas Meerza has ordered 30,000 men to march upon Herat, and that this movement is only preparatory to an advance upon India in conjunction with Russia. This is probably a mere rumour or the echo of a lie—but 'coming events cast their shadows before,' and many of these rumours, combined with the tone which now and then breaks out in the Russian journals,

the confederate armies of the two states into Khorassan, and thence upon Herat and India, generally discussed and believed. Such, indeed, at this time, was the ascendancy of Muscovite influence over the mind of Abbas Meerza, that it was reported he had married a Russian Princess, and adopted the Christian faith.

There was a British officer in the Persian camp, Captain Shee, whose interference brought about the postponement of the Khivan expedition, and in the following year it was determined to abandon the Oosbeg enterprise for the time, and to punish the offending Afghans. An expedition against Herat was then planned; but British interference, this time directed by the sagacity of Mr. M'Neill, was again successfully put forth, and the movement was suspended. In the mean while the Khorassan campaign was prosecuted with vigour. The arms of Abbas Meerza were triumphant. The independence which the province had endeavoured to assert could not be maintained in the face

show but too well the turn of men's thoughts and wishes, and should warn us to be prepared."—[*Bombay Gazette, August* 25, 1832.] About the same time, Dr. Wolff, who was then travelling in Central Asia, wrote: "It is remarkable that there is a current belief, not only throughout Khorassan, but, as I found it afterwards, throughout Toorkistan even to Caubul, that Abbas Meerza had married a Russian Princess, and adopted the Russian religion; and that 50,000 Russians would come to Khorassan by way of Khiva, and assist Abbas Meerza in conquering Khorassan. So much is true that Russia has written to Futteh Ali Shah, offering him 5000 men for taking Khorassan, and putting down the chupow—*i.e.*, plundering system of the Toorkomans; and I hope to prove it to a certainty that Russia will be very soon the mistress of Khiva, under the pretext that the King of Khiva has 8000 Russian slaves, whilst I know by the most authentic reports that there are not above 200 Russian slaves and 60 Russian deserters at Khiva."—[*Calcutta Christian Observer, September,* 1832.] It was stated at one time that Russia had consented to yield her claim to the balance of the indemnity money remaining then due by Persia, on condition of the latter joining in an expedition against Khiva.

of the battalions of the Prince Royal, aided, as they were, by European courage and skill.* Ameerabad and Koochan fell before him. The recusant chiefs made their submission; and before the close of 1832 all the objects of the campaign had been accomplished, and the subjugation of Khorassan was complete.

Emboldened by success, Abbas Meerza now contemplated new enterprises. The project of an expedition against Khiva, to be subsequently extended to Bokhara, was then revived; and the reduction of Herat, a design favoured alike by the ambition of the Prince and the insidious policy of Russia, was again brought under review. Herat, which lies on the western frontier of Afghanistan, had, on the partition of the Douranee Empire among the Barukzye Sirdars, afforded an asylum to Shah Mahmoud, and had ever since remained in the hands of that Prince and Kamran, his successor. To subjugate this tract of country was to open the gate to further Eastern conquest. The Russian agent was eager, therefore, to promote a movement which squared so well with the designs of his own Government. The expedition against Herat was no longer to be postponed. In 1833 it was actually put into execution; and the command of the invading force was entrusted to Mahomed Meerza, the son of the Prince Royal.

In the autumn of 1833 Abbas Meerza died at Meshed. Arrested in the prosecution of the siege of Herat by the tidings of his father's death, Mahomed Meerza returned, in no enviable frame of mind, and withdrew within the Persian frontier. There were some doubts, too, at that

* Abbas Meerza gratefully acknowledged the assistance he received from Captain Shee, Mr. Beek, and M. Berowski, the Pole, of whom subsequent mention will be made. At the siege of Koochan a sergeant of the Bombay Horse Artillery, named Washbrook, directed the mortar batteries, which mainly conduced to the reduction of the place.

time, regarding the succession; but these were soon set at rest. The Shah nominated Mahomed Meerza as his heir, and both the British and the Russian Governments gave their cordial assent to the choice.

A few months afterwards, in the autumn of 1834, Futteh Ali Shah died at Ispahan; and Mahomed Meerza ascended the throne. The change was not favourable to British interests. Futteh Ali had ever been our friend. From him the Russians had received little encouragement —but his son and his grandson had thrown themselves into the arms of the Muscovite; and now that the latter had ascended the throne, there was every prospect of Russian influence becoming paramount at the Persian Court. Great Britain had done for the young King all that he required. He believed that those good offices, which mainly had secured for him the succession to the throne, were employed only for the purpose of counteracting the dreaded ascendancy of Russia; and he was in no humour to display his gratitude towards a nation, the character and the resources of which he so little understood.

The thought of breaking down the monarchy of Herat still held possession of the mind of Mahomed Shah. Ever since, in the autumn of 1833, he had been arrested in his first expedition against that place by the death of his father, he had brooded over his disappointment, and meditated a renewal of the hostile undertaking. It is said, indeed, that he swore a solemn oath, sooner or later to retrace his steps to the eastward, and to wipe out his disgrace in Afghan blood. Seated on the throne of his grandfather, and upheld there by British influence, he dreamt of Eastern conquest, openly talked of it in durbar, and delighted to dwell upon his prospective triumphs over Oosbeg and Afghan hosts. He needed little prompting to push his armies across the Eastern frontier But there were promptings from without as well as from within. Russia was at the elbow of the Shah, ever ready to drop tempting suggestions into the young monarch's ear, and to keep alive within him the fire both of his ambition and his revenge. It was the policy of Russia at this time to compensate for its own encroachments on the Western frontier of Persia, by helping that country to new acquisitions of territory on the East. Mahomed Shah had little real love for his great Northern neighbour; but he profoundly reverenced the gigantic power of the Czar, and, mistaking quiescence for weakness, aggressiveness for strength, contrasted the resources of Russia and England in a manner very unfavourable to the pretensions of the latter.* The enormous wings of the Russian eagle seemed to overshadow the whole land of Iran; and the Shah was eager that they should be stretched over him in protection, and not descend upon him in wrath. He knew, by bitter experience, what was the might of the Northern army; he had fled before the Cossacks on the field of Ganjah, and narrowly escaped with his life. But of the English he knew little more than that some courteous and accomplished gentlemen were drilling his native troops, and doing their best to create for him a well-disciplined army out of the raw materials placed at their disposal.

And so it happened, that in 1835, when Lord Palmerston wrote to Mr. Ellis, who had been sent out from London to

* Nor did he scruple outwardly to evince the relative degrees of respect which he entertained for the two nations in the persons of their representatives. On one occasion, for example, when the Russian envoy, Count Simonich, was returning from an excursion, the foreign minister went out to meet him, but demurred to paying the same compliment to the British ambassador.—[*MS. Records.*] This incident, however, which created some sensation in the Calcutta Council-Chamber, may have had its source in the private feelings of Meerza Massoud, the foreign minister, who, having long resided at St. Petersburgh, was a mere creature of the Russian State.

assume charge of the Mission on the part of the Crown, that he was "especially to warn the Persian Government against allowing themselves to be pushed on to make war against the Afghans," he could obtain no more satisfactory reply from the ambassador than that the Shah had "very extended schemes of conquest in the direction of Afghanistan." " In common with all his subjects," added Mr. Ellis, "he conceives that the right of sovereignty over Herat and Candahar is as complete now as in the reign of the Suffarean dynasty." "This pretension," it was added, "is much sustained by the success of his father Abbas Meerza, in the Khorassan campaign, and the suggestions of General Berowski."* The Persian ministers declared that the rightful dominions of the Shah extended to Ghuzni; that an expedition against Herat would be undertaken in the following spring; that the capture of Candahar would shortly follow; and that then he would launch into new fields of enterprise among the Beloochees and the Toorkomans.

The Heratee campaign, however, was the most cherished, as it was the proximate of all these undertakings; and the Russian minister was ever ready with suggestions for the immediate march of the Persian army, lest the British Government should step in to discourage the undertaking, or take measures to thwart its success. It was urged, too, that the expedition would be rendered more difficult by delay, and at a later period more extensive military resources would be required to prosecute the war with success.

The British minister watched all these proceedings with interest and anxiety. It seemed to him, that whilst the restlessness of Russian intrigue was constantly threatening to educe a state of things in Central Asia, embarrassing to

Mr. Ellis to Lord Palmerston: Teheran, November 13, 1835.—[Published Papers relating to Persia and Afghanistan.]

the British-Indian Government, it became the British, on their parts, to make a counter-move that would keep her dangerous ally fairly in check. It had been seen, long before this, that the experiment of drilling the Persian army was nothing better than an expensive failure. It had, to some extent, the effect of excluding other European disciplinarians; but, beyond this, it did not increase our influence in the Persian dominions, or the security of our Indian frontier. It was advisable, therefore, to do something more. Never doubting that the network of Russian intrigue would soon extend itself beyond the Persian frontier, it appeared to the British minister expedient that we should anticipate the designs of Russia in Afghanistan by sending an envoy to Dost Mahomed, and offering to despatch British officers to Caubul to discipline the Ameer's army.* It was obvious that a decided movement was becoming every day more and more necessary. A mere conciliatory course of policy, dictating offers of quiet intervention, was found of no avail in such a conjuncture. The British minister offered to use his influence with Shah Kamran to induce that ruler to abstain from the commission of those acts which had offended the Shah-in-Shah of Persia, but the offer had been coldly received. It was evident that the aggressive designs of Mahomed Shah were largely promoted by the Russian minister, and that no peaceful mediation would induce the young King to abandon his projects of Eastern conquest.

In the spring of 1836 the plan of the campaign was laid down, but it was doubtful whether the Shah possessed the means of immediately reducing it to practice. An unhappy expedition against the Toorkomans in the course of the summer somewhat cooled his military ardour; and

* The officer whom he proposed to send was Lieutenant Todd, of the Bengal Artillery, who held the local rank of Major in Persia, and who had long been employed in instructing the artillery of the Persian army.

before the year had worn to a close, he opened negotiations with Herat. A gallant answer was sent back to his demands. "You demand hostages," said the Heratee minister. "We gave no hostages during the reign of the late Shah; and we will give none now. You demand a present; we are ready to give as large a present as we can afford. If the Shah is not satisfied with this, and is determined to attack us, let him come. We will defend our city as long as we can; and if we are driven from it, it will of course remain in your hands till we can find means to take it back again from you." The Shah was, at this time, on the way back to his capital. He at once summoned a council of war, laid the offensive answer of Yar Mahomed before the chief officers who attended him in his tent, and sought their advice. The result was a determination to return to Teheran for the winter months, and to commence the expedition against Herat early in the following spring.*

But the spring of 1837, like the spring of 1836, passed by, and the expedition was not commenced. There appeared to be some hope of bringing matters to an issue by peaceable negotiation. But the demands of Persia involved the sacrifice of the independence of the state of Herat, and Shah Kamran could not be persuaded to reduce himself to a state of vassalage. He had great respect for the Shah of Persia, he said; but he could not acknowledge him as his sovereign—could not coin money or suffer prayers to be read in his name. He consented that hostages should reside for two years at Meshed, as guarantees for the fulfilment of the terms of the proposed

* The Russian minister had urged the King to undertake a winter campaign against Herat. But Count Nesselrode always resolutely maintained that Simonich had endeavoured to persuade the Shah not to proceed against Herat at all; and Simonich told the same story in his letters to his own government.

treaty. He consented that certain sums of money, in the way of tribute, should be paid annually to the Persian Government. He consented to furnish troops in aid of any Persian expedition against Toorkistan. He consented to restrain his subjects from marauding and plundering, and capturing slaves on the Persian frontier. But he could not consent to relinquish the title of Shah, and acknowledge himself a dependant of Persia. The propositions submitted by Herat were moderate and reasonable, they called for nothing from the Persian Government beyond a pledge of non-interference in the internal affairs of Herat. But the pretensions of the King of Kings to the sovereignty of Western Afghanistan were not to be sobered down, even by the representations of the British minister, who endeavoured to reconcile conflicting interests, and to cement a friendly alliance between the contending parties. Mahomed Shah was determined, either to break down the independence of Herat, or to batter down its walls. So the enterprise, long projected—long brooded over, was undertaken in earnest at last.*

The Barukzye Sirdars of Candahar watched the advance of the Persians with evident satisfaction. They had never ceased to see in Shah Kamran the murderer of Futteh Khan. They had never ceased to regard with

* Though we need not seek the causes of this expedition in anything either nearer or more remote than the ambition of the young Shah and the intrigues of the Russian Government, a pretext was put forth by, or for Persia, of a more plausible kind. It was urged that the Heratees had carried off and sold into slavery the subjects of the Persian Shah. There is no doubt of the fact. But it was never put prominently forward by the Shah, who always urged that Herat had no right to be independent Another pretext, but a weak one, for undertaking the war was also alleged. Hulakoo, son of the Prince of Kerman, after his father was taken and blinded, and Kerman occupied by the Shah's troops, fled to Herat, and from thence endeavoured to excite disturbances in Kain, Khaf, and Eastern Kerman.

impatience and irritation that last remnant of Suddozye supremacy which marred the completeness of Barukzye rule, and at times even threatened to extend itself towards the East in an effort to restore the old dynasty of the successors of Ahmed Shah. The approach of the Persian army seemed now to promise at least the overthrow of Shah Kamran; and the Candahar brothers looked eagerly for the transfer of the Heratee principality to themselves.*

To cement the alliance with Mahomed Shah, and to secure the most advantageous terms for himself and his brothers, Kohun Dil Khan determined to send one of his own sons to the Persian camp. Dost Mahomed disapproved of the movement. "If you look upon me," he wrote to the Candahar chief, "as greater than yourself, do not send your son to Persia. In the event of your not attending to my advice, such circumstances will happen as will make you bite the finger of repentance." But the Candahar chief was not to be turned from his purpose by the remonstrances of the Ameer. The bait held out by Persia was too tempting to be resisted; and Russia was standing by, ready to guarantee the alluring promises of Mahomed Shah. M. Goutte, the Russian agent with the Persian army, wrote letters of encouragement to Kohun Dil Khan, and General Berowski endorsed the flattering assurances they contained. "It is better," wrote the former, "to despatch Omar Khan without apprehension, and I will write to the Persian Government to remove all apprehensions at your sending your son. He will be treated with great distinction by the Shah and his nobles."

---

* Kamran had threatened Candahar on more than one occasion; and at the end of 1835, Mr. Masson reported to the Supreme Government that the Sirdars of that place, despairing of obtaining any assistance from Dost Mahomed, had sent an emissary to the Bombay Government, offering to cede their country to the British !—[*MS. Records.*] I merely give this as a report sent down by the English news-writer.

"Nothing but good," said the latter, "will result from this your connexion with the Shah; so much good, indeed, that I cannot put it to paper. Be convinced that your serving the Shah will turn out every way to your advantage." The Candahar chief was easily convinced. He had fixed his eye upon Herat, and he fell readily into an alliance which he hoped would place that principality securely in his hands.

With very different feelings Dost Mahomed Khan viewed the advance of the Persian army. He wished Mahomed Shah to assist him in a religious war against the Sikhs; but even an alliance based upon these grounds he was willing to forego, if he could secure the friendly offices of the British. A new actor was by this time upon the scene, and new schemes of policy were beginning to unfold themselves before the Ameer. Little did he think, when he received with honour, and took friendly counsel with a British officer sent to his Court to discuss matters of commerce, how soon that officer would again enter the Afghan capital, accompanied by a British army. Burnes appeared at Caubul—Mahomed Shah at Herat; and the seeds of the Afghan war were sown.

⁎ *The various treaties referred to in this Introductory Book will be found in an Appendix at the end of the volume.*

BOOK II.

[1835—1838.]

CHAPTER I.

[1835—1837.]

The Commercial Mission to Caubul—Arrival of Lord Auckland—His Character—Alexander Burnes—His Travels in Central Asia—Deputation to the Court of Dost Mahomed—Reception by the Ameer—Negotiations at Caubul—Failure of the Mission.

In the autum of 1835, Lord Auckland was appointed Governor-General of India. The Whigs had just returned to power. The brief Tory interregnum which had preceded the restoration to office of Lord Melbourne and his associates, had been marked by the appointment to the Indian Viceroyship of Lord Heytesbury—a nobleman of high character and approved diplomatic skill. His official friends boasted largely of the excellence of the choice, and prophesied that the most beneficial results would flow from his government of India. But nothing of the Governor-Generalship ever devolved upon him, except the outfit. The Whig ministers cancelled the appointment, and, after a time, selected Lord Auckland to fill the rudely vacated place.

The appointment occasioned some surprise, but raised

little indignation. In India, the current knowledge of Lord Auckland and his antecedents was of the smallest possible amount. In England, the general impression was, that if not a brilliant or a profound man, he was at least a safe one. The son of an eminent diplomatist, who had been won over to the support of Pitt's administration, and had been raised to the peerage in reward for his services, he was generally regarded as one of the steadiest and most moderate of the Whig party. As an industrious and conscientious public servant, assiduous in his attention to business and anxious to compensate by increased application for the deficiencies of native genius, he was held in good esteem by his colleagues and respected by all who had official intercourse with him. India did not, it was supposed, at that time demand for the administration of her affairs, any large amount of masculine vigour or fertility of resource. The country was in a state of profound tranquillity. The treasury was overflowing. The quietest ruler was likely to be the best. There was abundant work to be done; but it was all of a pacific character. In entrusting that work to Lord Auckland, the ministry thought that they entrusted it to safe hands. The new Governor-General had everything to learn; but he was a man of methodical habits of business, apt in the acquisition of knowledge, with no overweening confidence in himself, and no arrogant contempt for others. His ambition was all of the most laudable kind. It was an ambition to do good. When he declared, at the farewell banquet given to him by the Directors of the East-India Company, that he "looked with exultation to the new prospects opening out before him, affording him an opportunity of doing good to his fellow-creatures—of promoting education and knowledge—of improving the administration of justice in India—of extending the blessings of good government and happiness to millions in India," it was felt by all who knew him, that the words were uttered with a grave sincerity, and expressed the genuine aspirations of the man.

Nor did the early days of his government disappoint the expectations of those who had looked for a painstaking, laborious administrator, zealous in the persecution of measures calculated to develope the resources of the country, and to advance the happiness of the people. It appeared, indeed, that with something less of the uncompromising energy and self-denying honesty of Lord William Bentinck, but with an equal purity of benevolence, he was treading in the footsteps of his predecessor. The promotion of native education, and the expansion of the industrial resources of the country, were pursuits far more congenial to his nature than the assembling of armies and the invasion of empires. He had no taste for the din and confusion of the camp; no appetite for foreign conquest. Quiet and unobtrusive in his manners, of a somewhat cold and impassive temperament, and altogether of a reserved and retiring nature, he was not one to court excitement or to desire notoriety. He would fain have passed his allotted years of office, in the prosecution of those small measures of domestic reform which, individually, attract little attention, but, in the aggregate, affect mightily the happiness of the people. He belonged, indeed, to that respectable class of governors whose merits are not sufficiently prominent to demand ample recognition by their contemporaries, but whose noiseless, unapplauded achievements entitled them to the praise of the historian and the gratitude of after ages.

It was not possible, however intently his mind might have been fixed upon the details of internal administration, that he should have wholly disregarded the aggressive designs of Persia and the obvious intrigues of the Russian Government. The letters written from time to time by the British minister at the Persian Court, were read at first, in the Calcutta Council-Chamber, with a vague interest rather than with any excited apprehensions. It was little anticipated that a British army would soon be encamped before the capital of Afghanistan, but it was plain that events were taking shape in Central Asia, over which the British-Indian Government could not afford to slumber. At all events, it was necessary in such a conjuncture to get together some little body of facts, to acquire some historical and geographical information relating to the countries lying between the Indian frontier and the eastern boundaries of the Russian Empire. Secretaries then began to write "notes," and members of Council to study them. Summaries of political events, genealogical trees, tables of routes and distances, were all in great requisition, during the first years of Lord Auckland's administration. The printed works of Elphinstone, Conolly, and Burnes; of Malcolm, Pottinger, and Fraser, were to be seen on the breakfast-tables of our Indian statesmen, or in their hands as they were driven to Council. Then came Sir John M'Neill's startling pamphlet on the "Progress and Present Position of Russia in the East." M'Neill, Urquhart, and others were writing up the Eastern question at home; reviewers and pamphleteers of smaller note were rushing into the field with their small collections of facts and arguments. It was demonstrated past contradiction, that if Russia were not herself advancing by stealthy steps towards India, she was pushing Persia forward in the same easterly direction. If all this was not very alarming, it was, at least, worth thinking about. It was plainly the duty of Indian statesmen to acquaint themselves with the politics of Central Asia, and the geography of the countries through which the invasion of India must be attempted. It was only right that they should have been seen tracing on incorrect maps the march of a Russian army from St. Petersburgh to Calcutta, by every possible and impossible route, now floundering among the inhospitable steppes, now parching on the desert of Merve. The Russian army might not come at last; but it was clearly the duty of an Indian statesman to know how it would endeavour to come.

It was in the spring of 1836 that Dost Mahomed addressed a letter of congratulation to Lord Auckland, on his assumption of the office of Governor-General. "The field of my hopes," he wrote, "which had before been chilled by the cold blast of wintry times, has by the happy tidings of your Lordship's arrival become the envy of the garden of paradise." Then adverting to the unhappy state of his relations with the Sikhs, he said: "The late transactions in this quarter, the conduct of reckless and misguided Sikhs, and their breach of treaty, are well known to your Lordship. Communicate to me whatever may suggest itself to your wisdom for the settlement of the affairs of this country, that it may serve as a rule for my guidance. I hope," said the Ameer, in conclusion, "that your Lordship will consider me and my country as your own;" but he little thought how in effect this Oriental compliment would be accepted as a solemn invitation, and the hope be literally fulfilled. Three years afterwards Lord Auckland, considering Dost Mahomed's country his own, had given it away to Shah Soojah.

To this friendly letter the Governor-General returned a friendly reply. It was his wish, he said, that the Afghans "should be a flourishing and united nation;" it was his wish, too, that Dost Mahomed should encourage a just idea of the expediency of promoting the navigation of the Indus. He hinted that he should probably soon "depute some gentlemen" to the Ameer's Court to discuss with him certain commercial topics; and added,

ORIGIN OF THE MISSION.

with reference to Dost Mahomed's unhappy relations with the Sikhs, and his eagerness to obtain assistance from any quarter: " My friend, you are aware that it is not the practice of the British Government to interfere with the affairs of other independent states " With what feelings three years afterwards, when a British army was marching upon his capital, the Ameer must have remembered these words, it is not difficult to conjecture.

This project of a commercial mission to Afghanistan was no new conception of which Lord Auckland was the parent. It had at least been thought of by Lord William Bentick—and, certainly, with no ulterior designs. It was suggested, I believe, to Lord William Bentinck by Sir John Malcolm. That Lord Auckland, when he wrote to Dost Mahomed about "deputing some gentlemen" to Caubul to talk over commercial matters with the Ameer, had much more intention than his predecessor of driving the Barukzye Sirdars into exile, is not to be asserted or believed. He may have seen that such a mission might be turned to other than commercial uses; he may have thought it desirable that the gentlemen employed should collect as much information at the Ameer's Court as the advantages of their position would enable them to acquire. But at this time he would have started back at the barest mention of a military expedition beyond the Indus, and would have scouted a proposal to substitute for the able and energetic ruler of Caubul, that luckless Suddozye Prince—the pensioner of Loodhianah,—whose whole career had been such a series of disasters as had never before been written down against the name of any one man.

Apart from the commercial bearings of the case, he had little more than a dim notion of obtaining a clearer insight into the politics of Central Asia. But vague and indefinite as were his conceptions, he was haunted, even at the commencement of his Indian career, by a feeling of insecurity, engendered by the aspect of affairs beyond the British frontier. There was a shadow of danger, but he knew not what the substance might be. Any one of the strange combinations which he was called upon to consider, might evolve a war;* so at least it behoved him to prepare for the possible contest, by obtaining all the knowledge that could be acquired, and securing the services of men competent to aid him in such a conjuncture.

Since distant rumours of an Afghan invasion had disturbed the strong mind of Lord Wellesley, much had been learnt both in India and in England concerning the countries between the Indus and the Oxus. The civil and military services of the East India Company, numbering in their ranks, as they ever have done, men of lofty enterprise and great ability, had, since the commencement of the century, brought, by their graphic writings, the countries and the people of Central Asia visibly before

* "I share with you," he wrote to Sir Charles Metcalfe, in September, 1836, "the apprehension of our being at no distant date involved in political, and possibly military operations upon our western frontier; and even since I have been here, more than one event has occurred, which has led me to think that the period of disturbance is nearer than I had either wished or expected. The constitutional restlessness of the old man of Lahore seems to increase with his age. His growing appetite for the treasures and jungles of Sindh—the obvious impolicy of allowing him to extend his dominions in that direction—the importance which is attached to the free navigation of the Indus, most justly I think, and yet perhaps with some exaggeration from its value not having been tried—the advance of the Persians towards Herat, and the link which may in consequence be formed between Indian and European politics,—all lead me to fear that the wish which I have had to confine my administration to objects of commerce, and finance, and improved institutions, and domestic policy, will be far indeed from being accomplished. But as you say, we must fulfil our destiny; and in the mean while I have entreated Runjeet Singh to be quiet, and in regard to his two last requests have refused to give him 50,000 musquets, and am ready to send him a doctor and a dentist."—[*M.S. Correspondence.*]

their home-staying countrymen. Before the close of the eighteenth century, but one English traveller—a Bengal civilian, named Forster—had made his way from the banks of the Ganges across the rivers of the Punjab to the lakes of Cashmere, and thence descending into the country below, had entered the formidable pass of the Khybur, and penetrated through the defiles of Jugdulluck and Koord-Caubul to the Afghan capital, whence he had journeyed on, by Ghuznee, Candahar, and Herat, to the borders of the Caspian Sea. The journey was undertaken in 1783 and the following year; but it was not until some fifteen years afterwards, that the account of his travels was given to the world. Honourable alike to his enterprise and his intelligence, the book exhibits at once how much, during the last seventy years, the Afghan Empire, and how little the Afghan character, is changed.

The great work of Mountstuart Elphinstone, published some fifteen years after the appearance of Mr. Forster's volume, soon became the text-book of all who sought for information relating to the history and geography of the Douranee Empire. But Elphinstone saw little of the country or the people of Afghanistan; he acquired information, and he reproduced it with marvellous fidelity and distinctness, and would probably not have written a better book if he had travelled and had seen more. It was left for a later generation to explore the tracts of country which were unvisited by the ambassador; and for a later still to elicit encouragement and reward.

Years passed away before government began to recognise the value of such inquiries. When Mr. Moorcroft, of the Company's Stud-Department, a man of high courage and enterprise, accompanied by Mr. Trebeck, the son of a Calcutta lawyer, set out in 1819, in the mixed character of a horse-dealer and a merchant, upon his long and perilous journey; spent the last six years of his life in exploring the countries of Ladakh, Cashmere, Afghanistan, Balkh, and Bokhara; and died at last in the inhospitable regions beyond the Hindoo-Koosh, nothing but absolute discouragement and opposition emanated from a government that had not the prescience to see the importance of such investigations.*

In 1828 Mr. Edward Stirling, an officer of the Bengal civil service, being in England on furlough, undertook to return to India by the route of Khorassan and Afghanistan. From Sir John Macdonald, the Resident Minister at Teheran, he received every encouragement and assistance; but the Indian Government looked slightingly upon his labours, and neglected the man. The information he had acquired was not wanted; and he was put out of employment, because he had over-stayed, by a few weeks, the period of his leave of absence. Those were days when no thought of an invasion from the westward overshadowed the minds of our Indian statesmen.† But when, a few

---

* Moorcroft seems to have been upheld only by the kindly encouragement of Sir Charles (then Mr.) Metcalfe, who, as Resident at Delhi, took the greatest interest in his enterprise, and afforded him all possible assistance. He attributed the unwillingness of our Government to explore the countries beyond our frontier, to some vague apprehension of alarming the Sikhs. "It is somewhat humiliating," he wrote to Metcalfe, "that we should know so little of countries which touch upon our frontier; and this in a great measure out of respect for a nation that is as despicable as insolent, whose origin was founded upon rapine, and which exists by acquiring conquests it only retains by depopulating the territory."—[*MS. Correspondence.*]

† "The greatest apathy," says Mr. Sterling, "prevailed, and the members of the government could not be roused to take an interest in the subject. The knowledge that I had been in these interesting countries produced no desire for intelligence regarding them, and my reception gave no encouragement for the production of it. Neglect had been preceded by the deprivation of my appointment. I was no longer collector of Agra; that situation had been disposed of nearly two months prior to my reaching the Presidency: my return was deemed hopeless, and my death anticipated."

years afterwards, a young officer of the Bengal cavalry, named Arthur Conolly—a man of an earnest and noble nature, running over with the most benevolent enthusiasm, and ever suffering his generous impulses to shoot far in advance of his prudence and discretion—set out from London, proceeded, through Russia, across the Caucasus, and thence through Persia and Khorassan, accompanying an Afghan army from Meshed to Herat, and journeyed on from the latter place to Candahar, and, southward, through Beloochistan and Sindh to India, there was little chance of the information which he collected on his travels being received with ingratitude and neglect. The period which elapsed between the time when those travels were completed and the date at which their written results were given to the world, deprived Arthur Conolly of some portion of the credit which he might otherwise have received, and of the interest which attached to his publication. Another officer had by this time made his way by another route, through the unexplored regions of Central Asia, and laid before the government and the country an account of his wanderings. On him, when Lord Auckland bethought himself of despatching a commercial agent to Caubul, the choice of the Governor-General fell.

Born in the year 1805, at Montrose, and educated in the academy of that town, Alexander Burnes proceeded to Bombay at the early age of sixteen, and, at a period of his career when the majority of young men are mastering the details of company-drill, and wasting their time in the strenuous idleness of cantonment life, had recommended himself, by his proficiency in the native languages, to the government under which he served. Whilst yet in his teens, he was employed to translate the Persian documents of the Suddur Court, and, at the age of twenty, was appointed Persian interpreter to a force assembled for a hostile demonstration against Sindh, rendered necessary by the continued border feuds which were disturbing the peace of our frontier. In a little while he became distinguished as a topographer no less than as a linguist; and as a writer of memoirs, and designer of maps of little-known tracts of country, soon rose into favour and repute. Attached to the department of the Quartermaster-General, he was employed upon the survey of the north-western frontier of the Bombay Presidency, and shortly afterwards was appointed Assistant Political Agent in Cutch, a province with which he had made himself intimately acquainted. In the young officer a spirit of enterprise was largely blended with the love of scientific research. He was eager to push his inquiries and to extend his travels into the countries watered by the Indus and its tributaries—the fabulous rivers on the banks of which the Macedonian had encamped his victorious legions. It was not long before occasion offered for the gratification of his cherished desires. A batch of splendid English horses had been despatched, in 1830, to Bombay, as a present to Runjeet Singh; and Sir John Malcolm, then Governor of that Presidency, selected Alexander Burnes to conduct the complimentary mission to Lahore.* Instructed, at the same time, to

* Sir William Napier says, that "an enlightened desire to ascertain the commercial capabilities of the Indus induced Lord Ellenborough, then President of the India Board of Control, to employ the late Sir Alexander Burnes to explore the river in 1831, under pretence of conveying presents to Runjeet Singh." But the enlightenment of this measure was questioned at the time by some of the ablest and most experienced of our Indian administrators. At the head of these Sir Charles Metcalfe emphatically protested against it. In October, 1810, he recorded a minute in Council, declaring "the scheme of surveying the Indus, under the pretence of conveying a present to Runjeet Singh," to be "a trick unworthy of our government, which cannot fail when detected, as most probably it will be, to excite the jealousy and indignation of the powers on whom we play it." "It is not impossible," he added, "that it may lead to war."—[*MS. Records.*] These opinions were repeated privately in letters to Lord William

neglect no opportunity of acquiring information relative to the geography of the Indus, he proceeded through the country of the Ameers of Sindh, though not without some obstruction, from the jealousy and suspicion of the Talpoor rulers.* At the Sikh capital he was received with becoming courtesy and consideration. The old lion of the Punjab flung himself into the arms of the young British officer, and retained him as an honoured guest for a month. Leaving Lahore, Burnes crossed the Sutlej, and visited Loodhianah, where, little dreaming of the closer connexion which would one day exist between them, he made the acquaintance of the ex-King, Soojah-ool-Moolk, and his blind brother, Zemaun Shah. "Had I but my kingdom," said the former to Burnes, "how glad I should be to see an Englishman at Caubul, and to open the road between Europe and India."

From Loodhianah the traveller proceeded to Simlah, to lay an account of his journeying and its results at the feet of the Governor-General. Lord William Bentinck was then recruiting his exhausted energies in the bracing

Bentinck, and, at a later date, to Lord Auckland. Metcalfe, indeed, as long as he remained in India, never ceased to point out the inexpediency of interfering with the states beyond the Indus.

* And doubtless, very absurd and uncalled for the jealousy was considered in those days. As Burnes ascended the Indus, a Syud on the water's edge lifted up his hands, and exclaimed, "Sindh is now gone, since the English have seen the river, which is the road to its conquest." Nearly twenty years before, Sir James Mackintosh had written in his journal: "A Hindoo merchant, named Derryana, under the mask of friendship, had been continually alarming the Sindh Government against the English mission. On being reproved, he said that although some of his reports respecting their immediate designs might not be quite correct, yet this tribe never began as friends without ending as enemies, by seizing the country which they entered with the most amicable professions." "A shrewd dog," said Mackintosh; but he did not live to see the depths of the man's shrewdness.

climate of that hill station. He received the traveller with kindly consideration, and listened to his narrations with interest and attention. Full of enthusiasm, with his appetite for enterprise stimulated by his recent adventures, Burnes pressed upon the Governor-General the expediency of extending the fields of geographical and commercial inquiry upon which he had entered, and succeeded in obtaining the sanction of the Governor-General to an expedition into Central Asia, to be undertaken under the patronage of Government, but not avowedly in connection with any public objects. He set out on his overland journey to England ostensibly as a private traveller, but protected by passports designed to show that he was travelling under the countenance of the government which he served.

Accompanied by Dr. Gerard, an assistant-surgeon on the Bengal establishment; by a young native surveyor, named Mahomed Ali; and by Mohun Lal, a Hindoo youth of Cashmerian descent, who had been educated at the Delhi College, and patronised by Mr. Trevelyan, Burnes set out on his long and perilous journey. Starting at the commencement of the new year of 1832, the travellers crossed the Punjab, and proceeded by the route of Peshawur and Jellalabad to Caubul. Here they were hospitably received by Dost Mahomed. The character of the Caubul chief and of the Afghan nation impressed themselves favourably upon the mind of Alexander Burnes. Of the latter he spoke as a simple-minded, sober people, of frank, open manners, impulsive and variable almost to childishness. He had seen and conversed with Shah Soojah at Loodhianah, and declared his conviction that the exiled Prince had not energy sufficient to empower him to regain his throne, or tact sufficient to enable him to keep it. The character of the Barukzye Sirdar now presented, in the eyes of the English officer, a favourable contrast to that of the Suddozye Prince. Burnes saw before him a man of no common ability, with a well-disciplined mind, a high sense of justice, and a general appreciation of his duties and responsibilities, as a ruler of the people, not unworthy of a Christian potentate. And I do not believe that from that time he ever changed his opinion.

Leaving Caubul, Burnes and his fellow-travellers ascended the mountain-paths of the Hindoo-Koosh, and journeying onward by the route of Syghan and Koondooz, debouched into the valley of the Oxus, followed the course of that river for many days, and then made their way to Bokhara. After two months spent in that city, they re-crossed the Oxus and journeyed westward to the Persian frontier. Visiting Meshed, Teheran, Ispahan, and Shiraz, and making the acquaintance on the way both of Abbas Meerza and the Shah-i-Shah, they proceeded to Bushire and Bombay. From Bombay, Burnes pushed on to Calcutta, and early in 1833 had laid before the Governor-General the results of his Central-Asian travels. Lord William Bentinck received him with marked attention and respect, and sent him to England, that he might impart, in person, to the home authorities the information with which he was laden.

His reception in England was of the most flattering character. The commendations of the East India Company and the Board of Control were endorsed by the commendations of the public. He published his book. It was read with avidity. In the coteries of London, "Bokhara Burnes" became one of the celebrities of the season. Learned societies did him honour. Fashionable dames sent him cards of invitation. Statesmen and savans sought his acquaintance. At Holland House and Bowood he was a favoured guest. He was no niggard of his information; he talked freely; and he had "some new thing" whereof to discourse. His fine talents and his genial social qualities recommended him to many; and there was more than enough in the overflowings of English hospitality to satisfy a vainer man.

These, however, were but unsubstantial rewards. He looked for promotion in the paths of Oriental diplomacy; and Lord Ellenborough, who then presided at the India Board, recommended him for the appointment of Secretary of Legation at the Persian Court.* This offer he was recommended to decline; and he returned to India, in the spring of 1835, to resume his duties as Assistant to the Resident at Cutch. Rescued in the autumn from the obscurity of this appointment, he was despatched to the Court of the Ameers of Sindh. The duties of the Mission were performed with judgment and ability. The Ameers consented to the proposal for the survey of the Indus, and would gladly have entered into more intimate relations with the British Government had it been considered, upon our part, desirable to strengthen the alliance.

Whilst still in the Sindh country, Burnes received instructions from the Supreme Government of India to hold himself in readiness to undertake the charge of the "commercial" mission which it had been determined to despatch to Afghanistan, and to proceed to Bombay to make preparations for the journey.† He reached that

---

* He was promised, too, the reversion of the office of minister.

† Burnes, when in England, had endeavoured to impress the Court of Directors with an idea of the expediency of sending him out as commercial agent to Caubul; but Mr. Tucker, who was then in the chair, could see only the evils of such a measure. "The late Sir Alexander Burnes," he wrote some years afterwards, "was introduced to me in 1834 as a talented and enterprising young officer, and it was suggested that he might be usefully employed as a commercial agent at Caubul, to encourage our commerce with that country and to aid in opening the river Indus to British industry and enterprise. . . . I declined then to propose or to concur in the appointment of Lieu-

Presidency in the course of October, 1836, and on the 26th of November, accompanied by Lieutenant Leech, of the Bombay Engineers, and Lieutenant Wood, of the Indian Navy,* Burnes sailed from Bombay to "work out the policy of opening the River Indus to commerce"—that policy, the splendid results of which, years afterwards, when our army, our treasury, and our reputation, had been buried in the passes of Afghanistan, Lord Palmerston openly boasted in Parliament amidst the derisive cheers of the House.

Taking the Sindh route, Burnes presented himself at the Court of the Ameers, and was hospitably received. The English officer explained the object of his mission; talked about the navigation of the Indus; and dwelt encouragingly upon the instructions which he had received, "to endeavour to infuse confidence into all classes by a declaration of the happy and close friendship which subsisted between the British and the powers on the Indus." From Hyderabad he proceeded to Bahwulpore; and thence to Dehra Gazee Khan. At the latter place he received intelligence of the battle of Jumrood; and, pushing on to the neighbourhood of Peshawur, soon found himself near the theatre of war. From Peshawur to Jumrood, Avitabile † drove the British officers in his carriage. The deputation that was to conduct them

---

tenant Burnes to a commercial agency in Caubul, feeling perfectly assured that it must soon degenerate into a political agency, and that we should as a necessary consequence be involved in all the entanglement of Afghan politics."— [*Memoirs of H. St. George Tucker*] Mr. Grant, who was then at the Board of Control, concurred in opinion with Mr. Tucker; Sir Charles Metcalfe also wrote a minute in council, emphatically pointing out the evils of this commercial agency.

* Mr. Percival Lord of the Bombay Medical Establishment, joined the Mission *in transitu*. Mohun Lal also accompanied it.

† Avitabile, an Italian by birth, was a General in the service of Runjeet Singh, and at that time Governor of Peshawur.

through the Khybur Pass had not made its appearance. They were suffering martyrdom from the effluvia of the putrifying corpses of the Afghan and Sikh soldiers who had fallen in the recent conflict; and, at all hazards, they determined to push on. The Khybur was cleared without accident or obstruction. Friendly deputations from the Ameer greeted the British officers as they advanced. On the 20th of September, they entered Caubul.

They were received "with great pomp and splendour." At the head of a fine body of Afghan cavalry Akbar Khan came out to meet them. Placing Burnes on an elephant beside him, he conducted the British officers to his father's Court. Nothing could have been more honourable than the reception of the British Mission. A spacious and beautiful garden within the Balla Hissar, and near the palace, was allotted as the residence of Burnes and his companions.

On the following day, "with many expressions of his high sense of the great honour conferred upon him," Dost Mahomed formally received the representatives of the British Government. Burnes submitted his credentials. The letters were opened by the Ameer himself, and read by his minister, Meerza Samee Khan. They introduced Burnes to his Highness solely as a commercial agent. The flimsy veil was soon dropped. It was evident from the first that whatever might have been his instructions—whatever might have been the proximate, or rather the ostensible object of the mission, Burnes had ulterior designs, and that he, in reality, went to Caubul either as a spy or a political diplomatist. He had not been three days at the Afghan capital, before he wrote to Mr. Macnaghten, that he should take an early opportunity of reporting what transpired at the Ameer's Court; and ten days afterwards we find him announcing "the result of his inquiries on the subject of Persian influence in Caubul, and the exact power which the Kuzzilbash, or Persian party resident in this city, have over the politics of Afghanistan." To a private friend he wrote more distinctly: "I came to look after commerce, to superintend surveys and examine passes of mountains, and likewise certainly *to see into affairs and judge of what was to be done hereafter;* but the hereafter has already arrived."* It is hard to say what our Oriental diplomatists would do if they were forbidden the use of the word "commerce." It launched Burnes fairly into the sea of Afghan politics, and then he cut it adrift.

On the 24th of September, Burnes was invited to a private conference with the Ameer. It took place in "the interior of the Harem" of the Balla Hissar, and in the presence only of Akbar Khan. Dinner was served; and "the interview lasted till midnight." The Ameer listened attentively to all that Burnes advanced relative to the navigation of the Indus and the trade of Afghanistan, but replied, that his resources were so crippled by his war with the Sikhs, that he was compelled to adopt measures injurious to commerce, for the mere purpose of raising revenue. He spoke with much warmth of the loss of Peshawur, which, he alleged, had been basely wrested from him, whilst he was engaged in war with Shah Soojah. Burnes replied with a number of cut-and-dried sentences about the ability and resources of Runjeet Singh. To all this the Ameer cheerfully assented. He acknowledged that he was not strong enough to cope with so powerful an adversary as the ruler of Lahore. "Instead of renewing the conflict," he said, "it would be a source of real gratification if the British Government would counsel me how to act: none of our other neighbours can avail me, and in return I would pledge myself to forward its commercial and its

* *Unpublished Correspondence of Sir Alexander Burnes.*

political views." Remarking that he heard with pleasure this acknowledgment, Burnes assured him that the British Government would exert itself to secure peace between the Punjab and Afghanistan; and added, that although he could not hold out any promise of interference for the restoration of Peshawur, which had been won and preserved by the sword, he believed that the "Maharajah intended to make some change in its management, but that it sprung from himself, and not from the British Government." The Ameer could not repress his eagerness to learn the precise character of these contemplated arrangements; but all that Burnes could offer was a conjecture that the Maharajah might be induced to restore the country, under certain restrictions, to Sultan Mahomed Khan and his brothers, to whom, and not to the Ameer, it had formerly belonged.

On the evening of the 4th of October, Burnes was again invited to the Balla Hissar. The Ameer had in the mean time waited upon him in his own quarters. At this second conference in the palace, the Newab Jubbar Khan was present. On this occasion, to the surprise of the British envoy, the Ameer carried his moderation and humility to an excess which might almost have aroused suspicion. He declared that if the representative of Great Britain recommended him to do so, he would express to Runjeet Singh his contrition for the past, and ask forgiveness; and that if the Maharajah "would consent to give up Peshawur to him, he would hold it tributary to Lahore; send the requisite presents of horses and rice; and in all things consider himself, in that part of his dominions, as holding under Lahore." Burnes suggested that such an arrangement would be destructive to the hopes of Sultan Mahomed, who ought to be regarded with compassion; and asked whether it would not be equally advantageous to the reputation of the Ameer that Peshawur should be restored to his brother. To this the Ameer replied, that the country might as well be in the hands of the Sikhs as in those of Sultan Mahomed, who had been to him both a treacherous friend and a bitter enemy. Little more passed at this meeting. Burnes retired to speculate upon the conduct of the Ameer and write letters to the political Secretary, Mr. Macnaghten, who was destined soon to play so conspicuous a part in the great drama, of which this "Commercial" mission was the prologue.

In the meanwhile the attention of the Mission was directed to the state of affairs at Candahar. The chief of that place, Kohun Dil Khan, had not only declared his willingness to embrace the Persian alliance, but had, as we have seen, determined on sending his second son, with the Persian agent, to Mahomed Shah, as the bearer of presents to the Shah and the Russian embassy. Against this course of procedure Dost Mahomed had protested. "Oh! my brother," he wrote, "if you will do these things without my concurrence, what will the world say to it?" There can be no doubt of the Ameer's sincerity. Indeed, it was the conviction that the Caubul chief was entering with his whole soul into the British alliance, to the exclusion, as it was believed, of the Candahar Sirdars, that drove the latter to strengthen their alliance with the Persian Court. Burnes himself had no doubt that the Ameer was at this time acting a straightforward part. On the 30th of October he wrote to a private friend: "Here a hundred things are passing of the highest interest. . . . . . . Dost Mahomed Khan has fallen into all our views, and in so doing has either thought for himself or followed my counsel, but for doing the former I give him every credit, and things now stand so that I think we are on the threshold of a negotiation with King Runjeet, the basis of which will be his withdrawal from Peshawur, and a Barukzye receiving it as a tributary of Lahore, the chief of Caubul sending his son to ask pardon. What say you to this after all that has been urged of Dost Mahomed Khan's putting forth extravagant pretensions? Runjeet will accede to the plan, I am certain. .... I have, in behalf of Government, agreed to stand as mediator with the parties, and Dost Mahomed has cut asunder all his connexion with Russia and Persia, and refused to receive the ambassador from the Shah now at Candahar. His brothers at that city have, however, caressed the Persian Elchee all the more for this, and I have sent them such a Junius as, I believe, will astonish them. I had, indeed, reason to act promptly, for they have a son setting out for Teheran with presents to the Shah and the Russian ambassador; and I hope I shall be in time to explain our hostility to such conduct. Everything here has, indeed, run well; and but for our deputation at the time it happened, the house we occupy would have been tenanted by a Russian Agent and a Persian Elchee." *

On the 31st of October, Burnes wrote to Mr. Macnaghten that another conference had taken place on the 24th between himself and the Ameer, and that what passed on that occasion "set Dost Mahomed's conduct in a light that must prove, as I believe, very gratifying to Government." On the British Envoy expressing the regret which he felt on being made acquainted with the misguided conduct of the Candahar Sirdars, the Ameer had declared that if such conduct was distressing to the British agent, it was much more distressing to him; that he himself repented of having ever listened to the overtures of Persia; that he would take care publicly to manifest his desire to strengthen his relations with the British Government, and do everything in his power to induce his Candahar brothers to adopt a wiser course of policy. Burnes replied that he

---

* *Unpublished Correspondence of Sir A. Burnes.*

was delighted to hear the expression of such sentiments; but distinctly stated "that neither he nor his brothers were to found hopes of receiving aid from the British Government," that so long as they conducted themselves with propriety they might rely upon the sympathy of the British Government, but that they must, by no means, expect to derive anything more substantial from the alliance.* Discouraging as this was, the Ameer still courted the British alliance—still declared that he would exert himself to the utmost to detach his Candahar brothers from their connexion with Persia, and even, if desired by the British agent, would commence active operations against them. Discountenancing the idea of an active movement against Candahar, Burnes commended the good feeling of the Ameer, and exhorted him to do his best, by pacific means, to break down Kohun Dil's connexion with Persia—an effort which "could not fail to be received by the British Government as a strong mark of his desire for our friendship, and of great good sense."

Burnes, who had gone to Caubul, as a commercial agent, was at this time without any political instructions.

* And, on the 30th December, Burnes, with reference to this promised sympathy, wrote, in the following words, to Mr. Macnaghten. The passage was not published in the official correspondence. It was thought better to suppress it.—"The present position of the British Government at this capital appears to me a most gratifying proof of the estimation in which it is held by the Afghan nation. Russia has come forward with offers which are certainly substantial. Persia has been lavish in her promises, and Bokhara and other States have not been backward. Yet, in all that has passed or is daily transpiring, *the chief of Caubul declares that he prefers the sympathy and friendly offices of the British to all these offers, however alluring they may seem, from Persia or from the Emperor*—which certainly places his good sense in a light more than prominent, and, in my humble judgment, proves that, by an earlier attention to these countries, we might have escaped the whole of these intrigues, and held long since a stable influence in Caubul."—[*Ungarbled Correspondence of Sir A. Burnes.*]

As he ascended the Indus, he had received letters from Government, somewhat modifying the character of his mission, and placing a larger amount of discretion in his hands.* But he did not feel that he was in a position to deal with the Peshawur question without positive instructions from the Supreme Government; so all that he could now do was to temporise, to amuse Dost Mahomed with vague assurances of sympathy and good-will, until the wishes of the Governor-General were conveyed to him in a specific shape. He could promise nothing substantial. He could only write for instructions, and await patiently the receipt of letters from Hindostan.

But Burnes, though he shrunk from compromising his government in the direction of Lahore, had no such scruples with regard to the proceedings of the Barukzye Sirdars in the countries to the westward. He thought that some latitude having been allowed him, he might take prompt measures to meet a pressing difficulty threatening us from a quarter so far removed from the ordinary circle embraced by the deliberations of the Calcutta Council. Before he entered Afghanistan the conduct of the Candahar chiefs had engaged his serious attention,

* "As I approached Caubul," he wrote to a private friend, on the 5th of July, "war broke out with the Afghans and Sikhs, and my position became embarrassing. I was even ordered by express to pause, and while hanging on my oars another express still cries *pause*, but places a vast latitude in my hands, and 'forward' is my motto—forward to the scene of carnage, where, instead of embarrassing my government, I feel myself in a situation to do good. It is this latitude throughout life that has made me what I am, if I am anything, and I can hardly say how grateful I feel to Lord Auckland. . . . . I have not as yet got the replies to my recommendation on our line of policy in Caubul, consequent on a discovered intrigue of Russia, and on the Caubul chief throwing himself in despair on Perso-Russian arms. I have at last something to do, and I hope to do it well."— [*Private Correspondence of Sir A. Burnes.*]

and he had written to the British minister at the Persian Court, saying that he should leave nothing undone to try and put a stop to their intercourse with the Russian mission. "If matters go rightly," he added, "we shall be able to neutralise the power of the Candahar chiefs, or at all events place them in complete subjection to Dost Mahomed Khan, whose influence increases daily." Burnes, as has been seen,* had despatched in October a letter to Kohun Dil Khan, threatening him with the displeasure of the British Government if he continued his intrigues with the Persian and Russian Court ; and the measures taken at this time were so far successful, that, encouraged by their result, the British agent determined to take further steps to secure the alliance of the chiefs of Candahar. On the 22nd of December, Burnes became convinced of the improved temper of Kohun Dil Khan, who declared that he had dismissed the Persian Elchee, had determined not to send his son to the Persian Court, and was anxious, above all things, for the counsel and assistance of the British Government, and of his brother, Dost Mahomed Khan. Mahomed Shah had by this time begun to cool down in his zeal for the Afghan alliance ; and it appeared

---

* *Ante, page* 186. In a letter to another correspondent, written about the same time, Burnes says : "With war came intrigues, and I have had the good fortune to find out all the doings of the Czar and his emissaries here, where they have sent letters and presents. After proving this, I plainly asked the Governor-General if such things were to be allowed, and I got a reply a week ago, altering all my instructions, giving me power to go on to Herat, and anywhere, indeed, I could do good. The first exercise of the authority has been to despatch a messenger to Candahar, to tell them to discontinue their intercourse with Persia and Russia, on pain of displeasure—and not before it was time, for a son of the chief of that city, with presents for the Russian ambassador, is ready to set out for Teheran."—[*Sir A. Burnes to Captain Jacob—Caubul,* 29*th of October,* 1837 : *MS. Correspondence.*]

to be at least possible that the Sirdar, instead of receiving Herat from the Shah, would, after the capture of that place, be threatened with the loss of Candahar. Seizing the opportunity afforded him by this favorable change in the aspect of affairs, Burnes wrote at once to Kohun Dil Khan, stating that if the Persian monarch threatened to subdue his chiefship, he would go at once to Candahar, accompanied by Dost Mahomed, and assist him by every means in his power, even to the extent of paying his troops.

In the meanwhile he determined to despatch at once an officer of the British Mission to Candahar. That officer was Lieutenant Leech. On Christmas-day, Burnes sat down and wrote him a long and clearly-worded letter of instructions. It was hoped that the presence of a British agent at Candahar would keep Persia in check, and if not, he could despatch to Caubul the earliest intelligence of the advance of the Persian army, and so enable Burnes to counteract the movement with the least possible delay.*

Burnes exceeded his instructions, and was severely censured by the Governor-General. Lord Auckland was then on his way to Simlah; and from Bareilly Mr. Secretary Macnaghten wrote a long letter to the Caubul agent, at the close of which he touched upon the

* "The chiefs of Candahar," he wrote a few days afterwards, to a private friend, "had gone over to Persia. I have detached them and offere them British protection and *cash* if they would recede, and if Persia attacked them. I have no authority to do so; but am I to stand by and see us ruined at Candahar, when the Government tell me an attack on Herat would be most unpalatable. Herat has been besieged fifty days, and if the Persians move on Candahar, I am off there with the Ameer and his forces, and mean to pay the piper myself. We have good stuff—forty-six guns and stout Afghans, as brave as irregular troops need be. am on stirring ground, and I am glad to say I am up to it in health and all that, and was never more braced in my life."—[*Correspondence of Sir A. Burnes—privately printed.*]

promises made to the Candahar chiefs. " It is with great pain," he said, "that his Lordship must next proceed to advert to the subject of the promises which you have held out to the chiefs of Candahar. These promises were entirely unauthorised by any part of your instructions. They are most unnecessarily made in unqualified terms, and they would, if supported, commit the Government upon the gravest questions of general policy. His Lordship is compelled, therefore, decidedly to disapprove them. He is only withheld from a direct disavowal of these engagements to the chiefs of Candahar, because such disavowal would carry with it the declaration of a difference between you and your Government, and might weaken your personal influence, and because events might, in this interval, have occurred which would render such a course unnecessary. But the rulers of Candahar must not be allowed to rest in confidence upon promises so given, and should affairs continue in the same uncertainty as that which prevailed at the date of your last despatches, you will endeavour to set yourself right with the chiefs, and will feel yourself bound in good faith to admit that you have exceeded your instructions and held out hopes, which you find, upon communication with your Government, cannot be realised. After what has been stated, his Lordship feels that he need not enlarge on his strict injunction that you in future conform punctually on all points to the orders issued for your guidance."*

* *Mr. W. H. Macnaghten to Captain A. Burnes—Camp, Bareilly, 20th January,* 1838 The letter from which this passage is taken consists of twenty-four paragraphs, of which three only appear in the published correspondence. There seems, indeed, to have been a studious suppression of the entire history of the offers made to the Candahar chiefs, and of the censure which they called down upon Captain Burnes. Lord Auckland subsequently, with praiseworthy candour, admitted that the best authorities at home were of opinion

And so Burnes was censured for a measure which, under all the circumstances of the case, was the very best that could have been adopted ; and the Candahar chiefs threw themselves again into the Persian alliance, and entered into a formal treaty with the Shah—under a Russian guarantee.

In the mean while a new actor had appeared on the political stage, ready to pick up the leavings of the British agent, and to appreciate what the British Government had been pleased to reject. On the afternoon of the 19th of December, a Russian officer named Vickovich,* entered the city of Caubul. Born of a good family in Lithuania, and educated in the national university of Wilna, he had attracted attention, whilst yet a student, by the liberality of his sentiments and the fearlessness with which he expressed them. Associated with others of kindred opinions and equal enthusiasm, he took part in a demonstration in favour of the Polish cause, which well-nigh ended in the suppression of the institution ; and, whilst other more formidable conspirators were condemned to end their days in Siberia, he and his immediate colleagues in the university were sent to Orenburgh, as a kind of honourable exile, to be employed in the military colony of the Ural. Here the general intelligence, the aptitude for instruction, the love of adventure, and the daring character of young Vickovich, soon distinguished him above his associates. Attached to the expeditions sent out for the survey of the Desht-i-Kipchak, he lived for some years among the Calmucks, gaining an acquaintance with the Nogai and Jaghatai dialects of the Turkish language,

---

that the measure which had evoked these expressions of the severe displeasure of his Lordship, was the very best that could have been adopted.

* I have given the vulgar orthography of the name. His real name was Viktevitch, or Wiktewitch.

and subsequently, during a residence of some months in Bokhara, whither he was sent with the Caravan from Orenburgh, acquired a sufficient knowledge of the Persian language to enable him to converse intelligibly, if not fluently, in it. When, therefore, the Russian Government began to meditate a mission to Caubul, and to cast about for a competent agent, there seemed to be no likelier man than Vickovich to perform, with advantage to the state, the dubious service required of him. He was at this time aide-de-camp to the Governor of Orenburgh. The Caubul agency was entrusted to him without hesitation. He was despatched at once to Astrakan, whence he crossed over to Resht, in Ghilan, and received his final instructions from Count Simonich, at Teheran, in September, 1837. Before the end of December he was at Caubul.*

* The first information relative to the fact of Vickovich's mission to Caubul was accidentally obtained by Major Rawlinson, when on his way to the camp of Mahomed Shah, who was then marching upon Herat. The circumstances, as set forth in a private letter, from that officer himself, are not unworthy of narration :—" *Teheran, November* 1, 1837. I have just returned from a journey of much interest. M'Neill had some business in the Persian camp which he thought I might help to arrange, and I was bid accordingly to make my way to the 'Royal Stirrup,' with all convenient despatch. I was obliged to ride day and night, as the post-horses on the road, owing to the constant passage of couriers, were almost unserviceable, and yet I was only able, after all, to accomplish the distance of something more than 700 miles in a week. The last morning of my ride I had an adventure. Our whole party were pretty well knocked up, and in the dark, between sleeping and waking, we had managed to lose the road. As morning dawned, we found ourselves wandering about on the broken plain which stretches up from Subzewar to the range containing the Turquoise mines, and shortly afterwards we perceived that we were close to another party of horsemen, who were also, apparently, trying to regain the high road. I was not anxious to accost these strangers, but on cantering past them, I saw, to my astonishment, men in Cossack dresses, and one of my attendants recognised among the party a servant of the Russian Mission. My curiosity was, of

On the day after the arrival of Vickovich at Caubul, Burnes reported the incident to the supreme Government,

course, excited, and on reaching the stage I told one of my men to watch for the arrival of the travellers, and find out who they were. Shortly afterwards the Russian party rode up, inquired who I was, and finding I was a British officer, declined to enter the Khan, but held on their road. In such a state of affairs as preceded the siege of Herat, the mere fact of a Russian gentleman travelling in Khorassan was suspicious. In the present case, however, there was evidently a desire for concealment. Nothing had been heard of this traveller by our Mission at Teheran. I had been told, indeed, absurd stories on the road, of a Muscovite Prince having been sent from Petersburgh to announce that 10,000 Russians would be landed at Asterabad, to cooperate with the Shah in reducing Herat; and this was evidently the man alluded to, but I knew not what to believe, and I thought it my duty, therefore, to try and unravel the mystery. Following the party, I tracked them for some distance along the high road, and then found that they had turned off to a gorge in the hills. There at length I came upon the group seated at breakfast by the side of a clear sparkling rivulet. The officer, for such he evidently was, was a young man of light make, very fair complexion, with bright eyes and a look of great animation. He rose and bowed to me as I rode up, but said nothing. I addressed him in French—the general language of communication between Europeans in the East, but he shook his head. I then spoke English, and he answered in Russian. When I tried Persian, he seemed not to understand a word; at last he expressed himself hesitatingly in Turcoman, or Uzbeg Turkish. I knew just sufficient of this language to carry on a simple conversation, but not enough to be inquisitive. This was evidently what my friend wanted, for when he found I was not strong enough in Jaghatai to proceed very rapidly, he rattled on with his rough Turkish as glibly as possible. All I could find out was, that he was a *bonâ fide* Russian officer, carrying presents from the Emperor to Mahomed Shah. More he would not admit; so, after smoking another pipe with him, I remounted, and reached the Royal Camp beyond Nishapoor before dark. I had an immediate audience of the Shah, and in the course of conversation, mentioning to his Majesty my adventure of the morning, he replied, 'Bringing presents to me! why, I have nothing to do with him; he is sent direct from the Emperor to Dost Mahomed, of Caubul, and I am merely asked to help him on his journey.' This is the first

and detailed the circumstances of his reception. Like almost everything in Burnes's public letters, which places the conduct of Dost Mahomed in a favourable light, the following passages were cut out of the correspondence before it was placed in the printer's hands ;—" On the morning of the 19th," wrote Burnes, "that is, yesterday, the Ameer came over from the Balla Hissar early in the morning with a letter from his son, the Governor of Ghuznee, reporting that the Russian agent had arrived at that city on his way to Caubul. Dost Mahomed Khan said that he had come for my counsel on the occasion; that he wished to have nothing to do with any other power than the British; that he did not wish to receive any agent of any power whatever so long as he had a hope of sympathy from us, and that he would order the Russian agent to be turned out, detained on the road, or act in any way I desired him. I asked the Ameer if he knew on what business the agent had come, and if he were really an agent from Russia. He replied that I had read all his letters from Candahar, and that he knew nothing more. I then stated that it was a sacred rule among civilised nations not to refuse to receive emissaries in time of peace, and that I could not take upon myself to advise him to refuse any one who declared himself duly accredited, but that the Ameer had it in his power to

information we have ever had of a direct communication between Petersburgh and Caubul, and it may be of great importance. The gentleman made his appearance in camp two days after my arrival, and I was then introduced to him by Mons. Goutte, as Captain Vitkavitch. He addressed me at once in good French, and in allusion to our former meeting, merely observed, with a smile, that 'It would not do to be too familiar with strangers in the desert.' I was so anxious to bring back to M'Neill intelligence of this Russian Mission to Caubul, that I remained but a very few days in camp; and here I am again in Teheran, after a second gallop of 750 miles, accomplished this time in about 150 consecutive hours."—[*MS. Correspondence*]

show his feeling on the occasion by making a full disclosure to the British Government of the errand on which the individual had come; to which he most readily assented. After this the Ameer despatched a servant on the road to Ghuznee to prevent the agent's entering Caubul without notice; but so rapid has been his journey, that he met him a few miles from the city, which he entered in the afternoon, attended by two of the Ameer's people. He has not yet seen the Ameer. He has sent a letter from Count Simonich, which I have seen, and states that he is the bearer of letters from Mahomed Shah and the Emperor of Russia. I shall take an early opportunity of reporting on the proceedings of the Russian agent, if he be so in reality; for, if not an impostor, it is a most uncalled-for proceeding, after the disavowal of the Russian Government, conveyed through Count Nesselrode, alluded to in Mr. M'Neill's letter of 19th of June last."*

* A few days afterwards, in one of those undress communications from which we often gather more significant truth than from the more formal official documents, Burnes wrote to a private friend: "We are in a mess here. Herat is besieged, and may fall; and the Emperor of Russia has sent an envoy to Caubul, to offer Dost Mahomed Khan money to fight Runjeet Singh!!!!! I could not believe my eyes or ears; but Captain Vickovich—for that is the agent's name—arrived here with a blazing letter, three feet long, and sent immediately to pay his respects to myself. I, of course, received him, and asked him to dinner. This is not the best of it. The Ameer came over to me sharp, and offered to do as I liked, kick him out, or anything: but I stood too much in fear of Vattel to do any such thing: and since he was so friendly to us, said I, give me the letters the agent has brought; all of which he surrendered sharp; and I sent an express at once to my Lord A., with a confidential letter to the Governor-General himself, bidding him look what his predecessors had brought upon him, and telling him that after this I knew not what might happen, and it was now a neck-and-neck race between Russia and us; and if his Lordship would hear reason, he would forthwith send agents to Bokhara, Herat, Candahar, and Koondooz, not forgetting Sindh. How all this pill will go down I

The letters of which Vickovich was the bearer, like those brought by Burnes, were purely of a commercial tendency. One was from the Emperor himself; the other from Count Simonich—written in the Russian and the Persian languages. The authenticity of the letter from the Emperor has been questioned.* The fact is, that

know not, but I know my duty too well to be silent."—[*Private Correspondence of Sir A. Burnes.*]

* Mohun Lal says that he translated the Persian copy of the letter from the Emperor, but that he lost the translation during the insurrection of 1841-42. "It plainly acknowledged," he states, "the receipt of the Ameer's letter, and assured him that all the Afghan merchants shall be well received in the empire of Russia, justice and protection shall be extended towards them, and their intercourse will cause to flourish the respective states."—[*Life of Dost Mahomed*, vol. i. p. 300.] Masson declares that it was a forgery, seal and all, alleging in proof, that it bore no signature. To this Mohun Lal replies, that the absence of the royal signature is a proof rather of the genuine than the counterfeit character of the document. The reasons given are not very conclusive, as regards the general usage of the Czar; but, under the circumstances of the case, he would have been more inclined to omit than to attach the signature. The following is the translated letter; it was excluded from the published papers:

"A.C. In a happy moment, the messenger of your Highness, Meerza Hosan, reached my Court, with your friendly letter. I was very much delighted to receive it, and highly gratified by its perusal. The contents of the letter prove that you are my well-wisher, and have friendly opinions towards me. It flattered me very much, and I was satisfied of your friendship to my everlasting government. In consequence of this, and preserving the terms of friendship (which are now commenced between you and myself) in my heart, I will feel always happy to assist the people of Caubul who may come to trade into my kingdom. On the arrival of your messenger I have ordered him to make preparations for his long journey back to you, and also appointed a man of dignity to accompany him on the part of my government. If it pleases God, and he reaches safe, he will present to you the rarities of my country, which I have sent through him. By the grace of God, may your days be prolonged.—*Sent from St. Petersburgh, the capital of Russia, on the 27th of April,* 1837 *A.D., and in the* 12*th year of my reign.*"

it was one to be acknowledged or repudiated, as most convenient. It was intended to satisfy Dost Mahomed on the one hand, and to be suspected by the European allies of Russia upon the other. That it came from the Cabinet of St. Petersburgh there is now little room to doubt.

Burnes, however, for some time, was doubtful of the real character of the agent and his credentials; but after some weeks of hesitation, he wrote to Mr. Macnaghten, "Though a month and upwards has elapsed since Mr. Vickovich reached Caubul, and my suspicions were from the first excited regarding his real character, I have been unable to discover anything to invalidate the credentials which he brought, or to cast a doubt on his being other than he gives himself out, and this, too, after much vigilance and inquiry."

This was written on the 22nd of January. In the same letter Burnes writes: "Mr. Vickovich himself has experienced but little attention from the Ameer, and has yet received no reply to his communications. He has been accommodated in a part of a house belonging to Meerza Samee Khan, and is entertained at the public expense. He paid his respects to the Ameer on the 12th of January, and has had no other personal intercourse with him. He has been urging the Ameer to send an agent to Count Simonich to receive the presents of the Emperor." Nothing, indeed, could have been more discouraging than the reception of the Russian agent. Dost Mahomed still clung to the belief that the British Government would look favourably upon his case, and was willing to receive a little from England, rather than much from any other state. But he soon began to perceive that even that little was not to be obtained. Before the close of the month of January, Burnes had received specific instructions from the Governor-General, and was compelled, with the strongest feelings of reluctance and mortification, to strangle the hopes Dost Mahomed had encouraged of the friendly mediation of the British Government between the Ameer and Runjeet Singh.

The whole question of Peshawur was now fully discussed. Burnes, with his instructions in his hand, miserably fettered and restrained, enunciated the opinions of his government, from which he inwardly dissented, and strove, in obedience to the orders he had received, to make the worse appear the better reason. Dost Mahomed was moderate and reasonable; and Burnes must have felt that the argument was all in favour of the Ameer. That others, in higher place, thought so too, is clearly indicated by the fact that pains have been taken to keep the world in ignorance of what Dost Mahomed, on this occasion, advanced with so much reason and moderation in reply to the official arguments of the British agent, who was compelled to utter words which were dictated neither by the feelings nor the judgment of the man.

In a letter of the 26th of January, which I now have before me in an ungarbled state, Burnes forwarded to the Governor-General a full account of the important conference between the Ameer and himself, held after the receipt, by the latter, of instructions from the Governor-General.* At this meeting Burnes communicated to Dost Mahomed the sentiments of the Governor-General, and recommended the Ameer, in accordance with the opinions

* An attempt, in the published Blue Book, was made to conceal the fact of the receipt of these letters, and to make it appear that Burnes acted entirely upon his own responsibility. The genuine letter commenced with the following words:—"I have now the honour to acknowledge the receipt of your (the Political Secretary's) letters of the 25th of November and 2nd of December last, which reached me about the same time, and conveyed the views of the Right Honourable the Governor-General regarding the overtures made by Dost Mahomed, &c., &c." In the published version the letter commences with the word "regarding."

expressed by Lord Auckland, to waive his own claims to Peshawur, and be content with such arrangements as Runjeet Singh might be inclined to enter into with Sultan Mahomed. The Ameer replied that he bore no enmity against his brother, though his brother was full of rancour against him, and would gladly compass his destruction; but that with Sultan Mahomed, at Peshawur, he would not be safe for a day; and that it would be less injurious to him to leave it directly in the hands of the Sikhs, than in the hands of an enemy ever ready to intrigue with the Sikhs for his overthrow.

"Peshawur," said he, "has been conquered by the Sikhs; it belongs to them; they may give it to whomsoever they please; if to Sultan Mahomed Khan, they place it in the hands of one who is bent on injuring me; and I cannot therefore acknowledge any degree of gratitude for your interference, or take upon myself to render services in return." And then follow these mollifying sentences, which it was a gross injustice to Dost Mahomed to omit from the published letter: "I admit," said the Ameer, "that it will be highly beneficial in many ways to see the Sikhs once more eastward of the Indus, but I still can dispense with none of my troops or relax in my precautionary measures, as equal if not greater anxieties will attach to me. I have unbosomed myself to you, and laid bare, without any suppression, my difficulties. I shall bear in lively remembrance the intended good offices of the British Government, and I shall deplore that my interest did not permit me to accept that which was tendered in a spirit so friendly, but which to me and my advisers has only seemed hastening my ruin. To Runjeet Singh your interference is beneficial, as he finds himself involved in serious difficulties by the possession of Peshawur, and he is too glad of your good offices to escape from a place which is a burden to his finances, but by that escape a debt of gratitude is exactible from him and not from me ; and if your government will look into this matter, they will soon discover my opinions to be far from groundless, and my conclusions the only safe policy I can pursue."

The Ameer ceased to speak, and Jubbar Khan followed, proposing a compromise. He suggested that it might be found advisable to deliver over Peshawur conjointly to the Ameer and Sultan Mahomed—Runjeet Singh receiving from the two chiefs the value which he might fix as the terms of surrender. The Ameer observed that such an arrangement * would remove his fears, and that if he appointed Jubbar Khan to represent him at Peshawur he would be sure of an equitable adjustment of affairs. Burnes replied in general terms that the withdrawal of the Sikhs to the eastward of the Indus would be a vast benefit to the Afghan nation ; and asked Dost Mahomed whether he would rather see the Sikhs or Sultan Mahomed in Peshawur. The Ameer replied that the question put in plain words was a startling one ; but he asked in return if that could be considered beneficial to the Afghan nation

* Burnes, commenting on the Newab's proposal, observes : "The observations coming from the Newab Jubbar Khan are the more remarkable, since he is devoted to his brother, Sultan Mahomed Khan, and would rejoice to see him restored to Peshawur. They consequently carried with me a conviction that the Ameer's fears are not groundless, and that they will deserve all due consideration before government entered upon any measures for attaching this chief to its interests." This passage was, of course, suppressed. Whether any attempt was made to bring about a settlement of the Peshawur question on the basis of this proposal, I have not been able to ascertain. But Captain Wade, considering it by no means unreasonable, declared his willingness, with the consent of the Supreme Government, to urge it upon the acceptance of Runjeet. It is doubtful, however, whether, even if Runjeet had consented to it, Sultan Mahomed would have fallen into the arrangement, although Jubbar Khan declared his ability to reconcile the brothers.

which was especially injurious to him who possessed the largest share of sovereignty in Afghanistan. He then observed, in evidence of the truth of his assertions relative to the dangers to which he was exposed from the supremacy of Sultan Mahomed at Peshawur: "Sultan Mahomed Khan has just sent an agent to the ex-King at Loodhianah (Shah Soojah) to offer his services to combine against me and to secure my brothers at Candahar, in support of this coalition." "What security," asked the Ameer, "am I to receive against a recurrence of such practices?" He then continued: "As for the ex-King himself, I fear him not; he has been too often worsted to make head, unless he has aid from the British Government, which I am now pretty certain he will never receive. If my brother at Peshawur, however, under a promise of being made his minister, and assisted with Sikh agents and money, appears in the field, I may find that in expressing my satisfaction at his restoration to Peshawur, I have been placing a snake in my bosom—and I may then, when too late, lament that I did not let the Sikhs do their worst, instead of replacing them by another description of enemies."

All this was carefully erased from the letter before it was allowed to form a part of the published Blue Book; and the following just observations of Captain Burnes shared no better fate: "It has appeared to me that they" (the opinions and views of the ruler of Caubul) "call for much deliberation. It will be seen that the chief is not bent on possessing Peshawur, or on gratifying an enmity towards his brothers, but simply pursuing the worldly maxim of securing himself from injury; the arguments which he has adduced seem deserving of every consideration, and the more so when an avowed partisan of Sultan Mahomed does not deny the justice of the Ameer's objection." And further on, our agent observes: "Since arriving here, I have seen an agent of Persia with alluring promises, after penetrating as far as Candahar, compelled to quit the country' because no one has sent to invite him to Caubul. Following him, an agent of Russia with letters highly complimentary, and promises more than substantial, has experienced no more civility than is due by the laws of hospitality and nations. It may be urged by some that the offers of one or both were fallacious, but such a *dictum* is certainly premature ; the Ameer of Caubul has sought no aid in his arguments from such offers, but declared that his interests are bound up in an alliance with the British Government, which he never will desert as long as there is a hope of securing one." There is much more in a similar strain — much more cancelled from the published correspondence—with the deliberate intention of injuring the character and misrepresenting the conduct of Dost Mahomed, and so justifying their after-conduct towards him—but enough has already been given to prove how mightily the Ameer has been wronged.

I cannot, indeed, suppress the utterance of my abhorrence of this system of garbling the official correspondence of public men—sending the letters of a statesman or diplomatist into the world mutilated, emasculated—the very pith and substance of them cut out by the unsparing hand of the state-anatomist. The dishonesty by which lie upon lie is palmed upon the world has not one redeeming feature. If public men are, without reprehension, to be permitted to lie in the face of nations—wilfully, elaborately, and maliciously to bear false-witness against their neighbours, what hope is there for private veracity? In the case before us, the *suppressio veri* is virtually the *assertio falsi*. The character of Dost Mahomed has been lied away ; the character of Burnes has been lied away. Both, by the mutilation of the correspondence of the latter, have been fearfully misrepresented—both have been set forth as doing what they did not, and omitting to do what they did. I care not whose knife—whose hand did the work of mutilation. And, indeed, I do not know. I deal with principles, not with persons; and have no party ends to serve. The cause of truth must be upheld. Official documents are the sheet-anchors of historians—the last courts of appeal to which the public resort. If these documents are tampered with; if they are made to misrepresent the words and actions of public men, the grave of truth is dug, and there is seldom a resurrection. It is not always that an afflicted parent is ready to step forward on behalf of an injured child, and to lay a memorial at the feet of his sovereign, exposing the cruelty by which an honourable man has been represented in state documents, as doing that which was abhorrent to his nature. In most cases the lie goes down, unassailed and often unsuspected, to posterity; and in place of sober history, we have a florid romance.

I ask pardon for this digression—In spite of the declarations of Burnes that Dost Mahomed had little to hope from the co-operation of the British Government, the Russian Mission made scant progress at the Afghan capital. Alluding to the negotiations of our agent, Vickovich wrote some time afterwards: "All this has occasioned Dost Mahomed Khan to conduct himself very coldly towards me; and then, as he daily converses with Burnes, from my arrival here to the 20th of February I have hardly been two or three times in his presence." The fact is, that up to this time, as we are assured on the concurrent testimony of the British and the Russian agent, the latter was received in a scurvy and discouraging manner. But on the 21st of February letters were opened from the Governor-General, stating, in the most decisive language, that there was no intention to accede to the proposals of the Ameer, and that Peshawur must be left to the Sikhs. Then, but not till then, a change came over the conduct of Dost Mahomed, and the Russian Mission began to rise in importance.

LAST EFFORTS OF THE AMEER.

But still another effort was to be made by the Barukzyes to secure the friendship of the British Government. On the 1st of March, Jubbar Khan came in from his country-seat, and next morning called upon Burnes. He had read Lord Auckland's discouraging letter; but he still believed that, through his agency, for he was notoriously friendly to the British, something might yet be done. His efforts, however, were fruitless. Burnes, tied down by his instructions, could give the Newab no encouragement. The British Government called upon Dost Mahomed to abstain from connecting himself with every other state; and promised, as the price of this isolation, that they would restrain Runjeet Singh from attacking his dominions; "And that," said Jubbar Khan, "amounts to nothing, for we are not under the apprehension of any aggressions from the side of Lahore."* The Peshawur difficulty, he said, might be got over; but the offer of so little, in return for so much that was asked from the Ameer, placed him in a most humiliating

* Lord Auckland's offers to restrain Runjeet from attacking the country of the Sirdars were laughed at by them. Jubbar Khan said that they indicated very little knowledge of the state of Afghanistan; for that, "so far from the proffered protection from Runjeet being of the value stated, the Maharajah never sought to attack Caubul, and that hitherto all the aggression had been on the part of the Ameer, and not the ruler of Lahore." He added with undeniable truth, that "it appeared we valued our offers at a very high rate, since we expected, in return, that the Afghans would desist from all intercourse with Persia, Russia, Toorkistan," &c. "Were the Afghans," he asked, "to make all these powers hostile, and receive no protection against the enmity raised for their adhering to the British?" "As for Peshawur," he added, "being withheld from the Ameer, it might be got over; and he believed he did not overrate his influence with Sultan Mahomed Khan, when he stated that he might bring about a reconciliation between him and the Ameer; but he must say that the value of the Afghans had indeed been depressed, and he did not wonder at the Ameer's disappointment."—[*Ungarbled Correspondence of Sir A. Burnes.*]

position, and would, if accepted, lower him in the eyes of the world. Meerza Samee Khan, next day, told the same story;* but fettered by the orders of the Supreme Government, Burnes could give him no hope.

On the 5th of March, Jubbar Khan again appeared before Burnes with a string of specific demands, dictated by the Ameer. "These consisted of a promise to protect Caubul and Candahar from Persia; of the surrender of Peshawur by Runjeet Singh; of the interference of our government to protect, at that city, those who might return to it from Caubul, supposing it to be restored to Sultan Mahomed Khan; with several other proposals." Upon this Burnes, with an expression of astonishment, declared that, on the part of the British Government, he could accede to none of these propositions; and added, that as he saw no hope of a satisfactory adjustment, he should request his dismissal. "The Newab," said Burnes, "left me in sorrow."

The British agent then sat down, and drew up a formal letter to the Ameer, requesting leave to depart for Hindostan. In spite of what had taken place, the letter somewhat startled the Ameer, who summoned a meeting of his principal advisers, "which lasted till past midnight."†

* "The Meerza made nearly the same observation as the Newab about the expectations which the Ameer had cherished of doing service for the British, and devoting himself to it; that it was not the adjustment of Peshawur affairs that dissipated his hopes, but the indifference to his sufferings and station, which it was now clear we felt." The Meerza truly said that Dost Mahomed had often written to the British Government about his affairs, and that in reply they answered him about their own.—[*Ungarbled Correspondence of Sir A. Burnes.*],

† It is probably of this meeting, or one shortly preceding it, of which General Harlan, who has not much regard for dates, speaks in the following passage. Harlan had by this time quitted Runjeet Singh's camp, and taken service with Dost Mahomed :—"The document (Lord Auckland's ultimatum) was handed to me amongst others. I satisfied myself, by the Governor-General's signature, of its authenticity, sur-

On the following morning the conference was resumed; and about mid-day Meerza Samee Khan waited on Burnes, and invited him to attend the Ameer in the Balla Hissar. Gracious and friendly even beyond his ordinary courtesy and urbanity, Dost Mahomed expressed his regret that the Governor-General had shown so little inclination to meet his wishes; but added, that he did not even then despair of forming an alliance advantageous both to England and Afghanistan. A long argument then ensued; but it led to nothing. The old ground was travelled over again and again. Burnes asked for everything; but promised nothing. He had no power to make any concessions. The meeting, though it ended amicably, was productive of no good results. Burnes took his departure from the Balla Hissar. He might as well have departed from Caubul.

veying the contents with extreme surprise and disappointment. Dost Mahomed was mortified, but not terrified. . . . . The Governor-General's ultimatum was handed round, and an embarrassing silence ensued. A few minutes elapsed, when Abdul Sami Khan recalled the party from abstraction. . . . . *He* proclaimed that the Governor-General's ultimatum left no other alternative than the dismission of the English agent, for the spirit of the Kuzzilbash party was supercilious and unyielding, though full of duplicity. . . . . Nieb Mahomed Ameer Khan, Akhondzadeh, openly opposed the Kuzzilbash party, and urged many weighty arguments in favour of a pacific settlement of the Ameer's relations with the British Government, which had now assumed a position so inauspicious. He concluded his oration with these words, addressing the Ameer: 'There is no other recourse for you but to introduce Mr. Harlan in the negotiations with Mr. Burnes, and he, through his own facilities and wisdom, will arrange a treaty according to their European usage, for the pacific and advantageous settlement of your affairs;' and to this proposition the council *unanimously* assented." The proposition, it appears, was made to Burnes; but Burnes declined the honour of negotiating with the doctor-general. Harland says that he then wrote to the British envoy, offering to "negotiate upon his own terms;" but Burnes sent "a reply personally friendly," but "evincing a deficiency of knowledge of first principles concerning the rights of independent powers in political negotiations." Burnes says nothing about this in his official or private letters.

On the 21st of March, the Ameer wrote a friendly letter to Lord Auckland, imploring him, in language almost of humility, to "remedy the grievances of the Afghans;" to "give them a little encouragement and power." It was the last despairing effort of the Afghan chief to conciliate the good-will of the British Government. It failed. The *fiat* had gone forth. The judgment against him was not to be reversed. Other meetings took place; but Burnes knew them to be mere formalities. He remained at Caubul with no hope of bringing matters to a favourable issue; but because it was convenient to remain. He was awaiting the return from Koondooz of Dr. Lord and Lieutenant Wood. The month of March passed away, and the greater part of April. These officers did not rejoin the Mission. But one of the Candahar Sirdars, Mehr Dil Khan, appeared at Caubul, with the object of winning over the Ameer to the Persian alliance. The "do-nothing policy," as Burnes subsequently characterised it, had done its work. The Russians, as he said, had given us the *coup-de-grace*. Vickovich was publicly sent for, and paraded through the streets of Caubul. So Burnes determined to depart. Accordingly, on the 26th of April, he turned his back upon the Afghan capital.*

Burnes went; and Vickovich, who had risen greatly in favour, soon took his departure for Herat, promising everything that Dost Mahomed wanted—engaging to furnish money to the Barukzye chiefs, and undertaking to propitiate Runjeet Singh.† The Russian quitted Caubul,

---

* Mr. Masson says, that before its departure the Mission had fallen into contempt, and that the assassination of Burnes was talked of in Caubul. He explains too, what, according to his account, were the real causes of Burnes's departure without his companions; but it does not come within our province to investigate Masson's charges against the envoy.

† Overtures had been made to Runjeet by Vickovich, who offered to

accompanied by Aboo Khan Barukzye, a confidential friend of Dost Mahomed. It had been arranged that Azim Khan, the Ameer's son, accompanied by the minister, should be despatched to the Shah ; but this arrangement being set aside, in consequence of the scruples of the Meerza, Aboo Khan was sent in their place. There were now no half measures to be pursued. Dost Mahomed had flung himself into the arms of the Persian King.

Vickovich was received with all honour in Western Afghanistan * Russian promises now began to carry

---

visit the Maharajah's Court. But British influence at this time was too strong at Lahore for the Russian to make way against it. Runjeet, however, who was not ignorant of the Russo-phobia then rampant amongst us, turned the Cossack's overtures to some account, and probably pretended more uncertainty on the score of the answer to be returned to him than he in reality felt. Mackeson, to whom the business of counteracting the designs of Vickovich was entrusted, managed it with great address, and won from the Maharajah a promise to have nothing to do with the Muscovite agent. But the knowledge that the Russian agent was, as it were, knocking at the gates of Lahore, made our authorities especially anxious to conciliate the Maharajah, by refraining from entering into any negotiations with Caubul which might possibly give umbrage to Runjeet.

* What befel the unhappy agent after this, it is painful to relate. When he returned to Persia, in 1839, after giving a full report of his mission to M. Duhamel, the new minister at Teheran, he was instructed to proceed direct to St Petersburgh. On his arrival there, full of hope, for he had discharged the duty entrusted to him with admirable address, he reported himself, after the customary formality, to Count Nesselrode ; but the minister refused to see him. Instead of a flattering welcome, the unhappy envoy was received with a crushing message, to the effect that Count Nesselrode "knew no Captain Vickovich, except an adventurer of that name, who, it was reported, had been lately engaged in some unauthorised intrigues at Caubul and Candahar." Vickovich understood at once the dire portent of this message. He knew the character of his government. He was aware of the recent expostulations of Great Britain. And he saw clearly that he was to be sacrificed. He went back to his hotel, wrote a few bitter reproachful lines, burnt all his other papers, and blew out his brains.

everything before them. A treaty between the Candahar brothers and the Shah was drawn up and signed by the latter. The Russian ambassador to whom it was forwarded sent it back to the Sirdars, saying, "Mahomed Shah has promised to give you the possession of Herat: I sincerely tell you that you will also get Ghorian, on my account, from the Shah. . . . . . When Mahomed Omar Khan arrives here I will ask the Shah to quit Herat, and I will remain here with 12,000 troops, and, when you join, we will take Herat, which will afterwards be delivered to you,"—magnificent promises, most refreshing to the souls of the Candahar chiefs. The letter was sent on to Dost Mahomed; but it did not fill the heart of the Ameer with an equal measure of delight. The Russian alliance was unpopular at Caubul. It had "ruined him in the eyes of all Mahomedans." It soon became obvious, too, in spite of the fair beginning, that whilst he was losing everything by the dissolution of his friendship with the British, the Russians could really do nothing to assist him. Mahomed Shah was wasting his strength before Herat. The Persian army, under the command of the Sovereign himself, moved by Russian diplomacy and directed by Russian skill, was only precipitating itself into an abyss of failure, and the Candahar brethren, who had been promised so much, were linking themselves with a decrepit cause, from which they were likely to gain nothing. Soon other tidings came to alarm him. The Russian game was nearly played out; and the resentment of the British was about to break forth in a manner which threatened the total extinction of Barukzye supremacy in Afghanistan. He looked out towards the West, and he could plainly see that, in flinging himself upon Russo-Persian support, he had trusted to a foundation of sand. The ground was shifting under his feet. His new friends were not able to assist him. A subaltern of the British army within the walls of Herat was setting them at defiance.

CHAPTER II.

[1837—1839.]

The Siege of Herat—Shah Kamran and Yar Mahomed—Return of the Shah—Eldred Pottinger—Preparations for the Defence—Advance of the Persian Army—Progress of the Siege—Negotiations for Peace—Failure of the Attack—The Siege raised.

SURROUNDED by a fair expanse of country, where alternating corn-fields, vineyards, and gardens varied the richness and beauty of the scene; where little fortified villages studded the plain, and the bright waters of small running streams lightened the pleasant landscape, lay the city of Herat.* The beauty of the place was beyond the walls. Within, all was dirt and desolation. Strongly fortified on every side by a wet ditch and a solid outer wall, with five gates, each defended by a small outwork, the city presented but few claims to the admiration of the traveller. Four long bazaars, roofed with arched brickwork, meeting in a small domed quadrangle in the centre of the city, divided it into four quarters.† In each of these there may have

* Arthur Conolly. The correctness of this description is confirmed by Eldred Pottinger, in his unpublished journal. I have been obliged to write it in the past tense. "The late war," says Pottinger, "and its consequences have so changed the entire neighbourhood of the city, that, under its present appearance, it would not be recognised by its former visitants. Moreover, the city and its surrounding places have been so well described by Lieut. A. Conolly, that I need not repeat the description."—[*Eldred Pottinger's MS. Journal.*]

† Of these bazaars Pottinger writes: "The interior of the city is divided into four nearly equal divisions, by two streets which, at right

been about a thousand dwelling-houses and ten thousands of inhabitants. Mosques and caravanserais, public baths and public reservoirs, varied the wretched uniformity of the narrow dirty streets, which, roofed across, were often little better than dark tunnels or conduits, where every conceivable description of filth was suffered to collect and putrify. When Arthur Conolly expressed his wonder how the people could live in the midst of so much filth, he was answered, "The climate is fine; and if dirt killed people where would the Afghans be?"*

Such to the eye of an ordinary traveller, in search of the picturesque, was the aspect of the city and its environs at the time when the army of Mahomed Shah was marching upon Herat. To the mind of the military observer both the position and construction of the place were suggestive of much interesting speculation. Situated at that point of the great mountain-range which alone presents facilities to the transport of a train of heavy artillery,

angles, cross each other in the centre of the city. The principal one joins the gate of Candahar to the Pay-i-Hissar, and was formerly covered by a succession of small domes, springing from arches which cross the streets. About two-thirds of this magnificent bazaar still remain; but so choked up with rubbish, and so ruinous, that it has lost much of its attraction to the eye. This bazaar was about 1300 yards long and 6 in width. The solidity of the masonry of this work should have insured its stability; but unfortunately the arches are all defective—not one has a keystone. They are built, as all others in this country are, with a vacancy at the apex, filled merely with bits of broken bricks, ... The whole of the lower floors on each side are used as shops."—[*Eldred Pottinger's MS. Journal.*]

* Conolly says: "The town itself is, I should imagine, one of the dirtiest in the world. .... No drains having been contrived to carry off the rain which falls within the walls, it collects and stagnates in ponds which are dug in different parts of the city. The residents cast out the refuse of their houses into the streets, and dead cats and dogs are commonly seen lying upon heaps of the vilest filth."—[*Conolly's Journey to the North of India.*]

Herat has, with no impropriety of designation, been described as the "Gate of India." Within the limits of the Heratee territory all the great roads leading on India converge. At other points, between Herat and Caubul, a body of troops unencumbered with guns, or having only a light field artillery, might make good its passage, if not actively opposed, across the stupendous mountain-ranges of the Hindoo-Koosh; but it is only by the Herat route that a really formidable well-equipped army could make its way upon the Indian frontier from the regions on the north-west. Both the nature and the resources of the country are such as to favour the success of the invader. All the materials necessary for the organisation of a great army, and the formation of his dépôts, are to be found in the neighbourhood of Herat. The extraordinary fertility of the plain has fairly entitled it to be called the "Granary of Central Asia." Its mines supply lead, iron, and sulphur; the surface of the country, in almost every direction, is laden with saltpetre; the willow and poplar trees, which furnish the best charcoal, flourish in all parts of the country; whilst from the population might at any time be drawn hardy and docile soldiers to recruit the ranks of an invading army.* Upon the possession of such country would depend, in no small measure, the success of operations undertaken for the invasion or the defence of Hindostan.

The city of Herat, it has been said, stood within solid earthen walls, surrounded by a wet ditch. The four sides were of nearly equal length, a little less than a mile in extent, facing towards the four points of the compass. The most elevated quarter of the city was the north-east, from which it gradually sloped down to the south-west

* *Report of Major Eldred Pottinger to the Supreme Government of India on the defences of Herat. Calcutta: July,* 1840.—[*MS. Records.*]

corner, where it attained its lowest descent.* The real defences of the place were two covered ways, or *fausse-braies*, on the exterior slope of the embankments, one within and the other without the ditch. The lower one was on the level of the surrounding country, its parapet "partly covered by a mound of earth on the counter-scarp, the accumulation of rubbish from the cleansings of the ditch." On the northern side, surrounded by a wet ditch, the citadel, once known as the Kella-i-Aktyar-Aldyn, but now as the Ark, overlooked the city. Built entirely of good brick masonry, with lofty ramparts and numerous towers, it was a place of considerable strength; but now its defences, long neglected, were in a wretched state of repair. Indeed, when, in 1837, tidings of the advance of the Persian army reached Herat, the whole extent of the fortifications was crumbling into decay.

The population of Herat was estimated at about 45,000 inhabitants. A large majority of these were *Sheeahs*. It was said that there might have been 1000 Hindoos, of various callings, in the city; there were several families of Armenians, and a few families of Jews. The general appearance of the inhabitants was that of a poor and an oppressed people. Dirty and ill-clad, they went about in a hurried, anxious manner, each man looking with suspicion into his neighbour's face. Few women were to be seen in the streets. It was hardly safe for a stranger to be abroad after sunset. Unless protected by an armed escort, there was too great a likelihood of his being seized and sold into slavery. There was no protection for life, liberty, or property. They who should have protected the people were the foremost of their oppressors. During the absence of the King, in 1837, such was the frightful misrule—such the reign of terror that had been established by the char-

* *Eldred Pottinger's MS. Journal.*

tered violence of the rulers of the city, that the shops were closed before sunset, and all through the night the noise and uproar, the challengings and the cries for help were such as could scarcely have been exceeded if the place had been actually besieged. A son of Yar Mahomed Khan, the Wuzeer, was then governor of the city. Compelled to hold office upon a small salary, he enriched himself by plundering the houses of the inhabitants, and selling the people into slavery. All who were strong enough followed his example, and when detected, secured immunity for themselves by giving him a portion of the spoil.* So remorseless, indeed, was the tyranny exercised over the unhappy Sheeahs by their Afghan masters, that many of the inhabitants of Herat looked forward to the coming of the Persian King as to the advent of a deliverer, and would gladly have seen the city given over to the governance of one who, whatever may have been his political claims, was not an alien in his religious faith.†

* Eldred Pottinger, from whose manuscript journal the materials of this chapter are mainly drawn, gives a remarkable illustration of the manner in which justice was then administered. "During this period," he says, "a Heratee detected a noted robber in his outhouse, and with the aid of his neighbours arrested him. In the morning, when taken before the Sirdar by the cutwal, to request the order for punishment might be given as the case was proved, the robber declared, that on hearing the citizen call for aid, he had run to his help, and, being immediately laid hold of, made prisoner and accused. He also accused the cutwal of being a partner in the plan. The young Sirdar, with an acumen to be wondered at but not described, decided that his was the truth of the story—sold the accuser, and so severely fined the witnesses, that they were reduced to poverty and debt to the soldiers—the sure precursor of slavery. He then gave the thief, who was his own servant, a *khelat* (or dress of honour) and released him. Under such a governor the misery of the people would require a more eloquent pen than mine to narrate."

† It need scarcely be said that the Persians are generally of the

Such was the last remnant of the old Afghan monarchy in the hands of Shah Kamran—the only one of the Suddozye Princes who had retained his hold of the country he had governed. His government was at this time a pageant and a name. An old and a feeble man, broken down by long years of debauchery, he had resigned the active duties of administration into the hands of his Wuzeer. He was, perhaps, the worst of the royal princes —the worst of a bad race. His youth had been stained by the commission of every kind of Oriental crime; and now in his old age, if the evil passions of his nature were less prominently developed, it was only because physical decay had limited his power to indulge them. In his younger days he had set no restraint upon himself, and now it was nature only that restrained him. The violent gusts of passion, which had once threatened all who were within his influence, had given place to an almost incessant peevishness and petulance of manner, more pitiable to behold than it was dangerous to encounter. He had once played openly the part of the bandit—placing himself at the head of gangs of armed retainers, plundering houses by night and slaying all who opposed him; now he suffered others to commit the violence which he had before personally enacted, and oppressed, by deputy, the weakness which he could not see smitten before his face. He had once been immoderately addicted to sensual pleasure, and in the pursuit of such gratification—arrested by no feelings of compassion, by no visitings of remorse—had violently seized the objects of his desires, to whomsoever they belonged, and cast them adrift when his appetite was sated; now he

Sheeah, and the Afghans of the Soonee sect. At Herat the rulers and the soldiery were Soonees, whilst the shopkeepers and other peaceful citizens were Sheeahs. The oppression of the Sheeahs by their Afghan masters was one of the circumstances by a reference to which Mahomed Shah sought to justify his invasion of Herat.

sought excitement of another kind, to which age and feebleness were no impediments, and turned from the caresses of women to seek solace from the stimulants of wine. Unfaithful to his friends and unmerciful to his enemies, ingratitude and cruelty were conspicuous in his nature, and these darker features of his character there was little to lighten or relieve. Among his countrymen he was esteemed for a certain kind of courage, and in his younger days he had not been wanting in activity and address.* Though naturally haughty and arrogant, there were times when he could assume, for his own ends, a becoming courtesy of demeanour; and, as by assiduous attention to costume, he endeavoured to compensate for the deficiencies of an unattractive person, there was something of a high and princely aspect about the outward bearing even of this degraded man. Short and thickset, with misshapen limbs and an unseemly gait, his appearance was more comely in repose than in action. His face was pitted with the small-pox, and there was a harshness in his countenance stamped by the long possession of arbitrary power and the indulgence of unbridled passions; but he had a finer, more massive, more upright forehead, than the majority of his countrymen, with more of intellect impressed upon it. His voice had once been loud and deep; but the feebleness of age, much sickness, and much suffering, had given a querulousness to its tones which was equally undignified and unpleasing.

If in the character and the person of Shah Kamran there was little that was estimable or attractive, there was less in the person and character of his Wuzeer. Yar

* Pottinger says that "he was much devoted to field-sports, and spent the greater part of his time in their pursuit. He was an unerring shot with a matchlock; he could divide a sheep in two by a single cut of his sabre, and with a Lahore bow send an arrow through a cow."— [*MS. Journal.*]

Mahomed Khan was a stout, square-built man, of middle height, with a heavy, stern countenance, thick negro-like lips, bad straggling teeth, an overhanging brow, and an abruptly receding forehead. His face was redeemed from utter repulsiveness by the fineness of his eyes and the comeliness of his beard. Like his master he attired himself with care and propriety; but his manner was more attractive than his appearance. Affable in his demeanour, outwardly courteous and serene, he seldom gave the rein to his temper, but held it in habitual control. He talked freely and well, had a fund of anecdote at his command, was said to be well read in Mahomedan divinity, and was strict in his attention to the external formalities of his religion. His courage was never questioned; and his ability was as undoubted as his courage. Both were turned to the worst possible account. Of all the unscrupulous miscreants in Central Asia, Yar Mahomed was the most unscrupulous. His avarice and his ambition knew no bounds, and nothing was suffered to stand in the way of their gratification. Utterly without tenderness or compassion, he had no regard for the sufferings of others. Sparing neither sex nor age, he trod down the weak with an iron heel; and, a tyrant himself, encouraged the tyranny of his retainers. As faithless as he was cruel, there was no obligation which he had not violated, no treachery that had not stained his career. If there was an abler or a worse man in Central Asia, I have not yet heard his name.*

In the summer of 1837 the bazaars of Herat were

* Yar Mahomed was the nephew of Atta Mahomed, an influential Sirdar of the Alekozye tribe, who was Minister to Shah Mahmoud and Hadjee Feroz, and afterwards of Shah Kamran. This man left two sons, Deen Mahomed and Sultan Mahomed; but neither possessed the same capacious mind and energetic character which distinguished their cousin Yar Mahomed, who was always, more or less, at enmity with them, and at last drove them out of Herat, in 1841.

a-stir with rumours of the movements of the royal army. The King and the Wuzeer were absent from the city on a campaign in Seistan. To gratify the personal rancour of the latter they had laid siege to the fortress of Jowayn, and in the vain attempt to reduce a place of no political importance, had crippled their own military resources in a manner which they soon began bitterly to lament. The waste of so much strength on so small an enterprise was unworthy of a man so able and so astute as Yar Mahomed; but the feeling of personal resentment was stronger in him than either avarice or ambition. He had a larger game in hand at that time; and he should have husbanded all his resources for the great struggle by which he sought to restore to the Suddozye Princes the sovereignty of Caubul and Candahar.*

It was soon buzzed abroad in Herat that the army was about to return—that it had broken off from the siege of Jowayn—and was coming back to gird itself up for stirring work at home. Cossids were coming in daily from the royal camp with instructions for the collection of grain and the repair of the defences of the city. The meaning of this was involved in no obscurity. The ambassador who had been sent to Teheran to seek, among other objects, the assistance of Mahomed Shah in the projected enterprise for the recovery of Candahar and Caubul† had

* Pottinger says, with reference to this ill-judged movement, that "the Wuzeer played away the last stake of his master by which he could have hoped to recover his former dominions or to defend his present. Indeed, after-events have shown that the body of cavalry which he thus frittered away and destroyed was strong enough to have prevented the Persian army leaving its own frontier." There was, however, some compensation which, whether the result of the siege or not, is worth mentioning, in the fact that when Herat was attacked by the Persians, many of the old garrison of Jowayn came to the assistance of their former enemies.

† It is doubted by some, whose opinions are entitled to the highest

brought back an answer to the effect that the Persian monarch claimed both principalities for himself, and intended to take possession of Herat as a preliminary to further operations. It was said to be the intention of the King of Kings to proceed to Caubul, and, receiving as the price of his assistance the submission of the Ameer, to join Dost Mahomed in a religious war against the Sikhs. Herat was to be reduced on the road. Kamran was to be deprived of his regal titles. Prayers were to be said and coin struck in the name of the Persian King; and a Persian garrison was to be received into the city. These were the terms dictated by Mahomed Shah, and thrown back by Shah Kamran with defiance.

The greatest excitement now prevailed throughout the city. There was but one topic of discourse. Every man met his neighbour with a word about the coming of the Persian army. The *Sheeahs*, smarting under the tyranny to which they had long been subjected, spoke of the advent of the Persian monarch as of the coming of a deliverer, whilst the *Soonee* Afghans, whom they taunted with predictions of the success of the invading force, swore that they would defend, to the last drop of their blood, the only remnant of the old Afghan monarchy which had not been violently wrested from the hands of its legitimate possessors.

respect, whether either Kamran or Yar Mahomed ever really contemplated an expedition for the recovery of Candahar and Caubul; but it is certain that they talked about it. In the letter which Kamran sent to Mahomed Shah, by Futteh Mahomed Khan, he expressed a "hope of obtaining the favour of his Majesty, so that with the aid of the well-wishers of Persia he might subdue his hereditary dominions, and overwhelm his rebellious enemies;" and in a message which Pottinger was commissioned to deliver to the Persian monarch, it was distinctly declared that Futteh Mahomed Khan had been sent to Teheran to beg for aid towards the recovery of Kamran's paternal kingdom.

On the 17th of September the King returned to Herat. Moved by one common impulse of curiosity, the people went forth to meet him. The streets were lined with eager thousands, and the house-tops were alive with gazers. A procession of the true Oriental type, it presented, in vivid contrasts, strange alternations of the shabby and the superb. First came a few strong baggage-mules, and a few straggling horsemen, mounted on fine well-built animals, but lean, and often lame and wounded. Then, in their high red-cloth caps, appeared the criers and the executioners, bearing aloft the instruments of their calling; and, in spite of the grim suggestiveness of the large knives and tiger-headed brazen maces, presenting an appearance less solemn than grotesque. Next came a string of horses led by armed grooms, their fine stag-like heads telling the purity of their blood, and their handsome equipments the royal ownership they boasted. Then followed, close behind, in a covered litter of red cloth, carried by Hindostanee bearers, Shah Kamran himself. Very plainly, but tastefully attired, the golden bosses on his sword-belt, and the jewels on his dagger-hilt, being the only ornaments about the royal person, he returned, through the open curtains of his litter, with a kingly and a graceful courtesy, the salutations of the people. Next came the Royal Princes, with the eunuchs, and other personal attendants of the Shah,* and then, but at a long interval, a motley crowd of armed foot-men, the regular infantry of Herat, in all sorts of irregular costumes. These preceded the cavalcade of the Wuzeer, Yar Mahomed, who, with all the chiefs of note around him, headed the main body of the Afghan cavalry, whose low sheepskin caps and uniform attire made up a very soldierly appearance. Another body of infantry closed the procession. The guns had been left behind.

* Among these was M. Euler, the Shah's European physician.

Among the many who went forth on that September morning to witness the entrance of Shah Kamran into his capital, was a young European officer. Riding out a mile beyond the city walls, he picketed his horse in the courtyard of a deserted house, and joined a party of Afghans, who, sitting on the domed roof of the building, were watching the procession as it passed. He had entered Herat about a month before, after an adventurous journey from Caubul, through the Imauk and Hazareh countries. The name of this young officer was Eldred Pottinger. He was a Lieutenant in the Bombay Artillery; and had been despatched by his uncle, Colonel Pottinger, who was then Resident in Sindh, for the purpose of exploring the countries of Afghanistan, and collecting materials for a full report to be drawn up on his return. He started in no recognised official capacity, but travelled onward in the most unostentatious manner, assuming the disguise of a Cutch horse-dealer, and attracting little attention on his route. Journeying upwards by Shikarpoor and Dehra Ismael Khan to Peshawur, he proceeded thence to Caubul, and there changing his disguise for that of an Indian Syud, made his way through the rude country of the Imauks and Hazarehs to Herat. Though at this period he was but slightly acquainted with the Persian language, and was ignorant of the Mahomedan prayers, of their genuflexions, modes of worship, and similar observances, he passed on almost unquestioned by the credulous Afghans. In Herat itself, though he seems to have taken little pains to conceal his real character, he remained, for some time,* lodging in a caravanserai, and mixing freely

* "I have heard him," writes one who knew Pottinger well, "describe how on two occasions, when challenged about not praying or turning towards Mecca, he silenced all questioning by appealing to the usage of India."—[*Private Correspondence.*]

with its inmates, but seldom recognised as an European by those with whom he associated.

The King and the Wuzeer returned to Herat; and Eldred Pottinger soon sent a message to the latter, offering, as a stranger and a traveller, to wait upon him, if he desired to see him. To the surprise of the English officer, Yar Mahomed sent a messenger to him intimating that, early on the following morning, he would be happy to receive him. Pottinger went. The minister, who was seated in an alcove in the dressing-room of his bath, rose as the stranger entered, invited him to take a seat beside himself, and welcomed him with becoming courtesy. As the only articles he possessed worthy of the acceptance of the chief, Pottinger presented his detonating pistols; and the gift was graciously received. A few days afterwards he paid, "by desire," a visit to the King.* Little did

* Pottinger, who is provokingly chary, in his journal, of information about himself, does not say whether he appeared at these interviews in his true character of a British officer, but I conclude that he did not, on these occasions, attempt to conceal his nationality. Nor does it seem that, in his intercourse with the higher class of Heratees, he wore any disguise; for we soon find him taking part in a conversation about Arthur Conolly, and addressed as a countryman of that fine-hearted young Englishman. I cannot transcribe, without a glow of pleasure, the following passage in Pottinger's journal:—" I fell in with a number of Captain Conolly's acquaintances. Every person asked after him, and appeared disappointed when I told them I did not know him. In two places I crossed Mr. Conolly's route, and on his account received the greatest hospitality and attention—indeed, more than was pleasant, for such liberality required corresponding upon my part; and my funds were not well adapted for any extraordinary demand upon them In Herat, Mr. Conolly's fame was great. In a large party, where the subject of the Europeans who had visited Herat was mooted, Conolly's name being mentioned, I was asked if I knew him, and on replying, 'Merely by report,' Moollah Mahomed, a Sheeah Moollah of eminence, calling to me across the room, said, ' You have a great pleasure awaiting you. When you see him, give him my salutation, and tell him that I say he has done as much to give the

Shah Kamran and Yar Mahomed, when they received that unassuming traveller, think how much, under Providence, the future destinies of Herat were in the hands of the young Englishman.

The spirit of adventure was strong in Eldred Pottinger. It had brought him to the gates of Herat, and now it kept him there, eager to take a part in the coming struggle between the Heratees and their Persian invaders. And when the day of trial came—when the enemy were under the walls of the city—he threw himself into the contest, not merely in a spirit of adventure, as a young soldier rejoicing in the opportunity thus afforded him of taking part in the stirring scenes of active warfare, but as one profoundly impressed with the conviction that his duty to his country called upon him, in such a crisis, to put forth all his energies in aid of those who were striving to arrest a movement threatening not only the independence of Herat, but the stability of the British Empire in the East.

Scarcely had the King returned to Herat, when a proclamation went forth into the surrounding villages, decreeing that all the grain and forage should be brought into the city, and that the villagers should abide within its walls, on pain of the Shah's resentment. The danger seemed something dim and remote, and the order, at first, was little heeded. But when, towards the close of October, intelligence reached Herat that the Persian army had arrived at Toorbut, another more imperative edict was issued, commanding all the outstanding crops, grain, and forage, to be destroyed, and the fruit-trees to be cut down in the surrounding gardens. The soldiery were let loose upon the country to carry out the royal decree. The policy of this measure is apparent; but there was

English nation fame in Herat, as your ambassador, Mr. Elphinstone, did at Peshawur;' and in this he was seconded by the great mass present."—[*Eldred Pottinger's MS. Journal.*]

ADVANCE OF THE PERSIANS.

unlooked-for evil in the result. It was the object of the Heratee Government to keep all the available grain, forage, and firewood outside the city from falling into the hands of the invading army. If these necessaries could not be stored in Herat, the next best thing was to destroy them. But the licence thus given to the soldiery completely unhinged the little discipline that had before kept them together. They were, indeed, from that time so completely disorganised, that it was never afterwards found practicable to reduce them to order.

In the mean while, the city was alive with rumours of the progress of the Persian army. It was ascertained that they were moving forward in three bodies, the advance of which was a force of 10,000 or 12,000 men, under Alayar Khan.* Every now and then a prisoner was brought in; but the people, who seized them, bitterly complained that they could not make more captures. The Persian army, they loudly declared, was composed of a set of the most contemptible cowards, because they marched in compact bodies, defended by their guns, instead of straggling boldly about on purpose to be cut off by marauding Afghans.†

Early in November there was a hard frost, and the

---

* Better known by his title of Asoof-ood-dowlah. He was the head of the *Yukhaw-bash* division of the Kajjar tribe, and, according to the heraldry of the clans, was thus of higher rank than the Shah, who was merely the chief of the *Ashagha-bash*, or younger branch. Futteh Ali Shah, to stanch an old tribe feud, had married his son and heir-apparent, Abbas Meerza, to the heiress of the rival branch, and Mahomed Shah being the issue of this marriage, the Asoof-ood-dowlah was his maternal uncle. The Asoof was Governor of Khorassan, with almost independent powers, from 1835 to 1847. He is now in exile at Baghdad.

† As the army approached Herat some important captures were made. Among others, the secretary of the Asoof-ood-dowlah was carried off, with all his papers.

Heratees began hopefully to speculate on the chances of a severe winter. Never were the predictions of the weather-wise so cruelly falsified; but the hope buoyed them up for a time. Another cheering anticipation was belied in the same mortifying manner. It was long a matter of anxious conjecture whether the Persians would attack Ghorian. In 1834-35 they had left it untouched; and it was believed that now again they would mask it, for its reputed strength was greater than that of Herat, and it was defended by a picked garrison, under the command of the brother of Yar Mahomed. But these hopes were soon dispersed by the arrival of couriers from Ghorian, with tidings that the place was besieged. On the 15th of November it was announced that Ghorian had fallen.

Matters now began to wear a more alarming aspect. Cursing with his whole heart the cowardice or treachery of his brother, who, almost without a struggle, had shamefully surrendered his charge,* Yar Mahomed, with increased vigour, addressed himself to the defence of the city. The gates were closed against all egress. The people poured into Herat in floods from the surrounding country. In every house were huddled together the members of five or six families. The very ruins were thickly tenanted. But still the streets were alive with throngs of people seeking habitations in the city. Everywhere excitement and alarm were visible in the countenances and the gestures of the Heratees. It was a strange and fearful

* This was Yar Mahomed's first angry view of the case; but it may be doubted whether Shere Mahomed Khan was fairly to be censured for the loss of Ghorian. Of small dimensions, and unfurnished with bomb-proofs, the place was ill calculated to sustain the heavy vertical fire of shot and shell which the Persian artillery poured into it. A magazine and storehouse took fire; and at the time of its surrender Colonel Stoddart pronounced it to be quite untenable.

conjuncture, and no man felt himself secure. A fiat had gone forth for the apprehension of all persons of doubtful loyalty. Many suspected of infidelity were seized, their persons imprisoned, and their property confiscated, whilst others, in whom the spirit of rebellion had been more clearly evidenced, were plunged, with all their family and dependents, into one great sea of ruin. When it was known that Shums-ood-deen Khan,* an Afghan chief of note, had thrown off his allegiance to Herat, his Persian dependents were seized and stripped of all they possessed. Some were tortured, some were sent into slavery, and some were condemned to death. The women and children were sold or given away. Those of the Afghan tribes were more mercifully treated; but few escaped imprisonment and fine. Nor were even the priesthood spared. The Moollahs of the Sheeah sect were arrested and confined, lest they should stir up intrigue and disaffection among the people.

Whilst these precautions against internal revolt were taken by the Shah and his unscrupulous minister, actively and unceasingly they laboured to defend the city against the enemy advancing from without. The fortifications now began to bristle with armed soldiers The hammer of the artificer rang upon the guns in the embrasures. The spade of the workman was busy upon the ramparts.

* Shums-ood-deen Khan of Herat was a Populzye nobleman of very good family, and in great favour with Shah Kamran before the commencement of the siege of Herat. His sister was the Shah's favourite wife, and he was entirely in his Majesty's confidence. A position of so much power, however, made Yar Mahomed his enemy, and it was to escape the minister's persecution that he deserted to the Persian camp on the approach of the invading army. Had he remained in the city, he would certainly have been imprisoned or assassinated, for the Shah was powerless to protect him. It was surmised, indeed, that his Majesty counselled, or at any rate connived at, his flight, as his only means of escape.

Eager for the foray, the trooper mounted his horse and scoured the country to cut off stragglers. But still the Persian army moved forward in that compact and well-ordered mass which had baffled the efforts and kindled the indignation of marauders along their whole line of march. Soon the contest actually commenced. On the 22nd of November, the advanced guard of the Persian army took up its position on the plain to the north-west of the city. Watching its opportunity, the Afghan horse charged the enemy's cavalry with success, and then fell upon an infantry regiment, which stood firm, and repulsed the attack. The Persian field artillery opened briskly upon the Afghan force. A couple of guns in the city replied to them; whilst a party of Afghan horsemen, dismounted, crept under cover, and with their long rifle-barrelled matchlocks, fired on the Persian gunners. Upon this, skirmishers were sent out by the Persians, who turned the flank of the Afghans, and forced them back to the position which they had taken up before. No advantage was gained by either party. But the contest was now fairly commenced.

The following day witnessed the opening of the siege of Herat—one, whether we regard the protracted nature of the operations, the vigour of the resistance, the gallantry of the chief actors concerned in it, or the magnitude of the political results, of the most remarkable in modern history. It was on the 23rd of November that the siege actually commenced. Taking possession of all the gardens and enclosures to the west of the city, and establishing themselves in considerable force among a cluster of ruins that afforded them good shelter, the Persians began to make their preparations for the attack. The garrison sallied out as they advanced. The Afghan infantry disputed every inch of ground, and the cavalry hung on the flanks of the Persian army. But they could not dislodge the enemy from the position they had taken up; and after carrying off a few prisoners, were compelled at last to retire.

From the events, however, of that day, two significant facts were to be deduced. The Persians had tried their artillery upon the walls of Herat in answer to the guns which the garrison had fired in support of their skirmishers; and the rotten parapets had fallen like tinder even to the light shot that was poured upon them. It was plain that little reliance was to be placed upon the strength of the defences. It was plain, too, that the war thus commenced would be carried on in a spirit of unsparing hatred and savage inhumanity — that what was wanting, on either side, in science or in courage, would be made up for in cruelty and vindictiveness. The Afghan skirmishers that evening brought in some prisoners and some heads. The latter were paraded about the ramparts.* The former bartered for horses with the Toorkomans, and sent off to the slave-markets of Merve.

* Of this barbarous custom of bringing in the heads of the enemy, Pottinger speaks with becoming indignation. "I have not thought it necessary," he writes in his journal, "to recount the number of heads that were brought in daily, nor indeed do I know. I never could speak of this barbarous, disgusting, and inhuman conduct with any temper. The number, however, in these sorties was always insignificant, and the collecting them invariably broke the vigour of the pursuit, and prevented the destruction of the trenches. There is no doubt great terror was inspired by the mutilation of the bodies amongst their comrades. But there must have been, at least, equal indignation—and that a corresponding exaltation was felt by the victors at the sight of these barbarous trophies, and the spoils brought in."—[*MS. Journal.*]
As rewards were always given for these bloody trophies, the garrison were naturally very active in their endeavours to obtain them. Sometimes their avarice outstripped both their honesty and their nationality. On one occasion, after an unsuccessful sortie, an Afghan brought in a pair of ears. A cloak and some ducats were given him as a reward for his butchery. Before any questions could be put to the fellow, he

The siege was soon in full operation. Whilst the Heratees were busily at work strengthening their defences, the Persians were entrenching themselves, throwing up their batteries, planting their guns, and trying their effect upon the walls of the city. After a day or two, guns, mortars, and rocket batteries were all in full play upon Herat. The rockets ranged too widely to work any serious mischief to the besieged; but their grand fiery flight as they passed over the city struck terror into the hearts of the people, who clustered upon the roofs of the houses, praying and crying by turns. "The uproar and confusion inside was tremendous, whilst not a sound was heard from the ramparts which a few nights before had been shaken by clamour."* The defenders of the city had too much serious occupation on hand to expend themselves in much noise. It was no easy thing to repair the defences which were crumbling to pieces under the fire of the Persian batteries. Silently, but resolutely, they set about their work, repairing the mischief as it arose, and giving a new character of defence to the battered fortifications.†

suddenly vanished. About half an hour afterwards, another man, covered with mud, made his appearance with a head in his hand. The Wuzeer, thinking it looked as though it had no ears, ordered one of his retainers to examine it. On this the bearer of the ghastly trophy threw it down, and ran away with all the speed he could command. The head was picked up by one of the Wuzeer's retainers, and found to be that of a comrade, who had fallen during a sortie of the preceding night. The fellow was pursued, and soundly beaten and kicked—but the more successful bringer-in of the ears was not to be found, though several rough unscrupulous fellows were told by the Wuzeer that they might possess themselves of both cloak and ducats if they could.

* *MS. Journal of Eldred Pottinger.*

† "The enemy's fire being directed to the parapet at all points, the rubbish began to shelter the foot of the escarp. Strong working parties commenced building up backs to the rampart at the point fired

Day after day, with little change of circumstance and little gain to either party, the siege continued throughout the months of November and December. At the end of the former, Pottinger wrote in his journal, "The Persians have wasted some thousand rounds of ammunition, and are not more advanced than when the firing commenced." The dreaded artillery of Mahomed Shah was less formidable in reality than in the excited imaginations of the Heratees, and the besieged gathered new courage from the success of their resistance. The fire from the Persian batteries was irregular and spasmodic; sometimes maintained with exceeding spirit, and at others languid and uncertain. The round shot from the guns went over the batteries, often clearing the entire city, but sometimes falling within it. The vertical firing from the mortars told with better effect. The shells* were thrown less at random, and many houses were destroyed. The loss of life was not great in the city; but those domestic episodes of war, which give so painful an interest to the annals of an attack upon a fortified town, were not absent from the siege of Herat. In the next house to that in which Eldred Pottinger resided, a shell descended close to the spot on which an infant was sleeping. The terrified mother rushed between the deadly missile and her child. The shell exploding carried off her head, and the corpse of the mother fell upon the babe, and suffocated it.

In the mean while, with a vigour and a constancy worthy of any garrison, in ancient or in modern times,

at, so that the body of the old rampart may become a parapet, and the summit of the new back a terre-pleine from which to defend the breaches when formed."—[*MS Journal of Eldred Pottinger*]

* "A great number of these shells are carved out of slate-rock, and their chamber contains little more than a bursting charge Hence they are unable to do much execution."—[*MS. Journal of Eldred Pottinger.*]

the besieged continued to conduct their defensive operations. Three of the five gates of the city were kept open, and the communications with the surrounding country were preserved. The cattle were sent out to graze. Firewood and other commodities were brought into the city. Every night the garrison sallied out, attacked the working parties, carried off their tools, often destroyed their entrenchments, wounded and sometimes killed the workmen, and carried their bleeding heads, with barbarous triumph, into the city.

Whilst the activity of the garrison thus sensibly increased, that of the besiegers was plainly declining. Throughout the month of December little progress was made. The fire of the Persian batteries slackened—sometimes altogether ceased. When it was most lively, it was wild and eccentric—so slovenly, indeed, as to warrant the belief that every gun was pointed in a different direction, and every gunner firing at some particular mark of his own. At last, on Christmas Day, when the siege had been continued for more than a month, Eldred Pottinger wrote in his journal, "I could not help recollecting the three shots a day which the Spanish army before Gibraltar fired for some time, and which the garrison called after the Trinity."

The following day was one of barbarous retaliation. All the Persian prisoners in Herat were sent off for sale to Kurookh. There were Afghan prisoners, at this time, in the Persian camp; and Mahomed Shah had no refined Christian notions on the score of returning good for evil. He ripped up the bellies, or destroyed after some cruel fashion, all the prisoners who fell into his hands. After this, in spite of the heavy rains that fell during the two succeeding days, there were some demonstrations of increased vigour in the conduct of the siege. A mine was sprung, and a practicable breach effected; but the storming party was driven back with considerable loss. Hadjee Khan, who commanded the party, was severely wounded, and one Mahomed Sheriff, a deserter from Herat, and a soldier of very formidable reputation, was killed in the breach. So much was this man dreaded, and such throughout the city was the opinion of his prowess, that when intelligence of his death was conveyed to Kamran, the Shah exclaimed, with eager delight, " Mahomed Shah, I am well satisfied, will never take Herat *now*."

The 30th of December was the great day of the festival of the Eyd-i-Ramzan. On this day the long Mahomedan fast terminates ; and it is ordinarily one of feasting and rejoicing. Even now, with becoming festivity, was it observed both by besiegers and besieged. On either side there was a tacit suspension of hostilities Accompanied by the royal family, Shah Kamran went in procession to the Juma Musjid, or great mosque ,* and, after offering up the accustomed prayers, distributed sweetmeats among the Moollahs. The holy men scrambled for the delicacies with surprising activity ; but they were deprived of their accustomed banquet of more substantial food. The liberality of his Majesty, on this occasion, flowed in a different channel. It was not a time in which to distribute valuable provender among such unserviceable people as priests, nobles, and courtiers The customary entertainment to these worthies gave place, therefore, to a distribution of all the disposable provisions to the fighting men and operatives on the works.

The new year opened with some increase of activity on the part of the besiegers Their mining operations alarmed the garrison , and vigorous efforts were made by a corresponding activity in the works, to frustrate the designs of the assailants All true Mahomedans were called upon,

* "They made," says Pottinger, " but a beggarly appearance."

by proclamation, to aid in the defence of the city, as the danger was very pressing. The assistance of the Moollahs was called in to organise working parties from among the people; and the houses of the Sheeahs and all suspected persons were again searched for arms. In the midst of these preparations, an emissary from the Persian camp made his appearance in the trenches opposite to the south-west bastion, and demanded to speak with the Wuzeer. This was the brother of Yar Mahomed, Shere Mahomed Khan, who had delivered up Ghorian to the Persians. The Wuzeer refused to see him; but the Sirdar implored the soldiers at the post to tell his brother that if Herat were not surrendered to Mahomed Shah, the Persian monarch would put him to death, storm the city, hang Yar Mahomed like a dog, and give his women and children to be publicly dishonoured by the muleteers.

The Afghans replied with a volley of abuse, cursing the Sirdar and the Persians; but the message was delivered to the Wuzeer. It found the minister in no very gentle mood. The mention of his brother's name exasperated him beyond control. "Tell the Sirdar," he said, "I am glad that Mahomed Shah intends to save me the trouble of putting the traitor to death. He is no brother of mine. I disown him. He is not my father's son. He is not an Afghan, but a Cashmerian, after his mother. As for myself, when Mahomed Shah takes the city, he is at liberty to do with me what he likes. In all other respects, I am his Majesty's most obedient servant; but I cannot obey him in this matter, for the Afghans will not hear of surrender." * And with this message

* The Wuzeer was too crafty a man to do anything to exasperate the Shah of Persia whilst there was the least prospect of his success. Pottinger's opinion on the subject is worth quoting:—"The minister throughout all the negotiations constantly addressed Mahomed Shah as his sovereign, and called both Hadjee Akasy (the Persian prime minis-

Shere Mahomed returned, crest-fallen, to the Persian camp.*

ter) and Alayar Khan (Asoof-ood-dowlah) his father. He also invariably threw the blame of the defence on some one else, and regretted being obliged to fight. He constantly talked of his being bound in honour to serve his master, Kamran, but in inclination to serve Mahomed Shah. He also invariably avoided mixing himself up individually in any act decidedly hostile to Persian feelings or prejudices; allowing some of his friends to act, and then, under (to the Persians) a show of inquiry, sharing the advantages; so that in reality very few tangible instances could be mentioned of his hostility, and none but what, as a good talker, he could easily assert were not so; and that he had taken the Persian side. He knew that the King was aware that all the chiefs of the Persian army supported themselves by the same means as he did; and in many instances without adding the lip-loyalty which he always gave vent to—that, moreover, he could say that he did not oppress the Persian people—that it was the other chiefs who did so—that without aid, he could not check it in his equals, who would otherwise join to overthrow him—that the *aylayats* (wandering tribes) always acted so—that he would not desert the cause of his patron and benefactor. In a despot, who only looks in his followers for personal attachment, and prefers the hardiest and most unscrupulous, less than this would have secured favour; nay, more, among chiefs who support themselves in the same way, such arguments would have secured popularity; and as parties also ran high in the Persian camp, and he had secured the favour of the two chiefs, both sides would have been anxious to secure so knowing and powerful an assistant by exertions in procuring his liberty. Yar Mahomed, with that shrewdness which characterises the Afghan nation, saw the favourable position he was in, and availed himself of it to the utmost. He had an overweening idea of the valour of his countrymen in arms, and a corresponding low one of that of the Persians. From having failed in a siege with his own people, he thought no other army could succeed against his nation, and in the event of being taken, his eyes, overlooking the danger to which the Persian wrath might expose him, were dazzled with visions of the wealth, the power, and glory he might acquire in

---

* On the 10th of January, "money being wanted, the houses of the Persian followers of Shere Mahomed were confiscated on a charge of treason, in giving up Ghorian."—[*Pottinger's Journal: MS.*]

The siege operations were continued; but with little access of vigour. The Persians were conducting no less than five several attacks on different points of the fortifications. The work was not carried forward in a manner that would have gladdened the heart of the commanding officer of a corps of English sappers; but the real nature of the enemy's movements was so little understood, that the garrison often exaggerated the danger, and gave the Persians credit for stratagems that had never entered their minds. One example of this will suffice. From beneath the rampart opposite the attack, conducted by General Samson and the Russian regiment, a mysterious noise, as of mining, was heard to proceed. It was audible to very few, and then only from a particular point; but abundant confirmation of the worst apprehensions of the garrison was derived from the fact that there was a working party in constant activity, throwing out black mud from the trench in the neighbourhood of the spot whence the mysterious sounds were heard to issue. The greatest alarm was occasioned by this intelligence; and the Heratees began at once to take counsel as to the best means of counteracting the stratagems of the besiegers.

In this crisis, the advice of Eldred Pottinger was sought by the garrison. His activity was unfailing; he was always on the ramparts; always ready to assist with his

the service of what he thought a rich and ill-managed government. I do not mean to say that any persons had recommended this plan to Yar Mahomed, or that it had been [*obscure in MS.*]; but that from the multitude of his counsellors, some recommending war, some submission, this must have been the mean opinion; and, added to the knowledge that, whether he defended himself or not, his life was in the same danger, and that the promise of a Kajar was only to be trusted as a last resource. He, therefore, addressed himself to the task of defence; but, at the same time, took steps to secure his interest in case of a reverse. I do not think that he could have succeeded in the latter point but he, doubtless, had hopes of succeeding."—[*MS. Journal.*]

counsel—the counsel of an educated English officer—the ruder science of the responsible conductors of the defence, and to inspire with his animating presence new heart into the Afghan soldiery. They asked him now if it were possible to mine below the ditch His answer was in the affirmative; but he represented at the same time how much more feasible it was to fill up the ditch and sap across it. "The fear of stratagem, however," he says, "was predominant; and they took stronger measures to counteract the supposed danger, and went to greater trouble about it than they did with actions of vital importance to their preservation. I recommended that a gallery of envelope under the lower *fausse-braie* should be completed, and in it a few shafts sunk a little below the floor of the gallery. This did not satisfy them; so they sunk shafts on both sides of the wall and connected them by galleries; and dug a ditch inside the city, at the foot of the mound, till the water stood several feet deep in it." The sequel of all this is sufficiently diverting. It was not until some months afterwards, when these extensive and laborious works were nearly completed, that it was discovered that the mysterious noise, which had struck so great a terror into the hearts of the garrison, arose from nothing more formidable than "a poor woman, who was in the habit of using a hand-mill to grind her wheat, in an excavation at the back of the mound."*

On the 18th of January, Yar Mahomed besought Eldred Pottinger to proceed as an envoy, on the part of the

---

* "The digging a gallery," writes Pottinger, "under the wall, and entering in the midst of the town, appeared a most capital plan, and suited much better their cunning than any other. Consequently, they were seriously alarmed, and for a time serious consequences resulted to the Sheeah inhabitants; and many domiciliary visits were paid in search of the gallery, whilst the ruins and empty houses were particularly patrolled for many nights."—[*MS. Journal.*]

Afghans, to the Persian camp. The young English officer readily assented to the proposal; and it was arranged that on the morrow he should have an audience of Shah Kamran, and receive instructions for the conduct of his mission. Accordingly, on the following day, he was conducted to the residence of the Shah. As he went along, he observed with pain, in the interior of the city, the desolating effects of the siege. "Scarcely a shop had escaped destruction. The shutters, seats, shelves—nay, even the very beams and door-posts—had in general been torn out for firewood. Scarcely any business was going on. Here and there were gathered knots of the pale and anxious citizens, whispering their condolences and grievances—anxious that they might escape the notice of the rude Afghans, who were swaggering about the streets."*

The room in which the Shah received the English officer was a dreary, comfortless place. "I have seen nothing I can compare to it," wrote Pottinger, "but an empty store-room carpeted." Plainly, but richly attired, attended only by his eunuchs, the Shah welcomed the young Englishman. But he appeared ill at ease—unhappy about himself—peevish, and lost in thought; for he was sick. It was plain, indeed, that he was more concerned about his health than about the safety of the city. Sending for his chief physician, he consulted him about the royal symptoms, and in the intervals of this interesting personal conversation, coughed out, with considerable energy and warmth, his instructions to the British officer. His cough, indeed,

* *Eldred Pottinger's MS. Journal.* "No matter," he adds, "how the cowardice and meanness of these men might be despised, no one could help pitying the wretchedness they were suffering. Even the better class of the Afghans used to say, 'Afsoos ast, lekin chi koonym'—'It is a pity, but what can we do?' In the Pay Hissar (esplanade in front of the drawbridge) were lying half a dozen Persian heads lately brought in."

in all probability, saved him from something more serious. For when he had worked himself into a passion, it compelled him to pause, and whilst he was applying himself to the restoratives at hand, he cooled down till the next paroxysm of rage and coughing brought him to a full stop.

The interview was long and tedious. Much was said in a very wordy language by the Shah, about his own merits and his own wrongs, and the ingratitude and injustice of his enemies. Then Pottinger received his instructions regarding the message which he was to deliver in the Persian camp. It commenced with a string of reproaches, and ended in a strain of mingled invective and entreaty.

"How generous!" ran the message, after much more in the same style. "You look round to see who your neighbours are. I am your weakest one. You, therefore, assemble all your force to rob me of my last of eighty cities. You answer my supplication for aid by the roar of your cannon and bombs. Raise the siege; retire and give me the troops and guns I want to recover my kingdom; and I will give you Herat on my return. Send the Afghan traitors out of your camp. If you persist in your present purpose, future ages will call you a robber, who preyed upon the aged and helpless. If you do not act generously, God is great; and on him we rely. We have still got our swords."

Such was the pith of the message which Pottinger was commissioned to deliver to the Shah of Persia. It came out by snatches, in an excited spasmodic manner; but was understood by the British officer. Having heard all that was to be said, he took his departure, and joined the Wuzeer upon the works. But, for some time, the projected negotiations never advanced beyond the threshold. It occurred to Shah Kamran that it would be well to strike a blow, and to achieve some demonstrable success, before despatching an emissary to the Persian camp, lest the overtures should be attributed to conscious weakness, and rather increase than lower the pretensions of the Shah.

An attempt was soon made to strike an important blow, but it was singularly unsuccessful. On the 21st of January, the Afghans determined to make a night attack, in considerable force, upon the camp of Sirdar Mahomed Khan at Karta. Nearly the whole garrison turned out, and was reviewed by the Wuzeer. The King himself, looking out from a tower of the citadel, surveyed in secret the gathering below, as Yar Mahomed, on the *terre-pleine* of the rampart, surrounded by all the principal chiefs not absolutely on duty elsewhere, mustered the fighting men on the lower part of the works. Twelve hundred men were selected for the sortie, and told off in detachments, under the command of different chiefs. Divesting themselves of whatever could, in any way, encumber their movements—of everything, indeed, but their shirts, drawers, skull-caps, and swords—they filed out of the Kootoobchak gate, the chief of each party naming his men, one by one, as they crossed the drawbridge. Futteh Mahomed Khan, to whom the command of the entire party had been entrusted, followed last, upon foot. But of all these great preparations nothing came at last. "The business failed; no attack was made; and every one was blamed by his neighbour."*

This lamentable failure determined the Shah to postpone Pottinger's departure for the Persian camp. To commence negotiations immediately after a miscarriage of so formidable a nature, would have been a confession of weakness, very impolitic in such a conjuncture. The King, therefore, imperatively arrested the movements of the young English ambassador, whilst the Wuzeer began

* *MS. Journal of Eldred Pottinger.*

to bethink himself of the best means of removing the impediment which loomed so largely before the eyes of the King. Accordingly it was determined that, on the 26th of January, both the cavalry and the infantry should be sent out to draw the Persians into action. It was a fine, bright morning. The whole city was in an unusual state of excitement. Partly impelled by curiosity, partly moved by a more laudable ambition to fill the places of those whose services were required beyond the walls, the citizens flocked to the ramparts. Along the whole eastern face of the fortifications the parapets and towers were alive with men. "The old Afghans and relatives of the military," writes Pottinger, "in like manner crowded the *fausse-braies*. I do not think that less than 7000 men were assembled on one side in view of the enemy." The scene on which they looked down, was a most exciting one. It stirred the hearts of that eager multitude as the heart of one man. The Afghan cavalry, on issuing from the city, had spread themselves over the open country to the east, and the foot-men had taken possession of a neighbouring village and its surrounding gardens. The Persian videttes had fallen back ; the trenches and batteries had been manned; and the reserves had stood to their arms, when, looking down from the ramparts, the excited Heratees saw the Persian Sirdar, Mahomed Khan, with a large body of troops, prepare himself for an offensive movement, and push onward to the attack. At the head of the column were the Persian cavalry. As soon as they appeared in sight, the Afghan horse streamed across the plain, and poured themselves full upon the enemy.

The charge of the Afghans was a gallant and a successful one. Whilst the ramparts of Herat rang with the excited acclamation of "*Shabásh ! Shabásh ! Chi Roostumány !*" ("Bravo ! Bravo ! conduct worthy of Roostum himself !") the Persian column gave way before its impetuous assailants, and retreated amongst the buildings from which it had debouched. For a short time the progress of the struggle was lost sight of by the gazers on the ramparts; but the sharp, quick rattle of the musketry, the loud booming of the guns, and the columns of dust that rose against the clear sky, told that the infantry and artillery had covered the retreat of the Persian horsemen. The tide of victory now turned against the Afghan force. The Heratees, who before had driven back the Persian cavalry, were now in turn driven back by the enemy. The squadrons in the rear, instead of closing up, wheeled about, and the whole column was soon in flight. Recovering themselves, however, for a short time, the struggle was briefly renewed on the plain; but the Persian horse being well supported by the infantry planted in the gardens on both sides, whilst the rear of the Afghan cavalry afforded no support to the troops in front, the flight of the Heratees was renewed, and a gun was brought to bear upon their retreating columns. With varying success the battle was continued throughout the day. Towards evening the Afghans regained the advantage which they had lost at an earlier period of the engagement; and as the shades of evening fell over the scene, the Persians evacuated the posts they had occupied, and the Afghans were left in possession of the field.

The engagement, though a long, was not a sanguinary one. The loss on the side of the Afghans was not estimated at more than twenty-five or thirty killed. The Heratees, of course, claimed the victory; but the Sheeah inhabitants, who had made their way to the walls of the city, and were among the spectators of the fight, could not repress their inclination to sneer at a success of so dubious a character.* To the young English officer who had

* Contending emotions of sympathy, now with their co-religionists,

watched the events of the day, it was very clear that neither army was of a very formidable character. The Afghan cavalry made a better show than that of the enemy, but in the infantry branch the advantage was greatly on the side of the Persians. The whole affair was nothing better than a series of skirmishes, now resulting in favour of one party, now of the other. But the crafty Wuzeer boasted of it as a great triumph; and on the following morning went round to all those parts of the works from which the scene below could not be observed, rendering a highly embellished account of the events of that memorable day. "Though so changed," says Pottinger, "that scarcely any one could recognise it, those who had been present in the fight, finding themselves such heroes, commenced swelling and vapouring. The soldiery gathered round in the greatest excitement, and their opinion of their own superiority to the Persians was greatly increased. Many of them would say, "If we had but guns!" Others, evidently disliking the Persian cannon, would improve on this, and say, "Ah! if the infidels had no guns, we would soon send them away."

On the 8th of February, Pottinger received permission to visit the Persian camp. In the public baths of the city, where Yar Mahomed, with other men of note, in a state of almost entire nudity, was sitting at breakfast on the floor—his officers and servants standing around

and now with their fellow-citizens, agitated the breasts of the Heratees "I went," writes Pottinger, on the 2nd of February, "to see a Sheeah he was grieving over the fate which hung over him; one moment cursing Mahomed Shah's pusillanimity—the next, the Afghan tyranny. But through the whole of his discontent, I observed he felt a sort of pride and satisfaction in being the countryman of those who set the Persians at defiance. But he appeared fully impressed with the idea that the city must fall, whilst the Afghans I had just left were talking of plundering Teheran with the aid of our artillery and infantry."— [*MS Records*]

him armed to the teeth—the English officer took leave of the Wuzeer. "Tell Hadjee Meerza Aghassi" (the Persian minister), said Yar Mahomed, "that ever since he has honoured me with the title of son, and the Hadjee has assumed that of my father, I have been most desirous of showing him filial affection, and have endeavoured to do so. But the Hadjee, in a most unpaternal manner, has brought the Shah-in-Shah with an army to besiege Herat; and I am bound, by the salt I am eating, to stand by my old master. If, however, they will return to Persia, I will follow and show my obedience as the son of the Hadjee and the servant of the Shah-in-Shah. Further, tell him, that whatever may be my own wish, the Afghans would never surrender the city, nor dare I propose it to them. And you may tell him, too, that we have all heard of the bad treatment received by the Afghans who have joined the camp of Mahomed Shah, and are thereby deterred from joining his Persian Majesty."

Carrying this message with him, Pottinger left the city, accompanied by a small party of Afghans. They attended him some distance beyond the walls; and then shouting out their good wishes, left him to pursue his journey. A single attendant, Syud Ahmed, and a cossid went with him. Pushing on through narrow, tortuous lanes, bounded by high mud walls, and every moment expecting to be saluted by a bullet from some zealous sentinel posted on his line of road, the young English officer pushed on towards the Persian camp. "I kept a good look-out," he wrote in his journal; "and fortunately I did so, as, through one of the gaps in the wall, I observed the Persians running to occupy the road we were following. I therefore stopped and made Syud Ahmed wave his turban, for want of a better flag of truce. The Persians, on this, came towards us in a most irregular manner—so much so that, if twenty horsemen had been with me, the whole Persian picket might have been cut off. Some were loading as they ran; and one valiant hero, who came up in the rear after he had ascertained who we were, to prevent danger, I suppose, loaded his musket and fixed his bayonet. They were a most ragged-looking set, and, from their dress and want of beard, looked inferior to the Afghans. They were delighted at my coming; and the English appeared great favourites among them. A fancy got abroad that I was come with proposals to surrender, which made the great majority lose all command over themselves, at the prospect of revisiting their country so soon. They crowded round; some patting my legs, and others my horse, whilst those who were not successful in getting near enough, contented themselves with Syud Ahmed and the cossid—the whole, however, shouting, "Afreen! Afreen! Khoosh amedeed! Anglish hameshah dostan-i Shah-in-Shah." ("Bravo! Bravo! Welcome! The English were always friends of the King-of-Kings.")*

The officer who commanded the picket, a major in the Persian army who had served under Major Hart, who knew all the English officers recently connected with the Persian Court or the Persian army, and who had, moreover, been the custodian of Yar Mahomed when the Wuzeer was a prisoner at Meshid, conducted Pottinger to the guard-room Apologising, on the plea of military necessity, for any interference with his free progress, he stated that discipline required that the emissary should be taken to the Major-General commanding the attack. It happened that General Samson,† of the Russian regiment, was the officer in command. The way to the General's quarters was "through gardens and vineyards,

* *Eldred Pottinger's MS. Journal*

† Samson was a Russian in the Persian service, commanding a corps of Russian refugees.

in which not even the roots of the trees and shrubs were left." The General received the British officer with much courtesy, conceiving him at first to be an Afghan; and was greatly surprised to find that he was in the presence of an European soldier. Sending for tea and kalyans (pipes), he regaled his guest with becoming courtesy, and then sent him on in safety to the Persian camp.

Intelligence of Pottinger's arrival had preceded him, and the whole camp came out to meet the ambassador. None knew who or what he was. A report had gone forth that he was some great Afghan dignitary from Herat, who brought the submission of Kamran to the terms of Mahomed Shah. As he advanced, the torrent of people swelled and swelled, until in the main street of the camp the crowd was so dense that, if the escort had not plied their iron ramrods with good effect, it is doubtful whether the embassy would ever have reached the tent of the Persian Wuzeer. The quarters of the great man were gained at last, and the envoy was graciously received. The interview was a brief one. Readily obtaining permission to visit the tent of Colonel Stoddart, and to deliver the letters of which he was the bearer from the Government of India, the question of admission to the presence of Mahomed Shah was left to be decided by the monarch himself. It is easy to imagine the delight of the two English officers on finding themselves, in so strange a place and under such strange circumstances, in the presence of one another.* It was cruel to interrupt such a meeting;

* "I then proceeded to Colonel Stoddart's tent, whom I found in the greatest astonishment possible, as his servants, taking up the general report of my rank, had announced me as the Mooshtehid of Herat. He had been undressed; and putting on his coat to do honour to the high dignitary, gave me time to enter his tent before he could get out, so we met at the door, where he overwhelmed me with a most affectionate Persian welcome, to which I, to his great surprise, replied in English.

but before Stoddart and Pottinger had exchanged many words, and partaken of a cup of coffee in the former's tent, a peremptory message came from the minister to summon the latter to his presence. The two officers went together to Hadjee Meerza Aghassi's tent, where the Wuzeer, after the usual courtesies, asked what was the message brought by Pottinger from " Prince" Kamran to the King-of-Kings, and what was that which Yar Mahomed had sent to himself. " I replied," says Pottinger, "that the message from the Afghan *King* was to the Persian King, and that I could not deliver it to any one else ; that regarding his own message, probably a smaller number of auditors would be desirable." The tent accordingly was cleared ; and the Hadjee, a small, thin man apparently in a very bilious and excitable state, twisted himself into all kinds of undignified contortions, and prepared himself to receive the message of the Afghan Wuzeer.

Pottinger delivered his message. A long, animated, but profitless discussion then arose. The Hadjee refused to listen to the Afghan proposals, and declared that the English had themselves set down Herat on their maps as a part of the Persian dominions. In proof of the assertion, Burnes's map was produced, and, to his inexpressible chagrin, the Hadjee was shown to be wrong. Colonel Stoddart was then appealed to ; but his answers were shaped in true diplomatic fashion. He had no instructions on the subject—he would refer the case to the envoy at Teheran—he was not aware that the British Government had ever received official information from the Persian Government, of Herat being annexed to that state, whilst a branch of the Suddozye family, which the

No one who has not experienced it, can understand the pleasure which countrymen enjoy when they thus meet—particularly when of the same profession, and pursuing the same object."—[*Eldred Pottinger's MS. Journal.*]

British Government, in conjunction with Futteh Ali Shah, had acknowledged as sovereign in Afghanistan, still held possession of the place. The difficulty was not to be solved; and the English officers took their departure from the tent of the Wuzeer, to be summoned shortly to the presence of the Shah.

Under a tent, surrounded on all sides by an outer wall of red canvas, Mahomed Shah, plainly attired in a shawl vest, with a black Persian cap on his head, received with becoming courtesy the British officers. At the opposite end of the tent, in posture of profound reverence, heads bent, and arms folded, stood the personal attendants of the King. The message of Shah Kamran was delivered; and the Persian monarch, speaking at first with much dignity and calmness, stated in a clear and forcible manner, his complaints against Herat and its ruler. But, warming as he proceeded, he lashed himself into a passion; denounced Shah Kamran as a treacherous liar; and declared that he would not rest satisfied until he had planted a Persian garrison in the citadel of Herat. There was nothing more to be said upon the subject; and the British officers were formally dismissed.

A violent storm, which broke over Herat on the following day, prevented Pottinger's return to the city. But on the 10th of February, he turned his back upon the Persian camp. "I mounted," he writes, "and riding out by the flank of the Persian line, I returned to the city by the gate I come out at; and so avoided the points where hostilities were going on. On my coming back the whole town was in a ferment. What they had expected I do not pretend to know; but from the instant I entered the gate, I was surrounded by messengers requesting information. I, however, referred them all to the Wuzeer, and went there myself. After a short interview, I was summoned by a messenger from the

Shah. His Majesty having seen my return with his glass, was awaiting my arrival, anxious to hear Mahomed Shah's message. When he had heard it, he replied by a gasconading speech, abusing every one." And so terminated these first negotiations for a suspension of hostilities, in an utter and mortifying failure.

With little variation from the procedure of the two previous months, the siege operations were continued. The Persians had expected much from the addition to their siege train of an immense sixty-eight pounder, which was to batter down the defences of Herat as easily as though they had been walls of glass.* But the gun was so badly mounted that, after the fifth or sixth round, the light carriage gave way, and this formidable new enemy, that was to have done such great things, sank into an useless incumbrance.

The siege continued without intermission; but it was evident that both parties were anxious to conclude a peace. Not many days after Pottinger's return to Herat, a Persian officer† came into the city with instructions from General Samson, privately endorsed by the Wuzeer, to endeavour to persuade the Afghans to consent to the terms offered by Mahomed Shah. It was better, he said, for them to settle their differences among themselves, than to employ the mediation of infidels.‡ At the same time, he assured the Afghans that Mahomed Shah had no desire to interfere in the internal administration of Herat.

* They fired from this piece eight-inch shells full of lead, or twelve or eighteen-pound shot, with an outer case of copper. These were of so much value, that the garrison fought for them.

† The same man, a major in the army, whom Pottinger had first met in the Persian camp.

‡ "The man," says Pottinger, "was also instructed to say that warning should be taken from our conduct in India, where we had pretended friendship and trade to cover our ambition, and finally, by such deceit, had mastered all India."—[*MS. Journal.*]

What he required them to do was, to supply his army with soldiers, as they had, in times past, supplied the armies of Nadir Shah. The present movement, he said, was not an expedition against Herat, but an expedition against Hindostan, and that it behoved, therefore, all true Mahomedans to join the army of the King-of-Kings. Let them only unite themselves under the banner of the great defender of the faith, and he would lead them to the conquest and the plunder of India and Toorkistan.

The Persian emissary returned, on the following day, bearing promises of a vague and delusive kind, and suggestions that, if the Persians were really inclined for peace, the best proof they could give of the sincerity of their inclinations would be the retirement of the besieging force. Great was the excitement after his departure, and various the views taken of his mission. By some, the young and thoughtless, it was conjectured that his visit betokened a consciousness of weakness on the part of the enemy; and they already began to picture to themselves the flight and plunder of the Persian army. But the elder and more sensible shook their heads, and began, with manifest anxiety, to canvass the Persian terms. It mattered little, they said, whether Kamran were designated Prince or King—whether the supremacy of the Persian Shah were, or were not, acknowledged in Herat, so long as they did not endeavour to plant a Persian garrison in the city. But the Wuzeer declared that he had no confidence in the Persians—that he desired to be guided by the advice, and to be aided by the mediation of the English; and that if the Shah would place the conduct of negotiations in the hands of Colonel Stoddart, he on his part would trust everything to Lieutenant Pottinger, and agree to whatever was decided upon by the two English officers. "This," wrote the latter, "was a most politic measure. It threw all the odium of continuing the war off the shoulders of the Afghan war party on those of the Persians, whom every one would blame, if they declined to trust their guest, Colonel Stoddart ; and it would tend to make the Afghans believe that nothing but their destruction would satisfy Mahomed Shah."

On the 20th of February, the Persian emissary again appeared with a letter from the camp of the besiegers. It stated that the Shah had no desire to possess himself of Herat ; he only claimed that his sovereignty should be acknowledged. The answer, sent back on the following day, was full of compliments and promises. Everything asked for would be done, if the Persian army would only retire. On the 24th, the negotiations were continued—but with no result. The siege, in the mean while, proceeded. The garrison continued their sallies and sorties—sent out foraging parties—carried off large quantities of wood—and generally contrived to return to the city without suffering any injury from the activity of the investing force.

On the part of the latter, as time advanced, the firing became more steady ; but the severity and uncertainty of the weather, and the scarcity of food, which was now beginning to be painfully felt, damped the energy of the besiegers. Continuing, however, to push on their approaches, they did at least mischief enough to keep the garrison in a constant state of activity. Some unimportant outworks were carried ; and on the 8th of March, to the great mortification of the Wuzeer, the enemy gained possession of a fortified post about 300 yards from the north-east angle of the fort. The Afghans who manned the post were found wanting in the hour of danger, and were visited with summary punishment for this cowardly offence. Their faces were daubed with mud, and they were sent round the works and through the streets of the city, accompanied by a crier, commissioned to proclaim their cowardice to the world.

From the moment that this post fell into the hands of the enemy, "the investment," says Pottinger, "began to be really felt." The operations of the besiegers were pushed forward with some vigour, but the constancy of the garrison was not to be shaken.* Towards the end of March, the Asoof-ood-dowlah, whose force had encamped on the plain to the north-west of the city, sent in a message to the Afghan minister, offering to be the medium of negotiations for the suspension of hostilities. The Afghans sent word back that they were prepared to listen to any reasonable overtures; but that if peace were to be made, it must be made quickly. Seed-time, it was said, was passing; and once passed, peace was impossible. Their subsistence would then depend upon their plunder. After a few days, an interview was arranged between Yar Mahomed and the Asoof-ood-dowlah, and on the 2nd of April it was held on the edge of the ditch opposite the north-east tower. But the Wuzeer returned, hopeless of any arrangement.† On the following day a grand meeting of chiefs was held; but there was an end of all thought of peace.

On the 6th of April, Mr. M'Neill, the British minister at the Persian Court, arrived in the camp of Mahomed Shah. He had left Teheran on the 10th of March;

* It would be tedious to narrate all the details of the siege, and difficult to render them intelligible, even to the scientific reader, without the aid of a series of elaborate plans.

† "The point," says Mr. M'Neill, "on which the negotiation broke off was, I believe, the demand of the Shah, that Shah Kamran and Yar Mahomed should wait upon him in his camp, and there make their submission to him. I learn that the Persians did not, as on a former occasion, require that a garrison of their troops should be admitted into the town."—[*Mr. M'Neill to Lord Auckland, April* 11, 1838. *Published Correspondence.*]

and, in spite of efforts made by the Persian ministers to arrest his progress at Ghorian, had pushed on with all possible rapidity to the Persian camp. It was urged that his presence could not fail to encourage the Heratees in their resistance. But the British minister pleaded his duty to his sovereign, and was not to be detained. He was coldly received in the Persian camp; but he demanded and obtained admittance to the Shah, and having exacted the customary formalities of reception, presented his credentials recently received from the Queen. The impression made upon the King, and subsequently upon the minister, was favourable to the British envoy, and soon his discreet and conciliatory bearing smoothed down the irritation which had been engendered by his advance. But the Russian minister, Count Simonich, was also on his way from Teheran; and Mr M'Neill felt that the approach of this man might be fatal to his success *

On the 13th of April, Mr M'Neill had an audience of the Persian monarch, in the course of which he stated that the proceedings of Persia in Afghanistan were an obvious violation of the treaty between Great Britain and the former state; and that the British Government would be justified, therefore, in declaring it to be at an end, and in taking active measures to compel the withdrawal of the Persian army from Herat. The audience lasted two hours. The Shah solemnly protested that he had never meditated anything injurious to the interests of Great Britain; and the minister, with still stronger emphasis, repeated the declaration. At a subsequent interview, the Shah consented to accept the mediation of the British mission; and on the 16th of April, the Persian soldiers proclaimed from the trenches that

* *Mr M'Neill to Lord Auckland, April* 11, 1838. *Papers relating to Persia and Afghanistan.*

Mahomed Shah had determined to send Shere Mahomed Khan into Herat, accompanied by the British minister. But it was not Mr. M'Neill, but an inferior officer of the embassy, who was about to present himself on the morrow, in the character of a mediator, beneath the walls of the beleagured city.

The 18th of April was one of the most memorable days of the siege. The Persian batteries opened before noon, with unwonted activity, against the ramparts behind the great mosque. The walls soon began to crumble beneath the heavy fire of the enemy. First the thin parapets fell; then the *terre-plein* came down; "the old walls sliding into masses at every round." * Before evening, on the eastern and northern sides, the breaches were practicable, and that on the west was greatly enlarged. But the Afghans were in no way disheartened. They saw their walls crumbling beneath the heavy fire of the Persian batteries, and were neither alarmed nor discouraged by the spectacle. They had never trusted, they said, to their walls. The real defence, they declared, was the *fausse-braie*. About noon the Persians, having pushed on a gallery at this point, the garrison exploded it with a mine, and taking advantage of the alarm occasioned by the explosion, the Afghans rushed upon the besiegers, and at first carried everything before them. But in a short time the trenches of the enemy were lined with musketeers. The small-arm fire of the Persians overwhelmed that of the garrison, whilst the breaching batteries resumed their fire against the wall. Yar Mahomed and Pottinger were both upon the works. The Wuzeer ordered the men to cease firing, and to sit down, that they might be sheltered from the storm of musket-balls; but instead of this they drew

* *Eldred Pottinger's MS. Journal.*

their swords, brandished them over their heads, and calling to the Persians to come on, rushed down to the attack. They paid dearly for this bravado.* Pottinger himself narrowly escaped a bullet, which entered the lungs of Aga Ruhem, a favourite and devoted eunuch of Yar Mahomed, and sent him to his grave.

In the evening, the Persians in the trenches announced that an Englishman in their camp sought admittance to the city. The announcement was received with peals of derisive laughter and abuse. The Englishman was Major Todd, an officer of the Bengal artillery, who had been for many years employed with the Persian army, and whose great attainments and estimable personal qualities had won for him the respect of all with whom he had been associated. When a note was conveyed to the Wuzeer stating that the officer who sought admit-

* "Several men," says Pottinger, "received bullets through the hands and arms. One fellow, more fool-hardy than the rest, kept brandishing his huge Afghan knife, after the others had complied with the repeated orders to sheath their weapons, and had the knife destroyed by a bullet, which struck it just above his hand. I had gone down to the spot to see the mine sprung, and was sitting on the banquette with the Wuzeer and a party of chiefs, who, whilst tea was preparing, were bantering the man whose knife was broken, and who came to beg a sword instead, when a bullet came in through a loophole over my head, and, smashing a brick used for stopping it, lodged in Aga Ruhem's lungs, who was standing opposite—one of the splinters of the brick at the same time wounding him in the face. The poor fellow was an eunuch of Yar Mahomed's, and was always to be seen wherever any danger was. He died in two or three days. I had been but the moment before looking through the top of the parapet, with my breast resting against the loophole, watching the Persians, who were trying to establish themselves in the crater of the mine, and the Afghans on the counterscarp, who were trying to grapple the gabions and overset them, so that the scene was very interesting; and I had not sat down with the chiefs until Deen Mahomed Khan actually pulled me down by my cloak to listen to the jokes passed on the man who had his knife destroyed; and I thus escaped Aga Ruhem's bullet."—[*MS. Journal.*]

tance was the *naib* of the English ambassador, Yar Mahomed sent for his young English ally. Pottinger immediately joined him. The Wuzeer and many other chiefs were sitting on the *fausse-braie* near the breach. Making room for him on the charpoy on which he was seated, Yar Mahomed laughingly remarked, "Don't be angry with me. I have thrown ashes on it (the offered mediation), and blackened its face myself." Pottinger asked for an explanation, and was told that the Wuzeer had sent back word to the Persian camp that the Afghans wanted neither the Turks, the Russians, nor the English to interfere—that they trusted to their good swords; that at that hour of the evening they would not allow the Shah-in-Shah himself to enter; and that no one should be allowed to enter at that point. But if, they added, the English naib would present himself on the morrow at the south-east angle, he would be granted admittance to the city. Much of this was mere bravado. Yar Mahomed acknowledged that he only wished to impress the Persians with the belief that he was careless about British mediation.*

On the following day, Major Todd made his appearance. A vast crowd went out to gaze at him. He was the first European who had ever appeared in Herat in full regimentals; and now the tight-fitting coat, the glittering epaulettes, and the cocked hat, all excited unbounded admiration. The narrow streets were crowded, and the house-tops were swarming with curious spectators. The bearer as he was of a message from Mahomed Shah, announcing that the Persian sovereign was willing to accept the mediation of the British Government, he was

* "I was much annoyed," says Pottinger, "and told him he had probably prevented the English ambassador interfering, and he excused himself by saying that he acted so to make the Persians think he was not solicitous for the English to interfere."—[*MS. Journal.*]

received with becoming courtesy by Shah Kamran, who, after the interview, took the cloak from his own shoulders, and sent it by the Wuzeer to Major Todd, as a mark of the highest distinction he could confer upon him.* The English officer returned to the Persian camp with assurances of Kamran's desire to accept the mediation of the British minister. But there was no suspension of hostilities. That evening the aspect of affairs was more warlike than ever. "The Persian trenches were filled with men. The parties of horse and guards of the line of investment appeared stronger than usual; and everything betokened an assault of which at dusk the garrison received intelligence. The Afghans made all arrangements to meet it; the different chiefs were sent off to different points either to strengthen the posts or form reserves. Yar Mahomed's post was at the gate of Mulik, as the breach close to it was the most dangerous,

* "A horse," says Pottinger, "was also given; but Major Todd was as anxious not to accept presents, as the Afghans were to make them—so he would not wait for the horse, notwithstanding they set about cutting away the parapet of the *fausse-braie*, and making a ramp up the counterscarp to get the nag out. The Wuzeer was obstinately bent upon sending out the horse; but as there was no use in destroying a parapet in the only entire work left, or making an easy road across the ditch, when there were four practicable breaches. * * * As soon as the Persians were gone, my people led the horses off in another direction, and I told the workmen to stop and repair the damage done, so that the Wuzeer did not know of the ruse till late in the afternoon, when his master of the horse reported the return of the horses. He immediately sent them to me, saying he had given them to the English and would not take them. I told him I had not enough of grain to keep them: and suggested that if he did not like to keep them, they might be eaten. The people present, on the receipt of the message, highly approved of the latter part, and Yar Mahomed gave to the most clamorous the horse intended for the Persian, which was duly roasted. I believe the other one underwent the same fate a few weeks subsequently."—[*MS. Journal.*]

and the point was defended by the worst troops." It was agreed among the different chiefs that not a shot should be fired until the enemy reached the counterscarp, on pain of the immediate loss of the delinquent's ears.

The assembly had scarcely broken up when intelligence arrived that the British minister, Mr. M'Neill, had arrived at the edge of the ditch and sought entrance to the city. The report was presently confirmed by a messenger who brought letters from the envoy to Yar Mahomed and Lieutenant Pottinger. Pottinger, who was just composing himself to sleep, started up and proceeded with all haste to the Wuzeer's post. Yar Mahomed mustered the chiefs to receive the Envoy with becoming respect, and conducted him to his quarters. The greater part of the night was spent in discussion. It was nearly dawn when M'Neill accompanied Pottinger to his residence, and they lay down to sleep.

Pottinger rose before seven o'clock, and found M'Neill engaged in writing. The Wuzeer, having been sent for by the former officer, soon made his appearance grumbling at, but still honestly commending the vigilance of the British minister,* whom he conducted to the presence of Shah Kamran. The Shah, with the utmost

* "I was a good deal surprised on awaking at half-past six to see the Envoy already up and busy writing. At seven, according to engagement, I sent to let the Wuzeer know that his Excellency was ready to receive him. Yar Mahomed was asleep when the message arrived; but they awoke him, and he joined us in a short time with a whole posse of chiefs. On my meeting him at the door he asked me was it customary for our ministers not to sleep at night, declaring that he had scarcely closed his eyes when he was told that Mr. M'Neill was waiting for him; and further remarked, "I do not wonder your affairs prosper when men of such high rank as your minister plenipotentiary work harder than an Afghan private soldier would do even under the eye of the Shah."—[*Eldred Pottinger's MS. Journal.*]

frankness and unreserve, placed the negotiations in the hands of Mr. M'Neill, and said that he would gladly consent to any terms agreed upon by that officer. After partaking of some refreshment, the British minister took his departure; and the armistice ceased.

This was on the 21st of April. On the 23rd, Major Todd was despatched from the Persian camp with intelligence no less surprising than discouraging. Mahomed Shah had resolutely refused to submit to British arbitration the disputes between the states of Persia and Herat. In an abrupt and peremptory manner he had "refused the proposed agreement and spoke of prosecuting the siege." "Either," he said, "the whole people of Herat shall make their submission, and acknowledge themselves my subjects, or I will take possession of the fortress by force of arms, and make them obedient and submissive."[*] The British minister was deeply mortified at the result. He had been, however unwittingly, a party to the deception of the Government of Herat. He had told Yar Mahomed that the Shah would accept his intervention and abide his decision; and now his overtures had been peremptorily declined.[†] It was suggested by some whether it would be expedient to send any reply to the hostile declaration of Mahomed Shah; but as it had been forwarded by the British minister, etiquette demanded that an answer should be returned.[‡] That answer was

[*] *Mr. M'Neill to Yar Mahomed—Published Correspondence.*

[†] Pottinger explained to Kamran the manner in which Mr. M'Neill had been deceived. "On the 24th," he says, "I had an audience of Shah Kamran to explain the manner in which the Persians had deceived the British Envoy. His Majesty said that he never expected anything else—that the Kajars have been noted for their want of faith ever since they have been heard of—that his father and himself had several times tried their promises, but always been miserably deceived."—[*MS. Journal.*]

[‡] *Pottinger's MS. Journal.*

grave and dignified. "If the Persians," wrote Yar Mahomed, "will not attend to your words, we must answer with our bodies and leave the result to God. Be not distressed. Now that we have suffered so many injuries, and have been kept back from our tillage and cultivation, and have suffered that loss which should not have befallen us, what have we now to care for?"*

And now the siege was prosecuted with increased activity. A new actor had appeared on the stage. On the morning of the day which witnessed Mr. M'Neill's visit to the city of Shah Kamran, Count Simonich appeared in camp. He was not one to remain even for a day a passive spectator of the contest. Freely giving advice and rendering assistance, he soon began, in effect, to conduct the operations of the siege; whilst the officers of his suite were teaching the Persian soldiers how to construct more effective batteries. Nor was Russian skill all that was supplied, in this conjuncture, to raise the drooping spirits of Mahomed Shah. Russian money was freely distributed among the Persian soldiers; and a new impulse was given to them at a time when their energies were well-nigh exhausted, and their activity was beginning to fail.†

Mr. M'Neill remained in the Persian camp, and in spite of the failure of his endeavours to reconcile the contending parties, determined not to cease from his efforts, though all hope had well nigh departed of bringing

* *Yar Mahomed to Mr. M'Neill—Published Correspondence.*

† *Mr. M'Neill to Lord Palmerston—Published Correspondence.* Intelligence of Simonich's movements soon reached the beleaguered garrison. "We were told," says Pottinger, "that Count Simonich had reconnoitred the city, and had examined with a telescope from the top of the Masula, and given his opinion that all the points attacked were too strong to be taken; and that the only vulnerable side was the eastern side."

about a satisfactory arrangement. A strongly worded letter was addressed to the Persian ministers; and at one time it seemed likely that the Shah-in-Shah would accede to the terms offered by the Government of Herat; but the arrival of friendly letters from Kohun-dil Khan, the Candahar chief, offering to aid him in the prosecution of the siege, inflated him with new courage, and caused him to rise in his demands. He demanded compensation for the losses he had sustained; and the negotiations were again broken off at a time when they seemed likely, at last, to reach a favourable termination.

Nor was it only in the Persian camp that at this time Russian influence was making its way. The garrison was beginning to think whether it would not be expedient for Herat to fling itself into the arms of the great northern power. On the night of the 23rd of May, there was a consultation among the chiefs, when it was proposed that an envoy should be sent to the Russian ambassador, acknowledging the dependence of Herat upon that State. It was asserted, at the suggestion of M. Euler, Kamran's physician, that if such a step as this were taken the Persians dare not continue the siege, and that the English dare not interfere. The proposal was favourably received. It was with difficulty that the chiefs could be induced to listen to a suggestion for delay; but on the following day intelligence of the energetic course pursued by Mr. M'Neill found its way into the city. It was announced that the British minister had threatened Persia with hostilities if Herat should fall into its hands; that the city would be retaken, at any cost, by the British, army; and that Major Todd had been sent to India to make arrangements with the Governor-General for the sustenance of the people of Herat after the siege.

This intelligence, which was not wholly correct, changed at once the complexion of affairs. It was plain that the British were, after all, the best friends of the Afghans, and that it would be folly to reject their good offices for the sake of the problematical friendship and good faith of the Russian Government. The announcement, indeed, raised the spirits of the garrison, and inspired them with new courage. Even those who, the day before, had been loudest in their support of the Russian alliance, now abandoned it without reserve.

This feeling, however, was but short-lived. It soon appeared that the intentions of the British Government, as reported to have been set forth by Mr. M'Neill, had been over-stated; and again the chiefs began to bethink themselves of the advantages of a Russian alliance. Many meetings were held, at which the terms to be offered and accepted were warmly debated. At all of these Pottinger was present. Sometimes he was received and listened to with respect; at others he was treated with marked discourtesy. Now the value of the British alliance outweighed that of the Russian in the estimation of the chiefs; now it was held of far lighter account; and as the scale of their opinions turned, so varied with intelligible capriciousness their bearing towards the English officer. A man of temper and firmness, he was little disconcerted. The whole assembly might be against him; but he was not to be overawed.

On the evening of the 27th of May, Pottinger sought a private interview with Yar Mahomed. Telling the Wuzeer that his conduct towards the Persians had caused him to be suspected by the British ambassador, he insisted upon the necessity of acting decidedly upon two points—Kamran, he said, must never submit to be called the servant of Persia; nor must he on any account admit the interference of the Russians. Yar Mahomed assented to these conditions—declared that he would never sacrifice the independence of Herat, and, finally, with Pottinger's approval, despatched a letter into the Persian camp, intimating that "he agreed to the suppression of slavery, and would aid in its extinction; that he would release from bondage, and send back the people of Jam and Bakhurs if possible, and he would try to make the Soonee Hazarehs serve Persia; that he would pay a yearly present after the current year, and would also give his son and one of the King's sons as hostages. Persia should, on her part, restore Ghorian, and when his son joined the Persian camp, his brother, Shere Mahomed Khan, should be sent back, and that Mahomed Shah should give them an order for five or six thousand kurwars of grain on the Governor of Khorassan." "If these terms be not accepted," it was added, "nothing but the possession of Herat will satisfy you."

Pottinger had no easy part to play, at the best; but now his difficulties began to thicken around him. He could only hope to counteract Russian influence by impressing Yar Mahomed with a conviction that the British Government would do great things for Herat. But on the 29th of May he received instructions from Mr. M'Neill on no account to commit the government by any offers of aid to Herat as he had received no authority to make them. Startled and embarrassed by these injunctions, for, seeing that without such promises Yar Mahomed would have accepted the mediation of Russia, he had already committed the government, Pottinger went at once to the Tukht-i-pool, where the chiefs were assembled, and honestly stated that in his anxiety to bring affairs to a satisfactory adjustment, he had exceeded his powers. Exasperated by this announcement, the chiefs broke out into violent reproaches against Pottinger, M'Neill, and the whole British nation, and then began to discuss the advantages of the Russian alliance. Firm in the midst of all this storm of invective, the young British officer declared that he had only spoken the truth—that such were the instructions of the British minister—that he had no power to disobey them; but that a representation to Mr. M'Neill of the disappointment they had occasioned might induce him to depart from this cautious policy. To this the chiefs were induced to listen; and it was finally resolved to await the results of another reference to the British Envoy.*

But the influence of Mr. M'Neill at the Persian Court was now rapidly declining; and his departure was at hand. His position, ever since his arrival in the camp of Mahomed Shah, had been one of no little difficulty and embarrassment. Unhappily, at that time, one of those petty perplexities, which, arising between state and state, often evolve more serious misunderstandings than affairs of far higher moment, was constantly obtruding, in the way of a satisfactory adjustment of differences, an obstruction of a very annoying and irritating kind. A courier of the British minister, Ali Mahomed Beg by name, had been making his way from Herat to Teheran, bearing some letters from Yar Mahomed, Pottinger, and others, to Mr. M'Neill, and escorting some horses, sent by Futteh Mahomed Khan, the Herat agent, as presents to the same officer. Without any interruption he had passed the Persian camp and was within three stages of Meshed, when Berowski recognised the man and officiously reported him at head-quarters. Immediately, horsemen were despatched to carry him to the Persian camp. What followed could not be narrated better or more briefly than in the language of Mr. M'Neill:—"He was forced," wrote the minister to Lord

* "Notwithstanding," says Pottinger, "that I might then be considered a doubtful friend, it was never contemplated that I should be kept out of their assembly."—[*MS. Journal.*]

Palmerston, "to return with them ; a part of his clothes were taken from him ; the horses which he was bringing for me from Herat were seized ; he was dragged to camp, and there placed in custody. He succeeded, however, in making his way to the tent of Colonel Stoddart, and was by that officer conducted to the prime minister, who, after he had been informed by Colonel Stoddart that the man was in the service of this Mission, again placed him in custody, while Hadjee Khan, an officer of the rank of Brigadier in the service of the Shah, not only used offensive language in addressing Colonel Stoddart in presence of the prime minister, but after the messenger had been released by order of his Excellency, seized him again in the midst of the camp, stripped him to search for any letters he might have concealed about his person,* took from him Lieutenant Pottinger's letter, which was sent to the prime minister ; used to the messenger the most violent threats and the most disgusting and opprobrious language, and took from him a portion of his accoutrements."†

* *Published Correspondence relating to Persia and Afghanistan.*
† The Gholam's own account of the treatment he received from Hadjee Khan is worth quoting :—" Hadjee Khan then turned to me, and threatened me with instant death. I demanded the reason, but he gave me no other answer than abuse, calling me a traitor and a rascal, and said that he himself would be my executioner. He then began to unbutton his coat sleeves, threatening me all the while, and every now and then half unsheathing his dagger, 'I will be your executioner myself,' said the Khan. 'If there be an enemy to the English, I am the man—you are a traitor and a rascal—your eyes shall be plucked out ; the Shah has ordered me to kill you ; I will first cut off your hands. You must have papers from Herat, and unless you instantly deliver them up, you shall be cut to pieces.' Hadjee Khan went on in this strain for a long time, during which I was stripped nearly to my skin, the air being so cold that water, on being exposed, instantly froze. I was silent under all these threats and demonstrations, merely observing that, having such a noble executioner as Hadjee Khan, I was content to die, and I hoped the office

This was, doubtless, a grievous insult; and Mr. M'Neill believed that it was intended to be one. It was designed, he thought, " to exhibit to the Afghans and to the Persian army an apparent contempt for the English, with a view to diminish the moral effect which might have been produced on either party, by the general belief that we were opposed to the conquest of Herat by the Persians." It was an insult for which reparation, if not offered by one state, might be rightfully exacted by the other; and Mr. M'Neill was not a man to sit down tamely under such an outrage as this. But the incident had taken place in October, and now, in May, though the subject had been repeatedly forced upon the attention of Mahomed Shah and his ministers, no fitting reparation had been offered to the British Government. The Persian Government had, indeed, asserted their right to seize, punish, or put to death, without reference to the British minister, the Persian servants in his employment. The breach was thus palpably widening. The Governor of Bushire, too, had used offensive language towards the British Resident in the Persian Gulf; and the redress, which had been sought by Mr. M'Neill, had not been granted by the Persian Government. Then there was another grievance of which the British minister complained. The Persian Government had continued to evade the conclusion of the commercial treaty, which was guaranteed to us in the general treaty of friendship between the two states.

All these cumulative offences, added to the great subject of complaint—the conduct of Persia towards Herat—made up such an amount of provocation, that Mr. M'Neill felt his position at the Persian Court was little likely to be one of much longer continuance. The Shah had

would remain in his family."—*Statement of Ali Mahomed Beg.— Published Correspondence relating to Persia and Afghanistan.*]

declared that he would raise the siege, if the British minister would afford him a pretext for the retrograde movement, satisfactory in the eyes of his countrymen, by threatening, on the part of his government, to attack Persia if she continued her offensive operations against Herat; but from this promise he had receded, or thrown such difficulties in the way of its fulfilment, as practically to nullify the pledge. Mr. M'Neill massed all his demands upon the Persian Government. The Shah required that he should keep the question of Herat distinct from the others, and, on the British minister refusing to do so on his own responsibility, declared that he would do it himself, by acceding to all the demands except that which related to Herat. "The Shah then," says Mr. M'Neill, in his report of these proceedings to the Foreign Secretary, "immediately dismissed me, with an assurance that he should adopt that course, but before I had left the area on which the royal tent was pitched, he called after me, that on his agreeing to the other demands, he should expect me to avoid all further discussion of the affairs of Herat, and to order Mr. Pottinger to quit that city. In answer, I represented that I could not tie up the hands of my own government in respect to the question of Herat, and that Mr. Pottinger was not under my orders."

There was obviously now little hope of bringing these long-protracted negotiations to a favourable conclusion. The British Mission was fast falling into contempt. The Russians were exalted at the Persian Court. The British were slighted and humiliated. There was not a tent-pitcher in camp who did not know that the British Mission was treated with intentional disrespect. It was time, therefore, to bring matters to a crisis. So, on the 3rd of June,

* *Mr. M'Neill to Lord Palmerston. Meshed, June* 25, 1838

Mr. M'Neill addressed a letter to the Foreign minister in the Persian camp, announcing his intention to depart for the frontier on the following day. "I feel myself called upon," he concluded, "to inform you that, until the reparation and satisfaction I have demanded, for the indignities already offered, shall have been fully given, the Queen of England cannot receive at her Court any minister who may be sent thither by the Shah of Persia." The decisive language of the British minister called forth an evasive reply from the Persian Government. The Shah professed not to understand "his Excellency's object in all these writings," and declared that there had been no indignity or disrespect ever offered to him. But M'Neill was not to be thus appeased. He sent back, in a few plain words, a statement of his demands. He demanded that Hadjee Khan, who had outraged the servant of the British minister, should be removed from office; that Hadjee Meerza Aghassy, who had connived at the outrage, should go to the British minister's tent, and apologise for the insult; that a firman should be issued, commanding the servants of the Persian Government not to interfere with the dependants of the British Mission; that the Governor of Bushire should be removed from office for his insults to the British Resident; and that the commercial treaty should be forthwith concluded and ratified. All these demands but the last were to be carried into effect within three days of the date of the letter.

Again the Persian minister declared, on the part of the Shah, that no indignities had ever been offered to the British Mission; and again Mr. M'Neill requested his dismissal. The Shah was not ready to grant it. "No," he said; "never shall we consent to the departure of his Excellency. Let him by all means lay aside his intention, and let him not allow this idea to enter his mind." But he was not to be persuaded to lay aside his intentions. The Persian ministers continued to declare that no insults had been offered to the British Mission. So, reluctant as he was abruptly to terminate our diplomatic intercourse with Persia, Mr. M'Neill, on the 7th of June, took his departure from the Persian camp. From the ramparts of Herat they looked out upon the striking of the English ambassador's tents, and a large party of horsemen were seen making their way across the plain. The rupture was now complete Persia was no longer an ally of Great Britain.

In the mean while, as the year advanced, the miseries and privations of the siege were more and more severely felt by the inhabitants The wonder is, that at a still earlier period they had not become wholly unendurable. Houses were pulled down to supply fuel.* Horses were killed for food. The vast number of people assembled within the walls had not only created an extreme scarcity of provisions, but was in a fair way to generate a pestilence. The city was altogether without sewers or other means of drainage. The accumulations of filth had therefore become inconceivable, and the stench hardly to be borne. The decaying bodies of the dead had polluted the air to a still more horrible extent, so that there was every probability of some fearful epidemic breaking out among the people.† Indeed, at the beginning of May, famine

* The Jew's synagogue had been devoted to this unholy use; but they had contrived to accomplish its redemption.

† An amusing illustration of the unsavoury condition of the city at this time is given in Pottinger's Journal. He had made the acquaintance of a magician, and wished to have a specimen of his art. "People of his class," he writes, "are very careful of exposing themselves; and are excessively suspicious and bigoted. It was therefore a long time before I could venture to request a turn of his art. However, I at last did so, but was disappointed at finding he was not a regular practitioner; and as we had got now intimate he told me that he as yet had not commenced the practice; that he wanted to pursue the

and sickness pressed so severely upon the inhabitants, that it was debated whether it would not be expedient to suffer a number of them to depart out of the city. Fever and scurvy were rife among them; and it appeared that the enemies outside the gates were less terrible than the viewless ones within. In this extremity they mustered in large numbers, and petitioned the Shah to suffer them to depart. The Shah referred the matter to the Wuzeer; and the Wuseer consulted the chiefs. The discussion was long and animated. The decision was against the departure of the people. The petitioners were mainly women and children; and to suffer them to depart would be to throw them into the hands of the licentious Persian soldiery, and to expose them to a fate more terrible than famine and death.*

science allowed by the *Hudyth*; not the accursed magic—*Sihr Malown*; that he wished but for power to summon the *gins* and angels to his aid. Though this was not exactly what I wanted, I should have been most happy of an introduction to either of these classes; and, therefore, not to lose my labour, I used my utmost endeavours to get my friend to commence his incantations at once. He made many excuses. First, he had not got clean clothes to change, as the scarcity had obliged him to part with everything extra to buy grain whilst it was tolerably cheap. This and sundry other excuses were easily overcome; but he evidently wished to avoid the employment, or to make excuses for use when he failed. As soon as one objection was overruled another was raised; but I overcame all except that the stench of the dead bodies from the city would prevent these spirits from venturing, except under extraordinary strong incantations, within its walls; as angels and *gins* are said to be particularly fond of sweet odours, and excessively angered by the contrary. The argument was a clencher, and no ingenuity could overturn it, for certainly the smell was abominable, and in a calm, or when the wind came from the southward, in which direction the greatest number had been buried, the human kind could scarcely withstand the horrible effluvia of putrid flesh."—[*Eldred Pottinger's MS. Journal.*]

* A few days afterwards, however, a party of some 600 or 700, mostly old men, women, and children, were put out of the gates. "The enemy," says Pottinger, "opened a heavy fire on them until

The Persians now, under Russian direction, continued to prosecute the siege with increased vigour and judgment. The whole of the investing force, some portion of which had before been scattered over the great plain, was now drawn in more closely round the city.

On the 13th of June an assault was attempted at the south-west angle, but gallantly repulsed by the garrison. Informed by some deserters from Herat that the defence of the *fausse-braie* was comparatively neglected during the mid-day heats, the Persians surprised the guards at the outer works, and pushed on towards the *fausse-braie*. But a little party of Afghans—not more than three or four in number—stood at bay in the passages of the traverses, and heroically defended the post until assistance was at hand. The relieving party came down gallantly to the defence. Headed by Sultan Mahomed Omar, they flung themselves over the parapet of the upper *fausse-braie*, and pouring themselves down the exterior slope overwhelmed the assailants and dislodged them with great slaughter.*

Another attempt, made at the same time, to effect a lodgment at the south-east angle, was equally unsuccessful. Twice the storming column advanced, and twice it was repulsed. The fortune of the day was against the Persians.

In nowise disheartened by these failures, the besiegers

they found out who they were, when they tried to drive them back with sticks and stones; but Naib Dustoo, to whom the business was entrusted, liker a fiend than a man, opened a fire upon the wretched citizens from the works, and the Persians thus let them pass. From the besiegers' fire no one suffered, as a rising ground was between, but from that of the garrison it is said several fell."

* It was said that Mahomed Shah had come down in person to witness the assault; but the Royal amateur was only the Shah's brother, who, attended by a party of idlers, and a small body of horse, was a spectator of the defeat of his countrymen.

now redoubled their exertions, and pursued their mining operations with a vigour and an activity which the garrison could not match. The Afghans were now becoming dispirited and inert; even the chiefs began to despond, and the wonted constancy of the Wuzeer forsook him. Everywhere Pottinger saw with uneasiness signs of failing courage and impaired activity. He had been deputed by Mr. M'Neill to act as British Agent at Herat, and now, in his official capacity, he redoubled his exertions. There was need, indeed, of his best efforts. The siege was being pushed forward, not only with an energy, but with an intelligence that had not marked the earlier stages of the attack. The breaches had become more practicable. The Persians were filling up the ditch at some parts, and constructing bridges to span it at others. Another assault of a more formidable character than any before attempted was said to be in contemplation; and as these rumours were circulated through the works, and the obscure terms of the future were magnified by the palpable dangers of the present, the defenders scarcely strove to conceal the fear which had crept into their hearts.

The threatened assault was at hand. The 24th of June was a memorable day in the annals of the siege. It opened with a heavy fire from the Persian batteries on all the four sides of the city. Then there was a perfect lull, more ominous than the uproar that preceded it. The signs of the coming assault were plain and intelligible; but strangely were they disregarded. The Wuzeer was at his quarters. The garrison were off their guard. Many, indeed, had composed themselves to sleep. The enemy had been seen assembling in great force; but no heed was taken of the movement. Suddenly the stillness was broken by the booming of a gun and the flight of a rocket; another gun—then another—and presently a heavy fire of ordnance from all sides, supported by a discharge of musketry, which, feeble at first, grew presently more vigorous and sustained There was no longer any doubt of the intentions of the besieging force. The enemy had braced themselves up for a general assault upon the city, and were moving to the attack of five different points of the works.

At four of these points they were repulsed.* At the fifth, gallantly headed by their officers, the storming column threw itself into the trench of the lower *fausse-braie*. The struggle was brief, but bloody. The defenders fell at their post to a man, and the work was carried by the besiegers. Encouraged by this first success, the storming party pushed up the slope. A galling fire from the garrison met them as they advanced. The officers and leading men of the column were mown down ; there was a second brief and bloody struggle, and the upper *fausse-*

* "The assault on the gate of Candahar was repulsed, and the Persians chased back into their trenches ; but the danger at the south-east angle prevented them following up the advantage. At the south-west angle, or Pay-in-ab, the Persians can scarcely be said to have attacked, as they never advanced beyond the parapet of their own trenches. It was evidently a mere feint. At the western, or Arak gate, a column composed of the Russian regiment, and other troops under Samson, and those under Wully Khan, marched up to the counterscarp , but Wully Khan being killed, and Samson carried off the field wounded, the men broke and fled, leaving an immense number killed and wounded. The latter were nearly all shot by idlers on the ramparts, or murdered by the plunderers, who crept out to strip the slain. The other attack, on the centre of the north-west face, was repulsed in like manner, after reaching the counterscarp."—[*Eldred Pottinger's MS. Journal.*] Wully Khan's body was found on the following day, and his head was brought into the city. On his person were found several letters relating to the plan of assault, which satisfactorily proved that it had been designed by the Russian officers in the Persian camp. There were two letters among them from Mahomed Shah himself—one addressed to Wully Khan, ordering him to conform to the plan of the Russian ambassador, and another to Hadjee Meerza Aghassy, directing him to give similar instructions to Wully Khan.

braie was carried. A few of the most daring of the assailants pushing on in advance of their comrades gained the head of the breach. But now Deen Mahomed came down with the Afghan reserve. Thus recruited, the defenders gathered new heart. The Persians on the breach were driven back. Again and again, with desperate courage, they struggled to effect a lodgment, only to be repulsed and thrown back in confusion upon their comrades who were pressing on behind. The conflict was fierce; the issue was doubtful. Now the breach was well-nigh carried; and now the stormers, recoiling from the shock of the defence, fell back upon the exterior slope of the *fausse-braie*. It was an hour of intense excitement. The fate of Herat was trembling in the balance.

Startled by the first noise of the assault, Yar Mahomed had risen up, left his quarters, and ridden down to the works. Pottinger went forth at the same time, and on the same errand. There was a profound conviction in his mind that there was desperate work in hand, of which he might not live to see the end. Giving instructions to his dependents, to be carried out in the event of his falling in the defence, he hastened to join the Wuzeer. It was a crises that demanded all the energy and courage of those two resolute spirits. The English officer was equal to the occasion. The Afghan Sirdar was not.

As they neared the point of attack, the garrison were seen retreating by twos and threes; others were quitting the works on the pretext of carrying off the wounded. These signs of the waning courage of the defenders wrought differently on the minds of the two men who had hitherto seemed to be cast in the same heroic mould —soldiers of strong nerves and unfailing resolution. They saw that the garrison were giving way. Pottinger was eager to push on to the breach. Yar Mahomed sat himself down. The Wuzeer had lost heart. His wonted high courage and collectedness had deserted him in this emergency. Astonished and indignant at the pusillanimity of his companion, the English officer called upon the Wuzeer again and again to rouse himself—either to move down to the breach or to send his son, to inspire new heart into the yielding garrison. The energetic appeal of the young Englishman was not lost upon the Afghan chief. He rose up; advanced further into the works; and neared the breach where the contest was raging. Encouraged by the diminished opposition, the enemy were pushing on with renewed vigour. Yar Mahomed called upon his men, in God's name, to fight; but they wavered and stood still. Then his heart failed him again. He turned back; said he would go for aid; sought the place where he had before sat down, and looked around, irresolute and unnerved. Pointing to the men, who, alarmed by the backwardness of their chief, were now retreating in every direction, Pottinger in vehement language insisted upon the absolute ruin of all their hopes that must result from want of energy in such a conjuncture. Yar Mahomed roused himself; again advanced, but again waivered; and a third time the young English officer was compelled, by words and deeds alike, to shame the unmanned Wuzeer. The language of entreaty was powerless; he used the language of reproach. He reviled; he threatened; he seized him by the arm and dragged him forward to the breach. Such appeals were not to be resisted. The noble example of the young Englishman could not infuse any real courage into the Afghan chief; but it at least roused him into action. The men were retreating from the breach. The game was almost up. The irresolution of the Wuzeer had well-nigh played away the last stake. Had Yar Mahomed not been roused out of the paralysis that had descended upon him, Herat would have been carried by assault. But the indomitable courage of Eldred Pottinger saved the beleaguered city. He compelled the Wuzeer to appear before his men as one not utterly prostrate and helpless. The chief called upon the soldiery to fight; but they continued to fall back in dismay. Then seizing a large staff, Yar Mahomed rushed like a madman upon the hindmost of the party, and drove them forward under a shower of heavy blows. The nature of the works was such as to forbid their falling back in a body. Cooped up in a narrow passage, and seeing no other outlet of escape, many of them leapt wildly over the parapet, and rushed down the exterior slope full upon the Persian stormers. The effect of this sudden movement was magical. The Persians, seized with a panic, abandoned their position and fled. The crisis was over; Herat was saved.*

* There is nothing finer in the annals of the war in Afghanistan than the heroic conduct of Eldred Pottinger on this 24th of June. But I should as little discharge my duty as an historian, as I should gratify my inclinations as a man, if I were not to say that I have extracted, with some difficulty, from Pottinger's manuscript journal, the real history of the service that he rendered to his country on this memorable day. The young Bombay artilleryman was endowed with a rare modesty, which made him unwilling to speak or to write about himself. In the copy of the journal before me he has erased, throughout the entire record of this day, every entrance made in the first person; and only by giving rein to a curiosity, which I should not have indulged, or considered pardonable in any ordinary case, have I succeeded in extracting the real history of an incident which has already, in one or two incorrect shapes, been given to the world. Wherever Pottinger had written in the original copy of his journal "I," he had erased the egotistical monosyllable, and substituted the words, "the people about the Wuzeer," or had otherwise disguised the record of his own achievements. For example, the words, "I had several times to lay hold of the Vizier, and point to him the men, who turned as soon as he did," are altered into, "the people about abused, and several times had to lay hold of the Vizier, &c. &c." What was thought of Pottinger's conduct beyond the walls of Herat, may be gathered from the fact, that

But no exultation followed a victory so achieved. The bearing of the Afghans was that of men who had sustained a crushing defeat. The garrison were crest-fallen and dispirited. A general gloom seemed to hang over the city. Yar Mahomed, long after the danger was past, moved about as one confused and bewildered. There were few of the chiefs whose minds were not so wholly unhinged by the terrors of that great crisis as to be unable, for days afterwards, to perform calmly their wonted duties. A complete paralysis, indeed, descended upon men of all ranks. The loss on both sides had been severe; but if half the garrison had fallen in the defence of the breach, Herat could not have been more stunned and prostrated by the blow. The Persian camp was equally dispirited; and a week of inaction supervened.* Even the work of repairing the damaged fortifications was slowly recommenced by the garrison; and when at last the men returned to their accustomed duties it was plain that they

a few days afterwards a man came in from Kurookh, bringing some important intelligence, who immediately on his arrival, went up to Pottinger, seized his hands, kissed them, said he was indeed "rejoiced that he had made so great a pilgrimage," and spoke with enthusiastic praise of the repulse of the Persian stormers.

* The loss upon the Persian side was very heavy. A large number of officers, including several chiefs of note, were killed and wounded. Mr. M'Neill wrote from camp near Teheran, to Lord Palmerston: "The number of the killed and wounded of the Persian army is variously stated; but the best information I have been able to obtain leads me to believe that it cannot be less than 1700 or 1800 men. The loss in officers, and especially those of the higher ranks, has been very great in proportion to the whole number killed and wounded. Major-General Berowski and Sirteps Wully Khan and Nebbee Khan, have been killed; Sirteps Samson Khan, Hossein Pasha Khan, and Jaffier Kooli Khan, have been wounded; and almost all the field-officers of these brigades have been killed or wounded." There is little doubt, however, that the entire number of casualties is greatly overstated in this passage.

had no heart. Nor was there anything strange and unaccountable in this. The Afghans had repulsed the Persians on the 24th of June; but they felt that nothing but a miracle could enable them to withstand another such assault. The resources of the government had failed them. Food was scarce; money was scarce. The citizens could not be fed. The soldiers could not be paid.

In all of this there was much to disquiet with painful doubts and misgivings the mind of Eldred Pottinger. To protract the siege was to protract the sufferings of the Heratees. The misery of the people was past counting. The poor were perishing for want of food; the rich were dying under the hands of the torturers. The soldiers clamoured for their pay; and wherever money was known or suspected to be, there went the ruthless myrmidons of Yar Mahomed to demand it for their master, or to wring from the agonised victim the treasure which he sought to conceal. To tear from a wretched man, at the last gasp of life, all that he possessed; then, demanding more, to torture him anew, until, sinking under the accumulated agony, the miserable victim was released by death; and then to fling his emaciated corpse, wrapped in an old shawl or blanket down at the threshold of his desolated home, was no solitary achievement of the Wuzeer. Even ladies of rank were given over to the torturers. The very inmates of the Shah's Zenana were threatened. A reign of terror was established such as it sickened Pottinger to contemplate. He felt that he was the cause of this. Many reproached him openly. The despairing looks and gaunt figures of others reproached him more painfully still. All that he could do to redress the wrongs of the injured and alleviate the sufferings of the distressed he did in this fearful conjuncture. Men of all kinds came to him imploring his aid and importuning him for protection. Some he was able to save, stepping between the wrong-doer and the wronged; but from others he was powerless to avert by his intervention the ruin that was impending over them. Every day brought palpably before him new illustrations of the unsparing cruelty of the Wuzeer. But dire political necessity compelled him to protract a conjuncture laden with these terrible results. It is impossible to read the entrances in his journal at this time without feeling how great was the conflict within him between the soldier and the man.

The events of the 24th of June, though they had raised Pottinger's character, as a warrior, in the Afghan city, in the Persian camp, and in the surrounding country, had, greatly indeed, diminished his popularity in Herat and increased the difficulties of his position. In the negotiations which followed, Mahomed Shah insisted upon Pottinger's dismissal. The young English officer had excited the measureless indignation of the Persian King, and the Afghan Wuzeer was not disinclined to reproach him with presenting a new obstacle to the adjustment of the differences between the two states. The Afghan envoys said that they had always thought Pottinger was one man, but that the importance the Persians attached to his departure showed that he was equal to an army.* Pottinger was

* "The Wuzeer told me the whole business hung upon me; that the Persians made a point of obtaining my dismissal, without which they would not treat. They were so pressing, that he said he never before guessed my importance, and that the Afghan envoys who had gone to camp had told him they had always thought me one man, but the importance the Persians attached to my departure showed that I was equal to an army. The Afghans were very complimentary, and expressed loudly their gratitude to the British Government, to the exertions of which they attributed the change in the tone of the Persians. They, however, did not give the decided answers they should have done, but put the question off by saying I was a guest. The Persians offered to be security for my safe passage to any place I chose to go to."—[*Eldred Pottinger's MS. Journal.*]

always ready with a declaration that no thoughts of personal safety or convenience should ever suffer him to stand in the way of an arrangement conducive to the safety of Herat and the welfare of his country, and that if these objects were to be gained by his departure, he was willing to depart. But Yar Mahomed, whilst unwilling to retain him, was unwilling to persuade him to go. The dismissal of the man who had saved Herat from the grasp of the Persians, would have been an act that might have fixed a stain upon the character of the Wuzeer, prejudicial to the success of his after-career. Moreover, it was possible that Pottinger's assistance might be wanted at some future time—that the Persians, having obtained his dismissal, might hesitate to perform their promises, and rise in their demands on the strength of the advantage which they had thus gained.

The month of July was not distinguished by any great activity on the part of the besiegers. The siege, indeed, now began to assume the character of a blockade. The question of surrender had become a mere question of time. It seemed impossible much longer to protract the defence. Yar Mahomed, with all the resources of unscrupulous cruelty at his command, could not extort sufficient money from his victims to enable him to continue his defensive operations with any prospect of success. But it appeared to him, as it did to Pottinger, expedient to postpone the inevitable day of capitulation, in the hope that something might yet be written down in their favour in the " chapter of accidents," out of which so often had come unexpected aid. Yar Mahomed looked for the coming of an Oosbeg army. He had long anxiously expected the arrival of a relieving force from Toorkistan ; and scarcely a day had passed without some tidings, either to elevate or depress him, of the advent or delay of the looked-for succours. Pottinger, though unwilling to encourage in others expectations which might not be realised, was inwardly convinced that something of a decisive character respecting the intentions of his own government must soon be heard, and that the knowledge of those intentions would have an effect upon the Afghan garrison and the Persian camp very advantageous to the former. With the object, therefore, of gaining time, the Wuzeer renewed his exertions to raise money for the payment of the troops. Assemblies of the chiefs were held, at which every practicable method of recruiting their exhausted finances was discussed. The Sirdars addressed themselves to the discussion as men wholly in earnest, determined to do their best.* The resolutions of the chiefs in this conjuncture surprised and delighted Pottinger, who was little prepared for the unanimity with which they determined on protracting the defence. "With open breaches, trembling soldiery, and a disaffected populace, they determined to stand to the last. How I wished," exclaimed Pottinger, "to have the power of producing the money!"

The plan which was at last resolved upon—one which threw into the hands of a single chief the power of seizing the property of whomsoever he thought fit to mulct for the service of the state—under a written pledge

* At one of these consultations, held on the 18th of July, "Deen Mahomed," said Pottinger, "proposed that each chief should bring what he had to the Wuzeer. The Wuzeer proposed that each chief should retain his own men. The Topshee-Bashee said: 'As the Shah has money, and won't give it, we cannot force him; but if you allow me to seize whom I like, and the chiefs give me their promise that they will not interfere in favour of any one, I will undertake to provide the expense of the men for two months.' The chiefs immediately said 'Done!' and had an agreement made out, and those present sealed it. . . . . They were, or appeared well satisfied with me; and the Wuzeer quoted my anxiety and efforts as an example to those who had their women and children to defend."—[*Eldred Pottinger's MS. Journal.*]

from the other chiefs not to interfere, as had been their wont, for the protection of their own friends, threw the city into such confusion, and produced so many appeals to the assembly of chiefs, that Pottinger, anxious to establish a less arbitrary system of levying contributions, suggested that all who voluntarily brought their money would be reimbursed, at his recommendation, by the British Government. But money came in slowly. The difficulties of the garrison seemed to thicken around them. Negotiations were, therefore, again resumed, with a determination at last to bring them to an issue; and messengers were constantly passing and repassing between the city and the Persian camp.

But in the mean while, far beyond the walls of Herat, events were taking shape mightily affecting the issue of the contest. Lord Auckland, who had watched with much anxiety the progress of affairs in the West, had, in the course of the spring, determined on despatching an expedition to the Persian Gulf, to hold itself in readiness for any service which Mr. M'Neill might deem it expedient to employ it upon, "with a view to the maintenance of our interests in Persia." Instructions to this effect were forwarded to Bombay. In conjunction with Sir Charles Malcolm, the chief of the Indian navy, the Bombay Government despatched the *Semiramis* and *Hugh Lindsay* steamers, and some vessels of war, with detachments of the 15th, 23rd, and 24th Regiments, and the Marine battalion, to the Persian Gulf; and instructed the resident, Captain Hennell, to land the troops on the island of Karrack, and concentrate the squadron before it. On the 4th of June, the *Semiramis* steamed out of the Bombay harbour, and on the 19th anchored off Karrack. The troops were immediately landed. The governor of the island, greatly alarmed by the coming of the steamer and the fighting men, but somewhat reassured by the appearance of Captain

DEMONSTRATION IN THE PERSIAN GULF. 283

Hennell, said that the island and everything it contained, himself and its inhabitants, were at the disposal of the British Resident; and at once began to assist in the disembarkation of the troops.

The demonstration was an insignificant one in itself; but by the time that intelligence of the movement had reached the Persian camp, the expedition, gathering new dimensions at every stage, had swollen into bulk and significance. The most exaggerated reports of the doings and intentions of the British soon forced themselves into currency. The Persian camp was all alive with stories of the powerful British fleet that had sailed into the gulf, destroyed Bunder-Abassy and all the other ports on the coast, taken Bushire, and landed there a mighty army, which was advancing upon Shiraz, and had already taken divers towns in the province of Fars. Nothing could have been more opportune than the arrival of these reports. Mr M'Neill was making his way towards the frontier, when intelligence of the Karrack expedition met him on the road. About the same time he received letters of instruction from the Foreign-office, issued in anticipation of the refusal of Mahomed Shah to desist from his operations against Herat; and thinking the hour was favourable, he resolved to make another effort to secure the withdrawal of the Persian army, and to regain for the British Mission the ascendancy it had lost at the Persian Court.

Fortified by these instructions from the Foreign-office, Mr M'Neill despatched Colonel Stoddart to the Persian camp, with a message to the Shah. The language of this message was very intelligible and very decided. The Shah was informed that the occupation of Herat or any part of Afghanistan by the Persians would be considered in the light of a hostile demonstration against England; and that he could not persist in his present course without immediate danger and injury to Persia. It was stated, that already had a naval armament arrived in the Persian Gulf, and troops been landed on the island of Karrack, and that if the Shah desired the British Government to suspend the measures in progress for the vindication of its honour, he must at once retire from Herat, and make reparation for the injuries which had been inflicted upon the British Mission.

On the 11th of August, Colonel Stoddart arrived in the Persian camp. Repairing at once to the quarters of the minister, he found the son of the Candahar chief and a party of Afghans waiting in the tent. The Hadjee, on his return, received him with courtesy and friendliness, and fixed the following day for an interview with the Shah. Stoddart went at the appointed hour. The King was sitting in a raised room, up six or seven steps. Beckoning to the English officer to come up more closely to him, he welcomed him with much cordiality, and listened to the message from the British Government. Taking advantage of a pause in the recital, the King said: "The fact is, if I don't leave Herat, there will be war, is not that it?" "It is war," returned Stoddart; "all depends upon your Majesty's answer—God preserve your Majesty!" The message, written in the original English, was then given to the King. "It is all I wished for," he said. "I asked the minister plenipotentiary for it; but he would not give it to me. He said he was not authorized." "He was not authorized then," returned Stoddart; "but now he has been ordered to do it. No one could give such a message without especial authority from his Sovereign." The Shah complained that the paper was in English, which he could not understand; but said that his Meerzas should translate it for him, and then that he would give a positive answer to its demands. Two days afterwards Stoddart was again summoned to the royal presence. "We consent to the whole of the demands of the British

Government," said the Shah. "We will not go to war. Were it not for the sake of their friendship, we should not return from before Herat Had we known that our coming here might risk the loss of their friendship, we certainly would not have come at all."* The English officer thanked God that his Majesty had taken so wise a view of the real interests of Persia; but hinted to the Foreign Minister as he went out, that although the Shah's answer was very satisfactory, it would be more satisfactory still to see it at once reduced to practice.

Whilst, in the Persian camp, Mahomed Shah was promising the English diplomatists to withdraw his army from Herat, an officer of the Russian Mission—M. Goutte, who had approved himself an adept in intrigue —was busying himself in Herat to bring about an arrangement that would give a colour of victory to the achievements of the investing force. If Kamran could have been persuaded to come out and wait upon Mahomed Shah in token of submission, the army might have been withdrawn with some show of credit, and the Russian Mission might have claimed a diplomatic victory. The Afghans were not, in their present reduced state, disinclined to acknowledge the supremacy of Mahomed Shah, and to consent that Kamran should visit the Persian monarch at Ghorian: but the Russian envoy demanded that he should come out of Herat, and make his obeisance to the King of Kings, as a preliminary to the withdrawal of the Persian army.†

This was on the 17th of August. On the morning of the 18th, Yar Mahomed sent a messenger to Pottinger, requesting his attendance at the Wuzeer's quarters. The English officer was received with coldness almost amount-

* *Colonel Stoddart to Mr. M'Neill. Correspondence relating to Persia and Afghanistan.*
† *Eldred Pottinger's MS. Journal.*

ing to discourtesy. Scarcely a word was spoken to him whilst the levee lasted; but when the assembly broke up, Pottinger, in a tone of voice that showed he was not to be trifled with, asked him why he had sent for him if he had nothing to communicate and nothing to ask. The Wuzeer took him by the hand and was about to leave the room; when Pottinger, arresting his progress, demanded a private interview. The room was cleared. The young English officer and the Afghan Sirdar sate down together, and were soon in friendly discourse. Yar Mahomed, the most plausible and persuasive of men,* soon stilled the tempest that was rising in Pottinger's breast. All patience and gentleness now, he was ready to submit to any rebuke, and to utter any apology. They were soon in earnest conversation, as friends and brothers, regarding the general condition of the garrison and its available resources. The Wuzeer declared that "he regretted much the step he was obliged to take, but that indeed no alternative was left him—that every resource which even tyranny commanded was exhausted— that he dared not lay hands on the property of the combatants, though many of them had large funds." The chiefs, he declared, were misers. The eunuch, Hadjee Ferooz, he said, could easily contribute two lakhs of rupees towards the expenses of the war, and the Shah might contribute ten; but neither would advance a

---

* "Yar Mahomed is one of the most persuasive talkers I have met. It is scarcely possible to talk with him and retain anger. He is ready in a surprising degree, and is so patient under rebuke, that I never saw him fail to quiet the most violent of his countrymen, when he thought it worth his while. A person who disregards truth, and thinks nothing of denying what he has asserted a few minutes before, is a most puzzling person to argue with. Until you have thought over what has been said, you cannot understand the changeable colours which pass before you."—[*Eldred Pottinger's MS. Journal.*]

farthing. "They are all," he said, "equally niggardly. They have money, but they will not advance it. When their wives are being ravished before their faces, they will repent of their avarice; but now it is impossible to convince them of the folly and the danger of the course they are pursuing. With such people to deal with, and the soldiery crying out for pay and subsistence, how can I hold out longer by force?" He consented, however, to protract the negotiations to the utmost—to amuse the Persians—and to gain time. And in the mean while, he extracted from the weak and unresisting all that he could wring from them by torture. On the night after this conference with Pottinger, the Moonshee-Bashee died under the hands of the torturers.

The struggle, however, was now nearly at an end. The movements in the Persian camp appear, at this time, to have been but imperfectly known within the walls of Herat. Whilst Mahomed Shah was making preparations for the withdrawal of his army, Yar Mahomed and the Afghan Sirdars were busy with their financial operations for the continuance of the defence. A Finance Committee was appointed. Kamran was told that he must either provide money for the payment of the soldiery, or authorise the Committee to set about their work after their own manner. Eager to save his money, he sacrificed his people, and armed the Committee with full powers to search the houses of the inhabitants, to order the expulsion of all who had less than three months' provisions, and to take from those who had more all that they could find in excess. The Topshee-Bashee, or chief artilleryman, to whom the executive duties of the Committee were entrusted, contrived to extort from the inhabitants several days' food, and a large supply of jewels, with which he enriched the Wuzeer and himself. It was always believed that the former had amassed large sums of money during the siege; that he had turned the scarcity to good account, by retaining in his own coffers no small portion of the coin which he had wrung by torture from the wretched inhabitants. Now when the soldiery, lacking the means of subsistence, entered upon a course of plundering that threw the whole city into confusion, the Wuzeer, whilst issuing a proclamation forbidding such irregularities, and declaring severe penalties for the offence, allowed a continuation of the license to his own people, that he might avoid the necessity of paying them at his own cost. It is not strange, therefore, that when reports were circulated throughout the city that the Persian army was about to move, the *Soonee* Parsewans, scarcely less than the *Sheeahs*, should have received the intelligence, some with sorrow, and some with a forced incredulity, "preferring the miseries of the siege with the ultimate prospect of the city being taken and sacked, to the raising of the siege and the prospect of Kamran's and Yar Mahomed's paternal government." "All I wonder," said Pottinger, recording this fact, "is, that not a man is to be found among them bold enough to terminate their miseries by the death of their oppressors."*

But it was now becoming every day more obvious that Mahomed Shah was about to break up his camp. Some countrymen came into Herat and reported that the Persians were collecting their guns and mortars, and parking them as though in preparation for an immediate march. Parties of horsemen also had been seen moving out of camp. Others brought in word that the enemy had destroyed their 68-pounders, were assembling their carriage-cattle, and were about to raise the siege. The English, it was said, had taken Shiraz; but the Persians

* *Eldred Pottinger's MS. Journal.*

in the trenches, declaring that they were ready for another assault, cried out, that though the English army had advanced upon that city, the Prince-Governor had defeated it. All kinds of preposterous rumours were rife. Some asserted that the Russians had attacked and captured Tabreez; others that the Russians and English had formed an alliance for the overthrow of Mahomedanism, and the partition of the countries of the East between the two great European powers. But amidst all these rumours indicating the intended retrogression of the Persian army, the garrison was kept continually on the alert by alarming reports of another attack; and it was hard to say whether all these seeming preparations in Mahomed Shah's camp were nor designed to lull the Heratees into a sleep of delusive security, and render them an easier prey.

But the month of September brought with it intelligence of a more decided character. There was no longer any doubt in Herat, that Mahomed Shah was breaking up his camp. Letters came in from the Persian authorities intimating the probability of the "King-of-Kings" forgiving the rebellion of Prince Kamran on certain conditions which would give a better grace to the withdrawal of the Persian monarch. To some of these, mainly at Pottinger's suggestion, the Heratees demurred; but on the 4th of September, the Persian prisoners were sent into camp; and the Shah-in-Shah promised Colonel Stoddart that the march of the army should commence in a few days. There was, indeed, a pressing necessity for the immediate departure of the force. "The forage in camp," wrote Colonel Stoddart to Mr. M'Neill, "will only last for five or six days more, and as messengers have been sent to turn back all cafilas, no more flour or grain will arrive. The advanced guard under Humza Meerza leaves camp on Friday evening."

Everything was now ready for the retreat. The guns had been withdrawn from their advanced positions, and were now limbered up for the march. The baggage-cattle had been collected. The tents were being struck. The garrison of Herat looked out upon the stir in the Persian camp, and could no longer be doubtful of its import. The siege was now raised. The danger was at an end. Before the 9th of September, the Persian army had commenced its retrograde march to Teheran ; and on the morning of that day the Shah mounted his horse " Ameerj," and set his face towards his capital.

To Mahomed Shah this failure was mortifying indeed ; but the interests at stake were too large for him to sacrifice them at the shrine of his ambition. He had spent ten months before the walls of Herat, exhausting his soldiery in a vain endeavour to carry by assault a place of no real or reputed strength. He had succeeded only in reducing the garrison to very painful straits ; and had retired at last, not as one well-disposed to peaceful negotiation and reasonable concession, submitting to the friendly intervention of a neutral power, and willing to wave the chances of success ; but as one who saw before him *no* chance of success, and was moved by no feeling of moderation and forbearance, but by a cogent fear of the consequences resulting from the longer prosecution of the siege. On the whole, it had been little better than a lamentable demonstration of weakness. The Persian army under the eye of the sovereign himself, aided by the skill of Russian engineers and the wisdom of Russian statesmen, had failed, in ten months, to reduce a place which I believe, in no spirit of national self-love, a well-equipped English force, under a competent commander, would have reduced in as many days.

The real cause of the failure is not generally understood. The fact is, that there was no unity in the conduct of the siege. Instead of devising and adhering to some combined plan of operations, the Sirdars, or Generals, under Mahomed Shah, to whom the prosecution of the siege was entrusted, acted as so many independent commanders, and each followed his own plan of attack. The jealousy of the chiefs prevented them from acting in concert with each other. Each had his own independent point of attack, and they would not even move to the assistance of each other when attacked by the Heratees in the trenches Except when Mahomed Shah insisted on a combined assault, as on the 24th of June, and the Russian minister directed it, there was no union among them Each had his own game to follow up ; his own laurels to win ; and was rather pleased than disappointed by the failures of his brethren. It was not possible that operations so conducted should have resulted in anything but failure. But it was the deliberate opinion of Eldred Pottinger, expressed nearly two years after the withdrawal of the Persian army, that Mahomed Shah might have taken Herat by assault, within four-and-twenty hours after his appearance before its walls, if his troops had been efficiently commanded *

Whether Mahomed Shah ever rightly understood this

* "It is my firm belief that Mahomed Shah might have carried the city by assault the very first day that he reached Herat, and that even when the garrison gained confidence, and were flushed with the success of their sorties, he might have, by a proper use of the means at his disposal, taken the place in twenty-four hours. His troops were infinitely better soldiers, and quite as brave men, as the Afghans The non-success of their efforts was the fault of their generals We can never again calculate on such, and if the Persians again return, they will do so properly commanded and enlightened as to the causes of their former failure. Their material was on a scale sufficient to have reduced a powerful fortress. The men worked very well at the trenches, considering they were not trained sappers, and the practice of the artillery was really superb. They simply wanted engineers, and a general, to have proved a most formidable force "—[*Eldred Pottinger's Report on Herat: Calcutta, July*, 1840. *MS. Records.*]

matter I do not pretend to know, but he felt that it was necessary to make an effert to patch up the rents which this grievous failure had made in his reputation. So he issued a firman, setting forth all the great results of his expedition to the eastward, and attempted to demonstrate, after the following fashion, that he gained a victory, even at Herat :—"At last," so ran the royal proclamation, "when the city of Herat existed but in name, and the reality of the government of Kamran was reduced to four bare walls, the noble ambassadors of the illustrious British Government, notwithstanding that three separate treaties of peace between the two governments of England and Persia, negotiated respectively by Sir Harford Jones, Sir Gore Ouseley, and Mr. Ellis, were still in force, disregarding the observance of the conditions of these treaties, prepared to undertake hostilities, and as a warlike demonstration, despatched a naval armament with troops and forces to the Gulf of Persia. The winter season was now approaching, and if we protracted to a longer period our stay at Herat, there appeared a possibility that our victorious army might suffer from a scarcity of provisions, and that the maintenance of our troops might not be unaccompanied with difficulty; the tranquillity of our provinces was also a matter of serious attention to our benevolent thoughts; and thus, in sole consideration of the interest of our faith and country, and from a due regard to the welfare of our troops and subjects, we set in motion our world-subduing army upon the 19th of *Jumady-al-Akber*, and prepared to return to our capital. . . . . During the protracted siege of Herat, a vast number of the troops and inhabitants had perished, as well from the fire of our cannon and musketry as from constant hardship and starvation; the remainder of the people, amounting to about 50,000 families, with a large proportion of the Afghan and Persian chiefs, who had been treated with the most liberal kindness by the officers of our goverment, and who being compromised, could not possibly, therefore, hold any further intercourse with Yar Mahomed Khan, marched away with us, with zealous eagerness, to the regions of Khain and Khorassan, and there was no vestige of an inhabited spot left around Herat."

But although the failure of Mahomed Shah is mainly to be attributed to the jealousy, and consequent disunion, of his generals, it would be an injustice to the garrison of Herat not to acknowledge that they owed their safety, in some measure, to their own exertions. Their gallantry and perseverance, however, were not of the most sustained character, and might have yielded to the assaults of the Persians if there had been any union among the assailants. They gathered courage from the languid movements of the besiegers; and, surprised at the little progress made by the once dreaded army of Mahomed Shah, they came in time to regard themselves as heroes, and their successful sorties as great victories. When, on the other hand, the Persians really attempted anything like a combined movement against their works, the garrison began to lose heart, and were with difficulty brought to repulse them. To what extent they were indebted to the unfailing constancy and courage of Eldred Pottinger, has been set forth, but I believe very imperfectly, in this narrative of the siege. Enough, however, has been shown to demonstrate that, but for the heroism of this young Bombay artilleryman, Herat would have fallen into the hands of Mahomed Shah. The garrison were fast breaking down, not so much under the pressure from without as the pressure from within The chiefs were desponding — the people were starving. But still the continued cry of Eldred Pottinger was, "A little longer—a little longer yet." When the chiefs talked of surrender—when they set forth the hopelessness of further efforts of defence—

he counselled still a little further delay. His voice was ever for the manlier course ; and what he recommended in speech he was ever eager to demonstrate in action. Yar Mahomed did great things at Herat. It would be unjust to deny him the praise due to his energetic exertions in the prosecution of the defence, however unscrupulous the means he employed to sustain it. But his energies failed him at last ; and it was only by the powerful stimulants applied by his young European associate that he was supported and invigorated in the great crisis, when the fate of Herat was trembling in the balance. There was one true soldier in Herat, whose energies never failed him ; and History delights to record the fact that that one true soldier, young and inexperienced as he was, with no knowledge of active warfare that he had not derived from books, rescued Herat from the grasp of the Persian monarch, and baffled the intrigues of his great northern abettor.*

About these intrigues something more should be said. No sane man ever questions the assertion that Russian diplomatists encouraged Mahomed Shah to undertake the expedition against Herat, and that Russian officers aided the operations of the siege. No reasonable man doubts that, so encouraging and so aiding Persia in aggressive measures against the frontier of Afghanistan, Russia harboured ulterior designs not wholly unassociated with

* It will have been perceived that I have described the operations of the siege of Herat, almost entirely as from within the walls. I have done this partly, because I believe that the interest of such descriptions is greatly enhanced when the reader is led to identify himself more particularly with one contending party ; and partly because the outside movements of the Persian army have been already detailed in the published letters of Colonel Stoddart and Mr. M'Neill, whilst no account has ever yet been given to the public of the defensive operations of the Heratees. I have already stated that my information has been, for the most part, derived from the Manuscript Journals of Eldred Pottinger.

thoughts of the position of the British in Hindostan. At all events, it is certain that the first word, spoken or written in encouragement of the expedition against Herat, placed Russia in direct antagonism with Great Britain. "The British minister at Tcheran was instructed to dissuade the Shah from such an enterprise, urging reasons of indisputable force, and founded upon the interests of the Shah himself But the advice given by the Russian ambassador was all of an opposite tendency. For while Mr. M'Neill was appealing to the prudence and the reason of the Shah, Count Simonich was exciting the ambition and inflaming the passions of that Sovereign; whilst the one was preaching moderation and peace, the other was inciting to war and conquest, and whilst the one pointed out the difficulties and expense of the enterprise, the other inspired hopes of money and assistance." *

Such, very plainly stated, in grave, official language, had been the relative positions of Russia and Great Britain But when Lord Durham, in 1837, was directed to seek from the Russian minister an explanation of conduct so much at variance with the declarations of the Muscovite Government, the answer was, that if Count Simonich had encouraged Mahomed Shah to proceed against Herat, he acted in direct violation of his instructions

But for a man disobeying the instructions of an arbitrary government, Simonich acted with uncommon boldness. He advanced to the Persian ruler 50,000 tomauns, and promised, that if Mahomed Shah took Herat, the balance of the debt due by Persia to Russia should be remitted Thus encouraged, Mahomed Shah advanced upon Herat How Simonich followed M'Neill to the Persian camp, and how he thwarted the efforts of the

* *Draft of a Note to be presented by the Marquis of Clanricarde to Count Nesselrode. Published Papers.*

British diplomatist to bring about an accommodation of the differences between the two contending states, and how Russian officers subsequently directed the siege, has been already shown. It has been shown, how a Russian agent guaranteed a treaty injurious to British interests, between Mahomed Shah and the Sirdars of Candahar. It has been shown, too, how a Russian agent appeared at Caubul, and how he endeavoured to detach Dost Mahomed from an alliance with the British, and to encourage him to look for support from the Persian King and his Muscovite supporters.

Considering these things, the British Government asked whether the intentions of Russia towards Persia and Afghanistan were to be judged from Count Nesselrode's declarations, or from the actions of Simonich and Vickovich. The answer was, that Vickovich had been despatched to Caubul on a "Commercial Mission," and that, if he had treated of anything but commerce, he had exceeded his instructions; and that Simonich had been instructed, not only to discourage Mahomed Shah from prosecuting the expedition against Herat, but to withdraw the Russian-deserter regiment, which formed no insignificant portion of the invading army. "Not upon the cabinet of Russia," it was said, "can fall the reproach of having encouraged or suggested that fatal enterprise."* The proceedings of

* It is not very clear, however, that the Russian Government, though doubtless discredited by the failure, regarded it as "a fatal enterprise." Russia had a double game to play. In the familiar language of the turf, she "hedged." Whether the Persians won or lost, she was sure to gain something. The views of Russian statesmen have been thus set forth, not improbably in the very language of one of them:

"Russia," it is stated, "has played a very successful, as well as a very safe, game in the late proceedings. When she prompted the Shah to undertake the siege of Herat, she was certain of carrying an important point, however the expedition terminated. If Herat fell, which there was every reason to expect, then Candahar and Caubul

the agents were repudiated. Vickovich, being a person of no account, was remorselessly sacrificed, and he blew out his brains. But an apology was found for Count Simonich. It was said that he only assisted a friendly state when in extreme difficulty, and that any English officer would have done the same.*

There was some truth in this. At all events, when it was added by the Russian minister that his government had more reason to be alarmed by the movements of Great Britain, than Great Britain by the movements of Russia; and that England sought to monopolise the privilege of intrigue in Central Asia, it was difficult for any candid and unprejudiced observer of events to comment harshly upon the injustice of the imputation. When, too, some time afterwards, Baron Brunow said to Sir John Hobhouse, "If we go on at this rate, the Cossack and the Sepoy will soon meet on the banks of the Oxus,"† it would have been hard to have laid the contemplated collision wholly to the account of the restlessness of the Czar.

would certainly have made their submission. Russian influence would thus have been brought to the threshold of India; and England, however much she might desire peace, could not avoid being involved in a difficult and expensive war, in order to avert more serious dangers. If, on the other hand, England interfered to save Herat, she was compromised—not with the mere court of Mahomed Shah, but with Persia as a nation. Russia had contrived to bring all Persia to Herat, and to identify all Persia with the success or failure of the campaign; and she had thus gravelled the old system of partisanship, which would have linked Azerbijan with herself, and the rest of the nation with her rival."—[*Calcutta Review.*]

* *Count Nesselrode's Instructions to Count Pozzo di Borgo: November* 1, 1839.

† Sir John Hobhouse's answer is worth giving. "Very probably, Baron; but however much I should regret the collision, I should have no fear of the result." I give this on the authority of a distinguished writer on "Our Political Relations with Persia," in the *Calcutta Review.*

True it is, that the policy of Russia in the East had been distinguished for its aggressive tendencies;* and it is equally true, that in the plenitude of our national self-love, we encouraged the conviction that Great Britain had conquered the entire continent of Hindostan by a series of purely defensive measures. Looking merely at the recognised policy of the East India Company, the distinction may be admitted. For a century have this great body been steadfastly setting their face against the extension of their empire; but their empire has been extended in spite of them, and their agents have been less pacific than themselves. The general tendency of the Eastern policy worked out by the English in India, has not been purely defensive, and they are, perhaps, the last people in the world entitled to complain of the encroachments of their allies. England and Russia seemed at one time to be— and, perhaps, they are still—approaching each other on the vast Central-Asia battle-field; but when the account between the two great European states comes to be struck, it is doubtful whether History will set down against the Muscovite power any greater transgression than that which it is the object of these volumes to record.†

* For a very interesting and ably written summary of the progress of Russia in the East, and an elaborate investigation of the question of the possibility of a Russian invasion of India, see Mr. Robert Bell's excellent "History of Russia." It was written before the British crossed the Indus—before Russia entangled herself in the steppes, and England in the defiles of Central Asia. Neither country now, remembering these disasters, thinks of the meeting of the Sepoy and the Cossack without a shudder.

† I may as well mention here that the chasm between Persia and Great Britain, created by the events narrated in this chapter, was not bridged over until the spring of 1841, when Ghorian was given back to the Heratees. Before the close of that year, Mahomed Shah was collecting a great army, and contemplating extensive operations, the object of which, according to Sir John M'Neill, though disguised under the name of operations against Khiva, was another assault upon Herat. —

[*Sir John M'Neill to Sir Alexander Burnes: January* 5, 1842. *MS.*]
This letter was written more than two months after Burnes had fallen a victim to the policy which I am now about to elucidate. Sir John M'Neill wrote : "I have now to inform you, that since the arrival of Count Medem, the new Russian Minister, about a month ago, the Shah has given orders for collecting an army in the spring, about two months hence, which is intended to be numerous, and to be accompanied by two hundred pieces of Artillery; and he announces his intention to march in the direction of Meshed, for the purpose of attacking Khiva. The advance of the Shah with such an army to Meshed, may produce some commotion in Afghanistan, as you will no doubt hear of his proposing to go to Herat ; and I conclude, therefore, that you will be prepared to put down any movements that may be caused by the rumour of his approach, and for any ulterior measures that may be necessary." But in a postscript, dated January 6, the very day on which the British commenced their lamentable retreat from Caubul, he added : "Since writing the preceding lines, some circumstances which have come to my knowledge, lead me to think it quite possible that the Shah may not follow out his intention of going with an army into Khorassan, and it is even possible that no army may be sent in that direction ; but I am still of opinion, that it is considerably more probable that a force will be sent, than that it will not ; and if a large army should march to Meshed, its objects will, I think, have reference rather to Herat than to Khiva."—[*MS. Correspondence.*]

CHAPTER III.

[1837—1838.]

Policy of the British-Indian Government—Our Defensive Operations—Excitement in British India—Proposed Alliance with Dost Mahomed—Failure of Burnes's Mission considered—The claims of the Suddozye Princes—The Tripartite Treaty—Invasion of Afghanistan determined—Policy of the Movement.

WHILST the Persians were pushing on the siege of Herat to an unsuccessful termination, and the Russians were extending over them the wings of encouragement and assistance, the English in India were devising measures for the security of their own dominions, which seemed to be threatened by these movements on the frontier of Afghanistan.

But what these measures were to be it was not easy to determine. It was believed that the danger was great and imminent. There was a Persian army, under the command of the "King-of-Kings" himself, investing Herat, and threatening to march upon Candahar and Caubul. There were Russian diplomatists and Russian engineers in his camp, directing the counsels of the Shah and the operations of the siege. The Barukzye Sirdars of Afghanistan were intriguing with the Persian Court; and far out in the distance, beyond the mountains of the Hindoo-Koosh, there was the shadow of a great northern army, tremendous in its indistinctness, sweeping across the wilds and deserts of Central Asia, towards the frontiers of Hindostan.

The remoteness of the countries in which these incidents were passing, might have reconciled our Anglo-Indian statesmen to dangers of a character so vague, and an origin so distant; but the result of all these disturbing rumours was an after-growth of new perils springing up almost at our very doors. The Native States on our own borders were beginning to evince signs of feverish unrest From the hills of Nepaul and the jungles of Burmah came mutterings of threatened invasion, which compelled the British-Indian Government to look well to their lines of frontier Even in our own provinces, these rumours of mighty movements in the countries of the north-west disquieted the native mind ; there was an uneasy, restless feeling among all classes, scarcely amounting to actual disaffection, and perhaps best to be described as a state of ignorant expectancy—a looking outwards in the belief of some coming change, the nature of which no one clearly understood Among our Mussulman subjects the feeling was somewhat akin to that which had unsettled their minds at the time when the rumoured advent of Zemaun Shah made them look for the speedy restoration of Mahomedan supremacy in Hindostan. In their eyes, indeed, the movement beyond the Afghan frontier took the shape of a Mahomedan invasion, and it was believed that countless thousands of true believers were about to pour themselves over the plains of the Punjab and Hindostan, and to wrest all the country between the Indus and the sea from the hands of the infidel usurpers. The Mahomedan journals, at this time, teemed with the utterances of undisguised sedition. There was a decline in the value of public securities, and it went openly from mouth to mouth, in the streets and the bazaars, that the Company's Raj was nearly at an end

The dangers which threatened the security of our Anglo-Indian Empire, in 1837-38, were seen through the magnifying medium of ignorance, and greatly exaggerated in the recital. But the appearance of the Persian army before Herat; the presence of the Russian officers in the Persian camp; and the intrigues of the Barukzye Sirdars of Afghanistan, were, at all events, substantial facts. It was little doubted that Herat would fall. There seemed, indeed, no possibility of escape. The character of Mahomed Shah was well known; and it was not believed that, having conquered Herat, he would there stop short in his career of conquest. It had been long officially reported, by Mr. Ellis and others, to the Anglo-Indian Government, that Mahomed Shah encouraged very extensive ideas of Afghan conquest, and that the Russian officers about his Court were continually exerting themselves to foster the flame of his ambition. It seemed probable, therefore, that Herat, having fallen into the hands of Mahomed Shah, the Persian monarch would either push on his conquests to Candahar and Caubul, or, having transferred the Heratee principality to the hands of the Candahar Sirdars, and rendered Dost Mahomed such assistance in his wars against the Sikhs as would make him, in effect, the vassal of Persia, would erect, in Afghanistan, a platform of observation which might serve as the basis of future operations to be undertaken, not only by the Persians themselves, but also by their great northern allies.

It was plainly the policy of the British Government to preserve the independence of Afghanistan, and to cement a friendly alliance with the ruler or rulers of that country. But it was not very easy to discern how this was to be effected. Our Indian statesmen had never exhibited any very violent friendship for the Barukzye Sirdars. Lord William Bentinck had refused to connect himself in any way with the politics of Afghanistan; but he had suffered Shah Soojah to raise, in 1833-34, an army of invasion under the shadow of the British flag, and had done everything but openly assist the enterprise he was undertaking for the recovery of his lost dominions. Some nice ideas of legitimacy and usurpation, suggested by our own position in India, may have closed the sympathies of our Anglo-Indian rulers against men who were simply the *de facto* rulers of Afghanistan, and who laboured under 'the imputation of having rather acquired their dominions by right of conquest than possessed them by right of birth. The British-Indian Government had not concerned itself for a quarter of a century about the government of the Douranee Empire; but it now appeared that, because Zemaun Shah had threatened to invade India, and Shah Soojah had demonstrated his incapacity to maintain himself in security on the throne, and to preserve the integrity of his dominions, the English in India, when they thought of establishing a friendly and a permanent power in the country beyond the Indus, turned to the Suddozye Princes as the fittest instruments for the furtherance of these ends. Even in 1833-34 it was plain that the success of Shah Soojah would have delighted our Indian statesmen. Though we declined to aid him in a very substantial manner; our sympathies went with him; and now again it was obvious that we had very little desire to conciliate the friendship of the Barukzye Sirdars, who had long been eager for a closer alliance with the great European power beyond the waters of the Sutlej, but who had always been condemned to have their advances coldly received.

Before Mahomed Shah had advanced upon Herat, the British Minister at the Court of Teheran, well acquainted with the ambitious projects of the Persian monarch, had earnestly pressed upon the attention of the British Government the expediency of some counteracting movement in the country between Persia and Hindostan. And when it was known to Mr. M'Neill that Lord Auckland had despatched Captain Burnes upon a mission to the Court of Dost Mahomed, he wrote a long confidential letter to that officer, setting forth the advantages of subsidising the Ameer, and placing both Herat and Candahar under his rule. The letter was dated March 13th, 1837. "I sincerely wish," wrote Mr. M'Neill, "if the Ameer Dost Mahomed Khan and you come to a good understanding, that he were in possession of both Candahar and Herat." *

And again, in the same communication, he wrote more explicitly: "Dost Mahomed Khan, with a little aid from us, could be put in possession of both Candahar and Herat. I anxiously hope that aid will not be withheld. A loan of money would possibly enable him to do this, and would give us a great hold upon him. He ought to be precluded from receiving any other foreign representative or agent of any kind at his Court, and should agree to transact all business with foreign powers through the British agent. Unless something of this kind should be done, we shall never be secure; and until Dost Mahomed Khan or some other Afghan shall have got both Candahar and Herat into his hands, our position here must continue to be a false one." †

At this time, the Envoy in Persia, though profoundly convinced that the Candahar Sirdars were not to be trusted, and that the game they were playing was one injurious to the interests of Great Britain, seemed to repose confidence in the good feeling of Dost Mahomed, and to believe that it would be easy to secure his alliance. Of the intrigues of the former he wrote: "Kohun Dil Khan is playing a double game, and trying to strengthen himself by the alliance with Persia against both Caubul

---

* *Mr. M'Neill to Captain Burnes. MS. Records.*
† Id. ibid.

and Herat. He has put himself in communication with the Russian minister here, who has sent by the return envoy, Tej Mahomed Khan, Barukzye, a letter and presents. The letter will not find its way to the Khan,* for I am sending it to Lord Palmerston; but the presents have been forwarded, and it appears that Kohun Dil was the first to open the correspondence, and I think it not improbable that he had been advised to do so by Aziz Mahomed Khan, the agent formerly sent hither, who found the Court apparently devoted to Russia. I hope you will be able to put a stop to the intercourse, which I have only been able to impede and interrupt for a time."

Such were the views and recommendations of Mr. M'Neill. Among the few officers in the Company's service who at that time had any knowledge of the politics of Central Asia, not one was more conspicuous than Captain Claude Wade, who had held for some years the delicate and responsible office of Governor-General's agent on the North-Western Frontier. It was natural that, in such a conjuncture, the opinions of so well-informed and experienced an officer should have been sought by the Supreme Government. Captain Wade, through whose office the Trans-Indian correspondence passed, now therefore, on forwarding to government a copy of Mr. M'Neill's letter, freely expressed his opinion against the proposal to consolidate the Afghan Empire under the rule of the Caubul Ameer. "In my opinion," he wrote to Mr. Colvin, the private secretary of the Governor-General, "such an experiment on the part of our government would be to play into the hands of our rivals, and to deprive ourselves, as it were by a *felo-de-se*, of the powerful means which we have in reserve of controlling the present rulers

---

* Count Simonich's letter was intercepted, and taken to M'Neill by one Meer Mahomed, whom M'Neill subsequently placed at the disposal of Burnes.

of Afghanistan. The attempt to reduce the country to the sway of one of them would be an arduous enterprise. The chief obstacle in the way of Dost Mahomed would be in the opposition of those who are inimical to him and his family, and these include every other Douranee tribe in the country, to whom, therefore, the knowledge of such a design would render our name generally odious—whilst the attempt itself would undoubtedly lead the Toorkomans and other great bordering tribes to view with jealousy the powers of a chief whose interests they would soon have the sagacity to discover we had adopted for the purpose of serving our own interests at their expense."

"Our policy," continued Captain Wade, "ought not to be to destroy, but to use our endeavours to preserve and strengthen the different governments of Afghanistan as they at present stand; to promote among themselves a social compact, and to conduce, by our influence, to the establishment of that peace with their neighbours, which we are now endeavouring to produce between them and the Sikhs on one side, and the Sikhs and Sindhians on the other. Whilst distributed into several states, the Afghans are, in my opinion, more likely to subserve the views and interests of the British Government than if we attempted to impose on them the yoke of a ruler to whose authority they can never be expected to yield a passive obedience. Though undoubtedly weak, they would collectively be fully adequate to the defence of their country, when they have derived the advantages of a more decided intercourse with our government than at present exists. . . . Supposing that we were to aid Dost Mahomed to overthrow in the first place his brother at Candahar, and then his Suddozye rival at Herat, what would be the consequence? As the system, of which it is intended to be a part, would not go to gratify the longing wish of Mahomed Shah for the annexation of Herat to his dominions, the first results would be, that the Shah-zadah Kamran would apply to Persia, and offer, on the condition of her assistance to save him from the fate which impended over his head, to submit to all the demands of that general, which Kamran has hitherto so resolutely and successfully resisted, and between his fears and the attempts of Dost Mahomed Khan to take it (Herat), which is regarded by every one who has studied its situation as the key to Afghanistan, would inevitably fall prostrate before the arms of Persia, by the effect of the very measures which we had designed for her security from Persian thraldom "*

The expediency of maintaining the integrity of Herat was not at this time more palpable than the injustice of destroying it. But it hardly seems to have entered into the consideration of our Indian statesmen, that to transfer Herat, or any other unoffending principality from the hands of one ruler to those of another, was to perpetrate an act of political tyranny not to be justified by any reference to the advantages resulting from such a course. We had not, at that time, the shadow of a pretext for breaking down the independence of Herat. Kamran, indeed, was at this time about to play the very game that tended most to the advancement of British interests Had he formed an alliance with Persia, having for its end the recovery of his father's dominions—had he advanced, with a confederate Persian army, upon Caubul and Candahar, and consented to abandon Herat as the price of Kujjur assistance—some pretext might have been found in these aggressive measures for the confiscation of the principality. But Herat was now about to erect itself into a barrier against Russo-Persian invasion, and to fight single-handed the first great battle of resistance at the gates of Afghanistan.

* *Captain Wade to J. R. Colvin, Esq., June 27, 1837. MS. Records*

Mr. M'Neill's project for the consolidation of the Afghan Empire found little favour in the eyes of our Indian statesmen; but there were many who thought that, without any acts of spoliation and oppression, the *de facto* rulers of Afghanistan might be so encouraged and conciliated by small offers of assistance, as to secure their friendly co-operation in the great work of resisting invasion from the westward. But when Captain Burnes was despatched to Caubul, his powers were so limited, that, although he was profuse in his expressions of sympathy, he had not the authority to offer substantial assistance; and when he ventured to exceed the instructions of government, he was severely censured for his unauthorised proceedings.

His mission failed. What wonder? It could by no possibility have succeeded. If utter failure had been the great end sought to be accomplished, the whole business could not have been more cunningly devised. Burnes asked everything; and promised nothing. He was tied hand and foot. He had no power to treat with Dost Mahomed. All that he could do was to demand on one hand and refuse on the other. He talked about the friendship of the British Government. Dost Mahomed asked for some proof of it; and no proof was forthcoming. The wonder is, not that the Ameer at last listened to the overtures of others, but that he did not seek other assistance before.

No better proof of his earnest desire to cement an alliance with the British Government need be sought for than that involved in the fact of his extreme reluctance to abandon all hope of assistance from the British, and to turn his eyes in another direction. It was not until he was driven to despair by resolute refusals from the quarter whence he looked for aid, that he accepted the offers so freely made to him by other States, and set the seal upon his own destruction. "Our government," said Burnes, "would do nothing; but the Secretary of the Russian Legation came with the most direct offers of assistance and money, and as I had no power to counteract him by a similar offer, and got wigged for talking of it at a time when it would have been merely a dead letter to say Afghanistan was under our protection, I was obliged of course to give in."* What better result Lord Auckland could have anticipated, it is hard to say. If the failure of the Mission astonished him, he must have been the most sanguine of men.

I am unable to perceive that there was anything unreasonable or unfriendly in the conduct of Dost Mahomed at this time. That, from the very first, he was disappointed, there is no doubt. He had formed exaggerated ideas of the generosity and munificence of the British Government in the East, and, doubtless, expected great things from the contemplated alliance. The Mission had scarcely been a day in Caubul, when the feelings of the Ameer were shocked, the exuberance of his hopes somewhat straitened, and his dignity greatly offended, by the paltry character of the presents of which Burnes was the bearer. No one ignorant of the childish eagerness with which Oriental Princes examine the ceremonial gifts presented to them by foreign potentates, and the importance which they attach to the value of these presents, as indications of a greater or less degree of friendship and respect on the part of the donor, can appreciate the mortification of Dost Mahomed on discovering that the British Government, of whose immense resources and boundless liberality he had so exalted a notion, had sent him nothing but a few trumpery toys Burnes had been directed to "procure from Bombay such articles as would be required to be

* *Private Correspondence of Sir A. Burnes.*

given in presents to the different chiefs." And it had been characteristically added: "They ought not to be of a costly nature, but should be chosen particularly with a view to exhibit the superiority of British manufacturers." Accordingly the envoy had provided himself with a pistol and a telescope for Dost Mahomed, and a few trifles for the inmates of the Zenana—such as pins, needles, and playthings.* The costliness of the presents lavished upon Shah Soojah, when the Mission under Mountstuart Elphinstone had entered Afghanistan, was still a tradition throughout the country. The Ameer was disappointed. He thought that the niggardliness of the British Government, in this instance portended no good. Nor was he mistaken. He soon found that the intention to give little was manifest in all the proceedings of the Mission.

It has been said that the Ameer asked more than could reasonably be granted; that he had no right to look for the restoration of Peshawur, as that tract of country, since the dismemberment of the Douranee Empire, had fallen to the share of Sultan Mahomed. It is very true that the country had once been governed by Sultan Mahomed. Now to have re-established him at Peshawur would have been to have paved the way for the march of Runjeet Singh's army to Caubul. So thought Dost Mahomed. It was better to submit quietly to the unassisted enmity of the Maharajah, than to have an insidious enemy on the frontier, by whose agency Runjeet Singh might have accomplished that which he could not have achieved alone. It was the treachery of Sultan Mahomed that had lost Peshawur to the Afghans. It was the personal energy, the martial prowess, of Dost Mahomed that had secured the supremacy of the Barukzyes in

---

* See Harlan's account of the reception of these presents. I see no reason to question its veracity.

Afghanistan; and as Sultan Mahomed Khan wanted the ability, or the honesty, to hold his own at Peshawur, it was but natural and fitting that the chief of the Barukzyes should endeavour to enter into arrangements better calculated to preserve the integrity of the Afghan frontier. He desired, in the first instance, the absolute possession of Peshawur on his own account. He subsequently consented to hold it, conjointly with Sultan Mahomed, in vassalage to Runjeet Singh. Had the British Government endeavoured to effect an amicable arrangement between the Ameer and the Maharajah, there is no room to doubt that Dost Mahomed would have rejected all overtures from the westward, and proved to us a firm and faithful ally. But, instead of this, we offered him nothing but our sympathy; and Dost Mahomed, with all respect for the British Government, looked for something more substantial than mere meaningless words.

That his conduct throughout the long negotiations with Burnes was characterised by an entire singleness of purpose and straightforwardness of action is not to be maintained; but it may with truth be said that it evinced somewhat less than the ordinary amount of Afghan duplicity and deceit. Singleness and straightforwardness do not flourish in the near neighbourhood either of Eastern or Western diplomacy; and perhaps it is not wise, on our own account, to look too closely into these matters. The wonder is, not that the Ameer was so deceitful, so tortuous, so arrogant, and so exacting, but that he was so sincere, so straightforward, so patient, and so moderate. He might have possessed all these qualities in much scantier measure, and yet have been a very respectable Afghan chief.

It was, however, decreed that Dost Mahomed was a hostile chief; and the policy of the British Government soon made him one. Had Burnes been left to obey the dictates of his own reason and to use the light of his own experience, he would have conciliated both the Candahar Sirdars and the Caubul Ameer, and raised up an effective bulwark in Afghanistan against Persian invasion and Russian intrigue. We refused to detach Kohun Dil Khan from the Persian alliance, and we deliberately drove Dost Mahomed Khan into it. In fact, our policy, at this time, seems to have been directed to the creation of those very difficulties to encounter which the British Government launched into the Afghan war.

Unfortunately, at this time, Lord Auckland was separated from his Council. He was on his way to that pleasant hill Sanitarium, at Simlah, where our Governors-General, surrounded by irresponsible advisers, settle the destinies of empires without the aid of their legitimate fellow-counsellors, and which has been the cradle of more political insanity than any place within the limits of Hindostan. Just as Mahomed Shah was beginning to open his batteries upon Herat, and Captain Burnes was entering Caubul, Lord Auckland, taking with him three civilians, all men of ability and repute—Mr. William Macnaghten, Mr. Henry Torrens, and Mr. John Colvin — turned his back upon Calcutta.

Mr. Macnaghten was at this time chief secretary to Government. He had originally entered the service of the East India Company in the year 1809, as a cadet of cavalry on the Madras establishment; and whilst yet a boy acquired considerable reputation by the extent of his acquirements as an Oriental linguist. Transferred in 1814 to the Bengal civil service, he landed at Calcutta as the bearer of the highest testimonials from the government under which he had served; and soon justified by his distinguished scholarship in the college of Fort William the praises and recommendations of the authorities of Madras. It was publicly said of the young civilian by

Lord Hastings, that "there was not a language taught in the college in which he had not earned the highest distinctions which the Government or the College could bestow." On leaving college he was appointed an assistant in the office of the Register of the Sudder Dewany Adawlut, or High Court of Appeal; and in 1818 he quitted Calcutta to enter upon the practical duties of the magistracy, but after a few years was recalled to the Presidency and to his old office, and in a little while was at the head of the department in which he had commenced his career. During a period of eight years and a half, Mr Macnaghten continued to occupy the responsible post of Register of the Sudder Dewany Adawlut, and was only removed thence to accompany Lord William Bentinck, in the capacity of secretary, on the tour which that benevolent statesman was about to commence, at the close of 1830, through the Upper and Western Provinces of India. The objects of this journey were connected entirely with measures of internal reform; but having approached the territories of Runjeet Singh, the Governor-General met the old Sikh chief at Roopur, and there Macnaghten, who had up to this time been almost wholly associated with affairs of domestic administration, graduated in foreign politics, and began to fathom the secrets of the Lahore Durbar. Returning early in 1833 to Calcutta, with his experience greatly enlarged and his judgment matured by the opportunities afforded him on his journey, as well as by his intimate relationship with so enlightened and liberal a statesman as Lord William Bentinck, Macnaghten now took charge of the Secret and Political Department of the Government Secretariat, and remained in that office during the interregnum of Sir Charles Metcalfe, and the first year of Lord Auckland's administration, until summoned by the latter to accompany him on his tour to the North-Western Provinces.

Such, briefly narrated, were the antecedents of Macnaghten's official life. That he was one of the ablest and most assiduous of the many able and assiduous civil servants of the East India Company all men were ready to admit. With a profound knowledge of Oriental languages and Oriental customs, he combined an extensive acquaintance with all the practical details of government, and was scarcely more distinguished as an erudite scholar than as an expert secretary. In his colleague and assistant, Mr. Henry Torrens, there were some points of resemblance to Macnaghten; for the younger officer was also an accomplished linguist and a ready writer, but he was distinguished by a more mercurial temperament and more varied attainments. Perhaps there was not in all the presidencies of India a man—certainly not so young a man—with the lustre of so many accomplishments upon him. The facility with which he acquired every kind of information was scarcely more remarkable than the tenacity with which he retained it. With the languages of the East and the West he was equally familiar. He had read books of all kinds and in all tongues, and the airy grace with which he could throw off a French canzonet was something as perfect of its kind as the military genius with which he could sketch out the plan of a campaign, or the official pomp with which he could inflate a state paper. His gaiety and vivacity made him a welcome addition to the Governor-General's vice-regal court; and perhaps not the least of his recommendations as a travelling companion was that he could amuse the ladies of Lord Auckland's family with as much felicity as he could assist the labours of that nobleman himself.

Mr. John Colvin was the private secretary of the Governor-General, and his confidential adviser. Of all the men about Lord Auckland, he was believed to exercise the most direct influence over that statesman's mind.

Less versatile than Torrens, and less gifted with the lighter accomplishments of literature and art, he possessed a stronger will and a more powerful understanding. He was a man of much decision and resolution of character; not troubled with doubts and misgivings; and sometimes, perhaps, hasty in his judgments. But there was something noble and generous in his ambition. He never forgot either the claims of his country or the reputation of his chief. And if he were vain, his vanity was of the higher, but not the less dangerous class, which seeks rather to mould the measures and establish the fame of others than to acquire distinction for self.

Such were the men who accompanied Lord Auckland to the Upper Provinces of India. About him also clustered the common smaller staff of military *aides-de-camp;* and not very far in the back-ground were the two sisters of his lordship—ladies of remarkable intelligence and varied accomplishments, who are supposed to have exercised an influence not wholly confined to the social amenities of the vice-regal camp. Lord Auckland was not wanting in judgment or sagacity, and his integrity of purpose is undoubted; but he lacked decision of character; he too often mistrusted his own opinions, and yielded his assent to those of irresponsible advisers less single-minded and sagacious than himself. The men by whom he was surrounded were among the ablest and most accomplished in the country; but it was for the most part a dangerous kind of cleverness that they possessed; there was too much presumption in it. These secretaries, especially the two younger ones, were too ardent and impulsive—they were of too bold and ambitious a nature to be regarded as anything better than perilous and delusive guides. But Lord Auckland entrusted himself to their guidance. Perhaps, he scarcely knew to what extent he was swayed by their counsels; but it is my deliberate conviction, that if he had not quitted Calcutta, or if he had been surrounded by older and more experienced advisers, he would have followed a line of policy more in accordance with his own feelings and opinions, and less destructive to the interests of the empire.

But, so surrounded, Lord Auckland journeyed by easy stages towards the cool mountain-ranges of the Himalayah; and as he advanced, there came to the vice-regal camp tidings, from time to time, of the progress or no-progress of Mahomed Shah's army before Herat, and of Burnes's diplomatic movements at the Court of the Caubul Ameer. There was much in all this to perplex Lord Auckland. He was in all sincerity a man of peace. They who best knew his character and that of his chief secretary,* predicted that if war could, in any way, be avoided, there would be no war. But from all quarters came disturbing hints and dangerous promptings; and Lord Auckland thus assailed, had not resolution enough to be true to his own moderate and cautious character.† Mr. M'Neill had despatched Major Todd from Herat to the camp of the Governor-General; and had urgently solicited Lord Auckland to adopt vigorous measures for the intimidation of

* Lord William Bentinck is said to have exclaimed, "What! Lord Auckland and Macnaghten gone to war! The very last men in the world I should have suspected of such folly!"

† In the preceding year he had written to Sir Charles Metcalfe, "You are quite right in believing that I have not a thought of interference between the Afghans and the Sikhs. I should not be sorry to see strong, independent, and commercial powers established in Afghanistan; but short of Persian or Russian occupation, their present state is as unsatisfactory as possible, with national, family, and religious feuds so inveterate as almost to make one party ready to join any invader against another. It is out of the question that we can ever gain direct power or influence amongst them."—[*Life of Lord Metcalfe*, vol. ii. p. 307.] It was upon the basis of this assumption that he subsequently reared the delusive project of re-establishing "the integrity of the Douranee Empire."

Persia and the defence of Herat, which, it was alleged, could not much longer resist the efforts of the investing force. Nothing short of the march of a British army upon Herat was thought by some sufficient to stem the tide of Russo-Persian invasion. The British Government, seeing everywhere signs of the restless aggressive spirit of Russia, and the evident tendency of all her movements towards the East, had written strong letters to the Governor-General, urging him to adopt vigorous measures of defence. His own immediate advisers were at hand to second the suggestions both of Mr. M'Neill and the British Minister; and so Lord Auckland, though he hesitated to undertake a grand military expedition across the Indus, was persuaded to enter upon defensive measures of a dubious character, affecting the whole question of the sovereignty of the Douranee Empire.

The open, acknowledged danger, to be met by vigorous measures on the part of our Anglo-Indian statesmen, was the attempt of Mahomed Shah to destroy the integrity of Herat, and his asserted claims to the sovereignty of Ghuznee and Candahar. It is true that by the ninth article of the treaty with Persia, England was especially bound not to interfere in any quarrels between the Afghans and the Persians; but our statesmen both in the East and the West, saw a ready means of escape from these conditions in the circumstances of the assault on Mr. M'Neill's courier, which, however contemptible in themselves, were sufficient to bring about a temporary rupture between Persia and Great Britain. Lord Auckland was slow to encourage an idea of the expediency of such direct interference as would be involved in the passage of a British army across the great boundary line of the Indus. But he saw the necessity of so establishing our influence in Afghanistan as to erect a secure barrier against invasion from the westward; and now that he had abandoned all desire to propitiate Dost Mahomed and the Barukzye chiefs, and had begun to think of carrying out his objects through other agency, it was only natural that he should have turned his thoughts, in the first instance, to the Suddozye pensioner of Loodhianah, who had made so many unsuccessful efforts to reseat himself upon the throne of the Douranee Empire.

Shah Soojah had lived so long upon the bounty of the British Government, that it was only reasonable to believe that we should find in him a fast friend and a faithful ally. But when in the month of May, 1838, Lord Auckland, then at Simlah, wrote an elaborate minute, setting forth his opinions regarding the measures best calculated to secure the integrity of the western frontier of Afghanistan, and suggesting the restoration of the exiled Suddozye Prince, it was evident that he had not, at that time, grasped the grand, but perilous idea, of sending a British army into the fastnesses of Afghanistan to break down the dynasty of the Barukzyes, to set up a monarch of our own, and so to roll back for ever the tide of western invasion. He meditated nothing more at this time than the encouragement of an expedition to be undertaken by Shah Soojah and Runjeet Singh, the British Government supplying money, appointing an accredited agent to accompany the Shah's camp, and furnishing a certain number of British officers to direct the movements of the Shah's army.* It appeared to him that there were but three

* "Of plans, of this nature, that of granting our aid or countenance in concert with Runjeet Singh, to enable Shah Soojah-ool-Moolk to re-establish his sovereignty in the Eastern division of Afghanistan, under engagements which shall conciliate the feelings of the Sikh ruler, and bind the restored monarch to the support of our interests, appears to me to be decidedly the most deserving of attention. Shah Soojah-ool-Moolk and Maharajah Runjeet Singh would probably act readily upon such a plan, it being similar to that in which they were before engaged, but which failed principally from the want of pecuniary aid, and

courses open to him; "the first to confine our defensive measures to the line of the Indus, and to leave Afghanistan to its fate; the second, to attempt to save Afghanistan, by granting succour to the existing chiefships of Caubul and Candahar; the third, to permit or to encourage the advance of Runjeet Singh's armies upon Caubul, under counsel and restriction, and as subsidiary to his advance to organise an expedition headed by Shah Soojah, such as I have above explained." "The first course," argued Lord Auckland, "would be absolute defeat, and would leave a free opening to Russian and Persian intrigue upon our frontiers. The second would be only to give power to those who feel greater animosity against the Sikhs, than they do against the Persians, and who would probably use against the former the means placed at their disposal; and the third course, which in the event of the successful resistance of Herat, would appear to be most expedient, would, if the state were to fall into the hands of the Persians, have yet more to recommend it, and I cannot hesitate to say, that the inclination of my opinion is, for the reasons which will be gathered from this paper, very strongly in favour of it."*

All this is sufficiently moderate, if it is not sufficiently

---

the absence of our active sanction and support. In such an enterprise (which both from past experience, and from the circumstance that it would be undertaken in resistance of an attempt to establish *Sheeah* supremacy in the country, would, we believe, have many partisans in Afghanistan) Runjeet Singh would assist by the employment of a portion of his troops, and we by some contribution in money, and the presence of an accredited agent of the government, and of a sufficient number of officers for the direction of the Shah's army."—[*Minute of Lord Auckland's, Simlah, May* 12, 1838—*MS. Records.*] A portion of this minute is given in the published correspondence. The passage quoted, and indeed, all the latter and more practical portion of it, is omitted.

* *Minute of Lord Auckland—Unpublished portion: MS. Records.*

just. The whole question is argued simply as one of expediency. It appeared to Lord Auckland to be most expedient to construct an alliance between Runjeet Singh and Shah Soojah for the recovery of the lost dominions of the latter. England was to remain in the back-ground jingling the money-bag. At this time, it had been arranged that Macnaghten should proceed, with little delay, to the Court of Lahore. It had been intended, in the first instance, that the mission should be merely a complimentary one. But as events began to thicken in the north-west, it appeared impossible to confine to such narrow limits the communications which he was instructed to make to the Maharajah. He was now enjoined to sound Runjeet Singh on the subject of the proposed confederate expedition against the Barukzye Sirdars of Afghanistan. These instructions were written three days after the minute of the 12th of May. It seems that in this brief interval some idea of the employment of British troops in support of the Suddozye prince had dawned upon the understanding of the Governor-General. It is certain, at least, that the letter written by Mr. Torrens speaks of a demonstration to be made "by a division of the British army occupying Shikarpoor." * This was a step in advance. The great project to which Lord Auckland subsequently lent himself was only then beginning to take shape in his mind.

* It is worth while to quote some passages from this letter of instructions; only a grandiloquent passage setting forth generally the pacific views of Lord Auckland, and the power of the British Government having been inserted in the Blue Book. "You can then, as you observe the disposition of the Maharajah, listen to all he has to say, or, in the event of his showing no disposition to commence the conference, you can state to him the views of your own government—that two courses of proceeding had occurred to his lordship—the one that the treaty formerly executed between his Highness and Shah Soojah should be recognised by the British Government—that whilst the

The Mission crossed the Sutlej, and on the 31st of May were presented to Runjeet Singh at Adeena-nuggur. In a mango-grove—each under the shadow of its own tree—the Sikh ruler had ordered a number of mud-huts to be erected for the accommodation of Macnaghten and his companions. Small and comfortless as were these abodes, the officers of the Mission joyfully resorted to them for shelter from the intolerable summer-sun and the burning winds, which had scorched them in their own tents. Even now something horrible in the retrospect to the survivors of the Mission is the fiery heat of that June weather.

In the midst of much pomp and splendour, surrounded by his courtiers, the Maharajah received the English gentlemen* with befitting cordiality and respect. As

Sikhs advanced cautiously on Caubul, accompanied by British agents, a demonstration should be made by a division of the British army occupying Shikarpoor with Shah Soojah in their company, to whom the British Government would advance money to enable him to levy troops and purchase arms, and to whom also the services of British officers should be lent, that the same opportunity should be taken of securing to the Maharajah what it had been customary for him to receive from the Scindhians, and that with regard to Shikarpoor, the supplementary article in the treaty now proposed (and which with a second supplementary article relating to Herat is annexed to this despatch) should be substituted for Article IV. in the former treaty—that in the event of his Highness agreeing to this convention, the Governor-General would be prepared to ratify it, unless circumstances should intermediately have occurred to induce his Lordship to alter his views as to its expediency, and that in the event of the convention being ratified by his Lordship, the descent on Shikarpoor, for temporary occupation, should be directed as soon as due preparations could be made, and the season

---

* Captain Osborne, Lord Auckland's nephew and military secretary; Captain George Macgregor, of the artillery, one of his aides-de-camp, whose name has since become associated with some of the most honourable incidents of the Afghan war; and Dr. Drummond, accompanied Macnaghten.

Macnaghten entered the hall, the aged Prince rose from will permit. If his Highness also approved of this convention, and agreed that the operations of the allies should be conducted in concert with each other, by means of British agents in the camp of each, the Governor-General would be prepared to enter into a general defensive alliance with his Highness against the attacks of all enemies from the westward.

"You will, at the same time, propound the only other course of proceedings which, in the opinion of the Governor-General, the case admits of, which is to allow the Maharajah to take his own course against Dost Mahomed Khan without any reference to us. Should his Highness show a decided preference for this course, you are authorised to tell him at once, that he is at liberty to follow it ; but you should point out to him the possibility of defeat, by the combined army of the Persians and Afghans, and you will, as far as you can consistently with propriety, impress upon him the necessity of caution, and of using Afghan rather than Sikh influence or agency. Should he wish to make an instrument of Shah Soojah, you will apprise him that the Governor-General attaches too much importance to the person of the ex-King to admit of his going forth, otherwise than with the almost assured certainty of success ; but that the ex-King will be permitted to proceed to Caubul with a view of being re-instated in his sovereignty, should the Sikhs succeed in taking Caubul, and that arrangement be desired by his Highness.

"Of the relative advantages which may be derived from these two plans, you will be better able to judge after you shall have fully opened them, with the consideration which each has to recommend it to the Maharajah. His Highness may possibly be unwilling to commit his troops in the passes of the Khybur, and he may strongly feel the difficulty which religious and natural animosity will oppose to any measure mainly resting on Sikh power and Sikh influence. He may not, therefore, reject the plan that stands first in this paper ; and there can be little doubt that, for ultimate efficiency, and for bringing greater weight and greater strength to bear in concert upon the objects in view, that this plan should have the preference ; but it is cumbrous, and a considerable time may elapse before it can be set in motion ; and if it might conciliate Afghan opinion on one hand, on the other it might impair with the Sikhs that cordiality which would be so essential to the success of co-operation. His Lordship, on the whole, is disposed to think that the plan which is second in order is that which will be found most expedient."—[*MS. Records,*]

his seat, and tottering along the whole length of the presence-chamber, warmly embraced the British minister, and welcomed the other gentlemen of the Mission. After the usual compliments had been exchanged, and the presents sent by the British Government had been examined by the Maharajah with curious minuteness, a conversation ensued on an infinite variety of topics. "The Maharajah," wrote Macnaghten to the Governor-General, "passed from war to wine, and from learning to hunting, with breathless rapidity. He was particularly anxious to know how much each member of the Mission had drunk of some ardent liquor he had sent them the night before. He was equally anxious to know the distance at which a shrapnel shot could do execution. It is impossible to say on which of these subjects his interrogatives were most minute. He asked me if I was a good huntsman, and on replying in the negative, he asked me if I knew Arabic and Sanscrit. On receiving a reply in the affirmative, as if doubtful of what I had said, he insisted on my reciting a couplet of the former language. He asked about Herat—about Dost Mahomed Khan, about the Persian army and their connection with the Russians, and the possibility of their invading India." * It was not prudent to enter too minutely into this matter in open Durbar. Macnaghten replied, briefly and generally, to the questions about Russo-Persian invasion, and laughed the idea to scorn. "I can enter more fully into the question," he added, "at a private interview."

On the morning of the 3rd of June, Macnaghten and the other members of the Mission, accompanied also by Captain Wade and Lieutenant Mackeson,† appeared by

---

* *MS. Records.*

† Lieutenant (since Colonel) Mackeson was one of the assistants to the Governor-General's agent on the north-west frontier. Whilst Burnes was at Caubul he was directed to remain at Peshawur; a place

invitation at Durbar. There was some general conversation about the relations between Russia and Persia; and then a signal was made to the British officers to retire into an inner apartment. There the business of the conference was now to be transacted. On the part of the Lahore government there were present—Dhyan Singh, the minister; his son Heerat Singh, the favourite of the Maharajah; Lehna Singh, Adjeet Singh, and other Sirdars, with the doctor-secretary, the Fakir Aziz-ood-deen. On the part of the Mission, there were present with Macnaghten, Captains Osborne and Wade. Macgregor, Mackeson, and Dr. Drummond remained outside with some other officers of the Maharajah's Court.

Runjeet Singh commenced the conference. The letter of the Governor-General, he said, had been read to him, and he fully understood its contents. He desired that all present should hear it; and accordingly the Fakir Aziz-ood-deen, whose polished manners and admirable address presented a striking contrast to the ruder bearing of the Sikh chiefs by whom he was surrounded, read the letter aloud, and, with that unequalled power of interpretation of which he was the master, distinctly explained every sentence. Macnaghten was then requested to state what he had to say on the part of the British Government. This he did fluently and well. Whether

with which his name has since become historically, and now most painfully, associated. Some two months before the arrival of Macnaghten's Mission, he joined Runjeet Singh's camp and travelled with the Maharajah through different parts of the Sikh Empire. Runjeet conversed freely with the young officer regarding the progress of Burnes's negotiations at Caubul, the mission of Vickovich, and other matters connected with the politics of Afghanistan. Rumours had then reached him of the designs of the British Government to invite him to co-operate in measures for the overthrow of the Barukzye Sirdars. He discussed the subject with little reserve; and it was evident that the project had little attraction for him.

all he advanced was strictly true it is hardly necessary to inquire. Diplomacy is not intended to be subjected to such a test. The tender interest taken in the honour and dignity of the Maharajah were descanted upon, on the one side, and the unreasonableness of Dost Mahomed on the other. The failure of Burnes's Mission was spoken of as the result of the unwillingness of the Caubul Ameer to break off negotiations with other foreign agents, though even at that time Dost Mohamed, after Burnes's departure, was making a last despairing effort to win back the friendship of the British Government.* Then came a somewhat inflated eulogium on the resources of the British Government, and the 200,000 soldiers who could at any time be brought into the field to resist a simultaneous invasion from all the four sides of India If then, urged Macnaghten, such were the unaided power of the British Government, what must that power be when united with the strength of the Sikh Empire? There was nothing, indeed, of a palpable character to be apprehended from the movements of the Russians and Persians, or the hostility of the Barukzye Sirdars, but as

* I should not have thought that the drift of this passage could be misunderstood. And yet it has been said with reference to it [*Hume's Memoir of Henry Torrens*] that although I have "emphatically denounced the disgraceful act of mutilating official papers," I have "no single word of censure for diplomatic falsehoods," but have declared that "diplomacy *should not be* subjected to the test of truth." I said that it "is not intended to be," not that "it should not be," subjected to such a test. Every writer must be permitted to choose his own weapons of attack. At one time he may employ invective; at another, sarcasm; and the latter may express as strong a detestation of falsehood and baseness as the former Both in a previous and a subsequent chapter I have expressed my opinion of the manner in which Lord Auckland and his ministers misrepresented the conduct of Dost Mahomed; and in the present passage I do not seek to exculpate Macnaghten, by insinuating my belief that diplomacy is, in its general intent and practice, shamefully destitute of honesty and truth.

their intrigues, it was said, must have the effect of unsettling men's minds, both in the British and the Sikh dominions, it was desirable to concert measures for the future suppression of all these disturbing influences. He had, therefore, been despatched by the Governor-General of India to the Court of the Maharajah, to ascertain the wishes of his Highness.

Runjeet listened very patiently to this address, only interrupting the speaker now and then to express his assent to Macnaghten's statements; and when asked what were his wishes, replied that they were the wishes of the British Government. After some further interchange of compliments, Runjeet asked what were the wishes of the British Government; and the British Envoy then began guardedly to state them after the manner of the instructions he had received. There were two courses, he said, open to the Maharajah—the one was, to act independently; the other was, to act in concert with the British Government. A murmur of approbation arose from the assembled chiefs, when Runjeet broke in with the assertion that it was his wish to act in concert with the British Government. Entreating him not to decide hastily, but to weigh well the details of the two schemes, Macnaghten then said, "Your Highness some time ago formed a treaty with Shah Soojah-ool-Moolk. Do you think it would be still for your benefit that the treaty should stand good, and would it be agreeable to your wishes that the British Government should become a party to that treaty?" "This," replied Runjeet, "would be adding sugar to milk." "If such," said Macnaghten, "be decidedly the wish of your Highness, I do not think that the Governor-General would object to supply Shah Soojah with money and officers to enable him to recover his throne." He then proceeded to state what were the views of the Governor-General—that the Shah should advance by the route of Candahar, whilst the Sikh troops should advance upon Caubul through the Khybur Pass. "Circumstances," it was added, "might arise to render it necessary for the British Government to send some of its own troops down the Indus, to repel any threat of aggression in that direction." "How many?" asked Runjeet. The answer was, "As many as the exigency of the occasion may require; but their employment in that direction will only be temporary."

Macnaghten next launched into a panegyric on the general moderation of the British Government; and then having entered into some particulars relating to the necessary modification and extension of the treaty between Shah Soojah and Runjeet Singh,* proceeded to call the attention of the Maharajah to the second plan suggested by the Governor-General—the plan of independent action on the part of the Sikh ruler, which Lord Auckland declared that he was more inclined to favour than the other project. But it was with difficulty that Runjeet Singh could be induced to listen to this proposal. His impatience broke out openly. His mind, he said, was made up on the subject. He would have nothing to do with the independent expedition. The plan first set forth by the British Envoy was the one which he purposed to accept, and so Macnaghten could only say in reply, that though the Governor-General approved of the course last stated, his Lordship set too much value on the friendship of the Maharajah to wish to force it upon him.

* The greater part of the proposed treaty was substantially and literally the same as that negotiated in 1833—but some supplementary articles were added to it. One of these recognised the independence of the Ameers of Sindh (Runjeet thereby withdrawing all claims on Shikarpoor), in consideration of the payment by them of compensation-money to the amount of twenty lakhs of rupees; and another recognised the integrity of Herat.

It now only remained to settle the details of the project for the subversion of Barukzye ascendancy in Afghanistan. So little at this time was it in contemplation that the brunt of the expedition should fall upon the British army, that Runjeet, who soon began to have his misgivings regarding the success of an undertaking in which his own troops and the raw levies of Shah Soojah were to be the main actors, sent the Fakir Aziz-ood-een to ask Macnaghten whether, in the event of the allies sustaining a reverse, the British Government were prepared to support them. The affirmative reply hardly seemed to satisfy the Sikh agent, who spoke of the remoteness of our resourses from the scene of action ; and it was obviously then the desire of his master that the British troops should take a more prominent part in the coming expedition. He seemed, indeed, to think that too large a share of the danger* devolved upon him, and that he was to be allowed too little

* Runjeet was always doubtful whether his soldiers would not shrink from attempting to force the Khybur Pass. He told Mackeson, before the arrival of Macnaghten's Mission, that the Khalsa entertained very strong prejudices against that kind of warfare, of which it may be added, both he and his chiefs had the vaguest possible idea. He believed that to force the Khybur Pass was to push a column of troops into it, somewhat as you would push them over a narrow bridge, the men in the rear stepping over the bodies of their slaughtered comrades. He had no notion of turning the pass by flank movements—of crowning the heights on each side—and accomplishing by skilful dispositions what could not be done by brute force without a dreadful sacrifice of life. Subsequently, at his interviews with the officers of the British Mission, he reverted to this subject. He said that he had never tried the Khalsa at such work ; that he doubted whether they could be induced to march over the corpses of their countrymen ; and asked whether British troops could be depended on for such service. He added, that the Sirdars whom he had sent to command his troops at Peshawur, had often urged him to suffer them to move through the Khybur upon Jellalabad ; but that he had uniformly refused to listen to their proposals.—[*MS. Notes.*]

of the spoil.* The advantages to be derived from the alliance with Shah Soojah were not, he said, so great that he might not reasonably ask for something beyond what had been set forth in the proposals of the British Government; and it is not to be denied that there was at this time some show of truth in the assertion. Macnaghten continued to reply that the Maharajah, if he were not satisfied with the terms of the treaty, was at liberty to act independently, and that it would be no offence to the British Government if he preferred that scheme to the other. But he took the opportunity, in the course of one of his conferences with the Sikh agents, to hint that it was possible that "circumstances might occur to render it necessary for us to counteract danger, and that if it seriously threatened us, we might be compelled to arrest the advance of the Persians by the advance of our own troops; and in this case we might find it expedient to support the cause of Shah Soojah." This, however, was uttered in a precautionary spirit, "in order to guard against the possibility of its being supposed hereafter that we designedly concealed our intentions from his Highness, and that we had sinister and exclusive views of our own." †

* Runjeet put in a claim for more than a moiety of the tribute-money of twenty lakhs of rupees that was to be wrung from the Ameers of Sindh and divided between him and the Shah; and he ssked also for the transfer of Jellalabad to his own rule. The latter demand was steadfastly refused; but an arrangement was effected with regard to the former, at the expense of the Ameers of Sindh; Runjeet receiving a larger amount without detriment to the Shah.

† *Mr. Macnaghten to Government. Camp, near Lahore, June* 20 1838 : *MS. Records.* Captain Cunninghame [*History of the Sikhs,* says that Runjeet was informed that the expedition for the restoration of Shah Soojah would be undertaken, whether the Maharajah chose to share in it or not. "That Runjeet Singh," the author adds in a note, "was told he would be left out if he did not choose to come in, does not appear on public record. It was, however, the only convincing argu-

On the 23rd of June, by which time the Mission had followed the camp of the Maharajah to Lahore, and the ment used during the long discussions, and I think Major Mackeson was made the bearer of the message to that effect." But this is stated somewhat too broadly. Runjeet Singh was not told that the British, in the event of his refusing to co-operate with the Shah, would undertake by themselves the restoration of Shah Soojah, but that they *might* be compelled to do so in self-defence. Mackeson told Runjeet, as Macnaghten had before told the Fakir Aziz-ood-een, that in order "to guard against any reproach of reserve or concealment, hereafter," it was right "to inform him now of the possibility that might occur of our being compelled, in self-defence, to take our own measures to ward off approaching danger, and use our own troops to restore Shah Soojah to the throne." The Maharajah, receiving this communication as though he had not been prepared for it by the Fakir Aziz-ood-een, told Mackeson at once to prepare the treaty. "Not immediately understanding," says Mackeson, in his memorandum of this interview, "to what treaty he might allude, I asked the Fakir whether that with the supplementary articles presented by Mr. Macnaghten to the Maharajah's approval was the one alluded to. The Maharajah observed, 'That one;' and the Fakir recalled his attention to the point by asking how the question of Jellalabad was to be settled; to which his Highness replied, that if the Sikhs could not be allowed to hold possession of Jellalabad, some other arrangement could be made, which would have the effect of making the Khalsa-jee act in cordial co-operation—that the friendship between the Sikhs and the British was great, and had lasted many years—that the British and Sikh Governments had no care, and were both able to act independently, but that they had a care for the mutual friendship which had lasted so long. The Fakir hinted to me to suggest some other mode to supersede that of the Sikhs holding possession of Jellalabad. I observed that it now rested with the Maharajah to suggest any plan that might have occurred to his mind. After some further conversation, Runjeet Singh said that an annual tribute of two lakhs of rupees from Shah Soojah would satisfy him for the non-possession of Jellalabad; and this granted, he was willing to co-operate for the restoration of the Shah. The British agents objected to the payment of tribute, as it would be an acknowledgment of inferiority on the part of the Shah; but they consented that the two lakhs should be paid, in the shape of a subsidy, Runjeet Singh undertaking to keep up a force on the frontier, at the call of the Afghan monarch."—[*Lieutenant Mackeson's Memorandum of a con-*

patience of the British negotiators had been well-nigh exhausted by the vexatious claims and frivolous objections of the Sikh party, a statement to the same effect was made on Macnaghten's authority by Lieutenant Mackeson* to Runjeet Singh himself; and the Maharajah told the British officer at once, in his hurried, emphatic manner, to prepare the treaty. It seemed as though the many objections which had been started, had originated from the Maharajah's advisers rather than from himself, and that they had kept out of his way the probability of the British Government acting for themselves independently in the matter before him. But now that the case had been plainly stated in his own hearing, Runjeet at once grasped the whole question; fully comprehended his own position; and resolutely decided for himself. But, never forgetful of his own interests, he clamoured still for the cession of Jellalabad;† and, with seeming coquettishness consented to receive two lakhs of rupees in the shape of an annual subsidy, instead of the territorial accession, which the British agent had resolutely refused.

On the 26th of June, the treaty was formally signed by the Maharajah. It had been slightly modified since the original draft was prepared; but, with the exception of the introduction of the subsidy article, had undergone no

---

versation with the *Maharajah, Runjeet Singh, at Lahore, 23d of June,* 1838 *MS. Records*]

* Mackeson was the general messenger on the part of the British agent, as was the Fakir Aziz-ood-een, or Kishen Chund, on the part of the Maharajah. These functionaries were constantly going backwards and forwards, in the frightful heat, to communicate the suggestions or replies of their respective chiefs.

† It is probable that the demand for Jellalabad was intended to be refused, in order that the refusal might strengthen Runjeet's claims to increased pecuniary compensation; for before the arrival of the Mission he was in the habit of speaking of Jellalabad as a possession not to be coveted by the Khalsa.

essential alterations. It was, in effect, a treaty between Runjeet Singh and Shah Soojah, guaranteed by the British Government; and it ran in the following words:

Treaty of alliance and friendship executed between Maharajah Runjeet Singh and Shah Soojah-ool-Moolk, with the approbation of, and in concert with, the British Government.

Whereas a treaty was formerly concluded between Maharnjah Runjeet Singh and Soojah-ool-Moolk, consisting of fourteen articles, exclusive of the preamble and the conclusion; and whereas the execution of the provisions of the said treaty was suspended for certain reasons; and whereas at this time Mr. W. H. Macnaghten, having been deputed by the Right Honourable George Lord Auckland, Governor-General of India, to the presence of Maharajah Runjeet Singh, and vested with full powers to form a treaty in a manner consistent with the friendly engagements subsisting between the two states, the treaty aforesaid is revived and concluded with certain modifications, and four new articles have been added thereto, with the approbation of, and in concert with, the British Government, the provisions whereof as contained in the following eighteen articles, will be duly and faithfully observed.

1st. Shah Soojah-ool-Moolk disclaims all title on the part of himself, his heirs, successors, and all the Suddozyes, to whatever territories lying on either bank of the River Indus that may be possessed by the Maharajah—viz., Cashmere, including its limits, east, west, north, and south, together with the Fort of Attock, Chuch Hazara, Khebel, Amb, with its dependencies on the left bank of the aforesaid river; and on the right bank Peshawur, with the Eusafzae territory, Kheteks, Husht Nagger, Mechnee, Kohat, Himgoo, and all places dependent on Peshawur, as far as the Khybur Pass; Bunnoo, the Vezeree territory, Dour Tuwk, Goraug Kulabagh, and Kushulgher, with their dependent districts; Dera Ishmael Khan, and its dependency, together with Dera Ghazee Khan, Kut, Methen, Omerkoth, and their dependent territory; Secughur, Heren Dajel, Hajeepore, Rajenpore, and the three Ketchees, as well as Mankeera, with its districts, and the province of Mooltan, situated on the left bank. These countries and places are considered to be the property and to form the estate of the Maharajah; the Shah neither has, nor will have, any concern with them. They belong to the Maharajah and his posterity from generation to generation.

2nd. The people of the country on the other side of Khybur will not be suffered to commit robberies, or aggressions, or any disturbances on this side. If any defaulter of either state who has embezzled the revenue take refuge in the territory of the other, each party engages to surrender him, and no person shall obstruct the passage of the stream which issues out of the Khybur defile, and supplies the fort of Futtehgurh with water according to ancient usage.

3rd. As agreeably to the treaty established between the British Government and the Maharajah, no one can cross from the left to the right bank of the Sutlej without a passport from the Maharajah; the same rule shall be observed regarding the passage of the Indus whose waters join the Sutlej; and no one shall be allowed to cross the Indus without the Maharajah's permission.

4th. Regarding Shikarpoor and the territory of Sindh lying on the right bank of the Indus, the Shah will agree to abide by whatever may be settled as right and proper, in conformity with the happy relations of friendship subsisting between the British Government and the Maharajah, through Captain Wade.

5th. When the Shah shall have established his authority in Caubul and Candahar, he will annually send the Maharajah the following articles—viz., 55 high-bred horses of approved colour and pleasant paces, 11 Persian cimeters, 7 Persian poniards, 25 good mules; fruits of various kinds, both dry and fresh, and surdees or musk melons of a sweet and delicate flavour (to be sent throughout the year), by the way of Caubul River to Peshawur; grapes, pomegranates, apples, quinces, almonds, raisins, pistales or chronuts, an abundant supply of each; as well as pieces of satin of every colour, choghas of fur, kimkhobs wrought with gold and silver, and Persian carpets altogether to the number of 101 pieces; all these articles the Shah will continue to send every year to the Maharajah.

6th. Each party shall address the other in terms of equality.

7th. Merchants of Afghanistan, who will be desirous of trading to Lahore, Umritsur, or any other parts of the Maharajah's possessions, shall not be stopped or molested on their way. On the contrary, strict orders shall be issued to facilitate their intercourse, and the Maharajah engages to observe the same line of conduct on his part in respect to traders who may wish to proceed to Afghanistan.

8th. The Maharajah will yearly send to the Shah the following articles in the way of friendship: 55 pieces of shawls, 25 pieces of muslin, 11 dooputtas, 5 pieces of kinkhob, 5 scarves, 55 tinbuns, 55 loads of Bara rice (peculiar to Peshawur).

9th. Any of the Maharajah's officers who may be deputed to

Afghanistan to purchase horses, or on any other business, as well as those who may be sent by the Shah into the Punjab for the purpose of purchasing piece goods or shawls, &c., to the amount of 11,000 rupees, will be treated by both sides with due attention, and every facility will be afforded to them in the execution of their commission.

10th. Whenever the armies of the two states may happen to be assembled at the same place, on no account shall the slaughter of kine be permitted to take place.

11th. In the event of the Shah taking an auxiliary force from the Maharajah, whatever booty may be acquired from the Barukzyes in jewels, horses, and arms great and small, shall be equally divided between the two contracting parties. If the Shah should succeed in obtaining possession of their property without the assistance of the Maharajah's troops, the Shah agrees to send a portion of it by his own agents to the Maharajah, in the way of friendship.

12th. An exchange of missions, charged with letters and presents, shall constantly take place between the two parties.

13th. Should the Maharajah require the aid of any of the Shah's troops in furtherance of the object contemplated by this treaty, the Shah engages to send a force commanded by one of his principal officers; in like manner, the Maharajah will furnish the Shah, when required, with an auxiliary force composed of Mahomedans, and commanded by one of his principal officers as far as Caubul, in furtherance of the objects contemplated by this treaty. When the Maharajah may go to Peshawur, the Shah will depute a Shah-zadah to visit him; on which occasions the Maharajah will receive and dismiss him with the honour and consideration due to his rank and dignity.

14th. The friends and enemies of each of the three high powers—that is to say, the British and Sikh Governments and Shah Soojah-ool-Moolk, shall be the friends and enemies of all.

15th. Shah Soojah-ool-Moolk agrees to relinquish for himself, his heirs, and successors, all claims of supremacy and arrears of tribute over the country now held by the Ameers of Sindh (which will continue to belong to the Ameers and their successors in perpetuity), on condition of the payment to him by the Ameers of such a sum as may be determined, under the mediation of the British Government, of such payment being made over by him to Maharajah Runjeet Singh. On these payments being completed, article 4 of the treaty of the 12th of March, 1833, will be considered cancelled, and the customary interchange of letters and suitable presents between the

Maharajah and the Ameers of Sindh shall be maintained as heretofore

16th. Shah Soojah engages, after the attainment of his object, to pay without fail to the Maharajah the sum of two lakhs of rupees of the Nanukshahee or Kuldar currency, calculating from the date on which the Sikh troops may be despatched for the purpose of reinstating his Majesty in Caubul, in consideration of the Maharajah stationing a force of not less than 5000 men—cavalry and infantry —of the Mohamedan persuasion, within the limits of the Peshawur territory for the support of the Shah, and to be sent to the aid of his Majesty whenever the British Government, in concert and counsel with the Maharajah, shall deem the aid necessary; and when any matter of great importance may arise to the westward, such measures will be adopted with regard to it as may seem expedient and proper at the time to the British and Sikh Governments. In the event of the Maharajah requiring the aid of the Shah's troops, a deduction shall be made from the subsidy proportioned to the period for which such aid may be afforded; and the British Government holds itself responsible for the punctual payment of the above sum annually to the Maharajah, so long as the provisions of this treaty are duly observed.

17th When Shah Soojah-ool-Moolk shall have succeeded in establishing his authority in Afghanistan, he shall not attack or molest his nephew, the ruler of Herat, in the possession of his territories, now subject to his government.

18th Shah Soojah-ool-Moolk binds himself, his heirs, and successors, to refrain from entering into negotiations with any foreign state, without the knowledge and consent of the British and Sikh Governments, and to oppose any power having the design to invade the British and Sikh territories by force of arms, to the utmost of his ability

The three powers parties to this treaty—namely, the British Government, Maharajah Runjeet Singh, and Shah Soojah-ool-Moolk—cordially agree to the foregoing articles. There shall be no deviation from them, and in that case the present treaty shall be considered as binding for ever; and this treaty shall come into operation from and after the date on which the seals and signatures of the three contracting parties shall have been affixed thereto Done at Lahore, this 26th day of June, in the year of our Lord 1838, corresponding with the 15th of the month of Assar, 1895. Aera of Bekramajeet.

The treaty was despatched to Simlah for the signature of the Governor-General, which Runjeet Singh expressed some anxiety to obtain with the least possible delay. But Lord Auckland at once decided that he could with no propriety attach his name to the treaty until it had been santioned and signed by Shah Soojah. Anxious as he was to conclude the negotiation, Runjeet Singh could not demur to this decision. His patience, however, was not to be severely taxed. Macnaghten was directed to proceed with all possible expedition to obtain the consent of the Shah; and so, on the 13th of July, the Maharajah gave the English gentlemen their audience of leave; and, amidst the most profuse expressions of friendship and attachment, they took their departure from Runjeet's Court.

They turned their faces towards Loodhianah. A pensioner on the bounty of the British Government, Shah Soojah, ever since his last disastrous attempt to regain his empire, had dwelt there in the midst of his family as one not yet reconciled to a life of peaceful obscurity, but somewhat sobered down by the repeated failures which had beset his unfortunate career. It is probable that no political vicissitudes in Afghanistan, however favourable to the restoration of the monarchy, would have tempted him to head another expedition for the recovery of Caubul and Candahar. But when reports reached him of the designs of the British Government, and the probability that he would be supplied with British money and British skill for the support and conduct of the army which he was to lead against the Barukzye Sirdars, he saw more clearly his way to his old place in the Balla Hissar of Caubul; and long dormant hopes and expectations began to revive within him. But he could not wholly suppress his suspicions of the sincerity both of the British and the Sikhs; and his delight was straitened by the thought that he would, in effect, be little more than a passive instrument in the hands of his powerful and ambitious allies.

On the evening of the 15th of July, accompanied by Captain Wade and Lieutenant Mackeson, Mr. Macnaghten waited on Shah Soojah at Loodhianah. Seated on a musnud slightly elevated above the level of the room, the Shah received the British gentlemen with becoming cordiality, and desired them to seat themselves on a carpet beside him. Macnaghten commenced the conference. He spoke of the friendly feeling that had always existed between the British Government and the Suddozye Princes, since Mr. Elphinstone's mission to Afghanistan. He said that, although unable actively to co-operate with the Shah in his first attempts to regain his kingdom, the British Government had always desired the success of his undertakings. He explained the circumstances under which a mission had been sent to the Court of Dost Mahomed. And then, with as little truth as had marked his previous communications to Runjeet, commented upon the unfriendly manner in which the Mission had been received, and the conduct of the Ameer in "rejecting our good offices;" conduct which had rendered it necessary to counteract his hostile designs by establishing a friendly power in the territories of Afghanistan.

To all of this the Shah listened attentively, and then said that he had always foretold the result of the mission to the Court of Dost Mahomed—(which was a piece of good luck the Ameer was not able to appreciate)—that he who had not been true to his own master was little likely to be true to a foreign power; but that now he would see the result of his folly, and be baffled in his attempt to betray his country into the hands of the Persian invaders.

Upon this Macnaghten at once announced the intention of the British Government to restore Shah Soojah to his hereditary dominions. It would have been more agreeable, he said, to his government to act in such a matter without consulting any other state ; but that the Sikhs were now in actual possession of so many of the provinces of the old Douranee Empire, and their interests so intimately associated with those of the British in that part of the country, that it was impossible to omit them from the compact—that, consequently, the Governor-General had instructed him to wait on Runjeet Singh, and that the result had been the formation of a treaty which was now to be submitted for his Majesty's approval, together with a letter from Lord Auckland. The letter was then read ; and Macnaghten reverting first to the old treaty between Shah Soojah and Runjeet Singh, said that it was the intention of the British Government to become a party to its stipulations under certain alterations and additions. With the utmost unconcern the Shah said that a paper of some kind had been exchanged with Runjeet Singh, but that it was merely to the effect that if he regained his dominions there should be an interchange of friendly letters, presents, and missions between the two Courts.

Whether Macnaghten smiled at this version of the old alliance is not on record. But he began now to read and explain the articles of the amended treaty. The Shah's comments were frequent and emphatic. Sneering at the minuteness with which the possessions of Runjeet Singh were defined in the first article, he declared that Peshawur was only a burden to the Sikh government, and that Runjeet would willingly hand it over to any one but Dost Mahomed. Indeed, he said, that the Maharajah's vakeel had often pledged his word to him that, in the event of his recovering his throne, Peshawur should be reannexed to his dominions. But when Captain Wade and Moollah Shikore* recalled to his Majesty's recollection that Pesha-

* Moollah Shikore was at this time the Shah's agent and confidential

wur had been expressly named in the old treaty among the possessions of Runjeet Singh, the Shah acknowledged that it was so, and yielded the point.

Other articles were then commented on by the Shah and his agent; but that which seemed most to stagger them was the stipulation for the annual payment by Caubul of two lakhs to the state of Lahore. Little advantage, observed the Shah, could the British Government expect to derive from his restoration, if they placed him in a position inferior to that held by the present ruler of Caubul, who paid no tribute to the Sikhs. " He had long," he said, "indulged a hope that the day would come when the British Government, whose honoured guest he had been for more than twenty years, would restore him to the throne and possessions of his ancestors —that the British Government must be aware that, after such a period of dependence on them, in whatever manner they chose to send him forth, his fair name was identified with their own—that in this world a good name alone deserved to be prized—that half a loaf with a good name were better than abundance without it. He then alluded to the small revenues of Afghanistan—said that Caubul and Candahar yielded nothing—that when Shikarpoor paid its revenues regularly, the amount realised was only three lakhs—that to enable him to establish his government, and keep it, he would require to maintain 15,000 troops, and how were they to be paid?—that it would be less irksome if the money were only required to be paid whenever he had occasion to make use of the services of Runjeet Singh's troops."* To all this Macnaghten

adviser in exile. Further mention will be made of him in a subsequent portion of the narrative.

* *Memorandum, by Lieut. Mackeson, of Mr. Macnaghten's Interview with Shah Soojah-ool-Moolk, at Loodhianah, on the 15th of July, 1838; MS. Records.*

replied, that the payment was not by any means, to be regarded in the light of tribute from a weaker to a more powerful state, but simply as remuneration for services performed. Adroitly alluding to the subsidy recently paid by the British Government to the Persian state, the English Envoy said that a powerful government often subsidised, for its own uses, a weaker one; and that if Runjeet did not furnish the troops, the Shah would be exempted from paying the money; but that as the former was bound to hold them always in readiness for service, it would not be reasonable to pay them only when they were called into the field. Indeed, he urged, Runjeet Singh had with difficulty been persuaded to consent to the terms of this very article, which imposed upon him no light conditions, and had, moreover, been substituted as a compensation to the Maharajah for withdrawing the demands he had made for actual territorial concessions both at Shikarpoor and Jellalabad.

There was little to be said in reply to this. The Shah yielded a reluctant assent. The remaining articles of the treaty were read, and called forth but slight comment. Macnaghten then invited the Shah to state unreservedly his opinions on the whole question. Thus appealed to, the exiled King spoke out cordially and unrestrainedly, but with a full sense of what was due to himself. "He spoke of his long connexion with the British Government, of his fortune being entirely in their hands—said that he had entertained the hope, in his long exile, that it would sooner or later stretch out its arm to restore him to all the possessions and powers of his ancestors; but that if this hope could not at once be fulfilled, he must content himself with what now remained of the disjointed kingdom of Afghanistan; that in the event of the straitened revenue of Candahar and Caubul being further reduced by the payment of two lakhs of rupees annually to the Sikhs, he must look to support from the British Government to meet and oppose any increased danger from the approach of more powerful enemies from the westward. On this point full assurance was given him. He then observed that there were one or two other points in which he wished to have assurance given him, and that, in other respects, he was at the disposal of the British Government:—1st. That no interference should be exercised with his authority over those of his tribe and household; 2ndly. That he should be allowed to raise forces of his own to go with some show of power, and not as though he were a mere puppet in the hands of the British Government to work out their views. He then dwelt on the importance of this in the eyes of his people who would come to join his standard; said that if they found he was no longer the source of honour and reward, they would desert him and return to their homes, as they would have no object in connecting themselves with the schemes of foreigners—that he should therefore be allowed to commence recruiting men, as many were waiting to enter his service—that when his adherents flocked to his standard, he should be able to give them hopes of reward for their services." *

On all these points the fullest assurances were given to the Shah. Then Macnaghten began to set forth how it was the desire of the British Government that one of their own functionaries should be stationed at the Shah's Court; † and that British officers should be furnished to discipline the Shah's levies, to command them during the expedition, and to remain with him after his restoration. To all of this the Shah readily assented. Declaring himself confident of success, he then expressed an eager hope that no delay would be permitted, but that the expedition

* *Lieutenant Mackeson's Memorandum: MS. Records.*

† "Who would, however," it was added, "not interfere with the full exercise of his authority over his subjects."

would set out as soon as ever the troops could be raised for the purpose. When the beginning of the ensuing cold weather was named as the time for commencing operations, the Shah expressed surprise and regret that the movement should be so long delayed; and urged the expediency of moving whilst Herat was still holding out. His appearance in the neighbourhood of Candahar, he said, would doubtless compel Mahomed Shah to withdraw his investing army, and secure the frontier against all future attacks.*

Then Macnaghten asked the King whether it were his desire to advance by the Khybur Pass, or the route of Sindh. To this Shah Soojah replied that the Khyburees were his slaves—that they were willing to sacrifice themselves at his bidding—that he frequently received imploring letters from the Momunds, the Eusofzyes, and other tribes in the neighbourhood of Peshawur, but that there were so many solid advantages in the combined movement by Candahar and Peshawur, which would completely paralyse the movements of Dost Mahomed, that he gave it the preference. His own force, he said, should advance by Candahar, whilst his eldest son, Prince Timour, might accompany the Sikh army through the Khybur Pass.†

Little more now remained to be said. But before taking his leave of the Shah, Macnaghten invited him to state in writing the points on which he required the assurances of the British Government, and expressed a hope that, as

* "He mentioned having a few days before sent an emissary to Kamram to conjure him, for the honour of the Afghans, to hold out for two short months, and he would hear of miracles worked in his favour."—[*Lieutenant Mackeson's Memorandum: MS. Records.*]

† Some anxiety was expressed by the Shah lest Prince Timour should be consigned entirely to the guidance of the Sikhs, but he was assured that the presence of British officers in his camp would effectually prevent this.

the Mission had received instructions to return immediately to Simlah, his Majesty's wishes might be laid before him with the least possible delay. Desiring the British Envoy to call upon him again on the following evening, after leisure had been allowed him to study well the contents of the proposed treaty, the Shah then bade him adieu; and the English officers took their departure. It did not appear to those present, on this occasion, when the sovereignty of Afghanistan was offered to the long-exiled monarch, and now, for the first time since his dethronement, there dawned upon him something like a certainty of recovering his lost dominions, that he received the announcements of the English Mission with feelings of very earnest exultation and delight. There were evidently some misgivings in the mind of the Shah, who mistrusted both Runjeet Singh and the British Government. Everything seemed to have been already arranged between the two parties, whilst he himself, it appeared, was designed to be a passive instrument for the furtherance of their ends—a puppet in their hands, to give grace to the show and character to the expedition.

An hour before the time appointed for the second meeting between Shah Soojah and the British Emissary, Moollah Shikore waited upon the latter with a paper, setting forth the points upon which the Shah especially desired to have the assurances of the British Government. They ran to the following effect:

Firstly. That as regards the descendants of the King of the Douranees (Ahmed Shah), and the sons and relations of myself, whoever they may be, the right of providing for them or not, and the direction of all that concerns them, belong to me alone; in this matter neither the British Government nor other shall exercise any interference.*

---

* It will be more convenient for purposes of reference to append, as a note to each article, Macnaghten's replies to these several points, as

Secondly. After I have been reinstated in Caubul and Candahar, if, in consequence of the smallness of my possessions, I should desire to send an army against Balkh, Seistan, Beloochistan, and the neighbourhood and dependencies of Caubul and Candahar, and take possession of them, no hindrance shall be offered.*

Thirdly. When Caubul and Candahar become mine, the dependencies of those places, as they existed in the time of the monarchy, ought to belong to me.†

Fourthly. When I have been reinstated at Caubul, and the officers of the British Government prepare to return, should I desire to retain one of them as an envoy, and some others for the purpose of forming and disciplining my army, they will not be refused.‡

Fifthly. The British officers shall exercise no authority over the people of Afghanistan, whether soldiers or subjects, without my approbation and concurrence.§

Sixthly. With respect to giving two lakhs of rupees, and something besides from Shikarpoor, it appears to me very hard and difficult; firstly, because my country will not afford means sufficient for the expenses of my government and the maintenance of my troops; and secondly, because the measure will be considered by the world as payment of tribute. It rests, however, with the

---

given at the subsequent interview: "With regard to the *first* article," he writes, "I told the Shah that he might make his mind perfectly at ease, as the British Government had no intention or wish to interfere between his Majesty and his family and dependents."—[*Mr. Macnaghten to Government, July* 17, 1838: *MS. Records.*]

* "With regard to the *second* article, I pointed out to the Shah, that the conquest of Shikarpoor would be directly opposed to one of the articles of the treaty. To the rest of the article I could only say that it would be naturally the wish of the British Government to witness the consolidation and extension, to their proper limits, of his Majesty's dominions."—[*MS. Records.*]

† "On the subject of the *third* article, I observed that, of course, the Shah did not mean to include the territories ceded to Runjeet Singh by the new treaty, and that the mention of Shikarpoor was inadmissible."—[*MS. Records.*]

‡ "The *fourth* article I stated would doubtless be approved by the Governor-General."—[*MS. Records.*]

§ "The wish, I said, expressed in the *fifth* article would be scrupulously attended to."—[*MS. Records.*]

British Government, and if it is of opinion that the country has the means, and that the measure is a proper one, I do not object. The conduct of my affairs is in the hands of the British Government.*

Seventhly. After the decay of the monarchy, in the same manner as my servants rebelling usurped the country, so did the Sindhians place officers in possession of Shikarpoor; now that I shall regain possession of my kingdom, the Sindhians must release Shikarpoor. It is a royal possession, and must belong to me. †

Eighthly. With respect to slave-girls who ran away from their masters, although to deliver them up may be against the regulations, yet it is a matter of necessity, for respectable people (females) cannot dispense with servants, however the regulations may be enforced with other people, it is not right to apply them to a

---

* "With respect to the objection urged in the *sixth* article, to making money-payments to Maharajah Runjeet Singh, I reiterated the arguments formerly used, to show the distinctions between a tributary and a subsidiary obligation. These arguments, it will be observed, had due weight with his Majesty, for in the written article he brings forward the objection as one that may occur to the world, not as one to which he himself attaches any importance. Ultimately, however, his Majesty admitted that it would be impossible to satisfy all unreasonable objections, and that to those who understood the subject, and whose opinions alone were to be valued, the reciprocal nature of the subsidiary obligation would be sufficiently obvious. With regard to the objection specified in this article, founded on the anticipated want of means, I gave his Majesty encouragement to hope that the British Government would not permit him to be in distress for the means of discharging his necessary pecuniary obligations."—[*MS. Records.*]

† "The *seventh* article, I observed, was at variance with the proposed provisions in the new treaty regarding Shikarpoor. His Majesty, after some conversation, agreed to expunge the article, as well as to exclude the mention of Shikarpoor in other places where it had been introduced from his paper of requests; but he seemed to set great value on his claim to Shikarpoor and the Sindh possessions generally. The Ameers, he observed, had no legitimate title to their dominions but what they derived from him. Shikarpoor, he said, he was particularly desirous to obtain possession of, as being an appropriate place of refuge and escape for his family in case of reverses; but he ultimately admitted that the object would be sufficiently secured to him so long as the British influence prevailed with the Ameers."—[*MS. Records.*]

guest, it is proper that the slave-girls of the *Vilaitis* (native of Afghanistan) attached to me, who may run away from their masters, be made to return.*

Having mastered the contents of this paper, Macnaghten proceeded to the audience, and after the first salutations, began, with his Majesty's permission, to read over the several articles, and comment on them as he proceeded. He then went on to say that it was now plain that the Shah's mind had been set at rest on all the points which had before occasioned him doubt, and as his Majesty was now prepared without scruple to ratify the treaty, he hoped that he would furnish him with a written paper to this effect. To this the Shah readily assented, and the following postscript was then appended to the document:

After a reperusal of the treaty, and hearing the representations made by the British officers of high rank, it appeared to me right that, in the foregoing enumeration of the objects to be desired, the mention of Shikarpoor should not be introduced, and with respect to the objections which I have stated, to giving two lakhs of rupees to Runjeet Singh, in exchange for the services of his troops, as it does not appear to me injurious to my dignity, I have omitted all mention of that also, and am now prepared with willingness and satisfaction to sign the treaty.†

The negotiation now at an end; the Shah expressed his eagerness to commence work without delay; and was urgent in his solicitations for an immediate supply of money, arms, and ammunition. He again, too, expressed

* "On the very delicate subject introduced into the last article, I observed to his Majesty that its connexion with the treaty generally did not seem to me to be obvious, but that I would nevertheless bring it to the notice of the Governor-General, who would, I felt persuaded, take it into consideration with the same anxious desire to gratify his Majesty in this as in all other matters."—[*MS. Records.*]

† *MS. Records.*

his desire to conduct the expedition for the recovery of his dominions, as one relying mainly upon the strength of his own army. He wished to obtain the assistance of British officers in raising and disciplining his troops, but he hoped "that the immediate operations for regaining his throne might be conducted" by those troops. Such reliance on his own arms would raise, he said, his character in the estimation of the people, "while the fact of his being upheld by foreign force alone could not fail to detract, in a great measure, from his dignity and consequence."* He had already, he declared, in reply to a suggestion from the British Envoy, sent letters to many persons of influence in Afghanistan, calling upon them to join his standard, and he was certain that thousands would flock to it from all parts of the country † He appeared to be in the highest

* *Mr. Macnaghten to Government, July 17, 1838 MS. Records.*
† Many of these letters were promptly responded to, and in some instances voluntary tenders of service were made by chiefs discontented with the Barukzye rule. Among others, Khan Shereen Khan, chief of the Kuzzilbashes, wrote to Shah Soojah declaring his intention to join his standard. " Since we have been so unfortunate," said the chief, "as to be far from your royal household, it is only known to God how wretchedly we pass our days. We have now resolved, as soon as the troops of your Majesty arrive on the frontier, to lose no time in waiting upon your Majesty and proving our fidelity by sacrificing ourselves in your service. For God's sake do not make this letter public." Even before it was known that there was any intention on the part of the Shah to attempt to regain his kingdom, many of the chiefs, either offended by Dost Mahomed's alliance with the Persians, or warned by the failure of Burnes's Mission of the danger of clinging any longer to a falling house, wrote to the Shah, beseeching him to return. "The faggots," it was said, "are ready. It merely requires the lighted torch to be applied " It is remarkable that one of the first to tender his services to the Suddozye Prince was that very Abdoollah Khan, Achetzkye, who was the prime mover of the insurrection at Caubul, which brought about the restoration of the Barukzyes.—[*Captain Wade to Mr Macnaghten, June 5th,* 1838 · *MS. Records.*] At this time the Shah was restricted from corresponding with his Afghan

spirits, and spoke strongly of the debt of gratitude which he owed to the British Government, both for the protection that had been yielded him during past years, and for the more active assistance which was about to confer upon him so much power and grandeur.

Macnaghten now took his leave of the Shah, and proceeded with the officers of the Mission to pay a visit to Zemaun Shah, who, blind and powerless, had remained since his dethronement an appendage to the faded Court of his younger brother, dreaming over the past grandeur of his magnificent reign, and sighing to revisit the scene of his by-gone glories. Vague rumours of the intention of the British Government to restore the Suddozye Princes to the sovereignty of Afghanistan had reached him in his dreary exile; and now that the British Envoy was at his door, so eager was he to learn the whole truth, that almost before the ordinary salutations had been exchanged, he pressed Macnaghten for a full revelation of the glad tidings of which he was the bearer. The intelligence, which the English gentleman imparted to him, stirred the heart of the old blind Prince with joy and exultation. "He seemed filled with delight at the prospect of being permitted to revisit the land of his ancestors."* This was the first gleam of good fortune that had burst upon him for many years; and it was a curious and affecting sight to mark the effect which the announcement of the good offices of the British wrought upon one, who, forty years before, had threatened vast expeditions to the southward, which had filled the British in India with anxiety and alarm.

friends; but Captain Wade, whilst reporting to government the receipt of the letters from Abdoollah Khan and others, recommended that the restriction should be removed. The Shah seems to have laid before the British agent, in perfect good faith, all the letters he received from Afghanistan whilst a pensioner on the British Government.

* *Mr. Macnaghten to Government, July* 17, 1838 : *MS. Records.*

On the 17th of July, Macnaghten and his suite turned their backs upon Loodhianah, and repaired, with all possible haste, to Simlah, there to discuss with Lord Auckland and the secretaries who had remained with him, the measures now to be adopted for the restoration of Shah Soojah-ool-Moolk to the long-lost empire of Ahmed Shah.

CHAPTER IV.

[July—October, 1838.]

The Simlah Manifesto—The Simlah Council—Influence of Messrs. Colvin and Torrens—Views of Captains Burnes and Wade—Opinions of Sir Henry Fane—The Army of the Indus—The Governor-General's Manifesto—Its Policy considered.

IT is obvious that, in all the negotiations detailed in the preceding chapter, the paramount idea was that of an alliance between Runjeet Singh and Shah Soojah, guaranteed by the British Government, and a conjoint expedition into Afghanistan from the two sides of Peshawur and Shikarpoor, to be undertaken by the armies of the Lahore ruler and the Suddozye Prince. It was hinted to Runjeet Singh that events might be developed, which would render necessary the more active co-operation of the British army; but Shah Soojah, who was desirous above all things that the British should not take the foremost part in the coming expedition, was led to believe that, assisted by a few British officers, he would be left to recover for himself his old dominions, and that he would by no means become a puppet in the hands of his Feringhee allies.*

---

* It was, as I have shown, the first wish of the Governor-General that the Sikhs should undertake, single-handed, the invasion of Afghanistan (see Lord Auckland's Minute and instructions to Mr. Macnaghten in the preceding chapter). Macnaghten, on his way to Runjeet's Court, wrote to Mr. Masson: "You will have heard that I am proceeding on a mission to Runjeet Singh; and as at my interview with his Highness it is probable that the question of his relations with

But these moderate views were about now to be expanded into a political scheme of far wider scope and significance. Whilst Macnaghten was negotiating the tripartite treaty at Lahore and Loodhianah, John Colvin and Henry Torrens remained at Simlah, as the scribes and counsellors of the Governor-General. To what extent their bolder speculations wrought upon the plastic mind of Lord Auckland it is not easy, with due historical accuracy, to determine. But it is generally conjectured that the influences then set at work overcame the scruples of the cautious and peace-loving statesman, and induced him to sanction an enterprise of a magnitude commensurate with the bold and ambitious views of his irresponsible advisers. The direct influence mainly emanated from John Colvin. It is probable, indeed, that the counsels of a man so young and so erratic as Henry Torrens would have met with no acceptance from the sober-minded nobleman at the head of the government, but for a circumstance which gave weight to his opinions and cogency to his advice. By all the accidents of birth and early associations, as well as by the bent of his own genius, the young civilian was a true soldier. The son of a distinguished officer and an approved military teacher, he had graduated, whilst yet a boy, in the learning of the camp, and his after studies had done much to perfect his acquaintance with

the Afghans will come on the *tapis*, I am naturally desirous of obtaining the opinion of the best-informed men with respect to them. Would you oblige me, therefore, by stating what means of counteraction to the policy of Dost Mahomed Khan you would recommend for adoption ; and whether you think that the Sikhs, using any (and what ?) instrument of Afghan agency, could establish themselves in Caubul ?"—[*Masson's Narrative*, vol. iii.] A letter, with a similar suggestion, was sent to Captain Burnes, of whose reception of the project I shall speak more in detail. The matter is further noticeable as an indication of the unwillingness of Lord Auckland to interfere more actively in the politics of Afghanistan.

the tactics and strategy of modern warfare. He possessed, indeed, the very knowledge which the other members of the Simlah Council most wanted; and hence it was that he came to exercise considerable influence over Lord Auckland, more perhaps through his brother secretaries than directly brought to bear upon the mind of the Governor-General himself. It was urged that the expedition, if entrusted entirely to Shah Soojah and the Sikhs, would set in disastrous failure; and there was at least some probability in this. Runjeet Singh was no more than lukewarm in the cause; and the Sikhs were detested in Afghanistan. Lord Auckland shrunk from the responsibility of despatching a British army across the Indus; but, warned of the danger of identifying himself with a slighter measure promising little certainty of success, he halted, for a time, between two opinions, and slowly yielded to the assaults of his scribes.*

There were two other men then on the frontier whose opinions Lord Auckland had been naturally desirous to obtain. Captain Burnes and Captain Wade were at least acquainted with the history and politics of Afghanistan, and they had freely placed their sentiments on record. It has been advanced that the course of policy eventually pursued was in accordance with the views of these two officers. It is important, therefore, that it should be clearly ascertained what those views actually were.

On the 20th of July Captain Burnes joined the Simlah

* In this revised edition of the present work, I am bound to state that Mr. Henry Torrens, whose early death, in 1852, is an event to be deplored far beyond the circle of his own private friends, emphatically denied, on reading these statements, and the comments made upon them by the local press of India, his participation in the evil counsels which led Lord Auckland astray. I am bound to give currency to Mr. Torrens's explanations, which will be found in the Appendix to the present volume, with such comments of my own as they seem to demand.

Council. On the 29th of May, whilst halting at Peshawur, he had received a letter from Mr. Macnaghten, instructing him to proceed at once to join the British Mission, and in obedience to the summons had started at once on his downward journey. In the middle of June he had joined the camp of the British Envoy at Lahore, and taken part in the later deliberations which had preceded the acceptance by Runjeet Singh of the terms proposed by the British Government ; and on the departure of the Mission for Loodhianah had proceeded to join Lord Auckland and his advisers at Simlah.*

Burnes had already placed his opinions on record. At Hussan Abdool he had received Macnaghten's letter calling upon him for his views regarding the best means of counteracting the hostile influence of the Barukzye chiefs, and on the 2nd of June he had despatched a long demi-official letter, stating the policy which, under the then existing circumstances, he conceived it expedient to adopt, " not," in his own emphatic words, " what was best ; but what was best under the circumstances, which a series of blunders had produced."

It is plain that no advice offered by Burnes could have had any effect upon the question of the restoration of Shah Soojah. Macnaghten, on reaching Adeenanuggur, had determined not to await the arrival of the agent from Caubul before stating the views of the British Government

* Mr. Masson says (*Narrative*, vol. iii , p. 495) that Burnes told him that the expedition across the Indus "had been arranged before he reached Simlah, and that when he arrived Torrens and Colvin came running to him and prayed him to say nothing to unsettle his Lordship ; that they had all the trouble in the world to get him into the business, and that even now he would be glad of any pretext to retire from it." I was for a long time, very sceptical of the truth of this story ; and I do not now vouch for it But I know that some men, with far better opportunities than my own of determining the authenticity of the anecdote, are inclined to believe it.

to Runjeet Singh. He had, indeed, given the Maharajah the option of participating in an expedition for the restoration of Shah Soojah before he had received, either orally or by letter, the recommendations of Captain Burnes. When Burnes joined the British Mission, our Government was irretrievably committed to a course of policy which he either might or might not have supported. If he had any influence on the future out-turn of events, it was rather as the adviser of Runjeet Singh* than as the adviser of the British Mission. The fatal offer had been made to the Maharajah before Burnes joined the Mission camp.

What Burnes really recommended, as the growth of his own free and unfettered opinion was, that the case of Dost Mahomed should be reconsidered, and that the British Government should act with him and not against him. "It remains to be reconsidered," he wrote,† "why we cannot act with Dost Mahomed. He is a man of undoubted ability, and has at heart a high opinion of the British nation; and if half you must do for others were done for him, and offers made which he could see conduced

---

* Runjeet was very anxious to obtain Burnes's private opinion regarding the state of politics in Afghanistan, and the course which it was expedient for the Maharajah to adopt. The Fakir Noor-ood-deen had two or three conferences with Burnes upon these points. The whole history of the negotiations with Dost Mahomed were gone over and reported, from notes taken down at the time, by the Fakir to the Maharajah. Runjeet declared himself very grateful for this information; and sent again to ask Burnes to tell him, not as a public functionary, but as a private friend, whether the restoration of Shah Soojah would be really to his advantage. Burnes's answer was in the affirmative; and Runjeet seems to have been, to some extent, influenced by it. —[*Captain Burnes to Mr. Macnaghten, Lahore, June 20th,* 1838 : *MS. Records.*] I do not know whether this letter has ever been made public from any private source. Like almost everything else relating to the proceedings at Lahore and Loodhianah in June and July, 1830, it was studiously suppressed by government.

† To Mr. *Macnaghten, June* 2, 1838.

to his interests, he would abandon Russia and Persia to-morrow. It may be said that opportunity has been given him; but I would rather discuss this in person with you, for I think there is much to be said for him. Government have admitted that he had at best a choice of difficulties; and it should not be forgotten that we promised nothing, and Persia and Russia held out a great deal." But Burnes had been asked for his advice, not regarding the best means of counteracting Persian or Russian influence in Afghanistan, but the best means of counteracting Dost Mahomed; and he gave it as his opinion, that if Dost Mahomed were to be counteracted, the restoration of Shah Soojah was a more feasible project than the establishment of Sikh influence at Caubul. Captain Wade had declared his conviction that the disunion of the Afghan chiefs was an element of security to the British; but this opinion Burnes controverted, and pronounced himself in favour of the consolidation of the Afghan Empire. "As things stand," he wrote, "I maintain that it is the best of all policy to make Caubul in itself as strong as we can make it, and not weaken it by divided forces. It has already been too long divided. Caubul owed its strength in bygone days to the tribute of Cashmere and Sindh. Both are irrevocably gone, and while we do all we can to keep up the Sikhs, as a power east of the Indus, during the Maharajah's life or afterwards, we · should consolidate Afghan power west of the Indus, and have a king, and not a collection of chiefs. *Divide et impera* is a temporising creed at any time; and if the Afghans are united, we and they bid defiance to Persia, and instead of distant relations we have everything under our eye, and a steadily progressing influence all along the Indus."

Such were the general views that Burnes enunciated, in the knowledge that the Simlah Cabinet had determined on the deposition of Dost Mahomed. In fulfilment of the object thus contemplated, he recommended that the empire should be consolidated under Shah Soojah, rather than under Sultan Mahomed or any other chief. He believed that the restoration of the ex-King could be accomplished with the greatest facility, at a very trifling expenditure of the resources and display of the power of the British Government. "As for Shah Soojah-ool-Moolk, personally,"* he wrote, "the British Government have only to send him to Peshawur with an agent, and two of its own regiments as an honorary escort, and an avowal to the Afghans that we have taken up his cause, to ensure his being fixed for ever on the throne. The present time is perhaps better than any previous to it, for the Afghans, as a nation, detest Persia, and Dost Mahomed having gone over to the Court of Teheran, though he believes it to be from dire necessity, converts many a doubting Afghan into a bitter enemy. The Maharajah's opinion has only, therefore, to be asked for the ex-King's advance on Peshawur, granting him, at the same time, some four or five of the regiments which have no Sikhs in their ranks, and Soojah becomes King. He need not move from Peshawur, but address the Khyburrees, Kohistances of Caubul, and all the Afghans from that city, (stating) that he has the co-operation of the British and the Maharajah, and with but a little distribution of ready money—say, two or three lakhs of rupees—he will find himself the real King of the Afghans in a couple of months. It is, however,

* Burnes had originally written, "Of Shah Soojah-ool-Moolk, personally, I have, that is as ex-King of the Afghans, no very high opinion;" but he had scored out the words. I quote the passages in the text from a copy, the accuracy of which is certified by two Justices of the Peace at Bombay. This letter was cited by Sir John Hobhouse in the House of Commons, in verification of the assertion that Burnes had recommended the course adopted by Lord Auckland. That I may not be myself accused of garbling, I give the letter entire in the *Appendix*.

to be remembered always, that we must appear directly, for the Afghans are a superstitious people, and believe Shah Soojah to have no fortune—but our name will invest him with it."

Such were the sanguine expectations of Captain Burnes, and the very moderate policy which he was inclined to recommend, on the presumption that all amicable relations with Dost Mahomed had now been repudiated by the British Government. The opinions of Captain Wade were scarcely less in accordance with those which found favour in the Simlah Council-Chamber. It had ever been the belief of this officer that the consolidation of Afghanistan would prove injurious to British interests. He had insisted that it was the wisest policy to support the existing rulers, and to encourage the disunion among them. Of Dost Mahomed, personally, Captain Wade entertained no favourable opinion. He underrated both the character of the man and his influence over his countrymen; but so little was he disposed to counsel the subversion of the existing rule in Afghanistan, that he was always willing to endeavour to bring about an arrangement with Dost Mahomed, by recommending Runjeet Singh to accept the overtures of the Ameer.*

* With reference to the final offers of Dost Mahomed to hold Peshawur, conjointly with Sultan Mahomed, tributary to Lahore (Jebbar Khan acting as the Ameer's representative), Captain Wade wrote: "They seem to be in some accordance with the overture made by Runjeet Singh to Dost Mahomed before Captain Burnes's arrival at Caubul, as reported in my despatch of the 8th of August last, and appear, as far as I can judge of them at present, to be more reasonable than his former overtures, though the Maharajah's opinion of their operation on the Peshawur branch of the family remains to be disclosed. I am ready, with the sanction of the Governor-General, to communicate the proposition now made to Runjeet Singh, and to support by every argument that I can use the expediency of its acceptance by him."— [*Captain Wade to Mr. Macnaghten, March* 3, 1838.]

It was his opinion, that if the consolidation of the country were to be attempted at all, it would be more expedient to support the claims of Shah Soojah than of Dost Mahomed; but he regarded the restoration of the Shah only as a last resort, and would rather have seen the Barukzye chiefs left quietly in their own possessions. Indeed, in the very letter of the 1st of January, 1838, on which so much stress has been laid, Captain Wade, even in the printed version, says: "Shah Soojah's recognition could only, however, be justified or demanded of us, in the event of the prostration of Herat to the Persian Government;" and in the unprinted portion of this letter the writer says: "I can see nothing in the state of parties at present in the Punjab to deter us from pursuing a line of policy" (in Afghanistan), "every way consistent with our engagements, our reputation, and our interests—viz., that of recognising the present holders of power, and discouraging any ambitious schemes of one party to the detriment of another." And in conclusion, Captain Wade sums up what he believes to be the true policy of the British, declaring that "if Dost Mahomed is kept, as he now is, at Caubul, whether as a Governor of the province, under Shah Soojah, or in independence of him, and Peshawur be restored to Sultan Mahomed, or remain as at present, we might not only be safe from disturbances, or any sudden inroads from the western powers, but be enabled to secure the integrity of the Sikh nation as far as the Indus, and would mould these people and their already more than half-disciplined troops to our wishes."* Captain Wade over-estimated the popularity of Shah Soojah. He was in constant receipt of information to the effect that the

* *Captain Wade to Mr. Macnaghten: MS. Records.* Captain Wade's letters have been garbled almost as shamelessly as Captain Burnes's.

Douranees and other tribes were eager for his return; and he did not, perhaps, sufficiently consider that the Afghans always long for what they have not, and are seldom unripe for revolution. But although he believed it would be safer to attempt to re-establish the integrity of Afghanistan under Shah Soojah than under Dost Mahomed, he thought that it would be better policy still to leave untouched the disunion and antagonism of the Barukzye Sirdars.

Such, read by the light of their unmutilated despatches, were the genuine opinions of Burnes and Wade. But the Simlah Council had more ambitious views, and were disposed towards more extensive plans of operation. First one project, then another, had been discussed. It had been debated, firstly, whether the movement on Candahar could be undertaken by the Shah's raw levies, supported only, as originally intended, by a British army of reserve at Shikarpoor; and secondly, whether some two or three regiments of British troops would not be sufficient to escort the Shah's army into the heart of his old dominions. Both of these projects were abandoned.

Sir Henry Fane was at this time commander-in-chief of the British forces in India. He had pitched his tent at Simlah, and was in frequent consultation with the Governor-General. He was a fine old soldier of the Tory school, with very strong opinions regarding the general "shabbiness" of all Whig doings, and a strenuous dislike of half-measures, especially in military affairs. It is believed that he did not approve of the general policy of British interference in the affairs of Afghanistan,* but

* In 1837, he had written to Sir Charles Metcalfe, "Every advance you might make beyond the Sutlej to the Westward, in my opinion adds to your military weakness. .... If you want your empire to expand, expand it over Oude or over Gwalior, and the remains of the Mahratta

he was entirely of opinion that it was the duty of government, in the conjuncture that had arisen, either not to interfere at all, or to interfere in such a manner as to secure the success of our operations. Always by nature inclined towards moderate measures, the Governor-General for some time resisted the urgent recommendations of those who spoke of the formation of a grand army, drawn from our own regular establishment, to be headed by the commander-in-chief in person, and marched upon Candahar, perhaps upon Herat itself. But Lord Auckland was never the most resolute of men. His own confidential advisers had long been endeavouring to convince him of the necessity of adopting more vigorous measures. The commander-in-chief was not only recommending such measures, but insisting upon his right, as the first military authority in the country, to determine the number of British troops to be employed, and the manner of their employment. And the ministers of the Crown, fortified by the knowledge that the expenses of the war would fall upon the treasury of the East India Company, and that they would not be called by the British people to account for any expenditure, however lavish, upon remote warlike operations, which the public might easily be persuaded to regard as the growth of the most consummate wisdom, were exhorting Lord Auckland to adopt effectual measures for the counteraction of Russian intrigue and Persian hostility in the countries of Afghanistan. So, after some weeks of painful oscillation, Lord Auckland yielded his own judgment to the judgment of others, and an order went forth for the assembling of a grand army on the frontier, to be set in motion early in the coming cold

empire. Make yourselves complete sovereigns of all within your bounds. *But let alone the Far West.*"—[*Life of Lord Metcalfe,* Vol. ii. p. 306.]

weather, in support of Shah Soojah and his levies; to cross the Indus; and to march upon Candahar.

In August, the regiments selected by the commander-in-chief were warned for field-service, and on the 13th of September he published a general order, brigading the different components of the force, naming the staff-officers appointed, and ordering the whole to rendezvous at Kurnaul. The reports, which all through the dry summer months had been flitting about from cantonment to cantonment, and making the pulses of military aspirants, old and young, beat rapidly with the fever of expectancy, now took substantial shape; and everywhere the approaching expedition became the one topic of conversation. Peace had reigned over India for so many years, that the excitement of the coming contest was as novel as it was inspiriting. There was not an officer in the army who did not long to join the invading force; and many from the distant Presidency, or from remote provincial stations, leaving the quiet staff-appointments which had lapped them long in case and luxury, rushed upwards to join their regiments. Even in that unpropitious season of the year, when the country was flooded by the periodical rains, corps were set in motion towards Kurnaul, from stations as low down as Benares, and struggled manfully, often through wide sheets of water, to their destination at the great northern rallying point. There had been no such excitement in military circles since the grand army assembled for the reduction of Bhurtpore; and though the cause was not a popular one, and there was scarcely a mess-table in the country at which the political bearings of the invasion of Afghanistan were discussed without eliciting the plainest possible indications that the sympathies of our officers were rather with the Barukzye chief than the Suddozye monarch, there was everywhere the liveliest desire to join the ranks of an army that was to traverse new and almost fabulous regions, and visit the scenes rendered famous by the exploits of Mahmoud of Ghuzni and Nadir Shah.

The army now warned for field-service consisted of a brigade of artillery, a brigade of cavalry, and five brigades of infantry. Colonel Graham was to command the artillery; Colonel Arnold the cavalry; whilst the brigades of infantry were assigned respectively to Colonels Sale and Dennis, of the Queen's; and Colonels Nott, Roberts, and Worseley, of the Company's service. The infantry brigades were told off into two divisions under Sir Willoughby Cotton, an old and distinguished officer of the Queen's army, who had rendered good service in the Burmese war, and was now commanding the Presidency division of the Bengal army, and Major-General Duncan, an esteemed officer of the Company's service, who was then in command of the Sirhind division of the army, and was therefore on the spot to take the immediate management of details.

The regiments now ordered to assemble were her Majesty's 16th Lancers, 13th Infantry, and 3rd Buffs; the Company's European regiment; two regiments of Native light cavalry, and twelve picked Sepoy corps.* Two troops of horse artillery and three companies of foot, constituted the artillery brigade; and some details of sappers and miners, under Captain Thomson, completed the Bengal force. The usual staff-departments were formed to accompany the army,† the heads of

---

* The 2nd, 5th, 16th, 27th, 28th, 31st, 35th, 37th, 42nd, 43rd, 48th, and 53rd regiments.

† The principal staff-officers were Major P. Craigie, Deputy Adjutant-General; Major W. Garden, Deputy Quartermaster-General; Major J. D. Parsons, Deputy Commissary-General; Major Hough, Deputy Advocate-General; and Major T. Byrne, Assistant Adjutant-General of Queen's Troops.

departments remaining in the Presidency whilst their deputies accompanied the forces into the field.

Whilst the Bengal army was assembling on the northern frontier of India, under the personal command of Sir Henry Fane, another force was being collected at Bombay. It was composed of a brigade of cavalry, including her Majesty's 4th Dragoons, a brigade of artillery, and a brigade of foot, consisting of two Queen's regiments (the 2nd Royals and 17th Foot) and one Sepoy corps. Major-General Thackwell commanded the cavalry; Major-General Wiltshire the infantry; and Colonel Stevenson the artillery brigade. Sir John Keane, the commander-in-chief of the Bombay army, took command of the whole.

Such was the extent of the British force warned for field-service in the autumn of 1838. At the same time another force was being raised for service across the Indus—the force that was to be led by Shah Soojah into Afghanistan; that was to be known distinctively as *his* force; but to be raised in the Company's territories, to be commanded by the Company's officers, and to be paid by the Company's coin.

To this army was to have been entrusted the work of re-establishing the authority of the Suddozye Princes in Western Afghanistan; but it had now sunk into a mere appendage to the regular army which the British-Indian Government was about to despatch across the Indus; and it was plain that, whatever opposition was to be encountered, the weight of it would fall, not upon Shah Soojah's raw levies, but upon the disciplined troops of the Indian army that were to be sent with them, to secure the success of the otherwise doubtful campaign. Whatever work there might be in store for them, the recruiting went on bravely. For this new service there was no lack of candidates in the Upper Provinces of India. The Shah himself watched with eager pride the formation of the army which was to surround him on his return to his own dominions, but was fearful lest the undisguised assumption of entire control by the British officers appointed to raise his new regiments should deprive him of all the *éclat* of independence with which he was so anxious to invest his movements. It was, indeed, no easy matter, at this time, to shape our measures in accordance with the conflicting desires of the old king, who wished to have everything done for him, and yet to appear as though he did it himself. To Captain Wade was entrusted the difficult and delicate duty of managing one who, by nature not the most reasonable of men, was rendered doubly unreasonable by the anomalous position in which he found himself after the ratification of the tripartite treaty. It was difficult, indeed, to say what he was at this time. At Loodhianah he had hitherto been simply a private individual. He had held no recognised position. He had been received with no public honours. He had gone hither and thither, almost unnoticed. He had excited little interest, and met with little attention. Some, perhaps, knew that he had once been an Afghan monarch, and that he received four thousand rupees a month from the British Government as a reward for his incapacity and a compensation for his bad fortune. Beyond this little was known and nothing was cared. But now, suddenly he, had risen up from the dust of Loodhianah as a recognised sovereign and framer of treaties—a potentate meeting on equal terms with the British Government and the Maharajah of the Punjab. He could not any longer be regarded as a mere tradition. He had been brought prominently forward into the light of the Present ; and it was necessary that he should now assume in men's eyes something of the form of royalty and the substance of power.

It was natural that, thus strangely and embarrassingly situated, the Shah should have earnestly desired to bring his sojourn at Loodhianah to a close, and to launch himself fairly upon his new enterprise. The interval between the signing of the treaty and the actual commencement of the expedition was irksome in the extreme to the expectant monarch. It was plain that he could not move without his army; he therefore did his best to expedite its information. Constantly attending the parade where the work of recruiting was going on, he desired personally to superintend both the payment and the enlistment of his men, and was fearful lest a belief should become rooted in the public mind that he was not about to return to Afghanistan as an independent Prince, ruling his own people on his own account. The tact and discretion of Captain Wade smoothed down all difficulties. Whilst preventing such interference on the part of Shah Soojah as might embarrass the movements of the British officers appointed to raise and discipline his regiments, he contrived to reconcile the mind of the King to the system in force by directing that certain reports should be made to him on parade, and at other times through an appointed agent, of the number of men enlisted into his service, and the amount of pay that was due to each.* At the same time, it was suggested to the commanding officer of the station that, as one entitled to the recognitions due to royalty, the Shah should be saluted by the troops when he appeared in public. The suggestion was promptly acted upon; and the King, whose inveterate love of forms and ceremonies clung to him to the end of his days, rejoiced in these new demonstrations of respect, and bore up till his time of trial was over.

In the meanwhile Lord Auckland, having thus mapped

* *Captain Wade to Mr. Macnaghten, Loodhianah, September 23rd, 1838. MS. Records.*

out a far more extensive scheme of invasion than had ever been dreamt of, a few months before, in his most speculative moments, was thinking of the agency which it was most desirable to employ for the political management of the ensuing campaign. It had been determined that a British Envoy should accompany Runjeet Singh's army by the Peshawur route, and that another should accompany Shâh Soojah's camp on its march towards the western provinces of Afghanistan. There was no difficulty in naming the officer who was to superintend the demonstration to be made by the Sikh troops through the formidable passes of the Khybur. Captain Wade was nominated to this office. He was to be accompanied by the eldest son of Shah Soojah, the Prince Timour, a man of respectable character, but not very brilliant parts, whose presence was to identify the Sikh movement with the immediate objects of his father's restoration, and to make obvious to the understandings of all men that Runjeet Singh was acting only as Shah Soojah's ally.

But it was not so easy to determine to whom should be entrusted the difficult and responsible duty of directing the mind of Shah Soojah, and shaping, in all beyond the immediate line of military operations, the course of this great campaign. It seemed at first that the claims of Alexander Burnes could not be set aside. No man knew the country and the people so well; no man had so fairly earned the right to be thus employed. But it soon appeared to Burnes himself, sanguine as he was, that Lord Auckland designed to place him in a subordinate position; and chafing under what appeared to him a slight and an injustice, he declared that he would either take the chief place in the British Mission, or go home to England in disgust.* But these feelings soon passed away. It had

* "We are now planning a grand campaign," he wrote on the 22nd of July, "to restore the Shah to the throne of Caubul—Russia having

been debated whether the chief political control should not be placed in the hands of the commander-in-chief; and Sir Henry Fane, naturally favouring an arrangement which would have left him free to act as his own judgment or his own impulses might dictate, wished to take Burnes with him as his confidential adviser. But this plan met with little or no encouragement. The Governor-General appreciated Burnes's talents, but mistrusted his discretion. He thought it advisable to place at the stirrup of Shah Soojah an older head and a steadier hand. Men, who at this time watched calmly the progress of events, and had no prejudices and predilections to gratify, and no personal objects to serve, thought that the choice of the Governor-

come down upon us. What exact part I am to play I know not, but if full confidence and hourly consultation be any pledge, I am to be chief. I can plainly tell them that it is *aut Cæsar aut nullus*, and if I get not what I have a right to, you will soon see me *en route* to England." On the 23rd of August he wrote: "Of myself I cannot tell you what is to become. The commander-in-chief wants to go and to take me—but this will not be, and I believe the chief and Macnaghten will be made a commission—Wade and myself political agents under them. I plainly told Lord Auckland that this does not please, and I am disappointed. He replied that I could scarcely be appointed with the chief in equality, and pledged himself to leave me independent quickly, and in the highest appointment. What can I do when he tells me I am a man he cannot spare. It is an honour, not a disgrace to go under Sir Henry; and as for Macnaghten, he is secretary for all India, and goes *pro tem*. Besides, I am not sorry to see Dost Mahomed ousted by another hand than mine."—[*Private Correspondence of Sir A. Burnes.*] These letters were written to his brother. In another letter addressed to Captain Duncan, also on the 23rd of August, Burnes wrote: "Of my own destinies, even, I cannot as yet give an account. I go as a Political Agent with the Shah, but whether as *the* Political Agent remains to be seen. I find I bask in favour, but Sir Henry Fane is to go, and he must be the Agent; but it is even hinted that they will place a civilian with him, and employ me in advance. Be it so. I succeed to the permanent employ after all is over. . . . . The chief wishes to go, and to take me with him, and I am highly obliged for his appreciation."
—[*Private Correspondence of Sir A. Burnes: MS.*]

General would fall upon Colonel Henry Pottinger, who had been familiar from early youth with the countries beyond the Indus, and was now in charge of our political relations with the Court of Hyderabad, in Sindh. But Lord Auckland had no personal knowledge of Colonel Pottinger. There was little identity of opinion between them; and the Governor-General recognised the expediency of appointing to such an office a functionary with whom he had been in habitual intercourse, who was necessarily, therefore, conversant with his views, and who would not scruple to carry them out to the utmost.

The choice fell on Mr. Macnaghten. It seems, at one time, to have been the design of the Governor-General to associate this gentleman with the Commander-in-Chief, in a kind of Commission for the management of our political relations throughout the coming expedition;[*] but this idea seems to have been abandoned. It was finally determined that Mr. W. H. Macnaghten should be gazetted as "Envoy and Minister on the part of the Government of India at the Court of Shah Soojah-ool-Moolk." And at the same time it was resolved that Captain Burnes should be employed, "under Mr. Macnaghten's directions, as Envoy to the chief of Kelat or other states." It was believed, at this time, that Shah Soojah having been reseated on the throne, Macnaghten would return to Hindostan, leaving Burnes at Caubul, as the permanent representative of the British-Indian Government at the Court of the Shah. It was this belief that reconciled Burnes to the subordinate office which was conferred upon him in the first instance, and made him set about the work entrusted to his charge with all the zeal and enthusiasm which were so conspicuous in his character.[†]

---

[*] See Burnes's correspondence, quoted in a preceding note.
[†] Lord Auckland, with characteristic kindliness, exerted himself to allay any feelings of mortification that may have welled up in Burnes's

And so Burnes was sent on in advance to smooth the way for the progress of the Shah through Sindh, whilst Macnaghten remained at Simlah to assist the Governor-General in the preparation of the great official manifesto which was to declare to all the nations of the East and of the West the grounds upon which the British Government had determined to destroy the power of the Barukzye Sirdars, and to restore Shah Soojah-ool-Moolk to the throne of his ancestors.

On the 1st of October the manifesto, long and anxiously pondered over in the bureau of the Governor-General, received the official signature and was sent to the press. Never, since the English in India first began the work of King-making, had a more remarkable document issued from the council-chamber of an Anglo-Indian viceroy. It ran in the following words, not one of which should be omitted from such a narrative as this :

DECLARATION ON THE PART OF THE RIGHT
HONOURABLE THE GOVERNOR-GENERAL OF INDIA.

Simlah, *October*, 1, 1838.

The Right Hon. the Governor-General of India having, with the concurrence of the Supreme Council, directed the assemblage of a British force for service across the Indus, his Lordship deems it

---

mind ; and the latter wisely revoked his determination to be *aut Cæsar aut nullus*. The extracts from Burnes's letters, given in a preceding note, explain the motives that induced him to forego his original resolve ; and the following passage, from another private letter, shows still more plainly the feelings with which he regarded the considerate conduct of the Governor-General, of whom he writes : " 'I mean, therefore,' continued he (Lord Auckland), 'to gazette you as a Political Commissioner to Kelat, and when the army crosses, to regard you as an independent political officer to co-operate with Macnaghten.' Nothing could be more delicately kind, for I have permission, if I like, to send an assistant to Kelat. I start in a week, and drop down the Indus to Shikarpoor, where, with a brace of Commissaries, I prepare for the advance of the army and the disbursement of many lakhs of rupees. I

proper to publish the following exposition of the reasons which have led to this important measure.

It is a matter of notoriety that the treaties entered into by the British Government in the year 1832, with the Ameers of Sindh, the Newab of Bhawalpore, and Maharajah Runjeet Singh, had for their object, by opening the navigation of the Indus, to facilitate the extension of commercce, and to gain for the British nation in Central Asia that legitimate influence which an interchange of benefits would naturally produce.

With a view to invite the aid of the *de facto* rulers of Afghanistan to the measures necessary for giving full effect to those treaties, Captain Burnes was deputed, towards the close of the year 1836, on a mission to Dost Mahomed Khan, the chief of Caubul. The original objects of that officer's mission were purely of a commercial nature. Whilst Captain Burnes, however, was on his journey to Caubul, information was received by the Governor-General that the troops of Dost Mahomed Khan had made a sudden and unprovoked attack on those of our ancient ally, Maharajah Runjeet Singh. It was naturally to be apprehended that his Highness the Maharajah would not be slow to avenge the aggression; and it was to be feared that, the flames of war being once kindled in the very regions into which we were endeavouring to extend our commerce, the peaceful and beneficial purposes of the British Government would be altogether frustrated. In order to avert a result so calamitous, the Governor-General resolved on authorising Captain Burnes to intimate to Dost Mahomed Khan, that if he should evince a disposition to come to just and reasonable terms with the Maharajah, his Lordship would exert his good offices with his Highness for the restoration of an amicable understanding between the two powers. The Maharajah, with the characteristic confidence which he has uniformly placed in the faith and friendship of the British nation, at once assented to the proposition of the Governor-General, to the effect that, in the mean time, hostilities on his part should be suspended.

It subsequently came to the knowledge of the Governor-General that a Persian army was besieging Herat; that intrigues were actively prosecuted throughout Afghanistan, for the purpose of extending Persian influence and authority to the banks of, and even

---

care not for the responsibility; I am firm in the saddle, and have all confidence. I think you will hear the result of my negotiation to be, that the British flag flies at Bukkur."—[*Private Correspondence of Sir A. Burnes.*]

beyond, the Indus; and that the Court of Persia had not only commenced a course of injury and insult to the officers of her Majesty's Mission in the Persian territory, but had afforded evidence of being engaged in designs wholly at variance with the principles and objects of its alliance with Great Britain.

After much time spent by Captain Burnes in fruitless negotiation at Caubul, it appeared that Dost Mahomed Khan, chiefly in consequence of his reliance upon Persian encouragement and assistance, persisted, as respected his misunderstanding with the Sikhs, in urging the most unreasonable pretensions, such as the Governor-General could not, consistently with justice and his regard for the friendship of Maharajah Runjeet Singh, be the channel of submitting to the consideration of his Highness; that he avowed schemes of aggrandisement and ambition injurious to the security and peace of the frontiers of India; and that he openly threatened, in furtherance of those schemes, to call in every foreign aid which he could command. Ultimately he gave his undisguised support to the Persian designs in Afghanistan, of the unfriendly and injurious character of which, as concerned the British power in India, he was well apprised, and by his utter disregard of the views and interests of the British Government, compelled Captain Burnes to leave Caubul without having effected any of the objects of his mission.

It was now evident that no further interference could be exercised by the British Government to bring about a good understanding between the Sikh ruler and Dost Mahomed Khan, and the hostile policy of the latter chief showed too plainly that, so long as Caubul remained under his government, we could never hope that the tranquillity of our neighbourhood would be secured, or that the interests of our Indian Empire would be preserved inviolate.

The Governor-General deems it in this place necessary to revert to the siege of Herat, and the conduct of the Persian nation. The siege of that city has now been carried on by the Persian army for many months. The attack upon it was a most unjustifiable and cruel aggression, perpetrated and continued, notwithstanding the solemn and repeated remonstrances of the British Envoy at the Court of Persia, and after every just and becoming offer of accommodation had been made and rejected. The besieged have behaved with a gallantry and fortitude worthy of the justice of their cause; and the Governor-General would yet indulge the hope that their heroism may enable them to maintain a successful defence, until succours shall reach them from British India. In the meantime, the ulterior designs of Persia, affecting the interests of the British Government, have been, by a succession of events, more and more openly manifested. The Governor-General has recently ascertained by an official despatch from Mr. M'Neill, her Majesty's Envoy, that his Excellency has been compelled, by a refusal of his just demands, and by a systematic course of disrespect adopted towards him by the Persian Government, to quit the Court of the Shah, and to make a public declaration of the cessation of all intercourse between the two Governments. The necessity under which Great Britain is placed of regarding the present advance of the Persian arms into Afghanistan as an act of hostility towards herself, has also been officially communicated to the Shah, under the express order of her Majesty's Government.

The chiefs of Candahar (brothers of Dost Mahomed Khan of Caubul) have avowed their adherence to the Persian policy, with the same full knowledge of its opposition to the rights and interests of the British nation in India, and have been openly assisting in the operations against Herat.

In the crisis of affairs consequent upon the retirement of our Envoy from Caubul, the Governor-General felt the importance of taking immediate measures for arresting the rapid progress of foreign intrigue and aggression towards our own territories.

His attention was naturally drawn at this conjuncture to the position and claims of Shah Soojah-ool-Moolk, a monarch who, when in power, had cordially acceded to the measures of united resistance to external enmity, which were at that time judged necessary by the British Government, and who, on his empire being usurped by its present rulers, had found an honourable asylum in the British dominions.

It had been clearly ascertained, from the information furnished by the various officers who have visited Afghanistan, that the Barukzye chiefs, from their disunion and unpopularity, were ill fitted, under any circumstances, to be useful allies to the British Government, and to aid us in our just and necessary measures of national defence. Yet so long as they refrained from proceedings injurious to our interests and security, the British Government acknowledged and respected their authority; but a different policy appeared to be now more than justified by the conduct of those chiefs, and to be indispensable to our own safety. The welfare of our possessions in the East requires that we should have on our western frontier an ally who is interested in resisting aggression, and establishing tranquillity, in the place of chiefs ranging themselves in subservience to a hostile power, and seeking to promote schemes of conquest and aggrandisement

After serious and mature deliberation, the Governor-General was satisfied that a pressing necessity, as well as every consideration of policy and justice, warranted us in espousing the cause of Shah Soojah-ool-Moolk, whose popularity throughout Afghanistan had been proved to his Lordship by the strong and unanimous testimony of the best authorities. Having arrived at this determination, the Governor-General was further of opinion that it was just and proper, no less from the position of Maharajah Runjeet Singh, than from his undeviating friendship towards the British Government, that his Highness should have the offer of becoming a party to the contemplated operations.

Mr. Macnaghten was accordingly deputed in June last to the Court of his Highness, and the result of his mission has been the conclusion of a triplicate treaty by the British Government, the Maharajah, and Shah Soojah-ool-Moolk, whereby his Highness is guaranteed in his present possessions, and has bound himself to co-operate for the restoration of the Shah to the throne of his ancestors. The friends and enemies of any one of the contracting parties have been declared to be the friends and enemies of all.

Various points have been adjusted, which had been the subjects of discussion between the British Government and his Highness the Maharajah, the identity of whose interests with those of the Honourable Company has now been made apparent to all the surrounding States. A guaranteed independence will, upon favourable conditions, be tendered to the Ameers of Sindh, and the integrity of Herat, in the possession of its present ruler, will be fully respected; while by the measures completed, or in progress, it may reasonably be hoped that the general freedom and security of commerce will be promoted, that the name and just influence of the British Government will gain their proper footing among the nations of Central Asia; that tranquillity will be established upon the most important frontier of India; and that a lasting barrier will be raised against hostile intrigue and encroachment.

His Majesty, Shah Soojah-ool-Moolk will enter Afghanistan, surrounded by his own troops, and will be supported against foreign interference and factious opposition by a British army. The Governor-General confidently hopes that the Shah will be speedily replaced on his throne by his own subjects and adherents, and when once he shall be secured in power, and the independence and integrity of Afghanistan established, the British army will be withdrawn. The Governor-General has been led to these measures by the duty which is imposed upon him of providing for the security of the possessions of the British Crown; but, he rejoices that, in the discharge of his duty, he will be enabled to assist in restoring the union and prosperity of the Afghan people. Throughout the approaching operations, British influence will be sedulously employed to further every measure of general benefit, to reconcile differences, to secure oblivion of injuries, and to put an end to the distractions by which, for so many years, the welfare and happiness of the Afghans have been impaired. Even to the chiefs, whose hostile proceedings have given just cause of offence to the British Government, it will seek to secure liberal and honourable treatment, on their tendering early submission, and ceasing from opposition to that course of measures which may be judged the most suitable for the general advantage of their country.

By order of the Right Hon. Governor-General of India.

W. H. MACNAGHTEN,
Secretary to the Government of India, with the
Governor-General.

NOTIFICATION.

With reference to the preceding Declaration, the following appointments are made:—Mr. W. H. Macnaghten, Secretary to Government, will assume the functions of Envoy and Minister on the part of the Government of India at the Court of Shah Soojah-ool-Moolk. Mr. Macnaghten will be assisted by the following officers:—Captain A. Burnes, of the Bombay establishment, who will be employed, under Mr. Macnaghten's directions, as Envoy to the Chief of Kelat, or other States; Lieutenant E. d'Arcy Todd, Bengal Artillery, to be Political Assistant and Military Secretary to the Envoy and Minister; Lieutenant Eldred Pottinger, Bombay Artillery; Lieutenant R. Leech, of the Bombay Engineers; Mr. P. B. Lord, of the Bombay Medical Establishment, to be Political Assistants to ditto, ditto; Lieutenant E. B. Conolly, 6th Bengal Cavalry, to command the escort of the Envoy and Minister, and to be Military Assistant to ditto, ditto; Mr. G. J. Berwick, of the Bengal Medical Establishment, to be Surgeon to ditto, ditto.

W. H. MACNAGHTEN,
Secretary to the Government of India, with the
Governor-General.

It was not to be supposed that such a manifesto as this could be published in every newspaper in India and in Europe, and circulated, in an Oriental dress, throughout all the states of Hindostan and the adjoining countries, without provoking the keenest and the most searching criticism. In India there is, in reality, no Public; but if such a name can be given to the handful of English gentlemen who discuss with little reserve the affairs of the government under which they live, the public looked askance at it—doubting and questioning its truth. The Press seized upon it and tore it to pieces.* There was not a sentence in it that was not dissected with an unsparing hand. If it were not pronounced to be a collection of absolute falsehoods, it was described as a most disingenuous distortion of the truth. In India every war is more or less popular. The constitution of Anglo-Indian society renders it almost impossible that it should be otherwise. But many wished that they were about to draw their swords in a better cause; and openly criticised the Governor-General's declaration, whilst they inwardly rejoiced that it had been issued.

Had the relief of Herat been the one avowed object of the expedition, a war now to be undertaken for that purpose would have had many supporters.† The movement might have been a wise, or it might have been an unwise one; but it would have been an intelligible, straightforward movement, with nothing equivocal about

---

* I do not mean that the entire Press of India and England condemned it; but I believe that, at the time it had very few genuine supporters: and I know that now it has fewer still.

† Among others the Duke of Wellington, who wrote to Mr. Tucker: "I don't know that while the siege of Herat continued, particularly by the aid of Russian officers and troops, even in the form of deserters, the Government of India could have done otherwise than prepare for its defence."—[*Life and Correspondence of Henry St. George Tucker.*]

it. It would have been addressed to the counteraction of a real, or supposed danger, and would have been plainly justifiable as a measure of self-defence. But it was not equally clear that because Mahomed Shah made war upon Herat, England was justified in making war upon Dost Mahomed. The siege of Herat and the failure of the Caubul Mission were mixed up together in Lord Auckland's manifesto; but with all his own and his secretary's ingenuity, his Lordship could not contrive, any more than I have contrived in this narrative, to make the two events hang together by any other than the slenderest thread. It was believed at this time that Herat would fall; and that Candahar and Caubul would then make their obeisance to Mahomed Shah. But we had ourselves alienated the friendship of the Barukzye Sirdars. They had thrown themselves into the arms of the Persian King, only because we had thrust them off. We had forced them into an attitude of hostility which they were unwilling to assume; and had ourselves aggravated the dangers which we were now about to face on the western frontier of Afghanistan. That in the summer of 1838, there existed a state of things calling for active measures on the part of the British Government is not to be denied; but I believe it to be equally undeniable that this state of things was mainly induced by the feebleness of our own policy towards the Barukzye Sirdars.

The comments which might be made in this place on Lord Auckland's Simlah manifesto have been, for the most part, anticipated. How far Dost Mahomed "persisted in using the most unreasonable pretensions," and "avowed schemes of aggrandisement and ambition, injurious to the security and peace of the frontiers of India," I have shown in a former chapter. I have shown, too, how far the best authorities were of opinion that the Barukzye Sirdars were "ill-fitted, under any circumstances, to be useful allies to the British."* Little comment is called for beyond that involved in the recital of facts, the studious suppression of which by the Government of the day is the best proof of the importance attached to them.†

* The facts may be briefly repeated in a note. M'Neill recommended the consolidation of Afghanistan under Dost Mahomed. Burnes recommended the same course. Wade recommended the government to rely upon the disunion of the Barukzye Sirdars, and was opposed to consolidation of any kind.

† The responsibility of this famous manifesto belongs to Lord Auckland, though some of his colleagues in the government at home have declared themselves willing to share it with him. Sir John Hobhouse, in 1850, told the Official Salaries Committee, in reply to a question on the subject of the Afghan war, that he "did it himself;" and so far as the announcement went entirely to acquit the East India Company of taking part in the origination of the war, it is to be accepted as a laudable revelation of the truth; but although Lord Palmerston and Sir John Hobhouse saw the expediency of extricating the British Government from the difficulties into which the conduct of Mahomed Shah had thrown them, by encouraging a demonstration from the side of India, the expenses of which would be thrown upon the Indian exchequer, they are to be regarded rather as accessories after, than before, the fact. The truth is, that Lord Auckland had determined on the course of policy to be pursued, not before the India Board despatches were written, but before they were received. Sir John Hobhouse stated in the House of Commons (June 23, 1842) that Lord Auckland "must not bear the blame of the measure; it was the policy of government; and he might mention that the despatch which he wrote, stating his opinion of the course that ought to be taken in order to meet expected emergencies, and that written by Lord Auckland, informing him that the expedition had already been undertaken, crossed each other on the way." When the Whig ministry went out of office in the spring of 1839, it was believed that the Peel cabinet would repudiate the Simlah manifesto, and direct a considerable modification of the measures which were to follow the declaration of war. The bedchamber *émeute* arrested the formation of the Peel ministry; and it was at least surmised, that it was in no small measure to save Lord Auckland, and to escape the disgrace of a public reversal of their

The oldest, the most experienced, and the most sagacious Indian politicians were of opinion that the expedition, though it might be attended at the outset with some delusive success, would close in disaster and disgrace. Among those, who most emphatically disapproved of the movement and predicted its failure, were the Duke of Wellington, Lord Wellesley, Sir Charles Metcalfe, Mr. Edmonstone, Mountstuart Elphinstone, Sir Henry Willock, and Mr. Tucker.

The Duke of Wellington said that our difficulties would commence where our military successes ended. "The consequence of crossing the Indus," he wrote to Mr. Tucker, "once to settle a government in Afghanistan, will be a perennial march into that country." Lord Wellesley always spoke contemptuously of the folly of occupying a land of "rocks, sands, deserts, ice and snow." Sir Charles Metcalfe from the first protested against Lord Auckland's measures with respect to the trade of the Indus; and in 1835-36, when Mr. Ellis's proposal to assist Dost Mahomed with British officers and drill-instructors to discipline his army, came down to Calcutta, said, one day after council, "Depend upon it, the surest way to bring Russia down upon ourselves is for us to cross the Indus and meddle with the countries beyond it." Mr. Edmonstone always hung down his head, and almost groaned aloud, when the Afghan expedition was named. Mr. Elphinstone wrote in a private letter to Sir A. Burnes: "You will guess what I think of affairs in Caubul. You remember when I used to dispute with you against having even an agent in Caubul, and now we have assumed the protection of the

Indian policy, that the Whigs again took the reins of government. After this, Sir John Hobhouse never neglected an opportunity of publicly identifying himself with Lord Auckland's policy, and was not deterred, even by the disastrous termination of the war, from bravely declaring that he was the author of it.

state, as much as if it were one of the subsidiary allies in India. If you send 27,000 men up the *Durra-i-Bolan* to Candahar (as we hear is intended), and can feed them, I have no doubt you will take Candahar and Caubul and set up Soojah; but for maintaining him in a poor, cold, strong, and remote country, among a turbulent people like the Afghans, I own it seems to me to be hopeless. If you succeed, I fear you will weaken the position against Russia. The Afghans were neutral, and would have received your aid against invaders with gratitude—they will now be disaffected and glad to join any invader to drive you out. I never knew a close alliance between a civilised and an uncivilised state that did not end in mutual hatred in three years. If the restraint of a close connection with us were not enough to make us unpopular, the connection with Runjeet and our guarantee of his conquests must make us detested. These opinions formed at a distance may seem absurd on the spot; but I still retain them notwithstanding all I have yet heard." Sir Henry Willock, whose extensive local knowledge and long experience entitled his opinions to respect, addressed a long letter to the Foreign Secretary, in which he elaborately reviewed the mistake which had been committed. And Mr. Tucker, in the Court of Directors, and out of the Court, lost no opportunity of protesting against the expedition in his manly uncompromising way. "We have contracted an alliance with Shah Soojah," he wrote to the Duke of Wellington, "and have appointed a minister to his Court, although he does not possess a rood of ground in Afghanistan, nor a rupee which he does not derive from our bounty, as a quondam pensioner. We thus embroil ourselves in all the intricate and perplexed concerns of the Afghan tribes. We place Dost Mahomed, the *de facto* sovereign in open hostility against us; we alienate the Prince Kamran of Herat, who is nearer than Shah

Soojah in the line of succession of the Douranee Family; and even if we succeed in ousting Dost Mahomed and placing Shah Soojah on the throne of Caubul, we must maintain him in the government by a large military force, at the distance of 800 miles from our frontier and our resources."

As a body the Court of Directors of the East India Company were strongly opposed to the war, and had no part in its initiation beyond the performance of such mechanical duties as are prescribed by act of Parliament. The members of the Secret Committee are compelled to sign the despatches laid before them by the Board of Control; and the President of the Board of Control has unreservedly admitted that, beyond the mere mechanical act of signing the papers laid before them, they had no part in the recommendation or authorisation of the war. The policy of the East India Company is a policy of non-interference. They had seldom lost an opportunity of inculcating upon their governors the expediency of refraining from intermeddling with the Trans-Indian states.* The temper, indeed, of this great body is essentially pacific; all the instructions which emanate from them have a tendency towards the preservation of peace and the non-extension of empire; and when the merits and demerits of their government come to be weighed in the balance, it can never be imputed to them that they have been eager to draw the sword from the scabbard, or have willingly squandered the resources of India upon unjust and unprofitable wars.

* In a despatch from the Court of Directors to the Governor-General, dated September 20, 1837, there occurs this remarkable passage:—"With respect to the states west of the Indus, you have uniformly observed the proper course, which is to have no political connection with any state or party in those regions, to take no part in their quarrels, but to maintain so far as possible a friendly connection with all of them."

But it is stated in the manifesto itself that the war was undertaken "with the concurrence of the Supreme Council of India." It would be presumptuous to affirm the absolute untruth of a statement thus publicly made in the face of the world by a nobleman of Lord Auckland's unquestionable integrity; but so certain is it that the manifesto was not issued with the concurrence of the Supreme Council, that when the document was sent down to Calcutta to take its place among the records of the empire, there issued from the Council-Chamber a respectful remonstrance against the consummation of a measure of such grave importance, without an opportunity being afforded to the counsellors of recording their opinions upon it. The remonstrance went to England, and elicited an assurance to the effect that the Governor-General could have intended no personal slight to the members of the Supreme Council; but those members were far too high-minded to have thought for a moment about the personalities of the case; they thought only of the great national interests at stake, and regretted that they should ever be jeopardised by such disregard of the opinions of the Governor-General's legitimate advisers. Such a manifesto as this would never have been cradled in Calcutta.

It would not be just, however, to scrutinise the policy of Lord Auckland at this time by the light of our after experience. We know now, that before the Simlah manifesto was issued, the Persians had raised the siege of Herat,—that, for all purposes of defence against encroachments from the westward, the expedition to Kurrack, contemptible as it was in itself, had sufficed. We know that the handful of "rotten Hindoos," as Mahomed Shah subsequently designated them, magnified by report into an immense armament, had caused that monarch to strike his camp before Herat, and march back his baffled army to Teheran. But, on the 1st of October, 1838, Lord Auckland believed, and had good grounds for believing, that the fall of Herat was inevitable. At this time it may have been questioned whether the restoration of Shah Soojah to the sovereignty of the Douranee Empire were the best means of resisting Persian aggression and combating Russian intrigue, but few doubted the propriety of doing something to meet the dangers that threatened us from those sources. Had Herat fallen to the Persian arms, the Barukzye Sirdars, without some intervention on our part, would have prostrated themselves at the feet of the Persian monarch; and Russia would have established an influence in Afghanistan which we should have striven in vain to counteract. There was a real danger, therefore, to be feared. Though the means employed were of doubtful justice and expediency, the end to be accomplished was one of legitimate attainment.

But before the Simlah proclamation had obtained general currency throughout India, authentic intelligence of the retrograde movement of the Persian army had reached the camp of the Governor-General. The tidings which arrived, in the first instance, from various native sources, and had been conveyed to Lord Auckland by the political officers on the frontier, were now officially confirmed. The siege of Herat had been raised. Mahomed Shah had "mounted his horse, Ameerj," and turned his face towards his own capital. The legitimate object of the expedition across the Indus was gone. All that remained was usurpation and aggression. It was believed, therefore, that the army assembling on the north-western frontier would be broken up; and Shah Soojah and Runjeet Singh left to pursue their own policy, as might seem most expedient to them. The Simlah proclamation had placed the siege of Herat in the foreground as the main cause of the contemplated expedition; and now that the pretext for the invasion of Afghanistan was removed, political consistency seemed to require that the sword should be returned to the scabbard. With no common anxiety, therefore, was the result of this unexpected intelligence from Herat awaited by the regiments which had been warned for active service, and were now in all the excitement of preparation for a long and adventurous march. The disappointment anticipated by many descended only upon a few. On the 8th of November, all doubts were set at rest, and all anxieties removed by the publication of an order by the Governor-General, setting forth that, although the siege of Herat had been raised, the expedition across the Indus would not be abandoned:

ORDERS BY THE RIGHT HONOURABLE THE GOVERNOR-GENERAL OF INDIA. SECRET DEPARTMENT.

Camp de Buddee, 8*th November*.

The Right Honourable the Governor-General of India is pleased to publish, for general information, the subjoined extract of a letter from Lieutenant-Colonel Stoddart, dated Herat, the 10th September, 1838, and addressed to the Secretary to the Government of India.

"I have the honour, by direction of her Britannic Majesty's Envoy Extraordinary and Minister Plenipotentiary, and the Hon. East India Company's Envoy at the Court of Persia, to acquaint you, for the information of the Right Hon the Governor-General of India in Council, that his Majesty the Shah of Persia yesterday raised the siege of this city, and with the whole of the royal camp marched to Sangbust, about twelve miles, on his return to his own dominions. His Majesty proceeds without delay, by Torrbut Sheki Jaum and Meshid, to Teheran

"This is in fulfilment of his Majesty's compliance with the demands of the British Government, which I had the honour of delivering on the 12th inst., and of the whole of which his Majesty announced his acceptance on the 14th of August.

"His Majesty Shah Kamran and his Vuzeer, Yar Mahomed Khan, and the whole city, feel sensible of the sincerity of the friendship of the British Government, and Mr. Pottinger and myself fully participate in their gratitude to Providence for the happy event I have now the honour to report."

In giving publicity to this important intelligence, the Governor-General deems it proper at the same time to notify, that while he regards the relinquishment by the Shah of Persia of his hostile designs upon Herat as a just cause of congratulation to the Government of British India and its allies, he will continue to prosecute with vigour the measures which have been announced, with a view to the substitution of a friendly for a hostile power in the eastern provinces of Afghanistan, and to the establishment of a permanent barrier against schemes of aggression upon our north-west frontier.

The Right Hon. the Governor-General is pleased to appoint Lieutenant Eldred Pottinger, of the Bombay Artillery, to be Political Agent at Herat, subject to the orders of the Envoy and Minister at the Court of Shah Soojah-ool-Moolk. This appointment is to have effect from the 9th of September last, the date on which the siege of Herat was raised by the Shah of Persia.

In conferring the above appointment upon Lieutenant Pottinger, the Governor-General is glad of the opportunity afforded him of bestowing the high applause which is due to the signal merits of that officer, who was present in Herat during the whole period of its protracted siege, and who, under circumstances of peculiar danger and difficulty, has, by his fortitude, ability, and judgment, honourably sustained the reputation and interests of his country.

By order of the Right Hon. the Governor-General of India,

W. H. MACNAGHTEN,
Secretary to the Government of India, with the Governor-General.

When the Persian army was before Herat—when the Afghan garrison was on the eve of surrender—when the chiefs of Caubul and Candahar were prostrating themselves at the feet of Mahomed Shah, the expedition for the restoration of Shah Soojah was one of doubtful honesty and doubtful expediency. The retrogression of the Persian army removed it at once from the category of questionable acts. There was no longer any question about it. The failure of Mahomed Shah cut from under the feet of Lord Auckland all ground of justification, and rendered the expedition across the Indus at once a folly and a crime. The tripartite treaty did not pledge the British Government to send a single soldier beyond the frontier. The despatch of a British army into the heart of Afghanistan was no part of the covenant either with Runjeet Singh or Shah Soojah. It was wholly an after thought. When Macnaghten, after his conferences with the Maharajah of the Punjab and the ex-King of Caubul, returned to Simlah to lay the result of his mission before the Governor-General, the British Government had pledged itself only to furnish a handful of European officers to raise and discipline the Shah's regiments; and so little had any obligation been imposed upon us to surround the ex-King with our battalions, on his restoration to his old dominions, that he himself expressed an eager hope that he would be suffered to advance as an independent prince, and not as a mere puppet in our hands.*

To march a British army into Afghanistan was not, therefore, an obligation upon the Indian Government; it was their deliberate choice. The avowed object of the expedition, as set forth in the November declaration, was the establishment of a friendly power in Afghanistan But the subversion of an existing dynasty could only be justified on the ground that its hostility threatened to disturb the peace and tranquillity of our own dominions. Whatever the hostility of the Barukzye Sirdahs may have been when Mahomed Shah was before the gates of Herat, it had now ceased to be formidable. It was obvious that the chiefs of Caubul and Candahar were little likely to exaggerate the power of a Prince that had brought all his military resources to bear upon the

* A general assurance had been given to Runjeet Singh, in reply to a difficulty started by himself, that if the allies met with any reverses, the British Government would advance to their aid; but he had failed to elicit from Macnaghten any more specific promise of co-operation.

reduction of a place of no reputed strength, and, after an ineffectual struggle of nine months' duration, had retreated, either because he was unequal to the longer continuance of the contest, or because the British Government had landed 500 Sepoys on an island in the Persian Gulf. It was only in connection with the Russo-Persian movement that an alliance with the rulers of Afghanistan had become a matter of concernment to the British Government. It was only by a reference to the crisis which had thus arisen that the Indian Government could in any way justify their departure from the course of non-interference laid down by the Court of Directors, and recognised by Lord Auckland and his predecessors. But now that the danger, to the counteraction of which the expedition across the Indus was directed, had passed away, the expedition was still to be undertaken. A measure so hazardous, and so costly as the march of a British army to the foot of the Hindoo-Koosh, was only justifiable so long as it was absolutely indispensable to the defence of our Indian possessions; but if so extreme a measure had ever been, it was no longer necessary to the security of India, now that the army of Mahomed Shah, defeated and disgraced, was on its way back to the capital of Persia. The expedition now to be undertaken had no longer any other ostensible object than the substitution of a monarch, whom the people of Afghanistan had repeatedly, in emphatic, scriptural language, spued out, for those Barukzye chiefs who, whatever may have been the defects of their government, had contrived to maintain themselves in security, and their country in peace, with a vigour and a constancy unknown to the luckless Suddozye Princes. Had we started with the certainty of establishing a friendly power and a strong government in Afghanistan, the importance of the end would have borne no just relation to the magnitude of the means to be employed for its accomplishment. But at the best it was a mere experiment. There were more reasons why it should fail than why it should succeed.* It was commenced in defiance of every consideration of political and military expediency; and there were those who, arguing the matter on higher grounds than those of mere expediency, pronounced the certainty of its failure, because there was a canker of injustice at the core. It was, indeed, an experiment on the forbearance alike of God and of man; and therefore, though it might dawn in success and triumph, it was sure to set in failure and disgrace.

* Shah Soojah himself said that there would be little chance of his becoming popular in Afghanistan, if he returned to the country openly and avowedly supported, not by his own troops, but by those of the Feringhees. Even the less overt assistance of an infidel government was likely to cast discredit upon the undertaking in the eyes of "true believers." The Shah talked about the bigotry of the Mahomedans; but it was plain that he had his misgivings on the subject. "During a visit," says Captain Wade, "which I paid to the Shah, the day before yesterday, he informed me that some Mahomedans of Delhi had been writing to him, to inquire how he could reconcile it to his conscience, as a true believer in the Koran, to accept the assistance of a Christian people to recover his kingdom. The Shah said that he contemplated with pity the bigotry of these people, and began to quote a passage of the Koran to prove their ignorance of its doctrines with reference to the subject on which they had presumed to address him. Having a day or two previously received information that the Newab of Bhopal had made a particular request of his Lordship to be permitted to place a party of his kinsmen and retainers at the service of the British Government on the present occasion, from the desire which he had to testify his deep sense of gratitude to it for the manner in which it had watched and protected the interests of their family in every necessitude of their political existence, I mentioned the cirumstance to his Majesty, to show the different views that prevailed among the followers of the faith, both with regard to their duty to the state and to their religion."—[*Captain Wade to Mr. Macnaghten, October 5, 1838 : MS. Records.*]

BOOK III.

[1838—1839.]

CHAPTER I.

The Army of the Indus—Gathering at Ferozepore—Resignation of Sir Henry Fane—Route of the Army—Passage through Bahwulpore—The Ameers of Sindh—The Hyderabad Question—Passage of the Bolan Pass—Arrival at Candahar.

THE army destined for the occupation of Afghanistan assembled at Ferozepore, on the north-western frontier of the British dominions, in the latter part of the month of November. It had been agreed that the expedition across the Indus should be inaugurated by a grand ceremonial meeting between Lord Auckland and Runjeet Singh;[*] and that the troops of the two nations should be paraded before the illustrious personages then reciprocating hospitalities and interchanging marks of friendship and respect.

The Governor-General reached Ferozepore on the 27th

[*] The meeting was agreed upon before the British Government had determined to cross the Indus; and Runjeet complained of its tardy accomplishment, on the ground of the expense that he was obliged to incur in keeping his troops together.

of November. The Commander-in-Chief and the infantry of the Army of the Indus had arrived a day or two before, and on the following day the main body of the cavalry and artillery took up their ground on the plain.* On the 29th,† the first meeting between Lord Auckland and Runjeet Singh took place amidst a scene of indescribable uproar and confusion. The camp of the Governor-General was pitched at the distance of some four miles from the river Gharra. In the centre of a wide street of tents were those set apart for the purposes of the Durbar. A noble guard of honour lined the way, as amidst the roar of artillery and the clang of military music, Runjeet Singh, escorted by the English secretaries and some of the principal political and military officers in camp, rode up, in the centre of a line of elephants to the Durbar tent. The Governor-General and the Commander-in-Chief came forth to meet them. Then came the crush of the two lines of elephants, urged forward by the goads of their drivers, and meeting with a terrific shock—the clangour of a tumultuous crowd of Sikh horsemen and footmen—a rush of English officers eager to see the show; and presently, amidst such tumult and such noise as had seldom before been seen or heard, the elephants of the Governor-General and the Maharajah were brought side by side, and Lord Auckland, in his uniform of diplomatic blue, was seen to take a bundle of crimson cloth out of the Sikh howdah, and it was known that the lion of the Pun-

* It is generally acknowledged that nothing could have been more orderly or more creditable both to the regiments and their commanding officers, than the style in which all the components of the "Army of the Indus" made their way to Ferozepore. Captain Havelock, an excellent authority on such points, says. "A force has never been brought together in any country in a manner more creditable and soldier-like than was the Bengal portion of the Army of the Indus."

† Captain Havelock says the 28th—Colonel Fane, the 29th.

jab was then seated on the elephant of the English ruler. In a minute the little, tottering, one-eyed man, who had founded a vast empire on the banks of the fabulous rivers of the Macedonian conquests, was leaning over the side of the howdah, shaking hands with the principal officers of the British camp, as their elephants were wheeled up beside him. Then the huge phalanx of elephants was set in motion again. There was a rush towards the Durbar tent; the English and the Sikh *cortége* were mixed up together in one great mass of animal life. Such was the crush—such was the struggle—that many of the attendant Sikhs believed that there was a design to destroy their old decrepit chief, and " began to blow their matches and grasp their weapons with an air of mingled distrust and ferocity." * But in time a passage was made, and the imbecile little old man was to be seen tottering into the Durbar tent, supported on one side by the Governor-General, and on the other by Sir Henry Fane, whose fine manly proportions and length of limb, as he forced his way through the crowd, presented a strange contrast to the puny dimensions of the Sikh chieftain who leant upon his arm.

In the gorgeous tent of the Governor-General, the ladies of Lord Auckland's family, and of the principal military and political officers, were seated, ready to receive his Highness. The customary formalities were gone through, and civilities interchanged; and then the Maharajah was conducted into an inner chamber, where the presents intended for his reception were laid out in costly and curious array. Here, a picture of Queen Victoria, from the easel of Miss Eden, whose felicitous pencil has rendered the European eye familiar with the persons of many

---

* *Captain Havelock's Narrative*—from which this description has been mainly written. *Colonel Fane's Five Years in India*; and *Mr. Stocqueler's Memorials of Afghanistan* also contribute some details.

THE SIKH CAMP.   391

of the principal Sikh chieftains who graced the Ferozepore gathering, was presented to Runjeet Singh. Sir Willoughby Cotton bore it, with becoming reverence, into the tent, and as he presented it to the Maharajah, who bowed before it, the guns of the camel battery roared forth a royal salute. Then Runjeet was escorted to another tent, where specimens of British ordnance, caparisoned elephants, and horses of noble figure, stood ready for his Highness's acceptance. All these were inspected with due expressions of admiration and a becoming interchange of courtesies; and then, amidst an uproar of hurras, a crash of military music, and another scene of indescribable confusion, Runjeet Singh ascended his elephant and turned his back upon the British camp.*

On the following day, Lord Auckland returned the visit of Runjeet Singh. It was said by one present on this occasion, that the Sikhs "shone down the English."† The camp of the Maharajah was on the other side of the river; and there, amidst a scene of Oriental splendour, difficult to describe or imagine, the great Sikh chieftain received the representative of the British nation. The splendid costumes of the Sikh Sirdars—the gorgeous trappings of their horses—the glittering steel casques and corslets of chain armour—the scarlet and yellow dresses—the tents of crimson and gold—made up a show of Eastern magnificence equally grand and picturesque. As the Maharajah saluted the Governor-General, the familiar notes of

---

* "It is worthy of notice that a strange accident befel the old Maharajah in the tent containing the larger gifts of the British Government. He was not very firm on his legs at any time, but here he had the misfortune to stumble over a pile of shells, and fell prostrate before the British guns."—[*Havelock's Narrative.*] Remembering how the Sikh Empire fell before the British guns at Goojrat, we may at least observe that this was a curious type of the destiny then awaiting the great kingdom founded by Runjeet Singh.

† *Stocqueler's Memorials of Afghanistan.*

the national anthem arose from the instruments of a Sikh band, and the guns of the Khalsa poured forth their noisy welcome. In the splendid Durbar tent of the ruler of the Punjab, the British Statesman and British General, after the due formalities had been observed and some conversation had been carried on through the medium of interpreters, were regaled with an unseemly display of dancing girls, and the antics of some male buffoons. The evening entertainments were still less decorous. It was a melancholy thing to see the open exhibition, even on this great public occasion, of all those low vices which were destroying the life, and damning the reputation, of one in whom were some of the elements of heroism—who, indeed, but for these degrading sensualities, would have been really one of the greatest, as he was one of the most remarkable, men of modern times.

Then came a grand display of the military resources of the two nations. On one day the British force was manœuvred by Sir Henry Fane ; and on another the Sikh troops were exercised by the Sirdars. The consummate skill with which the British chief attacked an imaginary enemy was equalled by the gallantry with which he defeated it. He fought, indeed, a great battle on the plain, and only wanted another army in his front to render his victory a complete one. The Sikh Sirdars were contented with less elaborate movements ; but what their troops were ordered to do they did readily and well, and military critics in the British camp admitted that their allies made no contemptible show of the tactics which they had learnt from their French instructors.*

Runjeet Singh returned to Lahore, and the Governor-General followed him, on a complimentary visit, to the

* For an account of the manœuvres both of the British and Sikh divisions, see *Captain Havelock's Narrative.*

Sikh capital; whilst the British troops prepared to cross the frontier in furtherance of the objects mapped out in the great Simlah manifesto. But there was no longer a Persian army to be encountered at Herat—no longer a Russian force in the background. The expedition had lost half its popularity with the army, and the force that was to take the field had been shorn of a portion of its original dimensions. On the 27th of November it had been publicly announced by the Commander-in-Chief, "that circumstances in the countries west of the Indus had so greatly changed since the assembly of the army for service, that the Governor-General had deemed that it was not requisite to send forward the whole force; but that a part only would be equal to effecting the future objects in view." It had become the duty therefore of the Commander-in-Chief to determine what regiments should cross the Indus, and what should remain in Hindostan. Sir Henry Fane had selected for service the corps whose efficiency, on his recent tour of inspection, had been most clearly demonstrated; and now that it devolved upon him to dash the hopes of some of those regiments, unwilling to make an invidious choice, he had decided the difficult question by lot. Instead of two divisions, the Bengal army was now to consist of one, under the command of Sir Willoughby Cotton. The brigades of infantry commanded by Colonels Denniss and Paul were to be left behind;* the Irregular Cavalry, under that fine old veteran, Colonel Skinner, of the Local Horse, were to share

* These brigades consisted of the 3rd Buffs, the 2nd, 27th, 5th, 20th, and 53rd Regiments of Native Infantry. Captain Havelock and other military authorities have condemned this decision by lot. It is said that the principle of selection should have been adhered to on the reduction, as well as on the formation of the force. "Sir Henry Fane," says Captain Havelock, "need not thus have distrusted or paid so poor a compliment to his own sagacity and impartiality; the

the same fate; and the artillery force, greatly reduced in strength, now lost its Brigadier (Colonel Graham), and was ordered to go forward under Major Pew, who had organised the camel battery, and had joined the brigade in command of that experimental section of the ordnance corps. Nor were these the only changes which the intelligence of the defeat of Mahomed Shah had wrought upon the Bengal force. Sir Henry Fane, as Commander-in-Chief of the Indian army, had determined to take command in person of the forces assembled for the expedition across the frontier. The assemblage of regiments ordered upon this service was to be called "The Army of the Indus." Both the extent of the force, and the objects of the expedition, seemed to demand the supervision of the chief military authority in the country. But now that the force had been greatly reduced, and the objects of the campaign had dwindled down into a measure of interference with the internal government of an independent country, Sir Henry Fane had no ambition to command such a force, or to identify himself with such an expedition. There was no want of physical energy or mental vigour in the man, but his health was failing him at this time; and it was expedient that he should altogether escape from the fiery climate of the Eastern world. He determined, therefore,

one had seldom been at fault in India or in Europe, the other was above suspicion. Sortilege, after all, did little for the army in one instance; for it sent forward to the labours of the campaign, the 13th Light Infantry, then as ever zealous, indeed, and full of alacrity, but even at Ferozepore shattered by disease; the spirit of its soldiers willing, but unequal to the task; whilst it doomed to inactivity the Buffs, one of the most effective European corps in India." This is the impartial testimony of an officer of the 13th Light Infantry. It was written immediately after the first campaign of the Army of the Indus. No writer would now regret the chance which sent Sale and Dennie into Afghanistan, and associated the name of the 13th Light Infantry with some of the most illustrious incidents of the war.

to resign the command of the expedition into other hands, and to set his face towards his native land.

Sir John Keane, the Commander-in-Chief of the Bombay army, was coming round from the western presidency, in command of the Bombay division, which was to be conveyed by water from that port to Kurrachee. On the junction of the two divisions, the chief command would fall into his hands. In Sir Henry Fane the Bengal army had unbounded confidence. They knew him to be a strict, but a good officer. They may have thought that he made of too much account external forms and appearances, better suited to the mild, cloudy atmosphere of Great Britain, than to the fiery skies of Hindostan. But they admired the energy of his character; the decision of his judgment; the promptitude of all his actions. The initial measures which had been entrusted to him had been carried out with remarkable ability. There was a coolness in all that he did; a clearness in all that he said; which inspired with unlimited confidence the officers with whom he was associated. They knew that he had the welfare of the army at heart;—that their safety and honour could not be confided to one less likely to abuse the trust. It was with no common regret, therefore, that they saw him yield into other hands the command of the Army of the Indus. Of Sir John Keane they knew little, and what little they did know did not fill them with any very eager desire to place themselves under his command.

Such was the position of affairs at the commencement of December. The Bengal army, then encamped at Ferozepore, consisted of about 9500 men of all arms. The levy that had been raised for the immediate service of Shah Soojah was then passing through Ferozepore. It comprised two regiments of cavalry; four regiments of infantry; and a troop of horse artillery—in all about 6000 men. It had marched from Loodhianah on the

15th of November, under the command of Major-General Simpson; and was now about, on the 2nd of December, to commence its progress across the frontier. On the 10th of the same month the Bengal division was to break ground from Ferozepore.

The line of march to be followed by the invading army ran, in a south-westerly direction, through the territories of Bahwulpore, and thence crossed, near Subzulkote, the frontier of Sindh, striking down to the banks of the Indus, and crossing the river at Bukkur. It then took a north-westerly course, passing through Shikarpoor, Bhag, and Dadur to the mouth of the Bolan Pass; thence through the pass to Quettah, and from Quettah through the Kojuck, to Candahar. A glance at any map of the countries on the two sides of the Indus will satisfy the reader at once that this was a strangely devious route from Ferozepore to Candahar. The army was about to traverse two sides of a triangle, instead of shaping its course along the third.

But it was hardly a subject for after-consideration, when the tripartite treaty had been signed, what route should be taken by the army destined for the restoration of Shah Soojah to his old dominions. It had from the first been intended that the Shah should proceed through the Sindh country, whilst Runjeet's troops were advancing through the Khybur Pass. It was not, indeed, a geographical but a political question. It was necessary that the army should proceed through Sindh, for Runjeet Singh did not will that it should traverse the Punjab; and the Ameers were to be coerced.

It had been determined, in the first instance, that twenty lakhs of rupees should be paid by the Ameers of Sindh, as ransom-money, for Shikarpoor. Runjeet, as has been seen, asked for more than a moiety of the money, which it was proposed to divide equally between him and Shah Soojah; and, as it was not deemed expedient by the British Government to gratify Runjeet's cupidity at the expense of the King, it was determined that the amount demanded from the Ameers should be increased, and that Runjeet should receive fifteen instead of ten lakhs, without injury to the claims of his ally. But there seemed to be some doubt whether the Ameers would consent to pay the money thus appropriated to others' uses. The Shikarpoor question, indeed, required some definite settlement by Shah Soojah himself; and as Shah Soojah was to proceed through Sindh, for the purpose of bringing the Ameers to a proper understanding of their duties, it was necessary that the British army that escorted him should march by the same route.

That the Ameers should have demurred to the payment of the money claimed by an exile of thirty years' standing would, under any circumstances, have been a result of the demand, exciting no surprise in the mind of any reasonable being on one side of the Indus or on the other. But that, having already received a formal release from the Shah, they should have objected to the revival of an abandoned claim, is something so natural and so intelligible that it would have been a miracle if they had not resisted the demand. Colonel Pottinger saw this at once: he saw the injustice of the whole proceeding; and he wrote to the Supreme Government: "The question of a money-payment by the Ameers of Sindh to Shah Soojah-ool-Moolk is, in my humble opinion, rendered very puzzling by two releases written in Korans, and sealed and signed by his Majesty, which they have produced. Their argument now is, that they are sure the Governor-General does not intend to make them pay again for what they have already bought and obtained, in the most binding way, a receipt in full."*

* *Colonel H. Pottinger to Government. Published Papers relating to Sindh.*

Injustice ever begets injustice. It was determined by the Simlah Council that Shah Soojah and the Army of the Indus should be sent through the country of the Ameers. To accomplish this, it was necessary that, in the first instance, an existing treaty should be set aside. When the Ameers consented to open the navigation of the Indus, it was expressly stipulated that no military stores should be conveyed along the river. But as soon as ever Lord Auckland had resolved to erect a friendly power in Afghanistan, and to march a British army across the Indus, it became necessary to tear this prohibitory treaty to shreds, and to trample down the scruples of the Ameers. "Whilst the present exigency lasts," it was intimated to Colonel Pottinger, "you may apprise the Ameers that the article of the treaty with them, prohibiting the using of the Indus for the conveyance of military stores, must necessarily be suspended during the course of operations undertaken for the permanent establishment of security to all those who are a party to the treaty." And that there might be no miscomprehension of the general course of policy, which the Governor-General desired to pursue towards the Ameers, a letter was addressed to Colonel Pottinger, stating that "he (the Governor-General) deems it hardly necessary to remind you that in the important crisis at which we are arrived, we cannot permit our enemies to occupy the seat of power: the interests at stake are too great to admit of hesitation in our proceedings; and not only they who have shown a disposition to favour our adversaries, but they who display an unwillingness to aid us in the just and necessary* undertaking in which we are engaged,

---

* "Just and necessary!"
——— Earth is sick,
And Heaven is weary of the hollow words
Which States and Kingdoms utter when they talk
Of truth and justice.

must be displaced, and give way to others on whose friendship and co-operation we may be able implicitly to rely." This was the dragooning system now to be carried out in Sindh. Sensible of the injustice of such proceedings, and the discreditable breach of faith that they involved, Colonel Pottinger did his best to soften down these intimations; but still the naked fact remained, that if the Ameers of Sindh displayed any unwillingness to co-operate with the parties to a treaty under which they were to be fined a quarter of a million of money, they were at once to be dragooned into submission and deprived of their possessions, at the point of our bayonets and the muzzles of our guns.*

The system now to be adopted was one of universal intimidation and coercion. Along the whole line of country which the armies were to traverse, the will and pleasure of the British Government was to be the only principle of action recognisable in all our transactions with the weaker States, which were now to be dragooned into

* I do not intend to enter into the politics of Sindh more than is absolutely necessary to the elucidation of the history of the war in Afghanistan; but it ought to be mentioned here that the harsh and unjust treatment of the Ameers in 1838-39 has been defended or extenuated upon the grounds of an alleged traitorous correspondence with Mahomed Shah of Persia. A letter from one of the Ameers to the "King of Kings" was intercepted, but Colonel Pottinger declared that it was of no political importance, but simply an ebullition of Sheeahism, addressed to Mahomed Shah as Defender of the Faith.— [*Correspondence relating to Afghanistan.*] A letter, also said to have been written by the Persian King to two of the Ameers (Mahomed Khan and Nussur Khan), acknowledging the receipt of letters from them, and exhorting them to look to him for protection, was forwarded from Khelat to Runjeet Singh, who sent it in through Captain Wade to the Governor-General. But Major Todd, who by this time had joined Shah Soojah at Loodhianah, "did not hesitate to pronounce it, from its style and language, to be a palpable fabrication."—[*Captain Wade to Mr. Macnaghten, October* 24, 1838. *MS. Records.*]

prompt obedience. Their co-operation was not to be sought, but demanded. Anything short of hearty acquiescence was to be interpreted into a national offence. The Khan of Bahwulpore and the Ameers of Sindh were ordered not only to suffer the passage of our troops through their dominions but also to supply them on their way. The former had ever been regarded as one of the staunchest friends of the British Government; but when he was called upon to collect camels and to place supplies at the different stages for the use of the army, the work was carried on with obvious reluctance. It was found necessary to remind the Khan of his "obligations" and "responsibilities." His officers affected to believe that the British force would not march, and, whilst laying in supplies for the Shah's troops, hesitated to make an effort in behalf of our supporting columns. The "obstinacy and perversity"—the "duplicity and equivocation"—the "neglectful, if not reckless conduct of the Bahwulpore authorities," was severely commented upon by our political officers;* and it was apprehended that the march of the army would be delayed by the misguided conduct of our respectable ally.

The reluctance of the Bahwulpore authorities was soon overcome; but the demands made upon the forbearance of the Ameers of Sindh were of a more oppressive and irritating character. The Bahwul Khan has ever been held up to admiration as the most consistently friendly of all the allies of the British Government; but the expedition was distasteful to him and his people, and the real feeling broke out in the beginning, though, after a while, it was suppressed. It is not strange, therefore, that the Talpoor Ameers, of whom so much more was demanded, should have co-operated somewhat unwillingly in a measure

* *Captain Wade to Mr. Macnaghten, Nov.* 8 *and* 9, 1838. *MS. Records.*

which had openly exacted from them a large amount of treasure, and was not unlikely in the end to deprive them of all that they possessed. Interpreted into homely English, the language now to be addressed to these unhappy Princes was simply, "Your money or your life." Colonel Pottinger was the agent employed, in the first instance, to dictate terms to the Court of Hyderabad; but he was too clear-headed and too high-minded a man not to perceive the injustice of the course prescribed by his government, and to feel painfully unwilling to pursue it. The instructions he had received, divested of the specious outside dress of diplomatic phraseology, and rendered in plain English by Colonel Pottinger himself, were truly of a startling character. The British agent was directed to tell the Ameers that "the day they connected themselves with any other power than England would be the last of their independence, if not of their rule." "Neither," it was added, "the ready power to crush and annihilate them, nor the will to call it into action, were wanting, if it appeared requisite, however remotely, for the safety or integrity of the Anglo-Indian Empire or frontier." The Ameers were known to be weak, and they were believed to be wealthy. Their money was to be taken; their country to be occupied; their treaties to be set aside at the point of the bayonet—but amidst a shower of hypocritical expressions of friendship and goodwill.

Whilst Colonel Pottinger, not without some scruples, was enclosing the Ameers of Lower Sindh in the toils of his diplomacy, Captain Burnes, who by this time had reaped the reward of his services in knighthood and a lieutenant-colonelcy, was proceeding to operate upon the Princes of Beloochistan. Originally sent upon a mission to Mehrab Khan of Khelat, he had turned aside, however, to negotiate with the Ameers of Khyrpore, in Upper

Sindh, and had found them more tractable than the Hyderabad Princes in Colonel Pottinger's hands. It was deemed expedient that the British troops should cross the Indus at Bukkur, and Burnes was instructed to obtain the temporary cession of the island. The fortress stands on a rock, dividing the river into two channels. Apprehending that the incursion of British troops into their country would be followed by acts of territorial spoliation, the Ameers of Khyrpore, whilst expressing in general terms their willingness to co-operate with our government, expressly stipulated that the forts on either bank of the river were to be untouched. But as Bukkur stood on neither bank, but on an island, it appeared to the British diplomatist that the wording of the memorandum actually placed the fortress in his hands. Ashamed, however, of such an exhibition of legal acuteness, he declared that he had no intention to take advantage of such a reading of the document; he cited it merely as an instance of the manner in which very cunning people sometimes overreach themselves. There was no need, indeed, to look for flaws in a state paper, when the Army of the Indus was assembling to help itself to what it liked. The Ameers were told that, whatever might be their dislike to the march of our troops through Sindh, "the Sindhian who hoped to stop the approach of the British army might as well seek to dam up the Indus at Bukkur." The fiat had gone forth, an army was to march, and it was now on the road.

There was every reason why the restoration of Shah Soojah, who was famous for the extravagance of his pretensions in the direction of Sindh, should have been viewed with apprehension and alarm by the Talpoor Ameers. But the matter now began to wear a much more formidable aspect. The British Government had not only announced its intention to assist the long-exiled monarch in his attempt to regain his crown, but had encouraged him to assert long dormant claims, and had announced its intention to march an army into the country of the Ameers, to plant a subsidiary force there, to compel the Princes of Sindh to pay for it, to knock down and set up the Princes themselves at discretion, to take possession of any part of the country that might be wanted for our own purposes—in fact, to treat Sindh and Beloochistan in all respects as though they were petty principalities of our own. That the Ameers thus struggling in our grasp, conscious of their inability openly to resist oppression, should have writhed and twisted, and endeavoured to extricate themselves by the guile which might succeed, rather than by the strength which could not, was only to follow the universal law of nature in all such contests between the weak and the strong. Macnaghten complained, some time afterwards, that no civilised beings had ever been treated so badly as were the British by the Princes of Sindh. If it were so, it was only because no civilised beings had ever before committed themselves to acts of such gross provocation. Throughout the entire period of British connection with Afghanistan, a strange moral blindness clouded the visions of our statesmen: they saw only the natural, the inevitable results of their own measures, and forgot that those measures were the dragon's teeth from which sprung up the armed men. The Ameers of Sindh viewed all our proceedings at this time with mingled terror and indignation. Our conduct was calculated to alarm and incense them to the extremest point of fear and irritation; and yet we talked of their childish distrust and their unprovoked hostility.

The Ameers of Sindh were told that, whether they were friendly or unfriendly to the movement, the British army would cross the Indus when and where our government

directed, and do whatsoever our government pleased—
that resistance on their part would be not only useless,
but insane, as it would bring down inevitable destruction
on the head of all who stood up to oppose us. From that
time these unhappy Princes felt that they ruled only by
sufferance of the British. They knew their helplessness,
and if at any time they thought of open resistance, the
idea was speedily abandoned. Two British armies were
bearing down upon their dominions—the one from Upper
India; the other from the Sea. Burnes and the Commissariat officers were in advance, laying in supplies
for the consumption of the invading force, and threatening with heavy penalties all who refused to co-operate
with them. It would be difficult to conceive anything
more distressing and more irritating; and yet we expected
the Ameers to open their arms and to lay down their treasures at our feet.

The Bengal army moved from Ferozepore on the 10th
of December.* Availing themselves of the water-carriage,
they moved down parallel to the river. The sick, the
hospital stores, and a portion of our Commissariat supplies
were forwarded on boats, which were subsequently to be
used for the bridging of the Indus. The force consisted
of about 9500 men and 38,000 camp-followers. Some
30,000 camels accompanied the army.† There was an
immense assemblage of baggage. Sir Henry Fane had
exhorted the officers of the Army of the Indus not to

* Shah Soojah's force passed through Ferozepore on the 2nd.
Major Todd accompanied the Shah. Macnaghten joined the royal
camp at Shikarpoor.

† It had been no easy matter to provide carriage-cattle for that
immense assemblage. The camels, which constituted the bulk of the
beasts of burden, had been mostly drawn on hire from Bekaneer,
Jaysulmer, and the northern and north-western provinces of India;
but the country had been so drained, that at last it became necessary
to indent upon the brood-camels of the government stud at Hissar.

encumber themselves with large establishments and unnecessary equipages; but there is a natural disposition on the part of Englishmen, in all quarters of the globe, to carry their comforts with them. It requires a vast deal of exhortation to induce officers to move lightly equipped. The more difficult the country into which they are sent —the more barbarous the inhabitants—the more trying the climate—the greater is their anxiety to surround themselves with the comforts which remote countries and uncivilised people cannot supply, and which ungenial climates render more indispensable. In the turmoil of actual war, all these light matters may be forgotten; but a long, a wearisome, and unexciting march through a difficult but uninteresting country, tries the patience even of the best of soldiers, and fills him with unappeasable yearnings after the comforts which make endurable the tedium of barrack or cantonment life. It is natural that with the prospect of such a march before him, he should not be entirely forgetful of the pleasures of the mess-table, or regardless of the less social delights of the pleasant volume and the solacing pipe. Clean linen, too, is a luxury which a civilised man, without any imputation upon his soldierly qualities, may, in moderation, desire to enjoy. The rudeness and barrenness of the country compel him to supply himself at the commencement of his journey with everything that he will require in the course of it; and the exigencies of the climate necessarily increase the extent of these requirements The expedition across the Indus had been prospectively described as a "grand military promenade;" and if such were the opinion of some of the highest authorities, it is not strange that officers of inferior rank should have endorsed it, and hastened to act upon the suggestion it conveyed. And so marched the Army of the Indus, accompanied by thousands upon thousands of baggage-laden camels and other beasts of burden, spreading themselves for miles and miles over the country, and making up with the multitudinous followers of the camp one of those immense moving cities, which are only to be seen when an Indian army takes the field, and streams into an enemy's country.

It was clear, bright, invigorating weather—the glorious cold season of Northern India—when the army of the Indus entered the territories of Bahwul Khan. Nature seemed to smile on the expedition, and circumstance to favour its progress. There was a fine open country before them; they moved along a good road;* supplies were abundant everywhere. The coyness of the Bahwulpore authorities, which had threatened to delay the initial march of the army, had yielded in good time, and at every stage Mackeson and Gordon had laid up in depôt stores of grain, and fodder, and firewood, for the consumption of man and beast.† Officers and soldiers were in the highest spirits. "These," it was said by one who accompanied the army on the staff of its commander, and has chronicled all its operations,‡ "were the halcyon days of the movements of this force." To the greater number who now crossed the frontier this was

* This road, some 280 miles in length, had been prepared, under Mackeson's directions, to facilitate the march of our troops.

† As the army advanced, the Khan, to whose court Mackeson had been despatched to conclude a treaty of protective alliance, exerted himself to assist the enterprise, and exhibited the most friendly feeling towards Shah Soojah. He gave the Shah two guns—made him a present of money—sent a party of irregular horse, under one of his chief officers, to escort him through the Bahwulpore dominions; and allowed the officers of the Shah's contingent to recruit their regiment from the ranks of his own regular infantry. The Shah's regiments were in this way raised to their full strength, six hundred men having been drawn from the Bahwulpore army.—[*MS. Notes.*]

‡ Captain Havelock.

their virgin campaign. The excitement was as novel as it was inspiriting. They might be about to meet mighty armies and to subdue great principalities; or they might only be entering upon a " grand military promenade." Still in that bright December weather the very march through a strange country, with all that great and motley assemblage, was something joyous and animating. The army was in fine health, full of heart, and overflowing with spirits. It seemed as if an expedition so auspiciously commenced must be one great triumph to the end.

There was but one thing to detract from the general prosperity of the opening campaign. Desertion was going on apace—not from the ranks of the fighting men, but from the mass of officers' servants, camel drivers, and camp-followers which streamed out from the rear of the army. The cattle, too, were falling sick and dying by the way-side. The provisions with which they were supplied were not good, and dysentery broke out among them. Many were carried off by their owners, who shrunk from the long and trying journey before them; and it soon became manifest that the most formidable enemy with which the advancing army would have to contend, would be a scarcity of carriage and supplies.

Even in those early days the voice of complaint was not wholly silent;* but when the army began to make its toilsome way through Sindh and Beloochistan, there were few in its ranks who did not look back with regret to the march through Bahwulpore, when all their wants had been supplied in a manner which they were little likely to see again. It was on the 29th of December

* Some of the Shah's troops were very unreasonable in their expectations and their complaints. The raw levies of horse, just recruited from the grain districts of Upper India, made violent complaints because they found that to the westward barley was the food of horses.

that the head-quarters of the army reached the capital of Bahwul Khan's country. Sir Henry Fane, who had been proceeding down the river by water, landed from his boats, and held a Durbar on the following day; and on the 31st returned the visit of state which the Khan had paid him.* On the first day of the new year the army broke ground again, and set out for the frontier of Sindh.

On the 14th of January, the head-quarters of the Army of the Indus entered the Sindh territory near Subzulkote. On the preceding day, Sir Alexander Burnes had joined the British camp; and though he had obtained by his negotiations the cession of Bukkur to the British Government,† for such time as it might seem

* Sir Henry Fane was much pleased with the economy of Bahwul Khan's Court. Though not on an extensive scale, it was perhaps, better ordered, on the whole, than that of any native potentate at the time.

† The cession of Bukkur was extremely distasteful to Meer Roostum. It was calculated to lower him in the eyes both of the other Ameers and of his own subjects; and Burnes, fearing that he would be dissuaded by his relatives, made the stipulation for the surrender of the place a separate article of the treaty, in order that the Ameer might conceal it from them if he feared that they would remonstrate against it. When Burnes despached Mohun Lal to Khyrpore, to deliver the treaty and the separate article, "face to face," to the Ameer, and to demand his acceptance of its terms, "the consternation," says Burnes, "caused by this public declaration, was very great. The Ameer first offered another fort in its stead; next, to find security that our treasure and munitions were protected; but the Moonshee, as instructed, replied to all that nothing but the unqualified cession of the fortress of Bukkur, during the war, would satisfy me. He said it was the heart of his country, his honour was centred in keeping it, his family and children would have no confidence if it were given up, and that if I came to Khyrpore the Ameer could speak in person to me many things. To this I had instructed the Moonshee to say, that it was impossible till he signed the treaty, as I asked a plain question and wanted a plain answer."—[*Published Papers.*] Earnestly was Meer Roostum

expedient to us to retain it, and had thus secured the peaceful passage of the Indus, the report which he made of the general feeling of the Sindhians was not very encouraging. It was plain that our armed passage through the country of the Ameers was extremely distasteful to them ; and that if they did not break out into acts of open hostility, their conduct towards us was likely to be marked by subterfuges, evasions, and deceit of every possible kind.

And presently it began to be suspected that the temper of at least some of the Talpoor Princes was such, that a hostile demonstration against them was little likely to be avoided. The Hyderabad Ameers had assumed an attitude of defiance. They had insulted and outraged Colonel Pottinger, and were now collecting troops for the defence

entreated by his family not to sign the treaty, but to resist the unjust demand. Greatly perplexed and alarmed, he wrote a touching letter of entreaty to Burnes, but by this time his doom was sealed. It was useless for him any longer to struggle against his fate ; so on the morning of the 24th of December he sent for Mohun Lal, told him that Burnes had been the first and best friend of the Khyrpore state, but that he had made an unexpected demand upon him, and that his good name would be irrecoverably lost if Lord Auckland did not seize upon Kurachee, or some other place from the Hyderabad family ; who were our enemies, and now triumphing, whilst he, our dearest friend, was thus depressed If they were suffered to escape, he said, that his only course would be to commit suicide. "With this," wrote Burnes to Government, "and saying *Bismillah!* (in the name of God) he sealed the treaty and the separate article in the presence of Ali Morad Khan, Meer Zungee, Soolaman Abdur, and about twenty other people." A day or two afterwards, Burnes himself called on Meer Roostum and received his submission in person. The poor old man, declaring that he was irretrievably disgraced, asked what he could now do to prove the sincerity of his friendship for the British Government "The answer to this declaration," wrote Burnes, "was plain—to give us orders for supplies, and to *place all the country as far as he could at our command—and he has done so as far as he can.*"—[*Burnes to Government. Khyrpore, Dec.* 28, 1838. *Published Papers*.]

of their capital. Sir John Keane, with the Bombay army, had landed at Vikkur at the end of November, and, after a long and mortifying delay, had made his way on to Tattah. Having come by sea, he was necessarily without carriage. He had relied upon the friendly feelings of the Sindh rulers; but the Sindh rulers were not disposed to do anything for him, but everything against him. They regarded the British General as an enemy, and threw every obstacle in his way. Sir John Keane was compelled, therefore, to remain in inactivity on the banks of the river until the 24th of December. A supply of carriage from Cutch, by no means adequate to the wants of the force, but most welcome at such a time, came opportunely to release Sir John Keane from this local bondage, and the Bombay column then commenced its march into Sindh. Proceeding up the right bank of the Indus to Tattah, and thence to Jerruk, he awaited at the latter place the result of the negotiations which were going on at Hyderabad. Captain Outram and Lieutenant Eastwick had been despatched to the Court of the Ameers with Lord Auckland's ultimatum; and Keane with the Bombay column, was now, at the end of January, awaiting the result.

Surrounded by his own contingent, Shah Soojah had proceeded in advance of the Bengal column; and his force had crossed the Indus, in very creditable order, before the end of the third week of January. Shikarpoor had been fixed upon as the place of rendezvous. There the force was now encamped, and there the Envoy and Minister joined the suite of the Douranee monarch.

Cotton was to have crossed the Indus at Rohree, which lies opposite to the fort of Bukkur. Some delay had taken place in the cession of the fortress; for the Bengal column had arrived on the banks of the river before the treaty with the Ameer of Khyrpore, by which it was to be ceded, had arrived with the ratification of the Governor-General; and after its arrival, some further delay was occasioned, either by the mistrust or by the guile of the Sindh ruler. He was not ignorant of the state of affairs at Hyderabad. He knew, or suspected, that there was a likelihood of a large portion of the Bengal column being detached, and he was eager to temporise. Something might be written down in the chapter of accidents, that might enable him to retain possession of Bukkur; or something might be gained by the detention of Cotton's troops. It was not, therefore, till the 29th of January that the British flag waved from the fort of Bukkur—and even when the detachment of troops, which was to receive possession, crossed the river, opposition seemed so probable, that some powder-bags, wherewith to blow in the gates of the fort, were stowed away in one of the boats.

The military authorities now determined to despatch the greater part of the Bengal column down the left bank of the Indus to co-operate with Sir John Keane against Hyderabad. Burnes entirely approved of the movement.* It does not appear that Keane had then made any requisition for more troops.† The two columns,

* "The aspect of affairs to the south being anything but satisfactory, the Commander-in-Chief intimated to me, in the presence of General Cotton, that the passage of the army across the Indus, even had the bridge been ready, which it will not be for ten days, was inexpedient, whilst matters were unadjusted at Hyderabad—that it was further his decided opinion that a portion of the army should at once march down towards Hyderabad. Participating entirely in these sentiments, as far as political matters were concerned, I felt myself bound to give the fullest effect to the views of his Excellency, and notify the intended movement of the troops to the south to Meer Roostum Khan."—[*Sir A. Burnes to Government: Rohree, January* 28, 1839. *MS. Records.*]

† Some days after Cotton's force had moved down the river, a

indeed, were entirely ignorant of each other's operations. Thus early the want of an intelligence-department was painfully apparent; but up to the last day of our connection with Afghanistan nothing was done, nor has anything been done in more recent wars, to remedy the admitted evil. Down the left bank of the Indus went Cotton with his troops, glorying in the prospect before them. The treasures of Hyderabad seemed to lie at their feet. Never was there a more popular movement. The troops pushed on in the highest spirits, eager for the affray—confident of success. An unanticipated harvest of honour—an unexpected promise of abundant prize-money was within their reach. A march of a few days would bring them under the walls of Hyderabad, to humble the pride of the Ameers, and to gather up their accumulated wealth.

But there was one man then on the borders of the Indus to whom this movement down the left bank of the river was a source of unmixed dissatisfaction. Mr. Macnaghten, who, under the title of Envoy-and-Minister at the Court of Shah Soojah, had been appointed political director of the campaign, viewed with alarm the departure of Sir Willoughby Cotton from Rohree, just as it was hoped that the Bengal column was about to cross to the right bank of the river. The Shah, with his contingent, was at Shikarpoor. Macnaghten had joined the royal camp. The King and the Envoy were alike eager to push on to Candahar; but, deserted by the Bengal troops, they were compelled to remain in a state of absolute paralysis. Seldom has any public functionary been surrounded by more embarrassing circumstances than those which, at this time, beset Macnaghten. At the very

requisition came for a troop of horse artillery, a detachment of cavalry, and a brigade of infantry.—[*Havelock's Narrative.*]

outset of the campaign there was a probability of the civil and military authorities being brought into perilous collision. The Envoy looked aghast at the movement upon Hyderabad, for he believed it involved an entire sacrifice of the legitimate objects of the campaign. It appeared to him, in this conjuncture, to be plainly his duty, as the representative of the British-Indian Government, to take upon himself the responsibility of preventing the march for the restoration of Shah Soojah from being converted into a campaign in Sindh Yet to no man could the assertion of such authority be more painful than to one of Macnaghten's temper and habits. It was certain that the military chiefs would resent his interference, and that the whole army would be against him. But he turned his face steadfastly towards Candahar; and determined to arrest the progress of the Bengal column on its march to the Sindh capital.

In what light this diversion was viewed by him, and for what reasons he deprecated it, Macnaghten's letters, written at this time, indicate with sufficient distinctness; and it is just, therefore, that in a matter which has entailed some odium upon him, he should be suffered to speak for himself:

"The Governor-General," he wrote to Burnes, "never seems to have contemplated the diversion of the army of the Indus from its original purpose, except on emergency. No such emergency appears to have arisen. We are utterly ignorant of the state of affairs below It is hardly possible to conceive that matters should not have been settled, unless under the very improbable supposition that Sir J. Keane should be waiting for reinforcements, or that a suspension of hostilities may have been agreed upon, pending the receipt of further instructions from the Governor-General. In the first place it may be presumed that the Bombay reserve will reach Sir John Keane long ere Sir Willoughby Cotton can do so. In the latter case, it is probable that the suggestions with which I have this day furnished Colonel Pottinger, will bring matters to an amicable conclusion. As far as I have learnt the motives of Sir W. C.'s movement down the left bank of the Indus, it was with a view of creating a diversion, and never with any intention of actually proceeding all the way to Hyderabad. The effect of the movement whatever it may have been, must have been already produced. At all events, by crossing to this side of the river, the effect will rather be heightened than lessened; while, if the force should not be required further, it might be all ready to proceed at the proper season to its original destination in Afghanistan. I should hope in less than ten days from this date to receive a reply from Colonel Pottinger; and, in the mean time, the boats might be got ready to proceed with the troops downwards, should their services be required. Thus no time would be lost. But, as in that case there could be little hope of the return of the troops to proceed this season into Afghanistan, I would strongly urge that a force, to the extent specified in the second paragraph of this letter (one European regiment, one Native cavalry, a troop of horse artillery, with a suitable battering train), with a sufficiency of carriage-cattle for itself and Shah Soojah's army, should be directed to proceed to Shikarpoor. With such a force I am clearly of opinion that the views of the Governor-General, in regard to Afghanistan, could be carried into effect during the present season. The consequences of losing a whole season are not to be foreseen." *

In another letter he wrote to the Governor-General—and the passage has an additional interest, as affording, for the first time, a glimpse of the unreasonable character of Shah Soojah, and the extent to which his Majesty's peculiarities heightened the difficulties of Macnaghten's position:

We should not, I think, on any account, lose the season for advancing upon Candahar. With our European regiment, some more artillery, a couple of Native regiments, and a small battering train, we might not only occupy Candahar, but relieve Herat; and by money, if we have no disposable troops, make Caubul too hot for Dost Mahomed.

The Shah is very solicitous about future operations, and, I am sorry to say, talks foolishly every time I see him on the subject of

* *Unpublished Correspondence of Sir W. H. Macnaghten.*

his confined territories that are to be—and frequently says it would be much better for him to have remained at Loodhianah. The next time he touches on the subject, I intend to remind him of the verse of Sadi, "If a king conquers seven regions he would still be hankering after another territory." I have little doubt of being able to bring him into a more reasonable temper of mind. He is much delighted with the four six-pounders presented to him by your Lordship. . . . . . . I hardly think it probable that 50,000 rupees per mensem will suffice for the Shah's expenses, but on this point I will write to your Lordship more fully on another occasion.*

And again he wrote, soon afterwards, to Mr Colvin

I grieve to say that I have no consolation to afford you Our accounts from every quarter as to what is really passing are most unsatisfactory, and Sir Willoughby Cotton is clearly going on a wild-goose chase. He cannot possibly, I think, be at Hyderabad under twenty-five days from this date, and he seems to be travelling by a route which has no road He will soon, I fear, find himself in the jungle. If this goes on as it is now doing, what is to become of our Afghan expedition Burnes's letters are most unsatisfactory.†

He had hardly despatched the letter from which this last passage is taken, when a communication from the Governor-General was put into his hands, and it became more than ever obvious from its contents, that Lord Auckland's first wish was, that the Bengal column should accompany Shah Soojah and his contingent as expeditiously as possible to Candahar. Fortified by these advices, Macnaghten, on the following day, wrote, in emphatic language to Sir Willoughby Cotton, in virtue of the power vested in him by the Governor-General, requiring that military chief to furnish him with a force sufficient to enable him to give effect to his Lordship's plans in Afghanistan :

* *Unpublished Correspondence of Sir W. H. Macnaghten.*
† *Ibid.*, *Feb.* 5, 1839.

"I have already urged," he added, "in the strongest terms, your crossing over to this side of the river with your whole force. Of Sir John Keane's army there can be no apprehension. His Excellency will always be able to keep up his communication with the sea, whilst your presence on this side would enable us to establish a strong post at the extremity of the Sindh territories, and ensure the safety of the supplies for the Army of the Indus in its advance into Afghanistan. The Ameers cannot for any length of time keep up an army—they must be reduced to act on the defensive, and then the result could hardly be doubtful. Dangerous as the experiment might be, it would, in my opinion, be infinitely better that we should let loose fifteen or twenty thousand of Runjeet Singh's troops (who would march down upon Hyderabad in a very short space of time), than that the grand enterprise of restoring Shah Soojah to the throne of Caubul and Candahar should be postponed for an entire season. By such a postponement it might be frustrated altogether."

Thus were the military and political authorities brought into a state of undisguised antagonism. Circumstances, however, had already occurred to unravel the web of difficulty that had been cast around them. The progress of the Bengal column towards Hyderabad was arrested by the receipt of intelligence to the effect that the Ameers, awed by impending danger, had submitted to the demands of the British Government. Outram and Eastwick had been from the 20th of January to the 4th of February at Hyderabad negotiating with them, and after much reasonable doubt of the issue had received their submission.* They had consented to pay the money which had been required from them, and it was believed that it would soon be paid.† They had consented to the terms of a stringent treaty, which had been fastened upon them by the British authorities, and agreed to pay annually

---

* See *Outram's Rough Notes*.

† Their share was twenty lakhs of rupees, a moiety of which was paid down. Seven more lakhs, making up the gross amount to be paid by the Talpoor Princes, were paid by the Ameer of Khyrpore.

three lakhs of rupees for the support of a British subsidiary force in their dominions. Cotton was, therefore, instructed to halt his division; and on the very 7th of February on which Macnaghten had written and despatched the letter which I have above quoted, the hopes of the Bengal column were dashed by the announcement that Hyderabad and its treasures were no longer lying at their feet. The Ameers paid an instalment of the tribute-money, and Cotton, to the great joy of the Envoy, but to the extreme disappointment of his troops, retraced his steps to Rohree, and prepared to effect the passage of the river, whilst Keane, with the Bombay column, moved up along the right bank of the Indus, and saw, through the dusty atmosphere of Lower Sindh, the palace and the city where was stored the gathered wealth which was to have enriched his army.

Halting for some days opposite Hyderabad,[*] the Bombay troops received intelligence to the effect that the Reserve which had been sent to their assistance from the Presidency had arrived at Kurachee, under Brigadier Valiant. The 40th Queen's Regiment formed a portion of this brigade. It had been brought from Bombay in a seventy-four gun-ship—the *Wellesley*—and Admiral Sir Frederick Maitland was on board. In the position which affairs had assumed in Lower Sindh, it seemed desirable that the English should possess themselves of the fort of Kurachee; so the Admiral summoned it to sur-

---

[*] "The city of Hyderabad," says Dr. James Burnes, in his *Visit to the Court of Sindh*, an interesting and valuable work, "is a collection of wretched low mud hovels, as destitute of the means of defence as they are of external elegance or internal comfort; and even the boasted stronghold of the Ameer, which surmounts their capital, is but a paltry erection of ill-burnt bricks, crumbling gradually to decay, and perfectly incapable of withstanding for an hour the attack of regular troops."

render. The answer of the Commandant was a gallant one. "I am a Beloochee," he said, "and I will die first." With characteristic mendacity the Sindhian boatmen in the harbour declared that the place was prepared to withstand a siege, and that one of the Ameers had come down with an army of 3000 men. The English sailor had now an answer to give as gallant as that of the Beloochee chief. "The more the better," he said; "we shall have the first trial of them." Everything was soon ready for the attack. But British humanity again interposed, and Maitland a second time summoned the garrison to surrender. The reply was a word of defiance, and a shot from the fort. Then was heard by the garrison that which had never been heard there before, and of which they had no conception—a broadside from an English man-of-war. The *Wellesley's* guns did their work in less than an hour, and the British colours soon floated over the place. The garrison had consisted of only some twenty men. *

On the 20th of February, Sir Willoughby Cotton, with the head-quarters of his force, arrived at Shikarpoor. On the morning of that day the General and the Envoy were for some time in conference with each other. The discussion was a long and a stormy one. The General seems to have anticipated the interference of Macnaghten, and to have resented it before it took any really offensive shape. The two officers looked on each other with suspicion. The General leapt hastily to the conclusion that the civilian was determined to overrule his military authority; and the Envoy, on the other side, thought that the soldier regarded him, the King and the King's army, with something very like contempt. Macnaghten wanted carriage for the Shah's

* Kennedy.

force, and asked for 1000 camels. Sir Willoughby resented this as an act of interference; accused the Envoy of wishing to assume the command of the army, and declared that he knew no superior authority but that of Sir John Keane. At this, and at subsequent meetings, the Envoy urged that he had no intention of interfering with the military movements of the General, but that if he thought it for the good of the service that Shah Soojah should be left behind, the matter must be referred for the decision of the Governor-General. In the evening they met at dinner in the Envoy's tent. The meal was not over when important despatches from the Governor-General were placed in Macnaghten's hands. In the Envoy's private tent they were read and discussed. Burnes and Todd were present at the conference. Late at night the General and the Envoy parted "very good friends," *

* "Sir Willoughby," wrote the Envoy to Mr. Colvin, on the 24th of February, "made his appearance in camp yesterday morning. He is evidently disposed to look upon his Majesty and his disciplined troops and myself as mere cyphers. Any hint from me, however quietly and modestly given, was received with hauteur; and I was distinctly told that I wanted to assume the command of the army; that he, Sir Willoughby, knew no superior but Sir John Keane, and that he would not be interfered with, &c., &c. All this arose out of my requesting 1000 camels for the use of the Shah and his force. Sir Willoughby was ably backed by the Commissariat officers. My arguments were urged throughout in the most mild and conciliatory tone. I was determined on no account to lose my temper; and we parted at a late hour last night very good friends. I told him I was the last man in the world who would presume to interfere with his military arrangements; but I found it requisite to tell him, during one of our conversations, that if he thought it for the good of the service to leave Shah Soojah in the lurch, without the means of moving, I should esteem it my duty, as a political officer, to protest most strongly against the arrangement, and that the Governor-General would determine which of us was right. Sir Willoughby dined with me, and at dinner the important despatches from the Governor-General and yourself, dated the 5th instant, were

It was decreed that the Bengal column should at once move in advance. On the following day it was manœuvred in presence of the King. The parching heats of Sindh, and the evil effects of a failing Commissariat, had not then begun to impair our army; and, in full health and fine condition, the troops moved before the well-pleased Shah. On the 23rd, Sir Willoughby Cotton began to put his force again in motion. But the Shah's contingent remained halted at Shikarpoor. There was not carriage sufficient for its advance.

The difficulties of the march now began to obtrude themselves. Between Sukkur and Shikarpoor the camels had dropped down dead by scores. But there was a worse tract of country in advance. The officers looked at their maps, and traced with dismay the vast expanse of sandy desert, where no green pasture met the eye, and no sound of water spoke to the ear. But the season was favorable. Escaping the arid and pestilential blasts of April and May, and the noxious exhalations of the four succeeding months, the column advanced into Cutch-Gundawa. The hard, salt-mixed sand, crackled under their horses' feet as the General and his staff crossed the desert, on a fine bright night of early March —so cool that only, when in a full gallop, the riders ceased to long for the warmth of their cloaks.* The distance from Shikarpoor to Dadur is 146 miles. It was accomplished by the Bengal column in sixteen painful marches. Water and forage were so scarce that the cattle suffered terribly on the way. The camels fell dead by scores on the desert; and further on the Beloochee robbers carried them off with appalling dexterity.

put into my hands. We discussed their contents in my private tent afterwards—present Sir W. C. Todd, and Burnes."—[*Unpublished Correspondence of Sir W. H. Macnaghten.*]

* Havelock.

SCARCITY OF PROVISIONS. 421

When the column reached a cultivated tract of country, the green crops were used as forage for the horses. The *ryots* were liberally paid on the spot; but the agents of the Beloochee chiefs often plundered the unhappy cultivators of the money that had been paid to them, even in front of the British camp.

It was on the 10th of March that the Bengal column reached Dadur, which lies at the mouth of the Bolan Pass. Whatever doubts may before have been entertained regarding the provisionary prospects of the Army of the Indus, they were now painfully set at rest. Major Leech had been long endeavouring to collect supplies for the army at this place, but, in spite of all his zeal and all his ability, he had signally failed. Mehrab Khan of Khelat, under whose dominion lay the provinces through which the army was now passing, had thrown every impediment in the way of the collection of grain for our advancing troops. The prospect, therefore, before them was anything but an encouraging one. At Dadur they found themselves, on the 10th of March, with a month's supplies on their beasts of burden. Cotton saw that there was little chance of collecting more; so he determined to push on with all possible despatch.

On the 16th he resumed his march; and entered the Bolan Pass. Burnes had gone on in advance with a party under Major Cureton, to secure a safe passage for the column, and had been completely successful. The Beloochee authorities rendered him all the aid in their power;* and when Cotton appeared with his troops on a

* "The conduct of the officers of the Khelat chief has been most creditable and praiseworthy. Syud Mahomed Sheriff, the Governor of Gundava, and Moolla Ramzan, a slave of the Khan, have attended me the whole way, procured a band of eighty of the natives to escort us, and they likewise addressed the Ameers and the neighbouring Beloochee tribes to attempt at their peril to molest us. Such has been the confidence thus given, that a great body of the migratory inhabitants from

clear, still morning, at the mouth of the defile, there was little likelihood of any obstacle being opposed to his free progress. But the baggage-cattle were falling dead by the wayside; the artillery horses were showing painful symptoms of distress. The stream of the Bolan river was tainted by the bodies of the camels that had sunk beneath their loads. The Beloochee freebooters were hovering about, cutting off our couriers, murdering stragglers, carrying off our baggage and our cattle. Among the rocks of this stupendous defile our men pitched their tents; and toiled on again day after day, over a wretched road covered with loose flint stones, surmounting, at first, by a scarcely perceptible ascent, and afterwards by a difficult acclivity, the great Brahoo chain of hills. The Bolan Pass is nearly sixty miles in length. The passage was accomplished in six days. They were days of drear discomfort, but not of danger. A resolute enemy might have wrought mighty havoc among Cotton's regiments; but the enemies with which now they had to contend were the sharp flint stones which lamed our cattle, the scanty pasturage which destroyed them, and the marauding tribes who carried them off. The way was strewn with baggage—with abandoned tents, and stores; and luxuries which, a few weeks afterwards, would have fetched their weight twice counted in rupees, were left to be trampled down by the cattle in the rear, or carried off by the plunderers about them.

Happy was every man in the force when the army again emerged into the open country. The valley of Shawl lay before them, a favoured spot in a country of little favour. The clear crisp climate braced the European frame; and over the wide plain, bounded by noble mountain-ranges, intersected by many sparkling streams,

Cutchee availed themselves of our escort to ascend into Afghanistan."
—[*Burnes to Macnaghten: March* 16, 1839. *MS. Records.*]

and dotted with orchards and vineyards, the eye ranged with delight ; whilst the well-known carol of the lark, mounting up in the fresh morning air, broke with many home associations charmingly on the English ear.* On the 26th of March the Bengal column reached Quettah —" a most miserable mud town, with a small castle on a mound, on which there was a small gun on a rickety carriage † Here Sir Willoughby Cotton was to halt until further orders. Starvation was beginning to stare his troops in the face.

Seldom has a military commander found himself in the midst of more painful perplexities than those which now surrounded Cotton. It seemed to be equally impossible to stand still or to move forward. His supplies were now so reduced, that even upon famine allowances his troops could not have reached Candahar with provisions for more than a few days in store; and to remain halted at Quettah would necessarily aggravate the evil. There appeared to be no possibility of obtaining supplies. All the provisions stored in Quettah and the surrounding villages would not have fed our army for many days In this painful conjuncture, Cotton acted with becoming promptitude He despatched his Adjutant-General to Sir John Keane for orders, whilst Burnes proceeded to Khelat to work upon the fears or the cupidity of Mehrab Khan ; and, in the meanwhile, reduced to the scantiest dole the daily supplies meted out to our unfortunate fighting men and our more miserable camp-followers.‡ These privations soon began

* See *Havelock's Narrative.*

† *Hough's Narrative of the Operations of the Army of the Indus.*

‡ Captain Havelock says : "From the 28th of March, the loaf of the European soldier was diminished in weight, the Native troops received only half instead of a full seer of *ottah* (that is a pound of flour) *per diem*, and the camp-followers, who had hitherto found it difficult to subsist on half a seer, were of necessity reduced to the famine allowance of a quarter of a seer."

to tell fearfully upon their health and their spirits. The sufferings of the present were aggravated by the dread of the future; and as men looked at the shrunk frames and sunken cheeks of each other, and in their own feebleness and exhaustion felt what wrecks they had become, their hearts died within them at the thought that a day was coming when even the little that was now doled out to them might be wholly denied.

Burnes hastened to Khelat. He was courteously received. He found Mehrab Khan an able and sagacious man. Suspicious of others, but with more frankness and unreserve in his character than is commonly found in suspicious men, the Khan commented freely on our policy —said, with prophetic truth, that we might restore Shah Soojah to Afghanistan, but that we should not carry the Afghan people with us, and that we should, therefore, fail in the end; and then, after launching into an indignant commentary on the ingratitude of Shah Soojah, for whom he had suffered much and reaped nothing in return, he proceeded to set forth the evils which had resulted to him and his people from the passage of the British army through his dominions.* "The English,".

* "The Khan, with a good deal of earnestness, enlarged upon the undertaking the British had embarked in—declaring it to be one of vast magnitude and difficult accomplishment—that instead of relying on the Afghan nation, our government had cast them aside and inundated the country with foreign troops—that if it was our end to establish ourselves in Afghanistan, and give Shah Soojah the nominal sovereignty of Caubul and Candahar, we were pursuing an erroneous course—that all the Afghans were discontented with the Shah, and all Mahomedans alarmed and excited at what was passing—that, day by day, men returned discontented, and we might find ourselves awkwardly situated if we did not point out to Shah Soojah his errors, if the fault originated with him, and alter them if they sprung from ourselves— that the chief of Caubul was a man of ability and resource, and though we could easily put him down by Shah Soojah, even in our present

he said, "had now come, and by their march through his country, in different directions, destroyed the crops, poor as they were; helped themselves to the water which irrigated the lands, made doubly valuable in this year of scarcity;"—"but he had stood," he added, "quiescent, and hoped from the English justice, from the Shah justice; hoped that his claims might be regarded in a proper light, and he for ever relieved from the mastery of the Suddozye Kings." He then spoke freely and fluently of our policy in Central Asia, of the position in which we had placed ourselves at Herat by supporting such a miscreant as Yar Mahomed, and of the failure of our negotiations at Caubul and Candahar. "I might have allied myself," he said, "with Persia and Russia— but I have seen you safely through the great defile of the Bolan, and yet I am unrewarded."

Burnes had brought with him the draft of a treaty, which, on the following day, he sent to the Khan. He had made it a condition of all peaceable negotiation with the Beloochee Prince, that he should wait upon Shah Soojah in his camp—a condition which Mehrab Khan disliked and resisted, and from which he could extricate himself only by pleading sickness. The treaty, by which the supremacy of Shah Soojah was distinctly acknowledged, bound the British Government to pay Mehrab Khan a lakh and a half of rupees annually, in return for which the Khan engaged to "use his best endeavours to procure supplies, carriage, and guards to protect provisions and stores going and coming from Shikarpoor, by the route of Rozan, Dadur, the Pass of Bolan, through Shawl to Koochlak, from one frontier to another."

Mehrab Khan affixed his seal to the treaty. But he

mode of procedure, we could never win over the Afghan nation by it."
—[*Burnes to Macnaghten: Khelat, March* 30, 1839. *MS. Records.*]

disliked the bargain he had made. He was altogether suspicious of Shah Soojah and the Suddozyes. He was by no means certain of the success of the present enterprise. He believed that, by paying homage to the Shah, he would raise up a host of powerful enemies, and plunge himself into a sea of ruin. Striving to allay the apprehensions of the Khan, Burnes made some trifling concessions, which were not without their effect; and then proceeded to press upon him the subject which at that moment was of most immediate importance to British interests—the matter of supplies; and earnestly pointed out the imperative necessity of every possible exertion being made by the Khan to provide them. But it was easier to suggest such provision than to make it. Mehrab Khan said that he would do his best—that he would place men at Burnes's disposal to proceed to Nooshky and other places, where the crops were nearly ripe ("and," said Burnes, parenthetically, "he has done so")—that he would "give grain in Gundava and Cutchee, and if we would send for our stores at Shikarpoor to Dadur, he would actively aid in passing them through the Bolan—that he might also aid us at Moostung in getting a small quantity of grain; but that there was really very little grain at Khelat, or in the country—that he had reduced his escort to wait on the Shah to 1000 men, on account of the scarcity—and that he could not then furnish the grain, but each man must bring his own.'
"This intelligence," wrote Burnes to Macnaghten, "is very distressing in our present position; but my inquiries serve to convince me that there is but a small supply of grain in this country, and none certainly to be given us, without aggravating the present distress of the inhabitants—some of whom are feeding on herbs and grasses gathered in the jungle. It is with some difficulty we have supported ourselves, whilst the small quantities we

have procured have been got by stealth. This scarcity is corroborated by a blight in last year's harvest Under such circumstances, the only way of turning the Khan to account is in supplying sheep; and here he can and is willing to assist us to a great extent. Probably 10,000 or 15,000 may be procured, and arrangements are now being made for purchasing and sending them down to Shawl "*

In the meanwhile, the Shah's Contingent and the Bombay division of the Army of the Indus were making their way through Sindh.† Greatly straitened for carriage, it had been for some time doubtful whether the whole of the Shah's army would be able to proceed to Candahar. There had been a disposition on the part of Sir Willoughby Cotton to look with contempt upon the Suddozye levies, and to make the King and his regiments play a part in the coming drama, by no means in accordance with the estimate which Macnaghten had formed of their importance. And now Sir John Keane seemed equally inclined to throw into the background the King, the Envoy, and the Contingent. But Macnaghten had claimed for the Shah a prominent place in the coming operations,‡ and the military chief had yielded to his

* *Burnes to Macnaghten . Khelat, April* 2, 1839.

† The Shah and his Contingent moved from Shikarpoor on the 7th of March.

‡ "His Majesty the Shah is naturally anxious to occupy a prominent position in our movements, and it is very desirable, on political grounds, that he should do so : I trust, therefore, that your Excellency will see fit to attend to his Majesty's wishes in this particular, and to authorise his being in advance with at least a portion of his own troops, after the junction of the several divisions shall have been effected, or rather after you have made your final arrangements for the order of our advance. This you will observe will be conformable to the wishes of the Governor-General, as expressed in the accompanying extracts. His Lordship never contemplated the leaving behind any portion of

representations, and even placed at his disposal a number of baggage-cattle which he greatly needed for his own force. Anxious to conciliate the commander of the army, and never unmindful of the public interests, the Envoy gratefully declined the offer.* Keane was, at that time, "in a wretched plight for want of cattle," and the Bengal Commissariat were compelled to supply him largely both with camels and grain.

Sir Willoughby Cotton had suggested to Macnaghten the expediency of a movement upon Khelat; but the Envoy was then little inclined to take the same unfavourable view of the conduct of Mehrab Khan, which Cotton, smarting under the privations to which his force had been subjected, was prone to encourage. "With regard to moving upon Khelat," he wrote on the 15th of March to the Bengal General, "I am not prepared at present to take upon myself the responsibility of that measure; and I am in great hopes that Sir Alexander Burnes will be able to arrange everything satisfactorily."† The further he advanced, indeed, the more obvious it became that the Khan of Khelat had just grounds of complaint against the English army. Everywhere traces of the devastation —much of it unavoidable devastation—which our advanc-

---

the Shah's force, except in the case of opposition being shown by Sindh and Khelat."—[*Mr. Macnaghten to Sir J. Keane: Shikarpoor, Feb. 27, 1839. Unpublished Correspondence.*]

* "I am exceedingly obliged to you for the attention you have paid to my suggestions regarding the Shah's troops; but your want of camels is so pressing, that I feel it impossible to retain the 1000 camels placed at my disposal. Deeply as I regret, on political grounds, the necessity of leaving behind any portion of the troops of his Majesty, I feel that any scruples on this score must give way to the more urgent exigencies of the public service."—[*Mr. Macnaghten to Sir J. Keane: Shikarpoor, March 3, 1839. Unpublished Correspondence.*]

† *Mr. Macnaghten to Sir W. Cotton: March 15, 1839. Unpublished Correspondence.*

ing columns had left behind them, spoke out intelligibly to him; and he plainly saw how extremely distasteful both our officers and our measures had become to the Beloochees. Pondering these things, he sate down and wrote the following letter to Lord Auckland—a significant letter, which shows how early had burst upon Macnaghten the truth, that only by a liberal expenditure of money was there any hope of reconciling to our operations the chiefs and people beyond the Indus:

Camp Bagh, *March* 19.

I found the Khelat authorities in the worst possible humour. Our enemies have evidently been tampering with them, and they had good cause for dissatisfaction with us; their crops have been destroyed, and the water intended for the irrigation of their fields has been diverted to the use of our armies. A great portion of these evils was perhaps unavoidable, but little or no effort seems to have been made either to mitigate the calamity or to appease the discontent which has been created by our proceedings. Our officers and our measures are alike unpopular in this country, and I very much fear that Sir A. Burnes may be led, by vague rumours of the Khan's unfriendly disposition, to recommend offensive operations against him. In what difficulties we might be involved by such a proceeding it would be impossible to foretell. My most strenuous efforts have been day and night directed towards reconciling all persons of influence to our operations; and in this I have been successful; but considerable sums must be expended, not only in remunerating the people for the severe losses they have sustained, but in bribing the authorities. Your Lordship may rely upon it, that I shall not expend one rupee of the public money more than I deem indispensably necessary; but here we are quite at the mercy of the Beloochees. This very day, had they been inimically inclined, they might with the greatest ease have turned an inundation into our camp, which would have swept away our entire force and everything belonging to us. The change in the demeanour of the authorities since yesterday is wonderful. They are now our devoted servants, and the Vizier has promised to write off instantly to his master at Khelat, advising him to give us his entire and unqualified friendship and support. Sir John Keane is in a wretched plight for want of cattle, and I cannot help thinking he has been neglected in a very unwarrantable manner by the Bengal authorities. . . . I went out myself this morning to see what damage had been done to the crops. The devastation is grievous; but the interest which the people saw me take in their complaints has done more to pacify them than I ever expected. Another source of great dissatisfaction has been the seizure by our troops of different individuals, and even families, on the plea of being robbers. This I have done all in my power to remedy.*

More and more sensible, after every march, of the miserable country through which he was passing, and the difficulties which now beset the expedition, Macnaghten was anxious to push on with all possible expedition. But Sir John Keane, who was in the rear with the Bombay column, dreading the assemblage, on the same spot, of so large a body of troops as would be brought together by the junction of the three forces, urged upon him the expediency of halting, whilst his Excellency went forward to ascertain the chances of finding forage and provisions in the Bolan Pass. So the Shah and his Contingent halted for a few days at Bagh,† whilst Sir John Keane pushed on with his escort. On the 28th of March, the King, the Minister, and the Commander-in-Chief were all assembled together at Dadur. "Their united camps displayed all the pomp and circumstances of a triple head-quarter." The passage of the Bolan was accomplished without difficulty, and on the 4th of April, Sir Willoughby Cotton, having ridden out with his staff from Quettah, greeted

* *Unpublished Correspondence of Sir W. H. Macnaghten.*

† From Bagh, Macnaghten wrote to the Governor-General's Private Secretary : "This is a wretched country in every respect. It may be said to produce little else but plunderers; but with the knowledge we now have of it, we may bid defiance to the Russian hordes as far as this route is concerned. Any army might be annihilated in an hour by giving it either too much or too little water. The few wells that exist might easily be rendered unavailable, and by just cutting the Sewee bund the whole country might be deluged."—[*Mr. Macnaghten to Mr. Colvin : Camp Bagh, March* 22, 1839. *Unpublished Correspondence.*]

the General-in-Chief and his companions as they were resting at the entrance to the Shawl Valley, after the fatigues of the passage through the defile. The tidings which he had to communicate were of the gloomiest hue. He reported that his men were on quarter-rations, and that there was every prospect of the army, as it entered Afghanistan, being opposed at every step. Macnaghten, however, more sanguine, was already beginning to think and to write about the means of disposing of the Barukzye Sirdars. On that 4th of April he wrote to the Governor-General a letter, which indicates the tone of his own feelings and of those of the Afghan Prince :

April, 4, 1839.

We are now encamped within ten miles of Shawl. Sir Willoughby came in here this morning, and talks in a most gloomy strain of his prospects. He says he has but twelve days' supplies, and his men are already on quarter-rations. We cannot reckon on being at Candahar under a fortnight, and it will go hard with us if we cannot get supplied in the meantime from other quarters. Sir Willoughby is a sad croaker, not content with telling me we must all inevitably be starved, he assures me that Shah Soojah is very unpopular in Afghanistan, and that we shall be opposed at every step of our progress. I think I know a little better than this. My accounts from Candahar lead me to believe that the religious excitement is subsiding, and that the Sirdars are only thinking how they can make good terms for themselves, or, failing that, how they may best contrive to effect their escape. It will be as well not to reduce them to desperation; for though they cannot oppose us in the field, yet they make sad havoc with our supplies. Large bands of camel-plunderers kept hovering over our line of march, and it certainly looks as if they had been incited by some one of influence. The mistakes and contretemps which are constantly occurring in our motley camp, require the exercise of much patience and discrimination. The Shah is in good health and spirits, but says he never had so much trouble and bother in his lifetime as he has met with during this campaign. The reason is obvious, the people on former occasions helped themselves to everything they wanted, and no complaint was permitted to approach the sacred person of his Majesty. His opinion of the Afghans as a nation is, I regret to say, extremely low. He declares that they are a pack of dogs, one and all, and, as for the Barukzyes, it is utterly impossible that he can ever place the slightest confidence in any one of that accursed race. We must try and bring him gradually round to entertain a more favorable opinion of his subjects. I cannot yet say how the Barukzye chiefs shall be disposed of, but I am decidedly of opinion that it would be a wise measure to get them quietly out of Afghanistan and pension them, if we can do so at an expense not exceeding a lakh of rupees per annum. If they oppose us and are taken, the Shah must, I imagine, be permitted to do what he likes with them short of putting them to death; and his own human nature is a sufficient security that he will not proceed to extremities.*

On the 6th of April, Sir John Keane fixed his headquarters at Quettah, and assumed the personal command of the army. Reviewing all the circumstances of his position, he came to the determination to push forward with all possible despatch to Candahar. There was no prospect of obtaining supplies through the agency of Mehrab Khan. Already was the Envoy convinced of the treachery of that Prince—already was he beginning to talk about dismembering the Khanate of Khelat, and annexing the provinces of Shawl, Moostung, and Cutchee to the Douranee Empire. On that day he wrote to the Private Secretary of the Governor-General:

Camp Quettah, *April* 6, 1839.

* * * Sir John Keane has represented to me in the strongest terms the necessity for moving on. The fact is, the troops and followers are nearly in a state of mutiny for food, and the notion of waiting for such a person as Mehrab Khan, who has done his best to starve us, seems utterly preposterous. I trust the Governor-General will see fit to annex the provinces of Shawl, Moostung, and Cutchee to the Shah's dominions. This would be the place for cantoning a British regiment. It is so cold now that I can hardly hold my pen, and the climate is said to be delightful all the year round. I am certain the annexation could be made without the

* *Unpublished Correspondence of Sir W. H. Macnaghten.*

slightest difficulty. . . . . Now for Candahar. The game is clearly up with the Sirdars. I had a letter from the triumvirate yesterday, brought by Syud Muhun Shah, whom they have sent to treat, or rather to get the best terms for themselves they can. As to opposition, it is quite clear that they look upon that as hopeless, and they have not even the power to retreat. I am unwilling to reduce them to desperation, and shall try and get the Shah to make some provision for them; but he is very loth to do so. Their demands now are extravagant beyond measure; but I do not think that a lakh of rupees per annum, distributed among the three brothers, would be too much for the King to give, if they agreed upon that to sink into the retirement of private life. Notwithstanding all the croaking about Shah Soojah's want of popularity, feel certain that my prediction will be verified, and that his Majesty will be cordially welcomed by all classes of the people.*

On the 7th of April the army resumed its march.† On the 9th it was at Hykulzye, a spot rendered famous in the later annals of the war. From this place Macnaghten wrote again to the same correspondent :

Camp Hykulzye, *April*, 9.
* * * I have reason to believe that the Sirdars of Candahar are at their wit's end. They make resolutions one day and break them the next. But all accounts concur in reporting that they are abandoned by the priesthood, and that if there is any religious feeling extant, it is all in favour of Shah Soojah. In a fit of desperation the last resolve of Kohun-dil-Khan is stated to be, that he will make a

---

* *Unpublished Correspondence of Sir W. H. Macnaghten.*

† The head-quarters of the 2nd brigade were left in garrison at Quettah, under General William Nott, of the Company's army, who, at a later period, so distinguished himself in command of the troops at Candahar. Whilst Sir Willoughby Cotton was commanding the Bengal army in chief, Nott had commanded a division; but when Sir John Keane joined the Bengal column, Cotton fell back to the divisional command, and Nott returned to the brigade to which he had originally been posted. Out of this much controversy arose; the command of the other division of the "Army of the Indus" having been conferred on General Willshire, of the Queen's army, a junior major-general, but an older officer and lieutenant-colonel.

night attack on our camp with about 2000 followers who are still attached to his person. This I fully believe to be fudge. The whole of the force, from Sir W. Cotton downwards, are infected with exaggerated fears relating to the character of the King and the prospects of the campaign. They fancy that they see an enemy in every bush. The Khan of Khelat is our implacable enemy, and Sir J. Keane is burning with revenge. There never was such treatment inflicted upon human beings as we have been subjected to on our progress through the Khan's country. I will say nothing of Burnes's negotiations. His instructions were to conciliate, but I think he has adhered too strictly to the letter of them. The Commander-in-Chief is very angry. I would give something to be in Candahar; and there, *Inshallah*, we shall be in about a week; but, in the meantime, this union of strictly disciplined troops with lawless soldiers is very trying to my patience. With a less tractable king than Shah Soojah the consequences might be fatal. I have references every minute of the day, and we are compelled to tell his Majesty's people that they must not touch the green crops of the country. This they think very hard, and so I believe does the King, but he has, nevertheless, forbidden them. Supplies are now coming in, but they are yet very dear—2½ seers of flour for a rupee! But this price will, no doubt, daily fall. The great thing is to give people confidence. All the villages in the Khan of Khelat's territory were deserted at our approach, and not a soul came near us, except with the view of plundering and murdering our followers. The instant we crossed the frontier the scene was entirely changed. The inhabitants remained in their villages, and have manifested the greatest possible confidence in our justice and good faith. Is it possible to conceive that the difference of feeling in the Khelat country has not been brought about by design? * * *

Macnaghten was naturally of a sanguine temperament. Civilians seldom estimate military difficulties aright. It is true that our political difficulties were melting away. The Candahar Sirdars, deserted and betrayed, seemed to have given themselves up to despair, and there was little chance of the progress of our army being disputed by an Afghan force. But the scarcity, which had pressed so severely on our troops, and had nearly destroyed our horses, was not less a reality because no enemy appeared to educe all the disastrous results which were likely to flow from such deterioration of the *physique* of our army. The army of the Indus surmounted the Kojuck Pass as safely as it had traversed the Bolan. The Shah, with his Contingent, was now in advance, leading the way, as it became him, into his restored dominions; and many of the chiefs and people of Western Afghanistan were flocking to his standard.* There were not wanting those who said that, if there had been any prospect of opposition at Candahar, the King and his levies would not have been the first to appear under the walls of the city. But authentic intelligence had reached Macnaghten, to the effect that Kohun-dil-Khan and his brothers had fled from Candahar—that there was no union among the Barukzye brotherhood—and that, if a stand were to be made at all, the battle-field would be nearer the northern capital. The way, indeed, was clear for the entry of the Suddozye monarch; so he pushed on in advance of Sir John Keane and his army, to receive, it was said, the homage of his people. Money had been freely scattered about; and the Afghans had already begun to discover that the gold of the Feringhees was as serviceable as other gold, and that there was an unfailing supply of it. Early in the campaign, Macnaghten had encouraged the conviction that the allegiance of the Afghans was to be bought—that Afghan cupidity would not be proof against British gold. So he opened the treasure-chest; scattered abroad its contents with an ungrudging hand; and commenced a system of corruption which, though seemingly

* Foremost among these was the notorious Hadjee Khan, Khaukur, whose sudden defection broke up the Barukzye camp, just as Rahun-dil-Khan and Mehr-dil-Khan were meditating a night attack on the Shah's Contingent He joined the Shah on the 20th of April, and from this time the Sirdars saw that their cause was hopeless. Further mention of this chief will be found in a subsequent chapter.

successful at the outset, wrought, in the end, the utter ruin of the policy he had reared.*

* I have not attempted in this chapter to give a minute account of the march of the three columns of the invading army to Candahar. It is no part of my design to render this work conspicuous for the completeness of its military details. I do not underrate their importance; but the operations of the Army of the Indus have already been so minutely chronicled, that I have only to refer the reader to the works of Havelock, Kennedy, and Hough. The real history of the march is to be found in the records of the Commissariat department. The difficulty of obtaining carriage and supplies was almost unprecedented, and the expenditure incurred was enormous. There were two different Commissariat departments (the Bengal and the Shah's) sometimes to be found bidding against one another. Everything was paid for at a ruinous price. The sums paid for the hire and purchase of carriage-cattle were preposterous; and the loss incurred by government from the deaths of the animals may be surmised, when it is stated that the number of deaths between Ferozepore and Candahar has been estimated at not less than 20,000. Large sums, too, were often paid for demurrage. For example, on one batch of camels hired from Bekanier and Jaysulmere, 44,000 rupees were paid for demurrage and remuneration for losses before they reached the place (Shikarpoor) at which their services were required, or were even seen by our Commissariat officers.—[*MS. Notes.*

CHAPTER II.

[April—August, 1839.]

Arrival at Candahar—The Shah's Entry into the City—His Installation—Nature of his Reception—Behaviour of the Douranees—The English at Candahar—Mission to Herat—Difficulties of our Position—Advance to Ghuznee.

ON the 25th of April, Shah Soojah-ool-Moolk re-entered the chief city of Western Afghanistan. As he neared the walls of Candahar, riding in advance of his Contingent, some Douranee horsemen had gone out to welcome him; and as the cavalcade moved forward, others met him with their salutations and obeisances, and swelled the number of his adherents. It is said that some fifteen hundred men, for the most part well dressed and well mounted, joined him before he reached the city.

Accompanied by the British Envoy, his Staff, and the principal officers of his Contingent, and followed by a crowd of Afghans, the Shah entered Candahar. There was a vast assemblage of gazers. The women clustered in the balconies of the houses, or gathered upon the roofs. The men thronged the public streets. It was a busy and an exciting scene. The curiosity was intense. The enthusiasm may have been the same. As the royal *cortège* advanced, the people strewed flowers before the horses' feet, and loaves of bread were scattered in their way. There were shouts and the sound of music, and the noise of firing; and the faces of the crowd were bright with cheerful excitement. The popular exclamations which were flung into the air have been duly reported. The people shouted out, "Welcome to the son of Timour Shah!" "We look to you for protection!" "Candahar is rescued from the Barukzyes!" "May your enemies be destroyed!" It was said, by some who rode beside the Shah, to have been the most heart-stirring scene they ever witnessed in their lives. Thus greeted and thus attended, the King rode to the tomb of Ahmed Shah, and offered up thanksgivings and prayers. Then the procession returned again through the city, again to be greeted with joyous acclamations; and "the eventful day," as the Court chroniclers affirmed, "passed off without an accident."

The welcome thus given to the Shah, on his public entry into his western capital, filled Macnaghten with delight. The future appeared before him bright with the promise of unclouded success. It seemed to him that the enthusiastic reception of the Shah would be a death-blow to the hopes of Dost Mahomed, and that in all probability the Ameer would fly before us like his brothers. It was encouraging intelligence to communicate to the Governor-General; so on his return from the royal progress through the city, Macnaghten sate down and wrote thus to Lord Auckland:

Candahar, *April* 25, 1839.

We have, I think, been most fortunate in every way. The Shah made a grand public entry in the city this morning, and was received with feelings nearly amounting to adoration. I shall report the particulars officially. I have already had more than one ebullition of petulance to contend with. The latest I send herewith, and I trust that a soft answer will have the effect of turning away wrath. There are many things which I wish to mention, but I really have no leisure. Of this your Lordship may judge, when I state that for the last three days I have been out in the sun, and have not been able to get my breakfast before three in the afternoon. I think it would be in every way advantageous to the public interests if, after Shah Soojah gains possession of Caubul, I were to proceed across the Punjab to Simlah, having an interview with Runjeet Singh, and giving him a detail of all our proceedings; perhaps getting him to modify the treaty in one or two respects. I have broached the subject of our new treaty to his Majesty, but my negotiations are in too imperfect a state to be detailed. Of one thing I am certain, that we must be prepared to look upon Afghanistan for some years as an outwork yielding nothing, but requiring much expenditure to keep it in repair. His Majesty has not yet nominated a Prime Minister, nor has he as yet, I believe, determined his form of administration. His new adherents are all hungry for place ; and in answer to their premature solicitations, he tells me that he has informed them that, since it took God Almighty six days to make heaven and earth, it is very hard they will not allow him, a poor mortal, even the same time to settle the affairs of a kingdom. I am gratified at being able to assure your Lordship that the best feeling is manifested towards the British officers by the entire population here, and I devoutly hope that nothing may occur to disturb the present happy state of things. Dost Mahomed will, I doubt not, take himself off like his brothers, though not, perhaps, in quite so great a hurry, when the intelligence reaches him of the manner in which Shah Soojah has been received at Candahar. The Sirdars have carried off my elephants, and I am informed that the animals proved of the greatest service to them in crossing their ladies over a deep and rapid river not far from this. We have heard nothing since our arrival here of the embassy from Herat. If I go to Simlah from Caubul, Sir A. Burnes could be left to officiate for me, and in case of my return he might go to Candahar and relieve Major Leach, who might be left there in the first instance.

I remain, my Lord, yours, &c.

W. H. MACNAGHTEN.*

Encouraged by the presumed "adoration" of the people, it was now determined to give them another opportunity of testifying the overflowing abundance of their loyalty and affection. So the 8th of May was fixed upon for a general public recognition of the restored sovereign, on the plains before Candahar. Both columns of the British

* *Unpublished Correspondence of Sir W. H. Macnaghten.*

army had now arrived. The troops were to pass in review-order before the king; and other ceremonial observances were to give *éclat* to the inauguration. Upon a raised platform, under a showy canopy, sate the restored monarch of the Dourance Empire. He had ridden out at sunrise under a royal salute. The troops had presented arms to him on his ascending the musnud, and a salute of a hundred and one guns had been fired in honour of the occasion. Around him were the chief military and political officers of the British Government. Everything went off as it had been ordered and arranged, and most imposing was the spectacle of the review-march of the British troops. But the King had then been a fortnight at Candahar, and the curiosity of the people had subsided. There was no popular enthusiasm.* The whole affair was a painful failure. The English officers saluted the King; and the King made a speech about the disinterested benevolence of the British Government. Greatly pleased was his Majesty with the exhibition; and when the troops had been dismissed, he said that its moral influence would be felt from Pekin to Constantinople.† But the miserable paucity of Afghans who appeared to

---

* Captain Havelock, who is by no means disposed to take an unfavorable view of the policy out of which emanated the assembling of the Army of the Indus, says: "Unless I have been deceived, all the national enthusiasm of the scene was entirely confined to his Majesty's immediate retainers. The people of Candahar are said to have viewed the whole affair with the most mortifying indifference. Few of them quitted the city to be present in the plains; and it was remarked with justice, that the passage in the diplomatic programme which presented a place behind the throne for 'the populace restrained by the Shah's troops,' became rather a bitter satire on the display of the morning." Compare Dr. Kennedy's version of these proceedings. All the private accounts I have received, confirm the truth of the printed narratives.

† Kennedy.

do homage to the King, must have warned Shah Soojah, with ominous significance, of the feebleness of his tenure upon the affections of the people, as it bitterly disappointed and dismayed his principal European supporters. Every effort had been made to give publicity to the programme of the ceremony; and yet it is said, by the most trustworthy witnesses, that barely a hundred Afghans had been attracted, either by curiosity or by loyalty, to the installation of the adored King.

Such were the mere outward facts of Shah Soojah's reception as recorded by the chroniclers of the day. Surrounded by his own Contingent, and supported by the British army, he had advanced unopposed to Candahar. But the brief local excitement, which his entrance into the city had aroused, cannot be regarded as national enthusiasm. When the first outbreak of curiosity had subsided the feeling which greeted the restored King was rather that of sullen indifference than of active devotion. In the vicinity of Candahar the Douranee tribes constituted the most influential section of the inhabitants. They had been oppressed and impoverished by the Barukzye Sirdars, and had longed to rid themselves of the yoke of their oppressors. But when the representative of the Suddozye dynasty, under which they had been pampered and protected, appeared at the gates of the Douranee Empire, they had neither spirit nor strength to make a strenuous effort to support or to oppose the restored monarch. It is doubtful whether, in the conjuncture which had then arisen, the Douranees, had they possessed any military strength, would have openly arrayed themselves on the side of the Shah; for although they hated the Barukzyes who had oppressed them, there were the strongest national and religious feelings to excite them against a Prince who had brought an army of Franks to desolate their country. Had they stood erect in their old pride of conscious power, a mighty conflict would have raged within them. The antagonism of personal and national interests would have rent and convulsed them; and it is not improbable that in the end, abhorring the thought of an infidel invasion, they would have determined to support the cause of the Sirdars. But when Shah Soojah was advancing upon Candahar, the Douranees were in a state of absolute feebleness and paralysis. They held aloof, for they had neither power nor inclination to take any conspicuous part in the revolution which was then brooding over the empire.

But when, supported by his Feringhee allies, the Shah had established himself in Candahar, the Douranees, offering their congratulations and tendering their allegiance, gathered round the restored monarch. The issue of the contest seemed no longer doubtful. The dominion of the Barukzye Sirdars had received its death-blow. The restoration of the Suddozye dynasty was certain; and with whatever feelings the Douranees may have inwardly regarded it, it was politic to make an outward show of satisfaction and delight. The change had been effected without their agency; but they might turn it to good account. So they clustered around the throne, and began to clamour for the wages of their pretended forbearance. They put forward the most extravagant claims and pretensions; bargained for the restoration of all the old privileges and immunities which they had enjoyed under Ahmed Shah and his successors; and would fain have swept the entire revenues of the state into their own hands.

It was plain that the King could not recognise the claims which were thus profusely asserted. But it would have been imprudent, at such a time, to have offended or disappointed these powerful tribes. The Shah had established himself at Candahar. Kohun-dil-Khan and his brothers had fled for safety across the Helmund, and sought an asylum in Persia.* But Dost Mahomed was still dominant at Caubul. There was work yet to be done. There were dangers yet to be encountered. It was necessary, therefore, to conciliate the Douranees. So steering, as well as he could, a middle course, the Shah granted much that was sought from him; but he did not grant all. He restored the Sirdars to the chieftainships of their clans, and to the offices which they had been wont to hold about the Court. He gave them back the lands of which they had been denuded, and granted them allowances consistent with the rank which they had been suffered to reassume. Some vexatious and oppressive imposts were removed, and a considerable remission of taxation was proclaimed. But the system of assessment which the Barukzye Sirdars had introduced was continued in operation; and the same revenue officers continued to collect the tax. These men were thoroughly hateful to the Douranees. They had been the willing instruments of Barukzye oppression, and had carried out the work of their masters with a ferocity, strengthened by the recollection of one of those old hereditary blood-feuds, which keep up from generation to generation a growth of unextinguishable hate.

If any feelings of delight at the thought of the restoration of the Suddozye dynasty welled up anywhere in the breasts of the people of Afghanistan, it was among these Douranee tribes. As the grandson of Ahmed Shah, they were prepared to welcome Shah Soojah. They were prepared to welcome him as the enemy of the Barukzye Sirdars. But the ugly array of foreign bayonets in the background effectually held in control all their feelings of

---

* Where they remained as guests of Mahomed Shah until the withdrawal of the British from Afghanistan.

national enthusiasm. They regarded the movement for the restoration of the Suddozye Prince in the light of a foreign invasion; and chafed when they saw the English officers settling themselves in the palaces of their ancient Princes.

In the meanwhile, the Army of the Indus remained inactive at Candahar. The halt was a long and a weary one. Provisions were miserably scarce. It was necessary to remain under the city walls until a sufficiency could be obtained, and to obtain this sufficiency it was necessary to await the ripening of the crops. Every one was impatient to advance. The delay was painful and disheartening. There were no compensating advantages to be obtained from a halt under the walls of Candahar. Save a few who had the real artist's eye to appreciate the picturesque, the officers of the force were disappointed with the place. They had believed that they were advancing upon a splendid city; but they now found themselves before a walled town, presenting so few objects of interest that it was scarcely worth exploring. After the desolate tracts over which they had passed, the valley of Candahar appeared to the eye of our officers to be a pleasant and a favoured spot. There were green fields, and shady orchards, and running streams, to vary the surrounding landscape. But they found the city itself to be little better than a collection of mud-houses, forming very unimposing streets.* The city was in ruins. "The interior

* As at Herat, the four principal streets meet in the centre of the city, and at their junction are covered over with a great dome. The picturesque accessories of Candahar are by no one so well described as by Lieutenant Rattray, in his letter-press accompaniments to his admirable series of "Views in Affghanistan." With true artistic feeling, he writes; "Viewing Candahar from without, or at a distance, there is no peculiarity in its structure to strike the eye, as nothing appears above the long, high walls, but the top of Ahmed Shah's tomb,

consisted only of the relics of houses of forgotten Princes."* There was altogether an air of dreariness and desolation about the place. Many of the houses had been thrown down by repeated shocks of earthquake, and had not been rebuilt. The public buildings were few; but conspicuous among them was the tomb of Ahmed Shah, whose white dome, seen from a distance, stood up above the houses of the city, whilst a spacious mosque, with its domes and minarets, seen also from afar, enshrined a relict of extraordinary sanctity—the shirt of the Prophet Mahomed.

When the British arrived before Candahar in April, 1839, it was said that the principal inhabitants had forsaken the place. But enough remained to give an animated and picturesque aspect to the city. The streets and bazaars were crowded with people of different castes

the summits of a few minarets, and the upper parapets of the citadel. But the interior, as seen from the battlements, cannot fail to delight. Its irregular mud-houses, partly in ruins, varied with trees and minarets; the square red-brick dwellings, with doors and windows of Turkish arches; the lofty habitations of the Hindoo; the tents pitched here and there on the flat house-tops; the long terraces crowded with people, busied in their various callings in the open air; the dung and mud-plastered hut of the Khaukur, with his heavy, wild-looking buffaloes tethered round it; the high enclosures of the different tribes; the warlike castles of the chieftains; the gaily-decorated palace of some great Douranee Lord, with its fountains, squares, and court-yards; and the domed houses of the other inhabitants, the bazaars, mosques, turrets, and cupolas, rising up in the midst of stupendous and inaccessible mountains,—from the whole rise a panorama pleasing to look upon."

* Kennedy. The author adds: "Shah Soojah had sheltered himself in one, Mr. Macnaghten in another, and Sir Alexander Burnes in a third. The latter had been rebuilt by one of the chiefs of Candahar for his favourite wife. It had an air of magnificence and grandeur where it stood: but in the Mogul Serai of Surat, or in Ahmedabad, would be passed unobserved."

and different costumes—Afghans, Persians, Oosbegs, Beloochees, Armenians, and Hindoos; whilst strings of laden camels everywhere passing and repassing, enhanced the picturesque liveliness of the scene.

There was little to break the monotony of the halt at Candahar. The movements of the enemy, and the probabilities of a stirring or a languid campaign were discussed in our officers' tents; and when, on the 9th of May, a brigade under Colonel Sale—an officer who had already done much good service to his country, and was destined now to play a conspicuous part in the great Central-Asian drama—was despatched to Ghiresk, a place some seventy-five miles in a westerly direction from Candahar, in pursuit of the fugitive Sirdars, there were few officers in Keane's army who did not long to accompany it. But the campaign was a brief and an inglorious one—Sale marched to Ghiresk and returned to Candahar. The Sirdars had abandoned the place, and fled across the Persian frontier. They had but a handful of followers, and they were powerless to offer any resistance to our advancing troops. From Kohun-dil-Khan and his brothers nothing was to be apprehended. Their very names were soon almost forgotten by the Feringhees who had driven them from their homes. Candahar and the surrounding country was in possession of the restored Suddozye Princes. But Shah Soojah and his supporters still looked anxiously towards the north, where Dost Mahomed, the ablest and the most powerful of the Barukzye brotherhood, was still mustering his fighting men—still endeavouring to rouse the chiefs to aid him in the defence of his capital against the often-rejected King, who had now come back to them again, supported by the gold and bayonets of the infidels.

But the very circumstances which might be supposed to work to our disadvantage, and to give strength to the enemy, really favoured our cause. The protracted halt at Candahar gave Dost Mahomed and his adherents abundant time to mature their measures of defence. Whilst the British army was starving in that city, the Barukzyes at Caubul might have been collecting troops and strengthening their defences for a vigorous and well-organised opposition. But to Dost Mahomed this continued halt was altogether unintelligible. He could not understand why, if they really purposed to advance upon Caubul, Macnaghten and Keane were wasting their strength in utter idleness at Candahar. It was the Ameer's belief that the British were projecting a movement upon Herat; that the Army of the Indus would branch off to the westward; and that its operations against Caubul would be deferred to the following year. Believing this, Dost Mahomed turned his thoughts rather to the defence of the eastern than of the western line of road. It had been arranged, under the Tripartite treaty,* that Prince Timour, the eldest son of Shah Soojah, accompanied by Captain Wade and a Sikh force, should penetrate the passes beyond Peshawur, and advance upon Caubul by the road of Jellalabad and Jugdulluck. This force was now advancing. Dost Mahomed sent out against it some of his best fighting men, under the command of his favourite son, Akbar Khan—the young chief who was destined to stand out with such terrible prominence from among the leading personages distinguished in the later history of the war.

No thought, however, of a movement upon Herat weighed at this time on Macnaghten's mind. It appeared to him little desirable to march a British army into the dominions of Shah Kamran, so long as there was a possibility of attaining the desired results by any means less costly and hazardous. There was little

* See *ante*, page 332

immediate prospect then of Mahomed Shah returning for the re-investment of Herat. There was no pressing danger to be combated. So Macnaghten determined to send, instead of a British army, a British mission to Herat, with a handful of engineer and artillery officers, and a few lakhs of rupees, to be expended on the defences of the place.

It was in the month of September, 1838, that, after a nine months' investment of Herat, Mahomed Shah struck his camp, and turned his face towards his own capital. Eldred Pottinger had saved the city from the grasp of the Persians. But his work was not yet done. The wretched people were starving. The necessary evils of the protracted siege had been greatly enhanced by the grinding cruelty of Yar Mahomed. To have left Herat immediately on the departure of the Persian army would have been to have left the inhabitants to perish. Moreover, the accursed traffic in human flesh, which the Persian Prince had set forth as the just cause of his invasion of Herat, had not been suppressed. So Pottinger remained in Herat, and Stoddart, having witnessed the breaking up of the Persian camp, joined his brother-officer in the city, and then the two began to labour diligently together in the great cause of universal humanity.

But these labours were distasteful to the Wuzeer. Pottinger and Stoddart had done the work which Yar Mahomed required of them. The one had driven off, and the other had drawn off, the Persian army. He did not desire that they should interfere with his internal tyranny. To oppress the helpless people at his will seemed to be his rightful prerogative. The slave-trade, which he carried on with such barbarous activity, was the main source of the Heratee revenue. The English officers did not propose to effect its suppression without securing adequate compensation to the slave-dealing state But Yar Mahomed viewed all their proceedings with jealousy and suspicion, and two months after the close of the siege of Herat, they were grossly insulted in the presence of the King, and ordered to withdraw themselves beyond the limits of the Heratee territory.

Stoddart had work to do in another quarter. He quitted Herat and made his way to Bokhara. But Pottinger was solicited to postpone his departure, and the dawn of the new year still found him at the Court of Herat. He only remained to be insulted. In January, 1839, another outrage was committed upon him. His house was attacked by the retainers of Yar Mahomed One of his public servants was seized and mutilated As the year advanced, the hostile temper of the Wuzeer became more and more apparent Tidings of the advance of Shah Soojah and his British allies had reached Herat; and although the integrity of that state had been especially guaranteed by the Tripartite treaty, and British money was then maintaining both the government and the people of Herat, Yar Mahomed began to intrigue both with the Persian Court and the Candahar Sirdars, and endeavoured to form a confederacy for the expulsion of the Shah and his allies from Afghanistan.*

But the Persian Court was little inclined to commit itself to an act of such direct hostility against Great Britain. The Army of the Indus continued to advance ; there was no prospect of any organised opposition. Our success was sufficiently intelligible to Yar Mahomed. He respected success. So, when Shah Soojah entered

* "Facts regarding our Political Relations with Herat, and the Conduct of Yar Mahomed Khan, from November, 1837, to February, 1841," by Dr J. S. Login, attached to the Heratee Mission.

Candahar, and the British army encamped beneath its walls, the Wuzeer hastened to congratulate the Shah upon his restoration, and sent a friendly mission to the British camp. In return for this, Macnaghten now determined to despatch a British officer to Herat, to negotiate a friendly treaty with Shah Kamran. His first thought was to entrust the duty to Burnes; but Burnes was disinclined to undertake it; and Sir John Keane was of opinion that he could not be spared.

So the choice of the Envoy fell upon Major Todd, an officer of the Bengal Artillery, who had been for many years employed in Persia, instructing the artillerymen of Mahomed Shah in the mysteries of his profession, and assisting the British Mission in matters lying beyond the circle of mere military detail. Thoroughly acquainted with the languages and politics of Western Asia, a man of good capacity, good temper, and good principle, he appeared to be well fitted for the office which the Envoy now thought of delegating to him. He had been in the camp of Mahomed Shah during the siege of Herat, and had been employed in the negotiations which had arisen between the two contending states. He had subsequently travelled down through Afghanistan to India, charged with information for the Governor-General, and had then recommended himself, by the extent of his local knowledge and general acquirements, scarcely more than by the integrity of his character and the amiability of his disposition, for employment upon the Minister's staff. He was military secretary and political assistant to Mr. Macnaghten when the Envoy deputed him to Herat. There went at the same time other officers, whose names have since been honourably associated with the great events of the Central-Asian War—James Abbott and Richmond Shakespear, of the Bengal Artillery; and Sanders, of the Engineers, who fell nobly upon the field of Maharajhpore.* They went to strengthen the fortifications of the place, and they took with them guns and treasure.

A few days after the departure of the Mission to Herat, the army recommenced its march. It had been halted at Candahar from the 25th of April to the 27th of June. During this time the harvest had ripened; the carriage-cattle had gained strength; but sickness had broken out among our troops. The heat under canvass had been extreme. Fever, dysentery, and jaundice had been doing their work; and many a good soldier had been laid in a foreign grave. Money, too, had been painfully scarce. It had been scattered about so profusely on our first arrival at Candahar, that now an empty treasury stared Macnaghten in the face; and he tried in vain to negotiate a loan. All these were dispiriting circumstances; and there were others which pressed heavily upon the mind of the Envoy. It was becoming clearer to him every day that the Afghans regarded the intrusion of the British into their dominions with the strongest feelings of national hatred and religious abhorrence. A different class of men from the Belooch marauders, who had carried off our cattle and plundered our stores in the southern country, were now surrounding our camp. If our people straggled far from their supports, they did it at the peril of their lives. "Remember, gentlemen, you are not now in Hindostan,"† was the significant warning which broke from Shah Soojah, when two young officers, ‡ returning from a

* Lieutenant North, of the Bombay Engineers, and Drs. Login and Ritchie, also accompanied them. The Mission left Candahar on the 21st of June, and reached Herat on the 25th of July.

† Havelock.

‡ Inverarity and Wilmer. The former was murdered; the latter escaped with his life.

fishing excursion along the banks of the Urghundab, had been cut down by a party of assassins. It was plain, too, that the Ghilzyes of Western Afghanistan— the original lords of the land—were disinclined to bend their necks to the Suddozye yoke. They had rejected the overtures made to them. They were not to be bought by British gold, or deluded by British promises. Perhaps they may have doubted the sincerity of the latter. Already were Shah Soojah and Macnaghten scattering about those promises even more freely than their money; and already were they ceasing to respect the obligation of fulfilling them. The Ghilzyes now regarded us with unconquerable mistrust. There was every prospect of their long continuing to be a thorn in the flesh of the restored monarch and his supporters —a wild and lawless enemy, not to be reduced to loyalty by Douranee Kings, or to subjection by foreign bayonets.

This, at all events, had been learnt at Candahar during the two months' halt of our army, which, when everything has been said on the subject of supplies, seems still to demand from the pen of the historian something more in the way of explanation. The supplies had now come into camp. They might not be available for the troops on the line of march to Caubul;* but there was no longer

* A convoy of camels laden with grain had been for some time expected from the southward, under the charge of a Lohanee merchant, named Surwar Khan. Some efforts had been made by the enemy to intercept this convoy, or to corrupt the Lohanee chief; and it is said that nothing but the determined fidelity of the leader of the Irregular Horse sent to escort it into Candahar, saved the convoy from being carried off to the Barukzyes. It reached Candahar, but there a new difficulty presented itself. The camel-drivers refused to proceed. There were 20,000 maunds of grain now at the disposal of our Commissariat officers; but the contumacy of these men was now likely to render it wholly useless. Surwar Khan had contracted to bring the

any excuse for protracting the halt. So, on the 27th of June, as Runjeet Singh, the old Lion of Lahore, was wrestling with death at his own capital, the British army resumed its march; and on the 21st of July was before the famous fortress of Ghuznee.

convoy to Candahar; but the camel-drivers, afraid of the vengeance of Dost Mahomed, refused to proceed any further. There was no contending against this; so the supplies were made over to the Commissariat, and stored at Candahar, where a detachment of our troops was left.

CHAPTER III.

[June—August: 1839.]

The Disunion of the Barukzyes—Prospects of Dost Mahomed—Keane's Advance to Ghuznee—Massacre of the Prisoners—Fall of Ghuznee—Flight of Dost Mahomed—Hadjee Khan, Khaukur—Escape of Dost Mahomed—Entry of Shah Soojah into Caubul.

THE disunion of the Barukzye brethren lost Afghanistan to the Sirdars. The bloodless fall of Candahar struck no astonishment into the soul of Dost Mahomed. He had long mistrusted his kinsmen. Candahar, too, was the home of the Douranees. He knew that the Barukzyes had nothing to expect from the allegiance of that powerful tribe. He knew that they were little inclined to strike a blow for the existing dynasty; but he knew at the same time, that they were so prostrate and enfeebled, that the Suddozye Prince would derive no active assistance from them—that they would only throw into the scale the passive sullenness and harmless decrepitude of men broken down by a long course of oppression.

If Dost Mahomed and the Candahar Sirdars had leagued themselves firmly together, without jealousy and without suspicion—if they had declared a religious war, and appealed to the Mahomedan feelings of the people—if they had, by their own energy and activity, encouraged Mehrab Khan of Khelat to array himself against the invaders, and throwing themselves heart and soul into the cause, had opposed our passage through the Bolan and Kojuck Passes, they might have turned to the best count the sufferings of our famine-stricken army, and have given us, at the outset of the campaign, a check from which we should not have speedily recovered. But it seems to have been the design of Providence to paralyse our enemies at this time, and so to lure us into greater dangers than any that could have beset us at the opening of the campaign

But although with slight feelings of astonishment Dost Mahomed now contemplated the successful establishment of Shah Soojah at Candahar, it could not have been without emotions of bitterness and mortification that he beheld his countrymen either flying ignobly before the invaders, or bowing down without shame before the money-bags of the infidels. It was a sore trial to him to see how almost every chief in the country was now prepared to sell his birthright for a mess of pottage. He had not sufficient confidence in his own strength, or the loyalty of his people, to believe that he could offer any effectual resistance to the approach of the Suddozye King, supported as he was by British bayonets and British gold. His enemies were advancing upon Caubul, both along the eastern and western lines of approach; and he was necessitated to divide his strength. Nor could he even give his undivided attention to his foreign enemies. There were danger and disaffection at home. The Kohistan was in rebellion.[*] He could see plainly that the Kuzzilbashes were against him. Indeed, all the bulwarks of national defence which he could hope to oppose to the advancing enemy, were crumbling to pieces before his eyes Believing that all nationality of feeling was utterly extinct in the souls of his brethren, it had, ever since he had established himself at Caubul, been his policy to place the least possible amount of power in their hands, and to entrust all his delegated

[*] The Kohistan is the hill country to the north of Caubul, lying between the capital and the Hindoo-Koosh.

authority to the hands of his sons. His only trust now was in them. Akbar Khan had been despatched through the eastern passes to oppose the march of Wade and the Sikhs; Hyder Khan was in command of the garrison of Ghuznee; and Afzul Khan, with a body of horse, was in the neighbourhood of that fortress, instructed to operate against the flanks of our army in the open country. The Ameer himself was at the capital waiting the progress of events, and husbanding his strength for the final conflict.

In the Ameer's camp there seems to have been little knowledge of the movements and designs of the enemy. It had been for some time believed that it was the intention of the British chiefs to march upon Herat, and now again it was the opinion that they purposed to mask Ghuznee and move at once upon Caubul. It seems, therefore, to have been the design of Dost Mahomed that Afzul Khan and Hyder Khan, having suffered us to advance a march or two beyond Ghuznee, should fall upon our rear, whilst Dost Mahomed himself was to give us battle from the front.* But he had not measured aright the policy of the British Commander. It was not Sir John Keane's intention to mask Ghuznee, but to reduce it.

The strength of Ghuznee was the boast of the Afghans. They believed that it was not to be carried by assault. On the other hand, Sir John Keane, persuaded that it was not a place of any strength, had advanced upon Ghuznee without any siege guns. A battering train had been brought up, with great labour and at great expense, to Candahar, and now that it was likely to be brought into use, and so to repay the labour and the expense, Sir John

* This was the account of the Ameer's tactics given by Hyder Khan. Mohun Lal, upon whose authority I instance it, was in daily personal communication with the Prince after his capture, and ought to be well informed upon this point.

Keane dropped it by the way. He was nearing the strongest fortress in the country; he knew that it was garrisoned by the enemy, and that, if he advanced upon it, it would be vigorously defended. He determined to advance upon it; and yet, with an amount of infatuation which, although after-events have thrown it into the shade, at the time took the country by surprise, and was, perhaps, unexampled in Indian warfare, he left his heavy guns at Candahar, and advanced upon Ghuznee with nothing but light field-pieces. He had been told that it was a place of no considerable strength, and that it would give him no trouble to take it. Major Todd and Lieutenant Leech had seen Ghuznee, and their reports had dissipated the anxieties of the Commander-in-Chief. So he found himself before a place which he subsequently described as one of "great strength both by nature and by art," without any means of effecting a breach in its walls.

The city of Ghuznee lies between Candahar and Caubul—about 230 miles distant from the former, and ninety miles from the latter place. The entire line of country from Candahar to Caubul is, in comparison with that which lies between Caubul and Peshawur, an open and a level tract, opposing no difficulties to the march of an army encumbered with artillery and baggage. As a city, it was of less importance than either Caubul or Candahar.* But the

* "The town," says Lieutenant Rattray, "stands on the extreme point of a range of hills, which slope upwards and command the northeast angle of the Balla Hissar, near which is perched the tomb of Belool the Wise, among ruined mosques and grave-stones. As a city, it will not bear comparison with Caubul or Candahar; and a previous visit to the bazaars of either would spoil you for the darkened narrow streets and small charloo of Ghuznee. However, it possesses snug houses and capital stabling, sufficient for a cavalry brigade, within its walls; and in the citadel, particularly, the squares and residences of its former governors were in many instances spacious and even princely in their style and decorations."

strength of the citadel had been famous throughout many generations; and the first sight of the fortress, as it burst suddenly on the view of our advancing army, "with its fortifications rising up, as it were, on the side of a hill, which seemed to form the background to it," must have thrust upon every officer of the force the conviction that, at Candahar, they had all underrated the strength of the place. It obviously was not a fortress to be breached by nine-pounder and six-pounder guns.

From the fortifications of the citadel Hyder Khan looked out through a telescope, and beheld our British columns advancing slowly and steadily across the plain. Some preparations had been made for external defence; but not on any extensive scale. Parties of the enemy were posted in the villages and gardens around the fort; but our light companies soon dislodged them. The morning was spent in brisk skirmishing;* the range of the enemy's guns was tried; the engineers reconnoitred the place; and then it was determined that the camp should be pitched upon the Caubul side of the city. It was reported that Dost Mahomed himself was advancing from the capital, and it was expedient to cut off his direct communication with the fort. Not without some confusion the camp was pitched. Had Afzul Khan descended with his cavalry upon us at this time, he might have wrought dire mischief amongst us.

Day had scarcely dawned on the 22nd of July, when Sir John Keane, accompanied by Sir Willoughby Cotton and the engineers, ascended the heights commanding the eastern face of the works, and reconnoitred the fortress. He had determined on carrying the place by assault. In

* The enemy, dislodged from the garden, retreated to an outwork, whence they directed a heavy fire upon our people, and did some mischief among them. Captain Graves, of the 16th Native Infantry, and Lieutenant Homrigh, of the 48th, were wounded.

ignorance of the means whereby this was to be accomplished, the King had recommended that the army should leave Ghuznee to itself, and march on at once to Caubul. It was evident that the light field-pieces which Keane had brought up with him from Candahar could not breach the solid walls of Ghuznee. "If you once breach the place," said the Shah, "it is yours; but I cannot understand how you are to breach it—how you are to get into the fort." But Sir John Keane did understand this; for his engineers had taught him. He understood, though he had left his siege train behind, that there was still a resource remaining to him. Though the walls could not be breached, a gate, Captain Thomson assured him, might be blown in with gunpowder.

The gate to be blown in was the Caubul gate. All the others had been built up. The military historians leave it to be surmised by the reader that the knowledge of this important fact was derived from the *reconnaissances* of the British Commander and his engineers. The truth is, that the British had then in their camp a deserter from the Ghuznee garrison—a Barukzye of rank, who had been induced to turn his traitorous back upon his tribe. Abdool Reshed Khan was the nephew of Dost Mahomed. When the "Commercial Mission" was in Afghanistan, Mohun Lal had made the acquaintance of this man. The Moonshee seems to have been endowed with a genius for traitor-making, the lustre of which remained undimmed to the very end of the war. He now began to operate upon his friend; and he achieved a brilliant success. Abdool Reshed was not deaf to the voice of the charmer. Mohun Lal wrote him a seductive letter, and he determined to desert. As the British army approached Ghuznee he joined our camp. "I introduced him," says Mohun Lal, "to the Envoy, who placed him under the immediate disposal of Lord Keane. The information which he gave to Major Thomson, the chief engineer, relative to the fortifications of Ghuznee, was so valuable and necessary, that my friend Abdool Reshed Khan was requested to attend upon him in all his reconnoitring expeditions." He was precisely the man we wanted. He gave us all the information we required. He taught us how to capture Ghuznee.

Having determined to enter Ghuznee through an entrance effected by an explosion of gunpowder, Keane began to issue his instructions for the assault, which was to take place before daybreak on the following morning. Every preparation was made, and every precaution was taken to ensure success. It was a day of expectation and anxiety, and not wholly uneventful. On that 22nd of July was made known to us, with fearful demonstrativeness, the character of those fanatic soldiers of Islam, who have since become so terribly familiar to us under the name of *Ghazees*. Incited by the priesthood, they flock to the green banner, eager to win Paradise by the destruction of their infidel foes, or to forestall the predestined bliss by dying the martyr's death in the attempt. A party of these fearless followers of the Prophet had assembled in the neighbourhood of Ghuznee, and now they were about to pour down upon the Shah's camp, and to rid the country of a King who had outraged Mahomedanism by returning to his people borne aloft on the shoulders of the infidels. A gallant charge of the Shah's Horse, led by Peter Nicolson, who took no undistinguished part in the after-events of the war, checked the onslaught of these desperate fanatics; and Outram, with a party of foot, followed them to the heights where the cavalry had driven them, and captured their holy standard. Some fifty prisoners were taken. It is painful to relate what followed. Conducted into the presence of Shah Soojah, they gloried in their high calling, and openly reviled the

King. One of them, more audacious than the rest, stabbed one of the royal attendants. Upon this, a mandate went forth for the massacre of the whole.

The Shah ordered them to be beheaded, and they were hacked to death, with wanton barbarity, by the knives of his executioners. Coolly and deliberately the slaughter of these unhappy men proceeded, till the whole lay mangled and mutilated upon the blood-stained ground.* Macnaghten, a little time before, had been commending the humane instincts of the King. The humanity of Shah Soojah was nowhere to be found except in Macnaghten's letters. It is enough simply to recite the circumstances of a deed so terrible as this. It was an unhappy and an ominous commencement. The Shah had marched all the way from Loodhianah without encountering an enemy. And now

* There has been so much bitter controversy on this unhappy subject, that I have not written this bare outline of the event without instituting inquiries among those who were most likely to have had some personal cognizance of it. That I have rightly characterised these murders I know, for I have the evidence of one who saw the butchery going on. An officer of the highest character writes, in reply to my inquiries: "As regards what is called the Ghuznee massacre, I was walking one day in camp, and came upon the King's tents, at the rear of which I saw a fearfully bloody sight. There were forty or fifty men, young and old. Many were dead; others at their last gasp; others with their hands tied behind them; some sitting, others standing, awaiting their doom; and the King's executioners and other servants amusing themselves (for actually they were laughing and joking, and seemed to look upon the work as good fun) with hacking and maiming the poor wretches indiscriminately with their long swords and knives. I was so horrified at coming so suddenly on such a scene of blood, that I was for the instant as it were, spell-bound. On inquiry, I ascertained that the King had ordered this wholesale murder in consequence of one of the number (they were, or were said to be, all *Ghazees*, who had shortly before been taken prisoners) having stabbed, in his Majesty's presence, a Pesh-Khidmut, or body-attendant of the King. My friend and I made our exit; and he went direct to the Envoy's tent and reported the circumstance."—[*MS. Correspondence.*]

the first men taken in arms against him were cruelly butchered in cold blood by the "humane" monarch. The act, impolitic as it was unrighteous, brought its own sure retribution. That "martyrdom" was never forgotten. The day of reckoning came at last; and when our unholy policy sunk unburied in blood and ashes, the shrill cry of the *Ghazee* sounded as its funeral wail.

A gusty night had heralded a gusty morn, when Keane, inwardly bewailing the absence of his heavy guns, planted his light field-pieces on some commanding heights opposite the citadel, and filled the gardens near the city walls with his Sepoy musketeers. No sound issued from the fortress, nor was there any sign of life, whilst unseen under cover of the night, and unheard above the loud wailings of the wind, the storming column was gathering upon the Caubul road, and the engineers were carrying up their powder-bags to the gate. The advance was under Colonel Dennie, of the 13th Light Infantry; and the main column under Brigadier Sale.* Captain Thomson, of the Bengal Engineers, directed the movements of the explosion party; and with him were his two subalterns, Durand and Macleod, and Captain Peat, of the Bombay corps. Three hours after midnight everything was ready for the assault.

Then Keane ordered the light batteries to open upon the works of Ghuznee. It was a demonstration—harmless but not useless; for it fixed the attention of the enemy, and called forth a responsive fire. A row of blue lights along the walls now suddenly broke through the darkness and illuminated the place. The enemy had been beguiled by the false attack, and were now looking out towards our batteries, eager to learn the nature of the operations com-

* The advance consisted of the light companies of the four European regiments; the remaining companies composed the other sections of the storming columns. The regiments were: the 2nd, the 13th, and 17th (Queen's), and the Company's European Regiment.

THE ASSAULT.

menced by the investing force And whilst the Afghans were thus engaged, anticipating an escalade and manning their walls, the British engineers were quietly piling their powder-bags at the Caubul gate.

The work was done rapidly and well. The match was applied to the hose. The powder exploded.* Above the roaring of the guns and the rushing of the wind, the noise of the explosion was barely audible.† But the effect was as mighty as it was sudden. A column of black smoke arose; and down with a crush came heavy masses of masonry and shivered beams in awful ruin and confusion. Then the bugle sounded the advance. Dennie at the head of his stormers, pushed forward through the smoke and dust of the aperture; and soon the bayonets of his light companies were crossing the swords of the enemy who had rushed down to the point of attack. A few moments of darkness and confusion; and then the foremost soldiers caught a glimpse of the morning sky, and pushing gallantly on, were soon established in the fortress. Three hearty, animating cheers—so loud and clear that they were heard throughout the general camp ‡—announced to their excited comrades below that Dennie and his stormers had entered Ghuznee.

Then Sale pressed on with the main column, eager to support the stormers in advance; and as he went he met an engineer officer of the explosion party, who had been thrown to the ground, shattered and bewildered by the concussion,§ and who now announced that the gate was

---

* Hough says : "Lieutenant Durand was obliged to scrape the hose with his finger-nails, finding the powder failed to ignite on the first application of the port-fire."

† Havelock. Hough says. "The explosion was heard by nearly all"

‡ Havelock.

§ Captain Peat.

choked up, and that Dennie could not force an entrance. So Sale sounded the retreat. The column halted. There was a pause of painful doubt and anxiety; and then the cheering notes of the bugle, sounding the advance, again stirred the hearts of our people. Another engineer officer had reported that, though the aperture was crowded with fallen rubbish, Dennie had made good his entrance. Onward, therefore, went Sale; but the enemy had profited by the brief pause. The opposition at the gateway now was more resolute than it would have been if there had been no check. The Afghans were crowding to the gate; some for purposes of defence, others to escape the fire which Dennie was pouring in upon them. Sale met them amidst the ruins—amidst the crumbled masonry and the fallen timbers. There was a sturdy conflict. The Brigadier himself was cut down;*

* I give the circumstances of Sale's escape in the words of Captain Havelock, who has detailed them with trustworthy minuteness. "One of their number rushing over the fallen timbers, brought down Brigadier Sale by a cut in the face with his sharp *shunsheer* (sabre). The Afghan repeated his blow as his opponent was falling; but the pummel, not the edge of his sword, this time took effect, though with stunning violence. He lost his footing, however, in the effort, and Briton and Afghan rolled together amongst the fractured timbers. Thus situated, the first care of the Brigadier was to master the weapon of his adversary. He snatched at it, but one of his fingers met the edge of the trenchant blade. He quickly withdrew his wounded hand, and adroitly replaced it over that of his adversary, so as to keep fast the hilt of his *shunsheer*. But he had an active and powerful opponent, and was himself faint from the loss of blood." Captain Kershaw, of the 13th, aide-de-camp to Brigadier Baumgardt, happened in the *mêlée* to approach the scene of conflict: the wounded leader recognised and called to him for aid. Kershaw passed his drawn sabre through the body of the Afghan; but still the desperado continued to struggle with frantic violence. At length, in the fierce grapple, the Brigadier for a moment got uppermost. Still retaining the weapon of his enemy in his left hand, he dealt him with his right a cut from his own sabre, which cleft his skull from the crown to the eyebrows. The Mahomedan

THE LAST STRUGGLE.

but after a desperate struggle with his opponent, whose skull he clove with his sabre, he regained his feet, again issued his commands; and the main column was soon within the fortress. The support, under Colonel Croker, then pushed forward; the reserve in due course followed; the capture of Ghuznee was complete; and soon the colours of the 13th and 17th regiments were flapping in the strong morning breeze on the ramparts of the Afghans' last stronghold.*

But there was much hard fighting within the walls. In the frenzy of despair the Afghans rushed out from their hiding-places, sword in hand, upon our stormers, and plied their sabres with terrible effect, but only to meet with fearful retribution from the musket-fire or the bayonets of the British infantry. There was horrible confusion and much carnage. Some, in their frantic efforts to escape by the gateway, stumbled over the burning timbers, wounded and exhausted, and were slowly burnt to death. Some were bayoneted on the ground. Others were pursued and hunted into corners like mad dogs, and shot down, with the curse and the prayer on their lips. But never, it is said by the historians of the war, after the garrison had ceased to fight, did the wrath of their assailants overtake them. Many an Afghan sold his life dearly, and, though wounded and stricken down, still cut out at the hated enemy. But when resistance was over, mercy smiled down upon him. The appeals of the helpless were never disregarded by the victors in their hour of triumph. The women, too, were honourably treated. Hyder Khan's zenana was in the citadel; but not a woman was outraged by the captors.†

once shouted, '*Ne Ullah!*' (Oh! God!) and never moved or spoke again."—[*Captain Havelock's Narrative.*]

* Havelock. The colour of the 13th was first planted by the hand of Ensign Frere—a nephew of John Hookham Frere.

† Havelock. The military historian attributes the forbearance of the

Resistance over, the Commander-in-Chief and the Envoy entered Ghuznee by the Caubul gate. Shah Soojah, before the contest was over, had ridden down to the point of attack, and watched the progress of events with the deepest interest, but with no apparent want of collectedness and nerve.* Keane and Macnaghten now led him up to the citadel. The wife of Hyder Khan, and the other women of his zenana, were conducted, under the orders of the political and military chiefs, by John Conolly, a cousin of the Envoy, to a house in the town, where they were placed under the charge of the Moonshee Mohun Lal.† But Hyder Khan himself had not yet been discovered. The Suddozye Prince and the British chiefs were inquiring after the commander of the garrison; but no tidings of him were to be obtained. He might have been concealed in the fortress, or he might have effected his escape. Accident only betrayed the position of the young Sirdar. He was found in a house near the Can-

soldiery to the fact, that no spirit rations had been served out to them during the preceding fortnight. "No candid man," he says, "of any military experience, will deny that the character of the scene, in the fortress and the citadel, would have been far different if individual soldiers had entered the town primed with arrack, or if spirituous liquors had been discovered in the Afghan depôts."

* I have been assured by an officer on the staff of the Shah's army, that he was near his Majesty at the taking of Ghuznee, when under fire, and that he exhibited great coolness and courage. He is said by my informant, who was close beside him, to have sate "as firm as a rock, not showing the slightest alarm either by word or gesture, and seeming to think it derogatory to his kingly character to move an inch whilst the firing lasted."—[*MS. Correspondence.*]

† Mohun Lal says: "Captain John Conolly conducted them, with every mark of deference, to a house in the town, where it fell to my lot to provide them with everything necessary which they wanted: and that responsible charge of them I had for a long time, and executed it to the satisfaction of the ladies, until they were sent to India."—[*Life of Dost Mahomed.*]

dahar gate, by an officer of the Company's European regiment.* At once acknowledging that he was the governor of Ghuznee, he threw himself upon the mercy of his captors. Conducted to Keane's tent, the Sirdar was guaranteed his personal safety, and placed under the charge of Sir Alexander Burnes † He was unwilling at first to appear in the presence of Shah Soojah, but the assurances of the Commander-in-Chief overcame his reluctance, and Keane conducted him both to the Mission and to the King Instructed as to the reception he was to accord to the fallen Barukzye chief, the Suddozye monarch received him with an outward show of kindness, and, with a dignified courtesy which he so well knew how to assume, declared that he forgave the past, and told him to go in peace.

And so Ghuznee fell to the British army, and was made over to the Suddozye King. It cost the victors only seventeen killed and a hundred and sixty-five wounded. Of these last eighteen were officers. The carnage among the garrison was most fearful Upwards of five hundred men were buried by the besiegers; and many more are supposed to have fallen beyond the walls, under the

* Captain Tayler, Brigade-Major of the 4th Brigade. Mohun Lal says that "Major Macgregor found him concealed with an armed party in the tower, waiting for the night." Mr. Stocqueler (*Memorials of Afghanistan*) attributes the honour of the capture to Brigadier Roberts, who directed Captain Tayler to proceed to the house

† "The Sirdar, mounted on a small horse, and accompanied by a few of his companions, was conducted by Major Macgregor to the tent of the Commander-in-Chief. Sir Alexander Burnes and myself were sent for, and as soon as the Sirdar saw him he felt a little easy in his mind; and discovering me with him, the expression of his countenance was at once changed, and he asked me for a glass of water. Lord Keane allowed him to remain in my tent, under the charge of Sir A. Burnes. I clothed him with my own clothes every day, and he partook of my meals."—[*Mohun Lal's Life of Dost Mahomed.*]

sabres of the British horsemen. Sixteen hundred prisoners were taken. Immense stores of grain and flour, sufficient for a protracted defence, fell into our hands; and a large number of horses and arms swelled the value of the captured property.

The fall of Ghuznee—a fortress hitherto deemed by the Afghans impregnable—astounded Dost Mahomed and his sons, and struck terror into their souls. Afzul Khan, who was hovering about the neighbourhood, prepared to fall upon our baffled army, found, to his wonderment, that the British colours were waving over the far-famed citadel of Ghuznee, and immediately sought safety in flight. Abandoning his elephants and the whole of his camp-equipage which fell as booty into the hands of Shah Soojah, the Sirdar fled to Caubul. His father, greatly incensed, ordered him immediately to halt, and "peremptorily refused to receive him."* He had expected something better from one who had done such good service on the boasted battle-field of Jumrood.

In little more than four-and-twenty hours after the fall of Ghuznee, intelligence of the event reached the camp of the Ameer. He at once assembled his chiefs, spoke of the defection of some of his people, expressed his apprehension that others were about to desert him, and declared his conviction that, without the aid of treachery, Ghuznee would not have fallen before the Feringhees. Then he called upon all present, who wavered in their loyalty, at once to withdraw from his presence, that he might know the extent of his resources, and not rely upon the false friendship of men who would forsake him in the crisis of his fate. All protested their fidelity. A council of war was held, and the Newab Jubbar Khan was despatched to the British camp† to treat with Shah Soojah and his allies.

* Outram.
† Whether this step was taken by Dost Mahomed on his own account,

The Newab mounted his horse and rode with unaccustomed rapidity to Ghuznee. Mohun Lal went out to meet him some miles beyond the camp; and Burnes received him at the piquets. A tent was pitched for his accommodation near the Envoy's; and he was well received by the British Mission. The King received him, too, with the same well-trained courtesy that he had bestowed on Hyder Khan—but the efforts of the Newab were fruitless. He tendered on the part of the Ameer submission to the Suddozye Prince; but claimed, on the part of the brother of Futteh Khan, the hereditary office of Wuzeer, which had been held so long and so ably by the Barukzyes. The claim was at once rejected, and the mockery of an "honourable asylum" in the British dominions offered in its stead. Jubbar Khan spoke out plainly and bluntly, like an honest man. His brother had no ambition to surrender his freedom and become a pensioner on the bounty of the British Government. Had his cause been far more hopeless than it was, Dost Mahomed, at that time, would have rather flung himself upon the British bayonets than upon the protection of the Feringhees. Jubbar Khan then frankly stating his own determination to follow the fortunes of his brother, requested and received his dismissal.*

or whether it was recommended or agreed to by his principal partisans, does not very clearly appear.

* Mohun Lal says that the Newab, who had acted with the greatest friendliness towards Burnes and his Mission, and was known to have been at the head of the English party in Caubul, begged that the wife of Hyder Khan might be given up to him; but preferred the request in vain. He sought an interview, too, with his nephew; and it would have been granted to him, but the official references caused delay, and the Newab took his departure without seeing the Sirdar. He said significantly to the Envoy, in the course of conversation, "If Shah Soojah is really a King, and come to the kingdom of his ancestors, what is the use of your army and name? You have brought him, by your money

The Newab returned to the Ameer's camp. All hope of negotiation was now at an end, and Dost Mahomed, with resolution worthy of a better fate, marched out to dispute the progress of the invaders. At the head of an army, in which the seeds of dissolution had already been sown, he moved down upon Urghundeh. There he drew up his troops and parked his guns. But it was not on this ground that he had determined to give the Feringhees battle. The last stand was to have been made at Maidan, on the Caubul river—a spot, the natural advantages of which would have been greatly in his favour. But the battle was never fought. At Urghundeh it became too manifest that there was treachery in his camp. The venal Kuzzilbashes were fast deserting his standard. There was scarcely a true man left in his ranks. Hadjee Khan Khaukur, on whom he had placed great reliance, had gone over to the enemy, and others were fast following his example. This was the crisis of his fate. He looked around him and saw only perfidy on the right hand and on the left. Equal to the occasion, but basely deserted, what could the Ameer do? Never had the nobility of his nature shone forth more truly and more lustrously. In the hour of adversity, when all were false, he was true to his own manhood. Into the midst of his own perfidious troops he rode, with the Koran in his hand; and there called upon his followers, in the names of God and the Prophet, not to forget that they were true Mahomedans —not to disgrace their names and to dishonour their religion, by rushing into the arms of one who had filled the country with infidels and blasphemers. He besought them to make one stand, like brave men and true believers; to rally round the standard of the commander

and arms, into Afghanistan. Leave him now with us Afghans, and let him rule us if he can."

of the faithful; to beat back the invading Feringhees or die in the glorious attempt. He then reminded them of his own claims on their fidelity. "You have eaten my salt," he said, "these thirteen years. If, as is too plain, you are resolved to seek a new master, grant me but one favour in requital for that long period of maintenance and kindness—enable me to die with honour. Stand by the brother of Futteh Khan, whilst he executes one last charge against the cavalry of these Feringhee dogs, in that onset he will fall; then go and make your own terms with Shah Soojah"* The noble spirit-stirring appeal was vainly uttered; few responded to it There was scarcely a true heart left With despairing eyes he looked around upon his recreant followers. He saw that there was no hope of winning them back to their old allegiance he felt that he was surrounded by traitors and cowards, who were willing to abandon him to his fate. It was idle to struggle against his destiny. The first bitter pang was over; he resumed his serenity of demeanour, and, addressing himself to the Kuzzilbashes, formally gave them their discharge. He then dismissed all who were inclined to purchase safety by tendering allegiance to the Shah; and with a small handful of followers, leaving his guns still in position, turned his horse's head towards the regions of the Hindoo-Koosh.†

* Havelock.

† General Harlan, who was at Caubul at this time, has written an account of the desertion of Dost Mahomed by his followers at Urghundeh, which only wants a conviction of its entire truth to render it extremely interesting. According to this writer, the Ameer was not only deserted, but plundered by his followers at the last. "A crowd of noisy disorganised troops," he says, "insolently pressed close up to the royal pavilion—the guards had disappeared—the groom holding the Prince's horse was unceremoniously pushed to and fro—a servant audaciously pulled away the pillow which sustained the Prince's arm—another commenced cutting a piece of the splendid Persian carpet—the

It was on the evening of the 2nd of August that Dost Mahomed fled from Urghundeh. On the following day the British army, which had moved from Ghuznee on the 30th of July, received tidings of his flight. It was now determined to send a party in pursuit. It was mainly to consist of Afghan horsemen; but some details from our cavalry regiments were sent with them, and Captain Outram, ever ready for such service, volunteered for the command. Other officers—bold riders and dashing soldiers [*]—were eager to join in the pursuit; and a party of ten, with about five hundred mounted men, mustered that afternoon before the Mission tents, equipped for the raid.

If the success of this expedition had depended upon the zeal and activity of the officers, Dost Mahomed would have been brought back a prisoner to the British camp; for never did a finer set of men leap into their saddles, flushed with the thought of the stirring work before them. But when they set out in pursuit of the fallen Ameer, a traitor rode with them, intent on turning to very nothingness all their chivalry and devotion. There was an Afghan chief known as Hadjee Khan Khaukur, of whom mention has been made. He was a man of mean extraction, the son of a goat-herd,[†] but from

---

beautiful praying rug of the Prince was seized on by a third. . . . . 'Take all,' said he, 'that you find within, together with the tent.' In an instant the unruly crowd rushed upon the pavilion—swords gleamed in the air and descended upon the tent—the canvas, the ropes, the carpets, pillows, screens, &c., were seized and dispersed among the plunderers."

[*] The names of many of them were subsequently associated with the later incidents of the war. They were Captains Wheler, Troup, Lawrence, Backhouse, Christie, and Erskine; Lieutenants Broadfoot, Hogg, Ryves, and Dr. Worral. Captains Tayler and Trevor joined them on the 8th.

[†] Outram says he was a melon-seller.

this low estate had risen into notice, and obtained service with Dost Mahomed. It was not in his nature to be faithful. He deserted Dost Mahomed, and attached himself to the Candahar Sirdars. On the advance of the British army he deserted the Sirdars, and flung himself at the feet of the Suddozye. Delighted with such an accession to his strength, the King appointed him Nassur-ood-dowlah, or "Defender of the State," and conferred on him a Jaghire of the annual value of three lakhs of rupees.

At Candahar, whence the Sirdars had fled, the Hadjee, profoundly conscious of the hopelessness of their cause, broke out into loyalty and enthusiasm, and was, to all outward seeming, a faithful adherent of the Shah. But as he entered the principality of the Caubul Ameer, he seemed to stand upon more uncertain ground; the issue of the contest was yet doubtful. Dost Mahomed and his sons were in the field. So the Hadjee made many excuses; and fell in the rear of the British army. He was sick; it was necessary that he should march easily; he could not bear the bustle of the camp. Keeping, therefore, a few marches in the rear, he followed our advancing columns, with his retainers; and there, it is said, "enjoyed the congenial society of several discontented and intriguing noblemen." *

* See the "Life of Hadjee Khan Khaukur, the Talleyrand of the East," published originally in the *Delhi Gazette*. It is attributed to the pen of Arthur Conolly. The writer adds: "In the camp of those chiefs conspiracies against Shah Soojah and his allies were daily agitated. Their letters formed the pride, the comfort, the hope, and the amusement of the Caubul Court. . . . . Sometimes it was proposed by the traitors to attack the English camp in concert with the Ghilzyes at night. Fear prevented this plot ripening; but had the army met with a repulse, it would undoubtedly have been attacked in rear. At last, at a full meeting—I have it from the lips of one present at it—it was determined to join Dost Mahomed *en masse*. At this meeting

If Ghuznee had not fallen, Hadjee Khan and his friends would have gone over in a body to the Ameer, and on the slightest information of a reverse having befallen us, would have flung themselves on our rear. But the fall of this great Afghan stronghold brought the Hadjee again to the stirrup of the Shah ; and he was again all loyalty and devotion. Confident of his fidelity, and perhaps anxious to establish it in the eyes of all who had viewed with suspicion the proceedings of the Hadjee, the King now put it to the proof. The man had once been Governor of Bameean. He knew the country along which the Ameer had taken his flight. What could be better than to entrust the conduct of the expedition to the veteran chief? The King and Macnaghten were of the same mind ; so Hadjee Khan, who had been for some time in treasonable correspondence with Dost Mahomed, was now despatched to overtake him and bring him back a prisoner to the camp of the Shah.

The result may be easily anticipated. Hadjee Khan cheerfully undertook the duty entrusted to him. The enterprise required the utmost possible amount of energy and promptitude to secure its success. The Ameer and his party were more than a day's journey in advance of his pursuers. Every hour's delay lessened the chance of overtaking the fugitive. So the Hadjee began at once to delay. The pursuers were to have started four hours after noon ; Hadjee Khan was not ready till night-fall. Then he was eager to take the circuitous high road

---

were the Hadjee Khan, Hadjee Dost, Fyztullub Khan, Noorzye, and many others. They had been deceived by a false report of a partial action of cavalry the day before ; the opportunity had arrived, they thought, for giving us the *coup de grace*. Hardly had the conclave separated, when intelligence was received of the capture of Ghuznee. It need hardly be said that, a few hours afterwards, Hadjee Khan and the rest were congratulating his Majesty on the splendid victory."

instead of dashing across the hills. His people lagge
behind to plunder. He himself, when Outram was mo
eager to push on, always counselled a halt, and in tl
hour of need the guides deserted. The Ameer was no
but little in advance; he was encumbered with wome
and children, and much baggage. He had a sick son
on whose account it was necessary to diminish the spec
of his flight. Outram seemed almost to have the Amer
in his grasp; when Hadjee Khan again counselled dela
It was necessary, he said, to wait for reinforcements. Tl
Ameer had two thousand fighting men. The Afghar
under Hadjee Khan were not to be relied upon. The
had no food: their horses were knocked up; they wer
unwilling to advance. Angry and indignant, Outrar
broke from the Hadjee in the midst of his entreaties, an
declared that he would push on with his own men. Agai
and again there was the same contention between th
chivalrous earnestness of the British officer and the fou
treachery of the Afghan chief. At last, on the 9th (
August, they reached Bameean, where Hadjee Khan ha
repeatedly declared that Dost Mahomed would halt, onl
to learn that the fugitives were that morning to be a
Syghan, nearly thirty miles in advance. The Ameer wa
pushing on with increased rapidity, for the sick Prince
who had been carried in a litter, was now transferre
to the back of an elephant, and his escape was no
almost certain. The treachery of Hadjee Khan ha
done its work. Outram had been restricted in hi
operations to the limits of the Shah's dominions; an
the Ameer had now passed the borders. Furthe
pursuit, indeed, would have been hopeless. The horse

* Akbar Khan, who had by this time been withdrawn from the de
fence of the Khybur line, and had joined his father's camp prostrate
by sickness.

of our cavalry were exhausted by over-fatigue and want of food. They were unable any longer to continue their forced marches. The game, therefore, was up. Dost Mahomed had escaped. Hadjee Khan Khaukur had saved the Ameer; but he had sacrificed himself. He had over-reached himself in his career of treachery, and was now to pay the penalty of detection. Outram officially reported the circumstances of the Hadjee's conduct, which had baffled all his best efforts—efforts which, he believed, would have been crowned with success*—and the traitor, on his return to Caubul, was arrested by orders of the Shah. Other proofs of his treason were readily found; and he was sentenced to end a life of adventurous vicissitude as a state prisoner in the provinces of Hindostan.†

So fled Dost Mahomed Khan across the frontier of Afghanistan. His guns were found in position at Urghundeh by a party of cavalry and horse artillery sent forward to capture them. They were mostly light pieces;‡

* Others, however, thought that his failure was fortunate, it being only too probable, in their opinion, that, if he had come up with the fugitive, his little party would have been overwhelmed by the followers of the Ameers and the traitorous Afghan horsemen whom Hadjee Khan had taken with him.

† He was confined at Chunar, where he seems to have borne his imprisonment with considerable philosophy.

‡ "With regard to the ordnance captured at Urghundeh, the guns were of all calibres, chiefly below 6-pounder—one a 17-pounder, and a few of different sizes, between 17 and 12-pounders. . . . . The number of shot left at Urghundeh was 4270, of various sizes. . . . . The shot is hammered iron, and so uneven, that, unless weighed, their weight could not be told. They are chiefly much under 6-pounder shot. . . . . With regard to the other stores taken at Urghundeh, nothing was of the slightest service, except the old iron of the carriages, and the axle-trees, also good as old iron only, and to which purpose they have been appropriated."—[*Lieutenant Warburton to Sir W. H. Macnaghten; Caubul, August* 15, 1841. *MS. Records.*]

and neither the ordnance nor the position which ha been taken up, could be considered of a very fo midable character.* It has been already said, howeve that the Ameer had fixed upon another spot on whic to meet the advancing armies of the Shah and his allie —a spot well calculated for defence, which, three yea afterwards, Shumshoodeen Khan selected for his last stan against the battalions of General Nott; but on whicl like his distinguished clansman, he never gave us battle.

On the 6th of August, Shah Soojah and the Britis army appeared before the walls of Caubul. On the fo lowing day the King entered the capital of Afghanistar The exile of thirty years—the baffled and rejected repre sentative of the legitimacy of the Dourance Empire, wa now at the palace gates. The jingling of the money bags, and the gleaming of the bayonets of the British, ha restored him to the throne which, without these glittei ing aids, he had in vain striven to recover. The Ball Hissar of Caubul now reared its proud front before him It was truly a great occasion The King, gorgeous i regal apparel, and resplendent with jewels, rode a whit charger, whose equipments sparkled with Asiatic gold

---

* "Onward," says Captain Havelock, "moved the force, and a hour had not elapsed since the day broke when it came full upon tl abandoned ordnance of the fallen Barukzye Twenty-two pieces ‹ various calibre, but generally good guns, on field carriages, superior 1 those generally seen in the armies of Asiatic Princes, were parked in circle in the Ameer's late position. Two more were placed in battei in the village of Urghundeh, at the foot of the hills . . . The rou1 by which we had advanced was flanked by a deep, impracticab ravine, on which the Afghan left would have rested there the artillery had been parked, and would probably from this point hav swept the open plain, and searched the narrow defile by which w would have debouched upon. Their front was open for the exertions ‹ a bold and active cavalry, and here the Ameer might at least hav died with honour."

† Havelock.

It was a goodly sight to see the coronet, the girdle, and the bracelets which scintillated upon the person of the rider, and turned the fugitive and the outcast into a pageant and a show. There were those present to whom the absence of the *Koh-i-noor*, which, caged in Hyde Park, has since become so familiar to the sight-seers of Great Britain, suggested strange reminiscences of the King's eventful career. But the restored monarch, wanting the great diamond, still sparkled into royalty as he rode up to the Balla Hissar, with the white-faced Kings of Afghanistan beside him. In diplomatic costume, Macnaghten and Burnes accompanied the Suddozye puppet. The principal military officers of the British army rode with them. And Moonshee Mohun Lal, flaunting a majestic turban, and looking, in his spruceness, not at all as though his mission in Afghanistan were to do the dirty work of the British diplomatists, made a very conspicuous figure in the gay cavalcade.*

But never was there a duller procession. The King and his European supporters rode through the streets of Caubul to the palace in the citadel; but as they went there was no popular enthusiasm; the voice of welcome was still. The inhabitants came to the thresholds of the houses simply to look at the show. They stared at the European strangers more than at the King, who had been brought back to Caubul by the Feringhees; and scarcely

* I am indebted for this, as for much else, to Captain Havelock. There is but little in the pages of the military analist to disturb the gravity of the historical inquirer, but it is impossible to restrain a smile at the happy wording of the following: "Let me not forget to record that Moonshee Mohun Lal, a traveller and an author, as well as his talented master, appeared on horseback on this occasion in a new upper garment of a very gay colour, and under a turban of very admirable fold and majestic dimensions, and was one of the gayest as well as the most sagacious and successful personages in the whole *cortége*."

even took the trouble to greet the Suddozye Prince with a common salaam. It was more like a funeral procession than the entry of a King into the capital of his restored dominions. But when Shah Soojah reached the palace from which he had so long been absent, he broke out into a paroxysm of childish delight—visited the gardens and apartments with eager activity—commented on the signs of neglect which everywhere presented themselves to his eyes—and received with feelings of genial pleasure the congratulations of the British officers, who soon left his Majesty to himself to enjoy the sweets of restored dominion.

The restoration of Shah Soojah-ool Moolk to the sovereignty of Afghanistan had thus been outwardly accomplished. The Barukzye Sirdars had been expelled from their principalities; a British garrison had been planted in Candahar and in Ghuznee; and a British army was now encamping under the walls of Caubul. A great revolution had thus been perfected. The Douranee monarchy had been restored. The objects contemplated in the Simlah manifesto had been seemingly accomplished, and the originators of the policy which had sent our armies thus to triumph in Afghanistan shouted with exultation as they looked upon their first great blaze of success.

APPENDIX.

[Vol. I., page 70.]

Preliminary Treaty with Persia, concluded by Sir Harford Jones on the 12th of March, 1809.

In the Name of Him who is ever necessary, who is all-sufficient, who is everlasting, and who is the only Protector.

IN these times distinguished by felicity, the excellent Ambassador, Sir Harford Jones, Baronet, Member of the Honourable Imperial Ottoman Order of the Crescent, has arrived at the Royal City of Teheran, in quality of Ambassador from His Majesty the King of England (titles), bearing His Majesty's credential letter, and charged with full powers munited with the great seal of England, empowering him to strengthen the friendship and consolidate the strict union subsisting between the high states of England and Persia. His Majesty the King of Persia (titles) therefore, by a special firmaun delivered to the said Ambassador, has appointed the most excellent and noble Lords Meerza Mahomed Sheffeeh, qualified with the title of Moatumed-ed-Dowlah, his First Vizier, and Hajee Mahomed Hoossein Khan, qualified with the title of Ameen-ed-Dowlah, one of the Ministers of Record, ι be his Plenipotentiaries to confer and discuss with the aforesaid Ambassador of His Britannic Majesty, all matters and affairs touching the formation and consolidation of friendship, alliance, and strict union between the two high states, and to arrange and finally conclude the same for the benefit and advantage of both Kingdoms. In consequence whereof, after divers meetings and discussions, the aforesaid

Plenipotentiaries have resolved that the following Articles are for the benefit and advantage of both the high states, and are hereafter to be accordingly for ever observed:

ART. I.—That as some time will be required to arrange and form a definitive treaty of alliance and friendship between the two high states, and as the circumstances of the world make it necessary for something to be done without loss of time, it is agreed these Articles, which are to be regarded as preliminary, shall become a basis for establishing a sincere and everlasting definitive treaty of strict friendship and union; and it is agreed that the said definitive treaty, precisely expressing the wishes and obligations of each party, shall be signed and sealed by the said Plenipotentiaries, and afterwards become binding on both the high contracting parties.

II. It is agreed that the preliminary articles, formed with the hand of truth and sincerity, shall not be changed or altered, but there shall arise from them a daily increase of friendship, which shall last for ever between the two most serene Kings, their heirs, successors, their subjects, and their respective kingdoms, dominions, provinces, and countries.

III. His Majesty the King of Persia judges it necessary to declare that from the date of these preliminary articles, every treaty or agreement he may have made with any one of the powers of Europe, becomes null and void, and that he will not permit any European force whatever to pass through Persia, either towards India, or towards the ports of that country.

IV. In case any European forces have invaded, or shall invade, the territories of His Majesty the King of Persia, His Britannic Majesty will afford to His Majesty the King of Persia, a force, or, in lieu of it, a subsidy with warlike ammunition, such as guns, muskets, &c., and officers, to the amount that may be to the advantage of both parties, for the expulsion of the force so invading; and the number of these forces, or the amount of the subsidy, ammunition, &c., shall be hereafter regulated in the definitive treaty. In case His Majesty the King of England should make peace with such European power, His Britannic Majesty shall use his utmost endeavours to negotiate and procure a peace between His Persian Majesty and such power. But if (which God forbid) His Britannic Majesty's efforts for this purpose should fail of success, then the forces or subsidy, according to the amount mentioned in the definitive treaty, shall still continue in the service of the King of Persia as long as the said European forces shall remain in the territories of His Persian Majesty, or until peace is concluded between His Persian Majesty and the said European power. And it is further agreed, that in case the dominions of His Britannic Majesty in India are attacked or invaded by the Afghans or any other power, His Majesty the King of Persia shall afford a force for the protection of the said dominions, according to the stipulations contained in the definitive treaty.

V If a detachment of British troops has arrived from India in the Gulf of Persia, and by the consent of His Persian Majesty landed on the Island of Karrak, or at any of the Persian ports, they shall not in any manner possess themselves of such places ; and, from the date of these preliminary articles, the said detachment shall be at the disposal of His Majesty the King of Persia, except his Excellency the Governor-General of India judges such detachment necessary for the defence of India, in which case they shall be returned to India, and a subsidy, in lieu of the personal services of these troops, shall be paid to His Majesty the King of Persia, the amount of which shall be settled in the definitive treaty

VI. But if the said troops remain, by the desire of His Majesty the King of Persia, either at Karrak, or any other port in the Gulf of Persia, they shall be treated by the Governor there in the most friendly manner, and orders shall be given to all the Governors of Farsistan, that whatever quantity of provisions, &c., may be necessary, shall, on being paid for, be furnished to the said troops at the fair prices of the day.

VII. In case war takes place between His Persian Majesty and the Afghans, His Majesty the King of Great Britain shall not take any part therein, unless it be at the desire of both parties, to afford his mediation for peace.

VIII. It is acknowledged the intent and meaning of these preliminary articles are defensive. And it is likewise agreed, that as long as these preliminary articles remain in force,

His Majesty the King of Persia shall not enter into any engagements inimical to His Britannic Majesty, or pregnant with injury or disadvantage to the British territories in India.

This treaty is concluded by both parties, in the hope of its being everlasting, and that it may be productive of the most beautiful fruits of friendship between the two most serene Kings.

> In witness whereof we, the said Plenipotentiaries, have hereunto set our hands and seals in the Royal City of Teheran, this twelfth day of March, in the year of our Lord one thousand eight hundred and nine, answering to the twenty-fifth of Mohurrum el Haram, in the year of the Hegira one thousand two hundred and twenty-four.   (L.S.)   HARFORD JONES.
>   (L.S.)   MAHOMED SHEFFEEH.
>   (L.S.)   MAHOMED HOOSSEIN.

[Vol. I., page 85.]

Treaty with Runjeet Singh, the Rajah of Lahore, dated 25th April, 1809.

WHEREAS certain differences which had arisen between the British Government and the Rajah of Lahore, have been happily and amicably adjusted, and both parties being anxious to maintain the relations of perfect amity and concord, the following articles of treaty, which shall be binding on the heirs and successors of the two parties, have been concluded by Rajah Runjeet Singh on his own part, and by the agency of Charles Theophilus Metcalfe, Esquire, on the part of the British Government:

ART. I. Perpetual friendship shall subsist between the British Government and the State of Lahore. The latter shall be considered, with respect to the former, to be on the footing of the most favoured powers; and the British Government will have no concern with the territories and subjects of the Rajah to the northward of the river Sutlej.

II. The Rajah will never maintain, in the territory occupied by him and his dependents on the left bank of the river Sutlej, more troops than are necessary for the internal duties of that territory, nor commit, or suffer, any encroachment on the possessions or rights of the chiefs in its vicinity.

III. In the event of a violation of any of the preceding articles, or of a departure from the rules of friendship, on the part of either state, this treaty shall be considered null and void.

IV. This treaty, consisting of four articles, having been settled and concluded at Umritser, on the 25th day of April, 1809, Mr. Charles Theophilus Metcalfe has delivered to the Rajah of Lahore a copy of the same in English and Persian, under his seal and signature; and the said Rajah has delivered another copy of the same under his seal and signature; and Mr. Charles Theophilus Metcalfe engages to procure, within the space of two months, a copy of the same, duly ratified by the Right Honourable the Governor-General in Council, on the receipt of which by the Rajah, the present treaty shall be deemed complete and binding on both parties, and the copy of it now delivered to the Rajah shall be restored.

[Vol. I., page 92.]

Treaty with the King of Caubul, dated 17th June, 1809.

WHEREAS in consequence of the confederacy with the state of Persia, projected by the French for the purpose of invading the dominions of His Majesty the King of the Douranees, and ultimately, those of the British Government in India, the Honourable Mountstuart Elphinstone was despatched to the Court of His Majesty, in quality of Envoy Plenipotentiary, on the part of the Right Honourable Lord Minto, Governor-General, exercising the supreme authority over all affairs, civil, political, and military, in the British possessions in the East Indies, for the purpose of concerting with His Majesty's Ministers the means of mutual defence against the expected invasion of the French and Persians; and whereas the said Ambassador having had the honour of being presented to His Majesty, and of explaining the friendly and beneficial object of his mission, His Majesty, sensible of the advantages of alliance and co-operation between the two states, for the purpose above described, directed his Ministers to confer with the Honourable Mountstuart Elphinstone, and, consulting the welfare of both states, to conclude a friendly alliance; and certain articles of treaty having accordingly been agreed to between His Majesty's Ministers and the British Ambassador, and confirmed by the Royal Signet, a copy of the treaty so framed has been transmitted by the Ambassador for the ratification of the Governor-General, who, consenting to the stipulations therein contained without variation, a copy of these articles, as hereunder written, is now returned, duly ratified by the seal and signature of the Governor-General, and the signatures of the members of the British Government in India. And the obligations upon both governments, both now and for ever, shall be exclusively regulated and determined by the tenor of those Articles which are as follow:

ART. I. As the French and Persians have entered into a confederacy against the state of Caubul, if they should wish to pass through the King's dominions, the servants of the heavenly throne shall prevent their passage, and exerting themselves to the extent of their power in making war on them and repelling them, shall not permit them to cross into British India.

II. If the French and Persians, in pursuance of their confederacy, should advance towards the King of Caubul's country in a hostile manner, the British state, endeavouring heartily to repel them, shall hold themselves liable to afford the expenses necessary for the above-mentioned service, to the extent of their ability. While the confederacy between the French and Persians continues in force, these articles shall be in force, and be acted on by both parties.

III. Friendship and union shall continue for ever between these two states. The veil of separation shall be lifted up from between them, and they shall in no manner interfere in each other's countries ; and the King of Caubul shall permit no individual of the French to enter his territories.

The faithful servants of both states having agreed to this treaty, the conditions of confirmation and ratification have been performed, and this document has been sealed and signed by the Right Honourable the Governor-General and the Honourable the Members of the Supreme British Government in India, this 17th day of June, 1809, answering to the 1224 of the Hegira.

[Vol. I., p. 96.]

Treaty with the Ameers of Sindh, dated 22nd August, 1809.

ART I. THERE shall be eternal friendship between the British Government and that of Sindh, namely, Meer Gholam Alee, Meer Kurreem Alee, and Meer Murad Alee.

II. Enmity shall never appear between the two states

III. The mutual despatch of the Vakeels of both Governments, namely, the British Government and Sindhian Government, shall always continue.

IV. The Government of Sindh will not allow the establishment of the tribe of the French in Sindh.

Written on the 10th of the month of Rujeeb-ool-Moorujub, in the year of the Hegira, 1224, corresponding with the 22nd of August, 1809.

[Vol. I., p. 144.]

Definitive Treaty with Persia, concluded at Teheran, by Messrs. Morier and Ellis, on the 25th November, 1814.

PRAISE be to God, the all-perfect and all-sufficient

These happy leaves are a nosegay plucked from the thornless Garden of Concord, and tied by the hands of the Plenipotentiaries of the two great states in the form of a definitive treaty, in which the articles of friendship and amity are blended.

Previously to this period, the high in station, Sir Harford Jones, Baronet, Envoy Extraordinary from the English Government, came to this Court, to form an amicable alliance, and in conjunction with the Plenipotentiaries of Persia, their Excellencies (titles) Meerza Mahomed Sheffeeh and Hajee Mahomed Hussein Khan, concluded a preliminary treaty, the particulars of which were to be detailed and arranged in a definitive treaty; and the above-mentioned treaty, according to its articles, was ratified by the British Government.

Afterwards, when His Excellency Sir Gore Ouseley, Ambassador Extraordinary from His Britannic Majesty, arrived at this exalted and illustrious Court, for the purpose of completing the relations of amity between the two states, and was invested with full powers by his own government to arrange all the important affairs of friendship, the ministers of this victorious state, with the advice and approbation of the above-mentioned Ambassador, concluded a definitive treaty, consisting of fixed articles and stipulations.

That treaty having been submitted to the British Government, certain changes in its articles and provisions, consistent with friendship, appeared necessary, and Henry Ellis, Esquire, was accordingly despatched to this court, in charge of a letter explanatory of the above-mentioned alterations. Therefore, their Excellencies Meerza Mahomed Sheffeeh, Prime Minister, Meerza Bozoork, Caimacan (titles), and Meerza Abdul Wahab, Principal Secretary of State (titles), were duly appointed, and invested with full powers to negotiate with the Plenipotentiaries of His Britannic Majesty, James Morier, Esquire, recently appointed minister at this court, and the above-mentioned Henry Ellis, Esquire. These Plenipotentiaries having consulted on the terms most advisable for this alliance, have comprised them in eleven articles. What relates to commerce, trade, and other affairs, will be drawn up and concluded in a separate commercial treaty.

Art. I. The Persian Government judge it incumbent on them, after the conclusion of this definitive treaty, to declare all alliances contracted with European nations in a state of hostility with Great Britain, null and void, and hold themselves bound not to allow any European army to enter the Persian territory, nor to proceed towards India, nor to any of the ports of that country ; and also engage not to allow any individuals of such European nations, entertaining a design of invading India, or being at enmity with Great Britain, whatever, to enter Persia. Should any European powers wish to invade India by the road of Kharazm, Tartaristan, Bokhara, Samarcand, or other routes, His Persian Majesty engages to induce the Kings and Governors of those countries to oppose such invasion, as much as is in his power, either by the fear of his arms, or by conciliatory measures.

II. It is agreed, that these articles, formed with the hand of truth and sincerity, shall not be changed or altered ; but, there shall arise from them a daily increase of friendship, which shall last for ever between the two most serene Kings, their heirs, successors, their subjects and their respective kingdoms, dominions, provinces, and countries. And His Britannic Majesty further engages not to interfere in any dispute which may hereafter arise between the princes, noblemen, and great chiefs of Persia; and if one of the contending parties should even offer a province of Persia, with view of obtaining assistance, the English Government shall not agree to such a proposal, nor by adopting it, possess themselves of such part of Persia.

III. The purpose of this treaty is strictly defensive, and the object is that from their mutual assistance both states should derive stability and strength; and this treaty has only been concluded for the purpose of repelling the aggressions of enemies ; and the purport of the word aggression in this treaty is, an attack upon the territories of another state. The limits of the territory of the two states of Russia and Persia shall be determined according to the admission of Great Britain, Persia, and Russia.

IV. It having been agreed by an article in the preliminary treaty concluded between the high contracting parties, that in case of any European nation invading Persia, should the Persian Government require the assistance of the English, the Governor-General of India, on the part of Great Britain, shall comply with the wish of the Persian Government, by sending from India the force required, with officers, ammunition, and warlike stores, or, in lieu thereof, the English Government shall pay an annual subsidy, the amount of which shall be regulated in a definitive treaty to be concluded between the high contracting parties; it is hereby provided, that the amount of the said subsidy shall be two hundred thousand (200,000) tomauns annually. It is further agreed, that the said subsidy shall not be paid in case the war with such European nation shall have been produced by an aggression on the part of Persia; and since the payment of the above subsidy will be made solely for the purpose of raising and disciplining an army, it is agreed that the English minister shall be satisfied of its being duly applied to the purpose for which it is assigned.

V. Should the Persian Government wish to introduce European discipline among their troops, they are at liberty to employ European officers for that purpose, provided the said officers do not belong to nations in a state of war or enmity with Great Britain.

VI. Should any European power be engaged in war with Persia when at peace with England, His Britannic Majesty engages to use his best endeavours to bring Persia and such European power to a friendly understanding. If, however, His Majesty's cordial interference should fail of success, England shall still, if required, in conformity with the stipulations in the preceding articles, send a force from India, or, in lieu thereof, pay an annual subsidy of two hundred thousand (200,000) tomauns for the support of a Persian army, so long as a war in the supposed case shall continue, and until Persia shall make peace with such nation.

VII. Since it is the custom of Persia to pay the troops six months in advance, the English minister at that court shall do all in his power to pay the subsidy in as early instalments as may be convenient.

VIII. Should the Afghans be at war with the British nation, His Persian Majesty engages to send an army against them in such manner and of such force as may be concerted with the English Government. The expenses of such an army shall be defrayed by the British Government, in such manner as may be agreed upon at the period of its being required

IX. If war should be declared between the Afghans and Persians, the English Government shall not interfere with either party, unless their mediation to effect a peace shall be solicited by both parties.

X. Should any Persian subject of distinction, showing signs of hostility and rebellion, take refuge in the British dominions, the English Government shall, on intimation from the Persian Government, turn him out of their country, or, if he refuse to leave it, shall seize and send him to Persia.

Previously to the arrival of such fugitive in the English territory, should the governor of the district to which he may direct his flight receive intelligence of the wishes of the Persian Government respecting him, he shall refuse him admission. After such prohibition, should such person persist in his resolution, the said governor shall cause him to be seized and sent to Persia ; it being understood that the aforesaid obligations are reciprocal between the contracting parties

XI Should His Persian Majesty require assistance from the English Government in the Persian Gulf, they shall, if convenient and practicable, assist him with ships of war and troops. The expenses of such expedition shall be accounted for and defrayed by the Persian Government, and the above ships shall anchor in such ports as shall be pointed out by the Persian Government, and not enter other harbours without permission, except from absolute necessity.

The articles are thus auspiciously concluded :

A definitive treaty between the two states having formerly been prepared, consisting of twelve articles, and certain changes, not inconsistent with friendship, having appeared necessary, we the Plenipotentiaries of the two states comprising the said treaty in eleven articles, have hereunto set our hands and seals, in the royal city of Teheran, this twenty-fifth day of November, in the year of our Lord one thousand eight hundred and fourteen, corresponding with the twelfth Zealhajeh, in the year of the Hegira one thousand two hundred and twenty-nine.

   (L.S.) JAMES MORIER.
   (L.S.) HENRY ELLIS.
   (L.S.) MAHOMED SHEFFEEH.
   (L.S.) ABDUL WAHAB.
   (L.S.) ISAH (MEERZA BOZOORK).

[Vol. I., page 153.]

Bonds given by Abbas Meerza, Prince Royal of Persia, and by the Shah, cancelling the Subsidy Articles of the Treaty of 25th November, 1814.

Bond granted by Abbas Meerza, Prince Royal of Persia, to Lieutenant-Colonel Macdonald, British Envoy.

Be it known to Colonel Macdonald, British envoy at our Court, that we, the heir apparent to the Persian throne, in virtue of the full powers vested in us by the Shah, in all matters touching the foreign relations of this kingdom, do hereby pledge our solemn word and promise, that if the British Government will assist us with the sum of two hundred thousand tomauns (200,000), towards the liquidation of the indemnity due by us to Russia, we will expunge, and hereafter consider as annulled, the IIIrd and IVth articles of the definitive treaty, between the two states, concluded by Mr. Ellis, and obtain the royal sanction to the same.

This paper bears the seal of His Royal Highness Abbas Meerza, and that of His Persian Majesty's Minister, the Kaim-Mukam.

Dated in the month of Shaban, or March, 1828.

Ruckum of His Royal Highness the Heir Apparent, in ratification of the Annulment of the IIIrd and IVth Articles of the Treaty with England.

Relative to the articles III. and IV. of the propitious treaty between England and Persia, which was concluded by Mr. Ellis, in the month Zekaud, A.H. 1229, agreeably to the engagements entered into with your Excellency, that, in consequence of the sum of 200,000 tomauns, the currency of the country, presented as an aid to Persia, in consideration of the losses she has sustained in the war with Russia, we, the heir apparent, vested with full powers in all matters connected with the politics of this nation, have agreed that the said two articles shall be expunged, and have delivered a bond to your Excellency, which is now in your hands.

In the month of Zikeyla, A.H. 1243, on our going to wait upon His Majesty at Teheran, in consistence with the note addressed to your Excellency by Meerza Abul Hassan Khan, the Minister for Foreign Affairs, we were appointed sole agent in this matter by His Majesty, with unlimited authority; therefore, as the Government of England, through the medium of Colonel Macdonald, have afforded us the assistance of 200,000 tomauns, we, the representative of His Majesty, have, on this day, the 14th of the month Suffer, and the 24th of the Christian month August, annulled the two obnoxious articles of our propitious treaty. The envoy, considering this document as a ratification on the subject of the two articles, will know that it is liable to no further comment from the ministers of His Majesty's Court.

Sealed by
Month of Suffer, A.H. 1244.   H.R.H. ABBAS MEERZA.

Firmaun from His Majesty the Shah to Colonel Macdonald, British Envoy in Persia.

A.C.

Let it be known to Colonel Macdonald, the English envoy, exalted by our munificence, that our noble son having represented to us his having recently come to an arrangement relative to the two articles of the treaty with England, we have ordered that what has been executed by our son, touching this transaction, in conformity with the firmaun of full powers granted to him by us, be confirmed by our royal ratification and consent; and we duly appreciate the exertions of your Excellency during the last year, which have obtained you the goodwill of the Shah.

Regarding the crore of tomauns required for the redemption of Khoee, agreeably to what has been laid before us, H.R.H. Abbas Meerza has directed the payment of 400,000 tomauns by Mohamed Meerza; and we have besides instructed the remaining 100,000 tomauns to be delivered to Meerza Abul Hassan Khan, Minister for Foreign Affairs, for the purpose of being transmitted to you.

Your Excellency will, therefore, conceiving this firmaun as your security, become responsible for the payment of the above sum, which will be afterwards paid to you by the lord of exalted rank, Meerza Abul Hassan Khan. Also make known to us all your wishes.

Sealed by
HIS MAJESTY FUTTEH ALEE SHAH.

[Vol. I., page 352.]

[The following is the passage, from Mr. Henry Torrens' letters to the "Friend of India," cited by his biographer, (Mr. James Hume), and referred to in a note to the above page.]

"On the sound historical basis of 'general opinion' and 'well credited report' you do me the honour of ascribing to me the creation of a policy which was a sound and wise one, *had it been carried out as devised*, and of which I only wish I could claim the authorship; but you will perhaps allow me to cite against 'general opinion' and 'well credited report,' the assurance of a late Cabinet Minister, Lord de Broughton, that *he* was the author of the expedition, the which he undoubtedly was. Without this declaration publicly made, I could not state what follows.

"The facts now related for the first time are simply these. Mr. Macnaghten, with me for his under Secretary, most unwillingly accompanied the Governor-General in 1837 towards the North-West, in which his presence was not required. Mr. Macnaghten, in the conviction that with the peculiar turn of mind of the Governor-General, it were better for him to be with his Council, did his utmost to persuade his Lordship to return from Cawnpore to Calcutta, the rather that it was the famine year of 1837-38. Orders were at once given for our return, but countermanded. Before our arrival at Cawnpore, Mr Macnaghten, pressed by his Lordship's anxiety and uncertainties, had prepared a scheme, based upon the independent expedition of Shah Soojah in 1832—of which we often spoke together, with reference to the stormy aspect of the times,—which contained the germ of the famous Afghan expedition ; the scope of this scheme was · 1. According to the policy of this Government in 1809, to interpose a friendly power in Central Asia between us and any invasive force from the West. 2 To exhibit the military resources of the Government which had experienced a dangerous decline in a native estimation. 3. To set at rest the frontier wars between Afghans and Sikhs which interfered with the extension of our trade. 4. To effect these objects by means of our pensioner, Shah Soojah, acting in concert with Runjeet Singh ; settling through our mediation the claims of the latter on Scinde, and of the former on Cashmere and Peshawur ; satisfying Runjeet as to his demand for Swat and Booneer, and purchasing from the Ameers of Scinde, by relieving them of tribute and vassalage to the Douranee Crown (Shah Soojah's), the complete opening of the Indus navigation, and the abolition of all tolls. 5. To establish in the person of a subsidized Monarch in Afghanistan so firm an ally at the head of a military people as might assure us that, in the event of Runjeet's death, the Sikhs would find occupation on the frontiers of Peshawur, for so large a portion of their army as might materially interfere with the assemblage of an imposing force on our own frontier. 6. To pass into Afghanistan, as Shah Soojah had done in 1832, by the Bolan Pass, place him on his throne, subsidized at twenty lakhs a year, and march home through the Punjab, showing our power.

" Such was the project submitted, rather to propose *something* to the Governor-General in his uncertainty, than to suggest a plan for absolute adoption. A few days afterwards, Mr. Macnaghten told me, that his Lordship had peremptorily rejected it, saying, " *such a thing was not to be thought of.*"

Some fortnight or three weeks afterwards, letters arrived, I believe from Her Majesty's Ministers in England, suggesting various schemes of diversion in the East as respected the aggressive views of Persia in connection with a great European power;—one, I believe, was analagous to that suggested by Mr. Macnaghten, and it was then Lord Auckland asked for the paper which had been previously submitted to him. I never saw it again after that time; but on it was framed a scheme in consonance with the views of Her Majesty' Ministers *which was approved by them and acted on;* but which only contemplated the expedition to, not the occupation of, Afghanistan, and it was the change of policy which fathered our disasters. My duties, which as under and officiating Secretary were purely executive, brought me subsequently much into official contact with the Governor-General, but not until after the policy had been decided upon as respected Afghanistan, and so thoroughly decided, that Mr. Macnaghten was ascending the hill with the tripartite treaty in his pocket, at the time when 'well credited report' represents 'some body'—myself—as rushing down the hill *to tell him of the adoption during his absence, of the policy on which the treaty in his pocket was founded!* I well recollect the subsequent discussions and difficulties as to execution, and in these Clerk, Wade, Colvin, Mackeson, Burnes, D'Arcy Todd, Lord, and others had a share. Of those curious councils it does not behove me to speak—save that previous to one I remember poor Burnes making his fifth suggestion within the week, to the effect that 'we had but to send Shah Soojah to the mouth of the Khyber Pass with two battalions of Sepoys, and the Afghans would carry him through it in their arms,'* when I recollect saying with some asperity—'surely it is better not to confuse high authority with fresh plans, when all our energies are needed to carry out the one decided upon.' As you have honoured me with the title of adviser of Lord Auckland, and given me the opportunity of divesting my-

---

* Burnes was of this opinion: he erred on that point in common with many others; but his views from first to last were in favour of making the Dost our ally.—H.T.

self of the unreal credit or discredit, as you may decide i
to be, before the expedition was decided upon, I will i
justice to myself record with you, two of the few opinions
ever had the opportunity of delivering *after* it began ; th
one was strongly against the fortification of Herat, the othe
strongly against the admission of English women of an
rank into Afghanistan, for giving each of which I wa
strongly reprimanded, and from this anecdote I leave you t
conclude the slight amount of my utility out of my stric
line of duty."

[If there is anything in this at variance with the state
ments in my narrative, the reader will now have an oppor
tunity of comparing the one with the other, and formin
his own judgment. It is necessary only to observe tha
there are two distinct questions to be considered, and tha
it rather appears that Mr. Torrens has evaded the mor
important one, and the one, too, with which he is mor
immediately concerned. The scheme of the tripartit
treaty is one thing, the march of a British army on Caubu
by way of the Bolan Pass is another. Mr. Torrens appeal
triumphantly to the fact that at a time when he and other
are represented (by Mr. Masson) as rushing down the hill t
tell Mr. Macnaghten of the adoption of the policy of th
war, he (Mr. Macnaghten) was ascending the hill with th
treaty in his pocket founded on that policy. But, in th
first place, the story to which Mr. Torrens refers (and whic
will be found in a note at page 353 of this volume) was no
told with respect to Mr. Macnaghten's, but to Captai
Burnes's, arrival at Simlah, in Mr. Macnaghten's absence
And in the second place, the policy into which Lord Auck
land is said to have been persuaded at this time was no
the policy of the tripartite treaty, but the policy of marchin
a British army into Afghanistan. It will have been see
that when Mr. Macnaghten negociated the treaty wit
Runjeet Singh and Shah Soojah, it was no part of th
scheme that the restoration of the Shah should be mainl
accomplished by our British bayonets. This was obviousl
an after-thought. The question then is, how it arose—ho
" the army of the Indus," to which Macnaghten at Lahor

and Loodhianah had never once alluded, grew into a substantial fact. This is not explained by Mr. Torrens: I therefore leave the statements in the text of my narrative as they were originally written, and I will only add in this place—what I could produce living testimony of the highest order to prove—that when the war in Afghanistan was believed to be a grand success, Mr. Torrens boasted, not merely of his participation in the councils from which it emanated, but of the actual authorship of the war. He said, indeed, *totidem verbis,* that he "made the Afghan war," an assertion which need not be taken too literally, but which, at all events, warrants the presumption that he counselled and approved the war in the shape in which it was undertaken. K.]

[Vol. I., page 356.]

[The following is the letter from Sir A. Burnes referred to in this page.]

Husn Abdul, 2nd *June,* 1838,

MY DEAR MR. MACNAGHTEN,

Just as I was entering this place, I had the pleasure to receive your letter of the 23rd, requesting me to state my views on the means of counteraction which should be presented to Dost Mahomed Khan, in the policy that he is pursuing. I should have liked to have conversed with you on this important subject, for it has so many bearings, and involves so many conflicting interests, that it is impossible to do it justice; but I do not delay a moment in meeting your wishes, as far as can be done in a letter.

It is clear that the British Government cannot, with any credit or justice to itself, permit the present state of affairs at Caubul to continue. The counteraction applied must, however, extend beyond Dost Mahomed Khan, and to both Persia and Russia. A demand of explanation from the Cabinet of St. Petersburgh would, I conceive, be met by an evasive answer, and gain for us no end; besides, the policy of Russia is now fairly developed, and requires no explanation, for it explains itself, since that government is clearly resolved upon using the influence she possesses in Persia (which is as great there as what the British command in India), to extend her power eastward. It had better, therefore, be assumed at once that such are her plans, and remonstrate accordingly. If we can do but little with Russia, the cause is widely different with Persia. She should at once be warned off Afghanistan, and our continuance of an alliance with her should depend upon her compliance. I believe that a letter from the Governor-General of India, sent to the Shah of Persia at Herat, would gain our end, and this effected, there is nothing to fear from the proceedings of Dost Mahomed Khan, or any other of the Afghan chiefs. If this be left undone, they will succumb to Persia and Russia, and become the instruments for whatever those powers desire. I therefore distinctly state my conviction that the evil lies beyond Afghanistan itself, and must be dealt with accordingly.

If it is the object of government to destroy the power of the present chief of Caubul, it may be effected by the agency of his brother, Sultan Mahomed Khan, or of Soojah-ool-Moolk, but to ensure complete success to the plan, the British Government must appear directly in it; that is, it must not be left to the Sikhs themselves. Let us discuss the merits of these two plans; but first I must speak on the establishment of Sikh power in Afghanistan, to which you refer as a general question.

No one entertains a more exalted opinion than I do of the Maharajah's head to plan, and ability to achieve; but I look upon the power of the Sikhs beyond the Indus to be dependent on his life alone. It is mere temporising, therefore, to seek to follow up any such plan; and were this of itself not conclusive against it, the fact of its alienating the Afghan people, who are cordially disposed as a nation to join us, would be a sufficiently valid objection for not persevering in it. I conclude always that our object is to make the Afghans our own, and to guide Afghanistan by Afghans, not by foreigners. It is, I assure you, a mere visionary delusion to hope for establishing Sikh ascendancy in Caubul. For argument's sake, I will admit that the Maharajah may take it, but how is it to be retained? Why, he cannot keep his ground with credit in Peshawur, and the Sikhs themselves are averse to service beyond the Indus. But facts are more illustrative than arguments; the French officers could not with safety leave their homes to an evening dinner whilst we were at Peshawur and our intercourse was confined to breakfasts. I saw this morning two tumbrils of money the followers of dozens of others, on their way to Peshawur to pay the troops, and the Maharajah only wishes a road of honour to retreat from it. If you use him, therefore, as an agent to go further a-head, the first request he will make of the British will be for money, and we shall waste our treasure without gaining our ends, which, as I understand them, are an influence in Caubul, to exclude all intrigues from the West.

Of Sultan Mahomed Khan, the first instrument at command, you will remember that his brother Dost Mahomed, plainly confessed his dread of him if guided by Sikh gold, and with such aid the ruler of Caubul may be readily destroyed; but Sultan Mahomed has not the ability to rule Caubul; he is a very good man, but incapable of acting for himself; and though fit as an instrument in getting rid of a present evil, he would still leave affairs as unsettled as ever when fixed in Caubul, and he is consequently a very questionable agent to be used at all.

As for Soojah-ool-Moolk personally,[*] the British Government have only to send him to Peshawur with an agent, and two of its own regiments as an honorary escort, and an avowal to the Afghans that we have taken up his cause, to ensure his being fixed for ever on his throne. The present time is, perhaps, better than any previous to it, for the Afghans as a nation detest Persia, and Dost Mahomed having gone over to the Court of Teheran, though he believes it to be from dire necessity, converts many a doubting Afghan into a bitter enemy.

The Maharajah's permission has only, therefore, to be asked for the ex-king's advance on Peshawur, granting him at the same time some four or five of the regiments which have no Sikhs in their ranks, and Soojah becomes king. He need not remove from Peshawur, but address the Khyburees, Kohistanees of Caubul, and all the Afghans from that city, that he has the co-operation of the British and the Maharajah, and with but a little distribution of ready money—say two or three lakhs of rupees—he will find himself the real King of the Afghans in a couple of months. It is, however, to be remembered always that we must appear directly, for the Afghans are a superstitious people, and believe Soojah to have no fortune (bukht); but our name will invest him with it. You will also have a good argument with the Maharajah in the honour of "Taj Bukhshie;" but still his Highness will be more disposed to use Sultan Mahomed Khan as an instrument than Soojah, for he will, perhaps, have exaggerated notions of Afghan

---

[*] Here Sir A. Burnes had inserted the words, "I have—that is, as ex-King of the Afghans, no very high opinion;" and had drawn his pen through them. He had also originally written the word "Of" to begin the sentence, instead of "As for."

power in prospect; but our security must be given to him, and we must identify ourselves with all the proceedings to make arrangements durable.

I have thus pointed out to you how the chief of Caubul is to be destroyed, and the best means which have occurred to me for effecting it; but I am necessarily ignorant of the Governor-General's views on what his Lordship considers the best mode of hereafter managing Afghanistan. It has been notified to me in various despatches, that this end may best be gained by using one small state to balance another, to keep all at peace, and thus prevent any great Mahomedan power growing up beyond the Indus, which might cause future inconvenience. It is with every respect that I differ; but these are not my sentiments, and though in theory nothing may appear more just and beneficial, I doubt the possibility of putting the theory into practice, and more than doubt the practice producing the benefit expected from it; for while you were trying to bring it about, another power steps in, paves the way for destroying the chiefships in detail, and the policy along with it. Our fears of a powerful Mahomedan neighbour are quickened by what we read of Ahmed Shah's wars in India, and the alarms spread even by Shah Zemaun, so late as the days of Lord Wellesley; but our knowledge of these countries has wondrously improved since that time; and though the noble Marquis, in his splendid administration, made the Afghans feel our weight through Persia, and arrested the evil, we should have had none of these present vexations if we had dealt with the Afghans themselves. We then counteracted them through Persia. We now wish to do it through the Sikhs. But as things stand, I maintain it is the best of all policy to make Caubul *in itself as strong as we can make it,* and not weaken it by divided power; it has already been too long divided. Caubul owed its strength in bygone days to the tribute of Cashmere and Sindh. Both are irrevocably gone; and while we do all we can to keep up the Sikhs as a power east of the Indus during the Maharajah's life, or afterwards, we should consolidate Afghan power west of the Indus, and have a King and not a collection of chiefs. *Divide et impera* is a temporising creed at any time; and if the Afghans are united, we and they bid defiance to Persia, and instead of distant relations, we have everything under our eye, and a steadily progressing influence all along the Indus.

I have before said, that we cannot with justice to our position in India allow things to continue as at present in Caubul; and I have already, in my despatch of the 30th April, suggested a prompt and active counteraction of Dost Mahomed Khan, since we cannot act with him. But it remains to be reconsidered why we cannot act with Dost Mahomed. He is a man of undoubted ability, and has at heart a high opinion of the British nation; and if half you must do for others were done for him, and offers made which he could see conduced to his interests, he would abandon Persia and Russia to-morrow. It may be said that that opportunity has been given to him, but I would rather discuss this in person with you, for I think there is much to be said for him. Government have admitted that at best he had but a choice of difficulties; and it should not be forgotten that we promised nothing, and Persia and Russia held out a great deal. I am not now viewing the question in the light of what is to be said to the rejection of our good offices as far as they went, or to his doing so in the face of a threat held out to him; but these facts show the man has something in him; and if Afghans are proverbially not to be trusted, I see no reason for having greater mistrust of him than of others. My opinion of Asiatics is, that you can only rely upon them when their interests are identified with the line of procedure marked out to them; and this seems now to be a doctrine pretty general in all politics.

I shall say no more at present. It will give me great pleasure again to meet you. I shall be on the banks of the Jhelam on the 7th or 8th, and my progress beyond that depends on the dawk being laid: but if that goes right, I ought to join you in ten days at the furthest.

Believe me, my dear Mr. Macnaghten,
Yours sincerely,
ALEXANDER BURNES.

P.S.—I have thought it advisable to send a duplicate of this letter, which Mr. Lord has been so good as to copy for me, by the Maharajah's dawk, as it prevents accidents, and may reach you sooner.

END OF VOL. I.

LONDON: PRINTED BY WILLIAM CLOWES AND SONS, STAMFORD STREET AND CHARING CROSS.

BIBLIOLIFE

Old Books Deserve a New Life
www.bibliolife.com

Did you know that you can get most of our titles in our trademark **EasyScript**™ print format? **EasyScript**™ provides readers with a larger than average typeface, for a reading experience that's easier on the eyes.

Did you know that we have an ever-growing collection of books in many languages?

Order online:
www.bibliolife.com/store

Or to exclusively browse our **EasyScript**™ collection:
www.bibliogrande.com

At BiblioLife, we aim to make knowledge more accessible by making thousands of titles available to you – quickly and affordably.

Contact us:
BiblioLife
PO Box 21206
Charleston, SC 29413

Made in the USA
Lexington, KY
26 July 2012